Advance Praise for
Constructing Private Governance

"This is an important book on the evolution of certification systems, with unparalleled coverage of three key industries and a
number of more general implications. Auld constructs a powerful
account of how market conditions and early decisions influence
the maturation of certification initiatives, which helps to explain
why some fields have seen such a proliferation of eco and social
labels."

—**Tim Bartley**, Ohio State University

"Simply put, this is the single best comparative project regarding
different certification/private governance schemes I have seen.
Easily the best."

—**Stacy D. VanDeveer**, University of New Hampshire

"The broad comparative perspective, achieved in few other analyses
of private regulation to date, makes this book a major contribution
to the literature."

—**Tim Büthe**, author of *New Global Rulers: The Privatization of
Regulation in the World Economy*

"Comparing the evolution of environmental and social certifications, Auld sheds light on the new institutions regulating the coffee in our cups, fish on our plates, and wood in our tables."

—**Laura T. Raynolds**, Center for Fair & Alternative Trade, Colorado
State University

CONSTRUCTING PRIVATE GOVERNANCE

GRAEME AULD

Constructing Private Governance

THE RISE AND EVOLUTION OF FOREST,

COFFEE, AND FISHERIES CERTIFICATION

Yale UNIVERSITY PRESS

NEW HAVEN AND LONDON

Published with assistance from the foundation established in memory of
Philip Hamilton McMillan of the Class of 1894, Yale College.

Yale University Press books may be purchased in quantity for educational, business, or
promotional use. For information, please e-mail sales.press@yale.edu (U.S. office) or
sales@yaleup.co.uk (U.K. office).

Set in Scala type by Integrated Publishing Solutions.
Printed in the United States of America.

Library of Congress Cataloging-in-Publication Data
Auld, Graeme
Constructing private governance: the rise and evolution of forest, coffee, and fisheries
certification / Graeme Auld.
     pages   cm.
Includes bibliographical references and index.
ISBN 978-0-300-19053-3 (alk. paper)
    1. Trade regulation—Environmental aspects.   2. Sustainable agriculture—
Standards.   3. Sustainable forestry—Standards.   4. Forest products—
Certification.   5. Coffee industry—Certification.   6. Fisheries—Certification.   I. Title.
   HD3612.A95 2014
   333.76′160218—dc23   2014005499

A catalogue record for this book is available from the British Library.

This paper meets the requirements of ANSI/NISO Z39.48-1992 (Permanence of Paper).

10 9 8 7 6 5 4 3 2 1

To my parents—Ed and Joyce

CONTENTS

This book took form at the end of my PhD dissertation in 2009, yet its conceptual and empirical roots reach as far back as the beginning of my master's degree when I first began to examine certification as a global governance phenomenon. Indeed, the idea for this book arose from the previous book—*Governing Through Markets*—that I co-wrote (with Benjamin Cashore and Deanna Newsom) on certification. We explored the rise of forest certification over the 1990s with the aim of explaining why the forest industries of various countries were engaging certification in different ways. Companies had two conceptions of certification to choose between. One, exemplified by the Forest Stewardship Council, was started by a coalition that included extensive participation from environmental groups. The other programs, such as the Sustainable Forestry Initiative in the United States, were formed by industry, often in reaction to the Forest Stewardship Council. We sought to understand why companies in some countries decided to support the Forest Stewardship Council even though they had a more business-friendly program as an alternative.

Governing Through Markets offered important insights into the development of certification, which was gaining attention as a notable new form of governance that might help address global challenges such as promoting responsible forest management. Yet the book focused only on forestry and thus lacked a comparative perspective across sectors.

Certification was spreading. The fishery sector was adopting a similar approach, as were many products in the agriculture, apparel, and service sectors. This lacuna led me to questions about what differed between forestry and these other sectors. These questions became the focus of my dissertation research, which I conducted from 2004 to 2008, and this is an area of research I have continued since.

From my preliminary knowledge back in 2004, it was clear that the forest sector was the exception, not the rule. No other sectors appeared to have the two-program competition between NGO-backed and industry-backed options. Rather, most were more fragmented. My first look at the coffee sector, for instance, indicated that there were distinct issues that certification programs were seeking to address, such as social development versus environmental impacts of farming practices, which meant a greater diversity of programs were emerging. In fisheries, the Marine Stewardship Council had formed, in part modeled after the NGO-backed Forest Stewardship Council, but it didn't address aquaculture, which was beginning to engender its own certification initiatives, including organics and the Global Aquaculture Alliance. Moreover, at the time, fair-trade-labeled coffee was readily available in coffee shops and grocery stores, whereas it remained surprisingly difficult to find Forest Stewardship Council–labeled wood or paper products. These and other differences were curious and—I suspected—potentially quite important for the success of nascent certification programs across sectors.

Further research into the coffee, fisheries, and forest sectors revealed differences that served as the empirical puzzles examined in this book. To unlock these puzzles, I did extensive document research on the origins and evolution of forest, coffee, and fisheries certification programs. I traveled to Europe and in North America to interview individuals who had played a role in establishing and managing different programs. This book is the synthesis of the insights I've gained from taking a cross-program and cross-sector look at the rise and evolution of certification.

I remain intrigued by the potential of certification as a form of governance. It has weathered more than two decades of growth to date and appears to have potential for continued development. Indeed, when I began studying programs such as the Forest Stewardship Council in the late 1990s and early 2000s, few of my family and friends knew much about certification. I often found myself explaining what certification involved and why it had come about. I even collected the few examples of labeled products I could find as props to use in talks or to better explain the focus of my research. Much has changed. Products labeled by the programs examined in this book are now more pervasive. From catalogues, printer paper, and various building materials carrying the Forest Stewardship Council label to seafood at supermarkets labeled by the Marine Stewardship Council or the Global Aquaculture Alliance to "bird-friendly" or fair-trade coffee available at coffee shops and supermarkets, consumers are now exposed to these labels as never before.

Still, often the stories and organizations behind these labels are poorly understood. Media attention to labels is episodic and typically focuses on potential scams and problems. This misses the remarkable rise of a new governance model. In tracing the histories of programs in three sectors, I hope that this book's analysis will illuminate not only how certification works and why it has come about as an instrument but also how, at best, it might—and potentially can—be part of global efforts to address the social and environmental challenges of our time. There is a healthy skepticism about the potential of certification. At worst, certification may be a form of greenwashing that undermines effective government policies to address social and environmental issues while potentially rewarding companies for doing nothing more than what they were already doing. Though this book will not end debate on the risks and possibilities of this instrument, I hope it can foster greater care in understanding the distinct origins of different certification initiatives and what these differences may mean for their future potential.

ACKNOWLEDGMENTS

This book would not have been possible without the support and co-operation of many individuals who took time from their busy lives to answer my questions. I thank them immensely for sharing their insights and helping me understand a little bit more about the histories and operations of certification programs. For financial support, I would like to thank the Social Sciences and Humanities Research Council of Canada, the Yale Program on Non-profit Organizations, and Carleton University. I am also greatly indebted to Ros Buck and Chrissie Webb, who helped me access and secure permission to cite materials from the Oxfam Archive. The materials on pages 142, 144, and 145 are adapted by the publisher from Oxford, Bodleian Library, Oxfam archive (uncatalogued), Marketing Directorate correspondence, Fairtrade Foundation, 1989–98, with the permission of Oxfam GB, Oxfam House, John Smith Drive, Cowley, Oxford OX4 2JY UK www.oxfam.org.uk; Oxfam GB does not necessarily endorse any text or activities that accompany the materials, nor has it approved the adapted text.

Thanks as well to Ole, Constanze, Karen, Justin, Lindsay, Monica, Tom, Camillo, Tony, and Caroline for housing me on my European research stints, and to Stefan Renckens, Louise Overington, Leela Steiner, Chris Tenove, Lars Gulbrandsen, and Jennifer McKee for reading earlier versions of this book. Their constructive, critical, and often detailed comments greatly improved the flow and clarity of my ideas and prose.

Tim Bartley, Tim Büthe, and Stacy VanDeveer were also instrumental in providing extensive and cogent critiques of my arguments. And I'm extremely thankful for the support and assistance of Yale University Press, particularly Jean Thomson Black, Sara Hoover, and Samantha Ostrowski. Thanks as well to Robin DuBlanc for her careful and thorough copyediting.

I am tremendously lucky to have had wonderful mentors as I pursued my three academic degrees. At the University of British Columbia, George Hoberg provided an early and vital introduction to political science that redirected me toward the social sciences. My intellectual growth was also greatly helped by Gary Bull, Sally Aitken, David Haley, Peter Marshall, Valerie LeMay, Tony Kozak, and John Worrall. At Auburn University, Conner Bailey, Mark Dubois, Daowei Zhang, Murray Jardine, and Jill Crystal were all instrumental in furthering my understanding of the social sciences. Finally, at Yale University I found two homes. In the political science department, a special thanks to Stathis Kalyvas, Kenneth Scheve, Donald Green, and Pauline Jones-Luong. In the School of Forestry and Environmental Studies, there are simply too many people to thank; it truly was an amazing place to spend six years as a student. I thank the entire faculty and staff for their support, particularly Daniel Esty, Brad Gentry, Anthony Leiserowitz, Mark Ashton, Rob Mendelsohn, Chad Oliver, Graeme Berlin, Ann Camp, Oswald Schmitz, John Wargo, Elisabeth Barsa, Gus Speth, Erin Mansur, and Bethany Zemba. In addition, Nathaniel Keohane and Sheila Olmstead were a constant source of inspiration and support; each offered invaluable guidance and insights.

My PhD dissertation committee members—Benjamin Cashore, Jacob Hacker, Tim Bartley, Douglas Kysar, and Frances Rosenbluth—each contributed in important ways to the genesis and evolution of the project that led to this book. I'm thankful to all of them for their critical and constructive feedback along the way as my thoughts moved from nascent ideas to written words. Benjamin Cashore requires separate and additional thanks. His mentorship is unsurpassed, as he constantly challenges me to think more deeply and write more clearly. I've gained too much to describe from his long-standing support: as a supervisor, a colleague and, most important, as a friend.

Professionally, I am indebted to many others whom I have worked with over the years, particularly Deanna Newsom, Lars Gulbrandsen, Connie McDermott, Stefan Renckens, Steven Bernstein, Kelly Levin, Cristina

Balboa, Aseem Prakash, Erika Sasser, Jessica Green, Luc Fransen, Laura Bozzi, Cory McCruden, G. Cornelius van Kooten, Melissa Aronczyk, Alexandra Mallett, Robert Slater, Jamie Lawson, Justin Stead, Peter Glück, Jane Lister, Virginia Haufler, Aarti Gupta, Michael Mason, Robert Falkner, Peter Wood, Anastasia O'Rourke, Marisa Camargo, Jennifer McKee, Leela Steiner, Bozica Burlica, Igga Kurzydlo, and Francis Nolan Poupart. We have collaborated on many different research projects that directly or indirectly furthered my thinking on private governance and on certification in particular. Thanks as well to the entire Earth Negotiations Bulletin Reporting Service of the International Institute for Sustainable Development. Since 2009, I've had the great pleasure to work with inspiring teams covering intergovernmental processes on oceans and forests; I thank each of these teams for wonderful experiences and for deepening my understanding of multilateral environmental negotiations.

At Carleton University, I have met great colleagues, established new research collaborations, and been inspired by the energy and enthusiasm of students aspiring to work on public policy issues in Canada and abroad. I am greatly indebted to the School of Public Policy and Administration for the support and encouragement I've received in my five years on faculty. A particular thanks to Robert Slater, Susan Phillips, Saul Schwartz, Stanley Winer, Glen Toner, Les Pal, Stephan Schott, Alexandra Mallett, Lisa Mills, Frances Abele, Calum Carmichael, James Meadowcroft, Alan Maslove, Barbara Levine, Bruce Doern, and Christopher Stoney. Thanks as well to the faculty and staff at the Liu Institute for Global Issues—and particularly Peter Dauvergne—for hosting me for three consecutive summers. I can't think of a more enjoyable environment for summer writing.

The intellectual journey I've traveled in researching and writing this book is paralleled by a personal journey rich with supportive, kind, and amazing friends and family. The ideas contained in this book are as much a product of their support and encouragement as they are due to my time alone thinking, reading, and writing. I am forever grateful for the support I've received from the people in my life. To Louise, thank you for enriching my life and sustaining me through late nights of reading and writing. To my parents and family, thank you for your never-waning support. To my friends in Vancouver, New Haven, Ottawa, and elsewhere around the world, thank you for your patience, encouragement, understanding, and—ultimately—for the inspiring and remarkable things you each do.

ACC	Aquaculture Certification Council	CSA	Canadian Standards Association
AFPA	American Forest and Paper Association	CWG	Certification Working Group
ASC	Aquaculture Stewardship Council	EEZ	Exclusive economic zone
		EFAT	European Fair Trade Association
ASI	Accreditation Services International	EPA	U.S. Environmental Protection Agency
CAFOD	Catholic Fund for Overseas Development (now Catholic Agency for Overseas Development)	ETI	Ethical Trading Initiative
		EU	European Union
		FAO	Food and Agriculture Organization of the UN
CALM	Conservation and Land Management Act (Australia)	FIIT	Fundacíon interamericana de investigacíon tropical
C&I	Criteria and Indicators		
CCOF	California Certified Organic Farmers	FLO	Fairtrade Labeling Organizations International
CFPC	Certified Forest Products Council	FoE	Friends of the Earth
		FoS	Friend of the Sea
CI	Conservation International	4C	Common Code for the Coffee Community
CPPA	Canadian Pulp and Paper Association (now Forest Products Association of Canada)	FSC	Forest Stewardship Council
		FTO	Fair Trade Organization

GAA	Global Aquaculture Alliance	ITTA	International Tropical Timber Agreement
GAP	Good Agricultural Practices	ITTO	International Tropical Timber Organization
GATT	General Agreement on Tariffs and Trade	IUCN	International Union for the Conservation of Nature
GFTN	Global Forest and Trade Network	IUU	Illegal, unreported, and unregulated
IAF	International Accreditation Forum	IWC	International Whaling Commission
IAPB	IFOAM Accreditation Programme Board	LEI	Indonesian Ecolabel Institute
ICA	International Coffee Agreement	MAP	Mangrove Action Project
ICFA	International Coalition of Fisheries Associations	MPRA	Marine Reserve Protection Authority (Australia)
ICO	International Coffee Organization	MSC	Marine Stewardship Council
ICSF	International Collective in Support of Fishworkers	MTCC	Malaysian Timber Certification Council
IDH	Dutch Sustainable Trade Initiative	NFI	National Fisheries Institute
IEC	International Electrotechnical Commission	NGO	Nongovernmental organization
IFAT	International Fair Trade Association	NOSB	U.S. National Organic Standards Board
IFIR	International Forest Industry Roundtable	NRDC	Natural Resources Defense Council
IFMA	International Forestry Monitoring Agency	NSMD	Nonstate-market-driven
IFOAM	International Federation of Organic Agriculture Movements	OCIA	Organic Crop Improvement Association
IIED	International Institute for Environment and Development	OFPANA	Organic Food Production Association of North America
IOAS	International Organic Accreditation Service	P&C	Principles & Criteria
		P&G	Procter & Gamble
IPC	Integrated Programme for Commodities	PEFC	Program for the Endorsement of Forest Certification (formerly Pan European Forest Certification)
IPOA	International Plan of Action	RAN	Rainforest Action Network
ISO	International Organization for Standardization	RA-SAN	Rainforest Alliance and Sustainable Agriculture Network

RFMO   Regional Fisheries Management Organization

RFS   Responsible Fisheries Society

SCAA   Specialty Coffee Association of America

SCS   Scientific Certification Services

SFI   Sustainable Forestry Initiative

SFM   Sustainable forest management

SGS   Société générale de surveillance

SMBC   Smithsonian Migratory Bird Center

TFAP   Tropical Forestry Action Plan

UCIRI   Union of Indigenous Communities of the Isthmus Region

UNCED   UN Conference on Environment and Development (or Rio Earth Summit)

UNCHE   UN Conference on the Human Environment

UNCLOS   UN Convention on the Law of the Sea

UNCTAD   UN Conference on Trade and Development

UNDP   UN Development Programme

UNEP   UN Environment Programme

UNESCO   UN Educational, Scientific and Cultural Organization

UNFCCC   UN Framework Convention on Climate Change

USDA   U.S. Department of Agriculture

US/GLEP   U.S./Guatemala Labor Education Program

USLEAP   U.S. Labor Education in the Americas Project

WARP   Woodworkers' Alliance for Rainforest Protection

WBCSD   World Business Council for Sustainable Development

WFP   Western Forest Products

WFTO   World Fair Trade Organization

WRI   World Resources Institute

WRM   World Rainforest Movement

WTO   World Trade Organization

WWF   World Wide Fund for Nature or World Wildlife Fund (in the United States)

CONSTRUCTING PRIVATE GOVERNANCE

CHAPTER ONE

The Puzzle

CERTIFICATION PROGRAMS—a form of private governance established by nongovernmental organizations (NGOs) and businesses to advance responsible production practices—have emerged to make remarkable inroads in global markets. Nowhere is this more apparent than in
the forest, coffee, and fisheries sectors. Certified forests in over eighty
countries accounted for approximately 33 percent of the world's production forests in 2011. Recent estimates put production of certified sustainable coffee (which includes organic, fair trade, and other initiatives) at 16
percent of world production (Tropical Commodity Coalition 2012); for
fisheries, recent estimates are that as much as 17 percent of the world
ocean-capture production is certified (Washington and Ababouch 2011).
All of this certified production supplies the consumer market with thousands of labeled products, including all manner of paper, wood, seafood,
and coffee.

Behind these statistics lie fascinating stories of the construction of
private governance fraught with struggles to determine the distribution
of benefits and costs and the ultimate consequences of these initiatives
for global environmental and social problems. The stakes are high. Economic activities in the examined sectors support the livelihoods of millions; they provide employment, valuable foreign exchange, and basic
sustenance. Oceans cover over 70 percent of the planet's surface and are
home to diverse organisms and ecosystems. Forests cover 30 percent of

the earth's land area and are, in many parts of the world, teeming with bio-diversity. Likewise, coffee grows in more than seventy countries, many of which are among the most biologically rich on the planet. Each sector con-fronts the challenge of balancing the benefits of economic activity against the need for sustainable practices, environmental protection, and socially equitable access to resources and the economic returns they support.

Certification programs have sought to address these issues by setting standards for social and environmental practices to allow those operators that practice responsibly to differentiate their operations and products and thus create incentives for improved performance. As an example, coffee farms that leave trees standing to provide habitat for birds can be recognized by the market as different from farms that clear all standing forests. The same recognition can be given to forestry operations that set aside areas of productive forest for conservation or cultural benefits or to fisheries that work to ensure the sustainability of the target fish stock and minimize negative effects on nontarget species. A common intent is to use market incentives—customer loyalty, market access, or price premiums—to reward those operators that are deemed to be help-ing address global environmental and social challenges in their sectors. In the coffee example, certifying farms that retain trees is a way to help slow the declining populations of neotropical migratory birds such as the iconic Baltimore oriole; in the fisheries example, certification aims to ameliorate the negative effects on birds and sea turtles that get trapped in fishnets or hooked on fishing lines.

By tracing the rise and evolution of forest, coffee, and fisheries certi-fication, this book sheds light on the stories behind diverse certification pro-grams and how they have sought to play a role—often a highly contested one—in ameliorating social and environmental challenges. Although they are connected by their common purpose and overall organizational form—they each define standards of responsible business practices, require third-party audits and product tracking through global supply chains, and include on-product labels—there remain notable differences in their histories and trajectories that are poorly understood. Two strik-ing differences stand out.

First, all of the programs examined have evolved to serve as global certification programs, meaning simply that they seek to regulate a set of social or environmental issues in the global practices of an economic sector. However, there are dramatic differences in how quickly programs became global governors. Some programs immediately sought to certify operations around the world. One example is the Marine Stewardship Council (MSC), created to define global standards for ocean-capture fisheries in order to provide an eco label for seafood markets. The council was initiated in 1996 and the first certification occurred by 2000—just four years later. In other cases, national or regional standards existed and certifiers were conducting audits within these markets before a global program could form. One example is the Forest Stewardship Council (FSC). Before the FSC was officially established in 1994, organizations such as the Rainforest Alliance and Scientific Certification Services (SCS) were developing stand-alone forestry certification standards for their own auditing services. Seven programs from the sectors fit this local-first pattern. One of them, the International Federation of Organic Agriculture Movements (IFOAM), took thirty-two years to become a global certification program for coffee. The first organic coffee certification occurred in 1967; it was not until 1999 that the IFOAM agreed on a global coffee standard. In contrast, the FSC needed only six years to become a global program after the Rainforest Alliance conducted the first-ever forest management audit in 1990. By 1996, the FSC had a global standard, a global procedure for accrediting certifiers, and a global label.

The second striking difference is the number of programs that have formed in the three sectors. The forest sector has two overarching global programs: the FSC and the Program for the Endorsement of Forest Certification (PEFC, formerly Pan European Forest Certification). By contrast, both coffee and fisheries have several programs. Coffee has five. Notable examples include the IFOAM for organic coffee and Fairtrade International (FLO, formerly the Fairtrade Labeling Organizations International), which certifies fair-trade coffee from small-farm cooperatives. The fisheries sector has six programs, including the MSC, the IFOAM's work on organic aquaculture, the Global Aquaculture Alliance (GAA), and the more recently formed Friend of the Sea (FoS) and Aquaculture Stewardship Council (ASC).

What explains the two differences across the programs and sectors? Why have some programs more quickly become global governors compared with others? Why is the field of certification programs much more fragmented in some sectors than in others? The analysis to follow reveals that part of the explanation for these differences is the distinct origins of the individual certification programs. Features of the initial form that individual certification programs adopt combined with the degree of market demand early in a program's existence affect the evolution of individual programs and the patterns of programs that emerge in different sectors. That is, these early choices help explain, but do not entirely determine, the striking differences just discussed. The central task of this book, therefore, is to trace the explanation for these differences and reflect on their significance for the role of certification as a form of global governance.

CERTIFICATION AS PRIVATE GOVERNANCE

The book focuses on one form of private governance: social and environmental certification programs (Courville 2003; Gereffi, Garcia-Johnson, and Sasser 2001; O'Rourke 2003). Often variants of an ideal type termed non-state-market-driven (NSMD) governance by Cashore (2002), Cashore, Auld, and Newsom (2004), and Bernstein and Cashore (2007), they are initiatives that harness market incentives to encourage behavioral change by economic actors. They represent formalized governance arrangements for developing and promoting standards to give buyers information about products made through environmentally and socially responsible cultivation, extraction, production, and manufacturing processes. They are voluntary to the extent that producers, traders, manufacturers, and retailers may choose whether or not to participate.[1]

Certification programs have four key features. First, they have logos or labels that can be used on products sold to end consumers. Second, they have some form of inspection and monitoring, which may have begun as an internal process but over time typically becomes an independent, third-party verification process. Third, they have governance structures and procedures for overseeing operations, including rules for membership, decision making, setting and revising standards, accrediting auditors, and resolving disputes. Certain programs are highly centralized, with most decision-making authority controlled by an international office; other programs include national affiliates that perform various functions such as developing local-specific standards, performing outreach, or generating market demand. Finally, they establish standards for regulating social and environmental impacts of production processes as well as tracking requirements for following products through to the end consumer. The policy focus of these standards has two components: program scope, which is defined as the substantive policy problems a program regulates, and program domain, defined as the group of economic actors in a supply chain that the program's rules target (Auld 2014a).

This book conceptualizes private governance as both an institution and an organization. As an institution, private governance is understood as rules that prescribe particular practices and that are not backed by state authority (Cashore 2002).[2] Sometimes institutions are defined to include social conventions, norms, values, beliefs, and ideas (Hoffman 1999; Peter Hall 1986); here they are defined as formal, written rules (North 1991; Ostrom 1986; Jack Knight 1992). Private governance programs are institutions because they establish rules that are designed to govern the behavior of individuals and societal organizations (including corporations) and because these rules are known by the members of the relevant community in which the program operates (Jack Knight 1992). These governance programs are not just sets of rules, however. They are both collective entities and bundles of rules and procedures for guiding social interactions.[3] As an organization, once a private governor exists, it becomes an agent with interests in its future.

EXPLAINING DIFFERENT PATTERNS OF EMERGENCE

Certification has garnered considerable scholarly attention in part because of its distinctiveness from other forms of private governance (for example, Bartley 2007b; Bernstein and Cashore 2007). Considerable research focuses on inspection and monitoring and the character of program standards—particularly how stringent standards are and whether they are performance- or procedural-related and discretionary or non-discretionary in nature (Clapp 1998; Auld and Bull 2003; McDermott, Noah, and Cashore 2008). This book, by contrast, focuses on the consequences of early design choices taken by programs.

To recap, the central thrust of the empirical project is to explain two differences. The first is the variability in time it has taken different certification programs to organize as global governors for the issues their standards address. As noted earlier, some certification initiatives quickly became global programs; others have taken years and sometimes decades to serve in this capacity. The second is the different patterns of certification programs that exist across the sectors. Coffee and fisheries programs have proliferated to a larger degree than forestry programs. As foreshadowed above, I argue that the distinct origins of programs help explain but do not completely determine these two striking patterns of divergence.

To advance an analysis of these issues, the book focuses on and is structured to answer three questions.[4] The first focuses on the early design choices of certification programs by asking: *What explains variation in the initial form of certification programs?* The second and third questions then focus on the puzzling differences across programs and sectors sketched at the outset. They ask: *What explains change in certification programs after they are established, especially whether and how quickly an initially local program can be transformed into a global program?* and *What explains the overall structure of certification programs in a sector, specifically whether or not (and what kinds of) alternative programs will arise?*

All three questions are conditional on programs having emerged in a given sector. With the first two, the unit of analysis is the program; for the third, the unit is the sector. The first question focuses on four aspects of the initial program form: (1) whether a program is created to be local or global; (2) which actors the program seeks to regulate within a given economic sector (the program's regulatory domain); (3) which demands are placed on actors that seek to certify (the program's policy scope); and (4) how inclusive the opportunities are for participation in the program's governance processes.

The second research question aims to explain the varying time programs take to globalize. A global program is defined as having a global standard, a label, and systems for auditing against its standard around the world.[5] The third research question seeks explanations for how fragmented the field of programs has become in the three sectors.

The analysis does not assume that all certification programs must be global. Rather, the intention is to understand the mechanisms that shape the character of different certification programs in different sectors. This is a paramount task given the interest in certification initiatives as supplements and complements to intergovernmental processes tackling social and environmental problems (Bernstein and Cashore 2007; Gulbrandsen 2004; O'Rourke 2003; Pattberg 2005).

For the first two questions, the programs fall into two groups. One includes programs in which the founders immediately worked to create rules for setting global standards that would be used to guide later local (regional, national, or subnational) standards development, and for auditing against these standards around the world. This group includes

Table 1.1.

Differences in the development of programs across and within sectors

SECTOR	PROGRAM	SCALE OF INITIAL CERTIFICATION ACTIVITIES	TIME TAKEN TO DEVELOP FEATURES OF A GLOBAL PROGRAM		
			INITIATED	COMPLETED	TIME TAKEN (YEARS)
Forestry	FSC	Local	1990	1996	6
	PEFC	Local	1996	2003	7
Coffee	IFOAM	Local	1967	1999	32
	FLO	Local	1988	2003	15
	RA-SAN	Local	1996	2012	16
	Utz Kapeh	Global	1997	2005	8
	SMBC	Local	1997	2011	14
Fisheries	IFOAM	Local	1994	2005	11
	MSC	Global	1996	2000	4
	GAA-RFS	Global	1997	2002	5
	Global GAP	Local	1997	2007	10
	FoS	Global	2001	2006	5
	ASC	Global	2010	2012	2

the Marine Stewardship Council, the Global Aquaculture Alliance (and its early joint initiative with the Responsible Fisheries Society [RFS]), Utz Kapeh, Friend of the Sea, and the Aquaculture Stewardship Council. For these programs, the time lag from inception to the first certification of an operation—for example, a fishery for the MSC or a coffee farmer for Utz Kapeh—varied from two to eight years (table 1.1 and figure 1.1).

In the second group, local standards were developed and audits occurred before the founders could create a global program. This group includes the Forest Stewardship Council, the International Federation of Organic Agriculture Movements for both coffee and aquaculture, the Fairtrade International, the Rainforest Alliance and Sustainable Agriculture Network (RA-SAN, formerly Eco-OK) program, the Smithsonian Migratory Bird Center's (SMBC) "bird-friendly" program, the Global "Good Agricultural Practices" (Global GAP, formerly EurepGAP) initiative, and the Program for the Endorsement of Forest Certification. It took between six and thirty-two years for these initiatives to develop a global

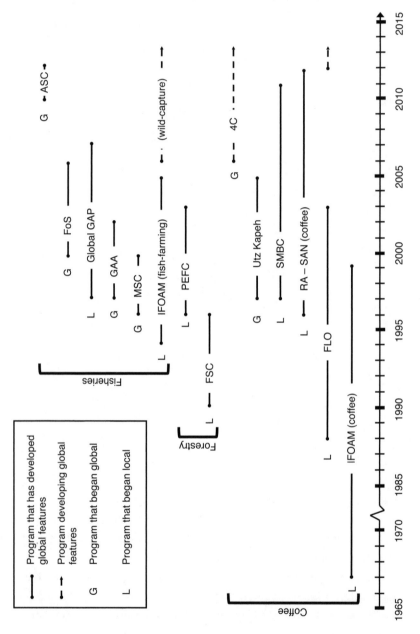

FIGURE 1.1. Development of certification programs in coffee, forestry, and fisheries sectors

standard, label, and rules for audits after local standards or certifications first occurred. The longest delays were with organic certification in the coffee and fisheries sectors. It is important to note that, since the start of 2012, Fair Trade USA ended its membership in FLO, meaning that what had been a global program since 2003 temporarily fell out of this category. Chapter 6 discusses these developments in detail.

The third research question focuses on variation in the patterns of programs in each sector (table 1.2). The forest sector has two overarching programs—the PEFC and FSC—both structured as federated systems with national affiliates and accredited certifiers. Both programs address similar forest management issues and will generally certify operations of any size. The coffee sector has five programs. FLO formed to address social development and market access, restricting its application to small-farm cooperatives. The IFOAM was established to deal with farm-level environmental considerations. Shade-grown coffee offered by the SMBC's "bird-friendly" program promotes the retention of overstory trees on coffee farms that are essential for bird habitat; the program developed primarily for coffee farms in Latin America. Sustainable coffee, such as that grown under the RA-SAN program, addresses each of these environmental concerns to a general degree. Utz Kapeh is similar, although it does not address shade, placing more emphasis on food safety.

The fisheries sector has six programs, with a notable split between ocean capture and aquaculture. The MSC focuses on ocean capture and has faced a few potential challengers. So far, the most notable has been the Friend of the Sea, which concentrates on environmental aspects of fisheries but also certifies aquaculture operations. It is the only program that does both. With aquaculture, certification began with organics, but here too there are recent entrants, including the ASC, which is concerned with the environmental and social impacts of aquaculture production. Before this, the GAA focused on shrimp; only in the last few years have standards for other farmed species been under development. In 2004, the Global GAP then launched its first integrated aquaculture standard, which addresses social, safety, and environmental aspects of fish-farming operations on a species-by-species basis. With the IFOAM, recent developments are opening the possibility for its expansion beyond aquaculture. Naturland, an organic certifier with IFOAM accreditation, has developed a program for ocean-capture fisheries, potentially setting on track future IFOAM attention to fish.

Table 1.2.

Policy scope and domain of actors regulated by programs in the forest, coffee, and fisheries sectors

SECTOR	PROGRAM	SCOPE OF STANDARDS	DOMAIN OF REGULATED ACTORS
Forestry	FSC	Environment, social, and economic	All producers
	PEFC	Environment, social, and economic	All producers
Coffee	IFOAM	Farm-level environmental impacts	All producers
	FLO	Social development	Smallholder groups
	RA-SAN	Social and farm-level and off-farm environmental impacts	All producers
	Utz Kapeh	Farm-level environment, social, and food safety	All producers
	SMBC	Off-farm environmental impacts	All producers
Fisheries	IFOAM	Environment	Aquaculture
	MSC	Environment	All wild-capture fisheries
	GAA-RFS	Environment	All operations (but early focus on shrimp farming)
	Global GAP	Farm-level environment, social, and food safety	Aquaculture
	FoS	Environment	Capture fisheries and aquaculture
	ASC	Environment and social	Aquaculture

How do we make sense of these patterns? To understand how certification programs have formed and evolved, it is necessary to examine how collective action in markets is affected by the degree of market demand, particularly during the early stages of program development, and to combine analyses of collective action with a recognition of path dependence, since early choices, though not entirely irreversible, create

lasting legacies.[6] Once collective action efforts in a sector create a certification program, the hypothesis is that independent conditions and
processes will then shape how individual programs internally evolve and
whether, and in what form, new programs emerge. Differences in the
conditions, processes, and programmatic origins, the argument holds,
will help explain variation in the time it takes programs to develop similar features, the rate at which new programs will enter a sector, and the
character of those new programs.

The book defends this overall argument by examining the three interrelated questions noted above. For the first question, what form programs take turns on a combination of the character of political and market opportunity structures and the way program founders understand
a sector's problems and how certification might serve as a solution. Political opportunity structures capture characteristics of a political system
that affords actors sources of influence over political and policy processes
(Tarrow 1998; Campbell 2005; Kitschelt 1986). Here the key features are
the relative openness of domestic versus international policy fora and
the role of openness in helping to generate and legitimate particular understandings of global problems.[7] Market opportunity structures define
characteristics of a sector's market that provide actors with better options
to develop particular forms of certification over others. High levels of
international trade, concentrations of multinational companies in global
supply chains, and high barriers to market entry are all hypothesized to
favor global programs. The focus of a program's standards and the regulatory targets it seeks to influence are shown to hinge on the founders'
understanding of a sector's problems and the necessary solutions.

The answer to the second question is then partly explained by the
initial form certification programs adopt. More precisely, the initial form
of programs interacts with the market to create incentives and disincen-
tives for early participants to support different evolutionary paths for
certification. Just as companies may try to have government regulate
the market entry of competitors to protect the incumbent companies'
profitability, when market demand exists for local certification programs,
early adopters may see change as threatening their use of certification
for competitive advantage. Thus, instead of supporting a global program
that could offer a consistent, industry-wide standard, early adopters will
have reason to prevent competitors from being able to certify. Similarly,
NGOs may resist efforts to scale up a program when they perceive that

the status quo better addresses problems salient to their organizations. Auditors that perform verification services for a certification program are also likely to resist a global program that would require making costly changes to their auditing procedures with no offsetting economic benefit. Hence, taken together, these actors may constitute a sufficiently influential coalition to resist, or at the very least slow down, the transformation of a locally focused certification initiative into one with global reach.

Turning to the third question, the initial form of programs also matters. Here, it interacts with the market conditions and the just-discussed struggles within programs to affect the pattern of programs that form in a sector. This occurs through two processes. First, early programs and participants generate information that makes it easier for later programs to develop and penetrate the market. This is known as learning by adoption. The promotional work of an early program and its supporters in fostering market demand for certified products will reduce uncertainty about the benefits of becoming certified. Early participants may also clarify the costs of certification, which assists others in determining whether it is worth becoming involved. Most important, however, market demand for an early certification program creates positive spillovers that increase the value of forming alternative programs. In this way, demand for certification is similar to an open-access good: it is depleted when more actors consume it (rival), but restricting higher consumption is hard or even impossible (nonexcludable). This means that those actors relevant to private governance systems—particularly NGOs, businesses, and auditors—have two options when evaluating how to be involved. They can either support an existing program or they can form a new program as a complement or substitute.

The second process brings in the influence of the initial form certification programs have adopted. The design of incumbent certification programs interacts with the incentives actors have to create new programs to influence whether a new program will be a complement or substitute. When incumbent programs focus on a narrow set of policy problems or seek to regulate only some producers in a sector, new programs are likely to form as complements by filling in the policy void. When existing programs have broad policy foci and seek to regulate all producers in a given sector, new programs will likely form as substitutes. In all situations, more opportunities for these actors to influence an existing program from within the program will reduce the incentives these actors have to create new programs. That is, how inclusive opportunities are for participation in a program's governance processes affects how likely actors are to develop alternative certification programs.[8]

CONTRIBUTIONS

The explanations offered for the three questions help make sense of the puzzling patterns that exist in the development of certification across programs and sectors. Three central contributions flow from the analysis.

Role of the Market

The first contribution is to recast and complicate the influence of market demand on the development of certification. The book finds that market demand—in a counterintuitive manner—can impede the ability of early programs to change and can foster the entry of alternative programs. This is a critical insight, as some see certification as possibly providing global collective benefits where governments have been unwilling or unable to act, and one lever available to achieve this is through increasing market demand for certified products (Cashore et al. 2007; Gulbrandsen 2004). Since participation by companies is voluntary, the theory of supply and demand predicts that certification will generate more collective benefits when businesses or individuals pay higher prices for certified products. However, the analysis adds nuance and thereby serves as a corrective to this simple economic model, which, while not wrong, is incomplete. The model does not explain which certifier, or certifiers, will emerge and persist. Will it be just one or two programs, something like the pattern in the forest sector? Or will it be many programs, more akin to the pattern in the fisheries or coffee sectors?

This counterintuitive role of market demand is also important for two other reasons. The first is because it shows that there will be different challenges facing programs that begin as global versus local. Programs that start with global structures face the top-down challenge of courting potential supporters and preventing entry by competitor programs. Programs that start local face similar threats of competitive entry but also must address the bottom-up challenge of coordinating preexisting standards development and auditing efforts that, for the reasons identified above, may be supported by actors hesitant to change.

The second reason relates to Prakash and Potoski's "club-good" model of voluntary environmental programs (Potoski and Prakash 2005; Prakash and Potoski 2006, 2007b).[9] They argue that certification programs produce excludable and nonrival benefits for their members (a positive environmental reputation) with the ancillary advantage that a club's standard, which members must meet to be in the club, generates public good benefits for society at large (Prakash and Potoski 2006, 17–25). In this application, they assume the key benefit is a shared reputational benefit, which grows—via network effects—with increased participation.[10]

However, the above role of market demand implies there are instances in which participants will have access to private benefits because of certification. Prakash and Potoski (2006, 48) do explain how private benefits can accrue to participating firms—for instance, realizing cost reductions in production processes—yet they dismiss this as a motive for participation on the logic that if private gains existed, a club would be unnecessary. Their discussion does not, however, adequately address or untangle the implications of private benefits coming from market demand. If there are profits to be made from end-product labeling, then participation in a program provides rival, excludable benefits (a private good), not only a nonrival, excludable good (a club good).[11] Indeed, Kotchen and van 't Veld (2009) show that when participating firms obtain a premium for a certified product (a private benefit), these firms have an incentive to participate to the point when their private marginal costs are equal to the marginal benefits (the per-unit premium) (see also Sandler and Tschirhart 1997). Hence, rather than more participants increasing reputation benefits through network effects, more participants may drive benefits to zero. This mechanism, in other words, should give earlier adopters incentives to limit participation by creating barriers to prevent growing participation in the program by their competitors. In more recent work (Prakash and Potoski 2010), the authors recognize this issue, and suggest that more work is needed to understand how different forms of incentives matter, and how the reputations of programs are generated and advertised. This book partly takes up this task.

Institutional Development and Change

The second contribution is found in the institutional analysis the book advances. The focus of certification on regulating externalities has implications for the challenges of institution building (Snidal 1985a; Knill and

Lehmkuhl 2002; Young 1999; Hardin 1982). Borrowing from economic theory, two market failures are important to distinguish. First, there is an information problem (Akerlof 1970). Companies have knowledge about how they extract resources or produce goods (for example, the size of a company's clear-cuts or forest set-asides for wildlife habitat) that is not available to buyers that may care about the impacts of these practices. Correcting the information problem entails providing this information through some policy mechanism, such as a testing procedure, disclosure policy, or product label. The second challenge is the public good problem (Hardin 1982). Faced with the decision to pay more for goods produced in a socially and environmentally responsible manner, all but a small segment of other-regarding citizens will not act on these concerns (Lober and Green 1994).[12] Given that only some consumers will pay more, producers all along the supply chain will have little incentive to absorb the cost of improved production practices.[13] Hence, society is left with an underprovision of a public good because the private cost of the socially or environmentally appropriate product outweighs the private benefit obtained from the infinitesimal increase in supply of the public good (Hardin 1982). This is partly the logic underpinning scholars' and strategists' emphasis on the critical need for market demand, as just discussed. Without it, this perspective makes it hard to explain how voluntary programs will ensure sufficient provision of a public good or check the production of a public bad.

Other private governors address coordination problems. In this case, producers will have an interest in creating some common set of standards for aspects of their production processes and products to smooth economic transactions and create common gains (Young 1999, 27; Büthe 2010). Distributional conflicts can arise over what standard to adopt since different producers are likely to gain relative to their competitors with one versus another standard (Jack Knight 1995, 1992; Salter 1999; Krasner 1991; Mattli and Büthe 2003; Büthe 2010). However, this coordination problem does not necessarily involve the production of externalities, and hence the challenge of institution building and that of attaining support is different.

The distinction between these two problem types becomes more complicated in a dynamic and multi-actor world, as explored in this book. Cooperation becomes easier when the shadow of the future is long or there are asymmetries among actors. A small group of states, for instance, may choose to provide the public good on its own (Hirshleifer 1983; Hardin 1982). It may also attempt to exclude noncontributors, providing members a club good (Sandler and Tschirhart 1997). By contrast, maintaining stable coordination gets harder when the shadow of the future is long (Snidal 1985a, 1996). When actors face relative losses from a coordinated agreement, the longer the agreement is to last, the higher the incentives are for these actors to find ways, sometime in the future, to argue for a new arrangement or to construct one. Hence, institutional designs relying only on third-party monitoring will be incomplete if different terms of cooperation entail relative gains (or losses) for the negotiating parties (Snidal 1996; Krasner 1991).[14] In these instances, the challenge to create a stable cooperative arrangement should become even more pronounced when substitutes exist; in this case, high demanders can "exit" a given institutional agreement rather than "voicing" their concerns from within (Hirschman 1970). Under these conditions, asymmetric demand and benefits will destabilize an institutional agreement (Hardin 1982).

Note the key difference here from analyses of standard setters such as the International Organization for Standardization (ISO), the International Electrotechnical Commission (IEC), or the International Accounting Standards Board—what Büthe and Mattli (2011) term private standards setters, selected by nonmarket means. Social and environmental certification programs operate in a regulatory marketplace where exits and entries occur. Unlike Büthe and Mattli, this book advances a perspective in which understanding the dynamics of private, market-based standards setters—using their term—requires looking at more than market power or the analogy of technology competitions (for example, VHS versus Betamax). The book follows Büthe and Mattli's careful attention to the distributional consequences of private standards. However, this study's contribution is unique because it examines these distributional consequences for standards dealing with externalities and for cases where no a priori hard-law preference exists for one standard setter over another or where network effects are unlikely to support compliance with a standard. By doing so, the framework further specifies the mechanisms affecting the possible global consolidation of programs and when and by what means new program entry occurs, thus providing new insights into the pathways whereby an important form of private governance may gain global status and potential policy authority.

A central thrust of the argument, therefore, is the need to understand the rise of certification as highly contested; the different possible forms and paths certification takes will involve distributional consequences for various actors, where some will win (or lose) relative to others (Jack Knight 1995; Snidal 1996; Krasner 1991). This is important since much of the existing work on certification emphasizes monitoring the compliance of participants (Prakash and Potoski 2006; Andrew A. King and Lenox 2000; Rivera, De Leon, and Koerber 2006) and performance-focused standards, but neglects to carefully consider the varied dynamics of conflict over what institution will perform this function and how this conflict may be significantly shaped by the early form of individual programs. Thus, while the stringency of certification standards does affect how NGOs and businesses evaluate these initiatives, including creating incentives to develop competitor programs (Cashore, Auld, and Newsom 2004), it cannot fully explain the pattern of programs that have developed across sectors, or the manner in which individual programs have evolved. Rather, the insights of work on institutional development and path dependence (Hacker 2002; Thelen 2003; Pierson 2004) provide a better understanding of the processes by which early design choices can generate hard-to-overcome inertia shaping subsequent developments.

Varieties of Private Governance

Considerable attention has been paid to parsing out the various forms of private governance. Typologies focus on the actors involved, the functions performed, the problems addressed, the character of the rules developed, and reasons why regulatory targets participate and choose to comply. This analysis makes two contributions to advancing understandings of certification in its various specific forms.

The first is to focus on the effects of particular design features that have been thus far inadequately examined. For instance, existing research argues that membership can bolster the legitimacy of certification organizations (Bernstein and Cashore 2007; Raynolds, Murray, and Heller 2007; Auld and Bull 2003; Cashore, Auld, and Newsom 2004; Boström 2006; Tollefson, Gale, and Haley 2008). However, the programs examined in the chapters to follow—and those in other sectors too—have notable differences in their membership rules. Some are highly inclusive; others are not. The theory sketched above and detailed further in chapter 2 hypothesizes about the specific way varied membership rules create different opportunities for voice within certification programs and should thus affect the evolution of individual programs and the patterns of programs in different sectors. In this respect, the analysis is laying the groundwork for further study theorizing certification programs as varied opportunity structures similar to the conception of political or market opportunity structures.

Second, aspects of the analysis should, if correct, help explain the patterns of behavior exhibited by other organizations within strategic action fields (Fligstein and McAdam 2012, 9–13). For instance, many of the same tensions and contentious issues facing certification may also help explain the rise and evolution of transnational environmental groups, including the break of Sea Shepherd from Greenpeace in the 1970s. In this way, the analysis is not arguing for an analytic approach to understanding certification that cannot travel to other organizational forms or substantive problem areas; still, a key condition that the discussion of path dependence highlights is that certification programs exist in a middle ground between markets and politics. Hence, many of the dynamics discussed in greater depth to follow may be found to hold only under these conditions.

RESEARCH APPROACH

This book examines coffee, forest, and fisheries programs for four main reasons. First, certification programs have operated in each sector for more than ten years. Second, they provide considerable temporal variation in program development and in the sector-level patterns of programs that have emerged. Together these features permit a comprehensive appraisal of the research questions.[15]

The third reason the sectors are selected concerns their economic, social, and ecological significance, as noted at the outset of this chapter. Devising institutions to manage and mitigate the effects of human activities is a fundamental challenge of our time, justifying problem-oriented scholarship on these issues (Shapiro 2002). This book contributes to our understanding of what to expect from these emerging initiatives, and how, going forward, their potential may be better realized.

The fourth reason the sectors are useful is that they were all affected by a shift to empowering consumers with information on the products they consumed. Boycotts were followed by the use of tools to inform consumers about "good" and "bad" companies. In December 1988, for instance, the U.S. Council on Economic Priorities released *Shopping for a Better World,* a guide to thousands of products sold by hundreds of companies that ranked each on their ethical performance, including environmental issues, charitable giving, women's advancement, and other concerns (Marlin et al. 1991). Roughly 4 million copies were sold in the first five years (Dickenson 1993).[16]

Such attempts to unlock the citizen trapped in the consumer's body coincided with a rise in public interest and concern for the environment (Dunlap 1992; Guber 2003; Wapner 1995, 324). Numerous surveys administered at the time found an upswing in the stated preferences for environmentally friendly products and public sentiments that corporate action on the environment was important (Auld 2009). Commentators did note that consumers often say they care and then continue to buy the cheapest item (Goldman 1991; Wetzstein 1990a). Yet there was still considerable excitement about this uptick in ethical consumerism.[17]

This upswing had consequences for the emergence of certification initiatives. In each of the sectors, there was some theoretical potential for premiums on labeled products. Certain forest products (for example, designer wood furniture), coffees (such as single-origin Arabica), and seafood (for example, bluefin tuna) exhibit luxury-good qualities. These are usually already marketed on the basis of some facet of prestige, such as the product's uniqueness, its conspicuous qualities, social or emotional value, or quality in use (Vigneron and Johnson 1999), meaning that adding ethics as an attribute might be reasonably easy. At the same time, the vast majority of products in each of the sectors are commodities competing on price, which makes premiums harder to obtain.[18] Thus, as cases, the sectors provide within-sector differences in how likely it is that products will elicit green or ethical premiums and across-sector differences in like categories of goods (commodities versus luxury goods). Both potential forms of variation are useful for exploring the emergence of certification. One can think of these as the latent potential of each sector; market demand is something that still would require efforts to build.

The research conducted for the analysis began in 2004, though it is also informed by the fieldwork and research done for *Governing Through Markets,* which I co-wrote with Benjamin Cashore and Deanna Newsom. Interviews conducted for this initial project on certification offered background insights into the rise of programs in the forest sector. The research built from this foundation, adding interviews with program officials and program developers in the three sectors. Documents from the early formation of the programs were also very significant sources, as were the archived Web pages of organizations available on the Web-based archive site the Wayback Machine.[19] This site was used to construct a careful and chronological narrative of the development of different programs, which was then woven together to form the backbone of the analytic narratives presented in chapters 3 through 8. In many instances, the analysis drew on insights from reports and the academic work of others to fill gaps in parts of the development of individual programs. Newswires, newspaper articles and editorials, and the trade press served as further sources providing essential details on the histories. Through triangulation, a more reliable and complete history could be constructed, which then served as the basis for the analytic process tracing done to examine the explanations sketched above and further detailed in chapter 2.

Outline of the Book

The remainder of the book proceeds in eight chapters. Chapter 2 begins by reviewing research on institutional development to advance an evolutionary perspective for private governance. The chapter then details an explanatory framework that identifies market, political, informational, and capacity factors that are expected to influence the initiation of certification programs in different sectors; expectations about how programs will evolve based on the interplay of actors' strategic decisions and the program's internal governance structures; and how this interplay combined with processes of learning shape the patterns of programs that emerge within different sectors.

Chapters 3 through 8 provide empirics on the developments in the three sectors examined. Two sequential chapters are dedicated to each sector. The first in the sequence describes the market and political opportunity structures hypothesized to affect program initiation. These chapters begin with the market by describing the organization, production, and trade in the sector's products; these chapters then sketch the structure of the sectors' supply chains. The discussion turns then to the political opportunity structures by detailing the character of intergovernmental processes relevant to each of the sectors; these details help to specify how the social and environmental problems were being framed when certification became an option.

The second chapter for each sector outlines the historical develop-ment of certification initiatives in that sector. These chapters are struc-tured to answer the three research questions, and they each begin by detailing how programs were initiated in each sector—assessing and tracing the influence of the conditions outlined in each of the sectors' complementary chapters on market and political opportunity structures. From here they explore the connection between the way programs initi-ated and the time programs have taken to globalize and the patterns of programs that have developed in each sector.

Chapter 9 gleans key lessons from a comparative assessment of the three cases. It carefully assesses the explanations posed in chapter 2 against the historical developments. The chapter closes by returning to the broader questions of institutional emergence, particular issues of path dependence, and what these mean for the rise and evolution of pri-vate governance.

CHAPTER TWO

Dynamics of Initiation, Consolidation, and Propagation

EVERY SOCIAL SCIENCE turns to history for some purpose.[1] History serves as a reservoir of data. It offers the context or background for studies, perhaps motivating a researcher's interest in a particular question. At other times, it is as an explanatory variable—distant historical events act as determinants of current outcomes. The term *path dependence* embodies this vision of history. However, the term has come to mean many different things—from a descriptive metaphor used to evoke the idea that history matters to a narrow process that involves the causal influence historical chance events have on the present. In all senses, historical events, and sometimes their timing and sequence, are treated as explanatory variables.

Do the origins of private governance initiatives shape their operation? This chapter develops an analytical framework to shed light on this question and to go beyond it by assessing the forces that influence the reproduction of early choices against those that push for change. Building from a review of work on path dependence, the chapter identifies key differences between political and economic uses of path-dependent arguments. Economic applications are typically coordination problems: efforts to move an industry from one technology or industry standard to another. In politics, the provision of collective goods is the perennial problem. Different mechanisms of reproduction apply in these cases, government laws and regulations being central. With coordination problems, in contrast, it is in the actor's own interest to eventually adhere to the equilibrium outcome, even if that outcome is suboptimal.

Yet, recall from chapter 1 that when cooperation occurs over longer time periods and involves relative gains (or losses) for actors, a twofold challenge ensues: overcoming the collective action problem (preventing free riding through third-party monitoring) and addressing distributional disputes (Martin and Simmons 1998; Snidal 1996; Krasner 1991; Büthe 2010; Büthe and Mattli 2011). Examining the former will be critical to understanding the evolution of certification programs. Following recent work in this area, the chapter underlines a need to clearly specify mechanisms of reproduction and mechanisms of change. The trajectory a certification program tracks will emerge as the concurrent operation of these mechanisms over time.

PRIVATE GOVERNANCE

Social science has long studied the development of and compliance with rules in the absence of the state (Ostrom 1990; Coase 1960). Work in new institutionalism, such as North (1991) and Jack Knight (1995), typify efforts to further understand the formation of rules via the interactions of individual actors, and how such rules are reproduced and diffused to become social institutions.[2]

Normally, regulations are considered the remit of states—states hold sovereign authority to enact and enforce laws within their territorial borders (Krasner 2001). Yet extensive research now explores and details contemporary and historical examples of regulations developing independent of—and sometimes in opposition to—the state (see Rodney Bruce Hall and Biersteker 2002; Webb 2002; Djelic and Sahlin-Andersson 2006; Micheletti 1999; Pattberg 2007; Büthe and Mattli 2011; Cutler, Haufler, and Porter 1999b). Braithwaite and Drahos (2000, 10), for instance, provides extensive evidence for why careful study of private rules is needed to understand the emergence of global business regulations; private activities often facilitate government regulation (see Vandenbergh 2005) or they can become stand-alone organizations that are largely autonomous of states and that dictate rules of practice for a given sector (see Cashore 2002; Bernstein and Cashore 2007; Colin Scott 2002).

Although the genealogy of private governance reaches far into the past, the field has broadened notably in recent decades, with numerous company and industry codes of conduct, self-regulatory programs, and

private-private partnerships forming to address aspects of business activities, including ethical and environmental practices (Kolk, Tulder, and
Welters 1999; Fliess and Matsudaira 1999; Bendell 2000; Börzel and
Risse 2005; Vogel 2008; Murphy and Bendell 1997; Auld, Bernstein,
and Cashore 2008; Pattberg 2007; Fransen and Kolk 2007; Haufler
2001; Bartley 2003). Explanations for this growth draw on social theory
and research that connects economic and social forces to periods of political instability and change. Many scholars examining private governance
draw parallels to Polanyi's (1944) discussion of the self-regulating market
and its creation of a spontaneous social backlash that helped efforts to
"embed" markets in national regulatory systems (Ruggie 2002). Forces
of globalization, accordingly, are seen to be "disembedding national
economies and generating a new mode of production and authority relations" (Cutler, Haufler, and Porter 1999a, 349).[3] Such forces include
rapid technological improvements to transportation and information
systems (Reich 2007) and greatly reduced monitoring and enforcement
costs (Esty 2004). The latter, among other things, facilitates using private
property rights to regulate many more open-access resource problems
(Rose 1991). As well, technological changes have spurred an increasing
scope of traded goods (that is, public goods being transformed into private ones), the general intensity of trading, and the extension of market
transactions more widely around the globe (Cerny 1995). These shifts
are also apparent in the strengthened position of neoliberal ideas and
norms embodied in the global free trade framework (Gilpin and Gilpin
2001), which has served to constrain the set of acceptable and feasible
policy options for addressing social and environmental problems (Bernstein 2002; Bartley 2003; Falkner 2003; Oberthür 2009; Kysar 2004).

All of these trends present challenges for states seeking to provide
collective goods (or reduce collective bads), including establishing a
working market framework (for example, protection of private property
rights); sponsoring or controlling production through the provision of
subsidies, infrastructure, and other public services; and redistributing
goods (for example, providing health services and protecting the environment). Concurrently, they have empowered and emboldened private
actors to collectively respond at scales both larger and smaller than state
boundaries, offering private solutions to social and environmental problems (Peter Evans 1997; Cerny 1995; Rodney Bruce Hall and Biersteker
2002; Wapner 1995; Keck and Sikkink 1998).

Private Governance and History Dependence

Although there is a sizable literature focused on certification as a form of private governance, probable links between *institutional emergence* and *institutional adaptation and change* have been largely neglected. This shortcoming flows from the simple fact that existing work does not adequately consider how initial differences among certification programs affect the evolution of these initiatives and potentially their effectiveness.[4]

The first contributing problem is how existing research understands emergence. At one extreme, it is given little attention. Work on the ISO, including that of Prakash and Potoski, often takes for granted the status of the standard-setting body, treating it as fixed and uncontested. This assumption is appropriate for certain standard-setting processes, where the standard setter has been delegated authority by states, what Büthe and Mattli (2011) term nonmarket-based private rules. The Agreement on Technical Barriers to Trade, for instance, explicitly references the ISO/IEC in its annex 3, Code of Good Practices for the Preparation, Adoption and Application of Standards (WTO 2005), and the agreement itself has provisions that encourage member countries to harmonize with existing or nearly complete standards in applicable situations (for example, article 2.4).[5] The Sanitary and Phytosanitary Agreement provides even stronger recognition of the Codex Alimentarius Commission as the default standard setter for global food safety issues, which Büthe and Harris (2011) explain has increased the salience of distributional disputes within the work of Codex.

When international law does not side with one standard setter or standard over others, by contrast, the political struggles to establish global standards will differ in important ways. For one, domestic laws or international agreements will not create lock-in effects (Pierson 2004). Thus, unlike situations in which first movers shape the international rules and followers face switching costs to comply (see, for example, Mattli and Büthe 2003; Clapp 1998), with private certification initiatives, provisions to protect first movers must be developed by the programs and the participants themselves (see Botzem and Quack 2006).

Other authors do examine emergence. Bartley's (2003) study on the emergence of the certification model in labor and forestry pays the most direct and extensive attention to questions of history dependence. Pattberg (2007) and Gulbrandsen (2010) adopted a similar analytic focus looking at, respectively, the FSC and the Coalition for Environmentally

Responsible Economies, and the FSC, PEFC, and MSC. Other work has also clarified the important and separate roles businesses, NGOs, certifiers, and foundations have played in the formation of certification programs (Klooster 2005; Bartley 2007b, 2003). Still others have identified the role of norms, such as technical and scientific rationality and neoliberalism, as foundational justification for the rise of private governors across issue areas (Büthe 2010; Bartley 2007b; Pattberg 2007; Bernstein 2002). Cashore, Auld, and Newsom (2004), by contrast, more carefully examined how programs adapted and changed over time, but they did not examine the legacy effects of different program origins, even though they speculated they were likely to matter.[6] Similarly, Rodney Bruce Hall and Biersteker (2002) and Cutler, Haufler, and Porter (1999a) focus more on how private initiatives, once in place, attempt to gain authority. Hall and Biersteker discuss "the reversibility of private authority" (213), but do so only generally by commenting on the possibility of the state superseding these new arrangements or how environmental programs might lose their moral authority to address some salient political problem. Reversibility, in this way, is a consequence of how well the private authority performs some function or how well the authority fits accepted norms.

Hence, while work does look at the origins of programs and at how programs garner support from businesses and NGOs, little research has considered how certain institutional features—laid down when a program forms—may matter for how programs evolve. Scholars have advanced various phase and stage models to examine private governance—from modified versions of the policy cycle model (Avant, Finnemore, and Sell 2010; Abbott and Snidal 2009a; Büthe 2010) to differently conceptualized phases of evolution or development (Klooster 2005; Bernstein and Cashore 2007)—yet these models typically serve only as heuristics, constructing a story line for the development or operation of individual private governors or the interactions among private governors in a specific sector. They move us only partially toward an understanding of how private governance, as institutions and organizations, evolves over time.

In summary, there are two key gaps in the existing work on the development of social and environmental certification programs. First, the dynamic and evolutionary implications of different program designs are poorly understood. Second, and related, little work traces the effects different program origins have for processes of internal program consolidation and the patterns of programs that emerge within different sectors. The next section turns to literature on path dependence for insights on how best to evaluate these neglected processes.

THEORIES OF PATH DEPENDENCE

There is considerable variation in the application of path-dependent theories (Griffin 1993). David's (1985) work explaining the adoption and continued use of the less efficient QWERTY keyboard defined path dependence as occurring when "important influences upon the eventual outcome can be exerted by temporally remote events, including happenings dominated by chance elements rather than systematic forces" (332). A "branching tree" metaphor is popular among scholars of political development in which "institutional choices made at 'critical junctures' lay down a given state's course of development for decades and even centuries to come" (Ertman 1997, 320).[7] To paraphrase Levi's (1997) description: think of a tree with many branches; choosing to climb one branch does not mean other branches are impossible to reach, but getting to them may be difficult. Decision makers in the future, in other words, will be limited to certain options (nearby branches) dictated by far-removed historical events (which branch was originally chosen).

Although some stress the importance of chance events at the original branching point (see Mahoney 2000), both Hacker (2002) and Thelen (2003, 1999) suggest the focus on contingent events is unfortunate; they argue that path dependence simply requires "an initial set of causes set in motion a self-reinforcing process that is at least partially independent of the original causes" (Hacker 2002, 309). Rather than resolve these debates about the defining features of path dependence, the analytical framework advanced below builds from the growing attention to mechanisms of change and reproduction.

Mechanisms of Path Dependence

Path-dependent arguments typically specify the processes of history dependence, referencing one or more of several mechanisms: large fixed costs relative to variable costs; learning effects; coordination (that is, network) effects; and adaptive expectations (table 2.1).

These mechanisms are often then seen to create larger processes such as increasing returns, self-reinforcing processes, and positive feed-

Table 2.1.

Mechanisms underlying path-dependent processes

MECHANISM	OPERATION OF THE MECHANISM
Large fixed costs relative to variable costs	With high fixed costs but low variable costs, once the decision to invest is made, it becomes rational to increase an activity to gain from reduced per-unit costs.
Learning effects	There are specific assets associated with the process of carrying out an activity. By doing the activity (learning by doing), learning occurs that can be captured only by the actor doing the activity. Learning can also reduce uncertainty about a product or an institution's performance (learning by adoption).[a]
Coordination effects	There is increasing value of a specific activity (or good) as more people do it (or consume it). This is also referred to as a positive network externality.
Adaptive expectations	Peoples' expectations about which of a set of activities will be broadly accepted will lead them to choose one option. As more people choose one, expectations will increasingly favor it as the accepted option.

Sources: Pierson 2004; North 1991; David 1985; Krugman 1991; Cowan 1990; Arthur 1989; and Arthur, Ermoliev, and Kaniovski 1987.

[a]This mechanism appears in the resource-based view of the firm. Conner (1991) details how this view explains the existence of firms, their scope, and their differences as functions of the specific knowledge and assets held by individual firms. A concrete example would be the relative value of research done by a company department versus that done by an outside consultant. The argument holds that specific value is obtained in the act of conducting the research that is not captured by the value of the product itself in completed form.

backs. For instance, North (1991, 94–95) uses self-reinforcing and increasing returns largely as interchangeable processes, which are the emergent pattern that results from learning effects, coordination effects, and adaptive expectations. Pierson (2004) provides a specific definition of increasing returns: "Each increment added to a particular line of activity yields larger rather than smaller benefits" (22). But in subsequent discussion, increasing returns and self-reinforcing processes are also used ostensibly as synonyms. Page (2006) offers a detailed critique of the limited consistency in the application of these different terms, setting out separate definitions in the hopes of unpacking possibly different processes by which history dependence occurs. It is beyond the scope of this book to weigh in on this debate. However, one important point Page makes is that constraint should be considered central to path dependence. He argues that increasing returns are neither necessary nor sufficient for path dependence. Rather, the loss of alternative options is a function of constraint, not increasing returns associated with the chosen option. North (1991) followed a similar logic. Two forces shape the course of institutional change: transaction costs and processes of increasing returns. North argued that with increasing returns, so long as markets were competitive, institutions would not matter.[8] Even though actors operate with incorrect models and face bounded rationality, in the long run, given these settings, they would either learn and adapt or be eliminated.[9] The outcome could still be efficient, since inefficiency comes from high transaction costs and incomplete information. Where increasing returns are combined with incomplete markets (that is, information problems, nonzero transaction costs), conversely, "the subjective models of actors modified by very imperfect feedback and by ideology will shape the path" (95). In these conditions, North argues, "not only can both divergent paths and persistently poor performance prevail, the historically derived perceptions of the actors shape the choice that they make" (95–96).

The branching-tree notion of path dependence proves much closer to this understanding of path-dependent mechanisms. It stresses constraints, costs of reversal, and negative externalities that make a particular choice or action the only one reasonably available to a network of actors. These points underline that the mechanisms of reproduction and change require simultaneous attention.

Path Dependence and Change

Path dependence implies an inability to change. This focus is a central point of critique, particularly for work that focuses on increasing returns. As Thelen (2003, 231) explains: "Increasing returns cannot tell the whole story because, in politics, losers do not necessarily disappear and their 'adaptation' to prevailing institutions can mean something very different from 'embracing and reproducing' those institutions, as in the worlds of technologies and markets. Precisely in the political realm, we should expect institutions to be not just the site but also the object of ongoing contestation." This critique highlights how analysis of institutional dynamics must pay attention to forces for stability and *change*. Pierson (2004) suggests that institutional development can, in simple terms, be expressed as a function of conversion and replacement costs (with costs not simply being monetary). Rather than assuming that certain rules will be hard to change, this approach views it as an empirical question. Stability is hypothesized to occur where costs are high for conversion and replacement.

One factor that influences these processes is the notion of redundancy, or slack resources (Cyert and March 1963). Crouch and Farrell (2004) explain that, although one path may be chosen, this does not mean other options are discarded; they may rest dormant, poised for use in the future. Indeed, when actors operate in different normative and institutional environments, the competencies, capabilities, and interests they therein develop are a foundation from which new paths can emerge. We can see this highlighted in the recent work on technology path dependence where niche markets allow competitors to develop sufficient returns to scale before entering the larger market (Cowan 1990; Kemp, Rip, and Schot 2001). Likewise, innovative companies frequently give employees leeway to pursue projects not driven purely by short-run profit motives (Garud and Karnoe 2001). Indeed, work on technological lock-in clarifies how a dominant technology can be and often is ousted. Early models such as Arthur's (1989) did not consider complementarities between competing technologies or what occurs when they develop at different times (Islas 1997). These models also neglected strategic efforts to create new technologies.

Path Dependence in Markets and Politics
Building from the last sections, the point about increasing returns is important. It implies that there are instances when dominance occurs that have nothing to do with path dependence. Rather, certain institutions or technologies may be superior and hence outcompete other options. This outcome is likely when the standard economic assumptions hold: transaction costs are negligible, information moves freely, actors are be-

haviorally consistent, and variation exists in technological alternatives (Nelson and Winter 2002).

These assumptions highlight the need for care in distinguishing between politics and markets. Pierson (2004) offers several features of politics that are important in this regard. First, politics involves authority, not exchange: "Both formal institutions (such as constitutional arrangements) and public policies place extensive, legally binding constraints on behavior" (34). Once a legally binding decision has been made, the exit option becomes largely unavailable, creating incentives for individuals to "invest in specialized skills, deepen relationships with other individuals and organizations, and develop particular political and social identities" (35). In other words, and relating this back to Nelson and Winter (2002), there are insufficient alternative institutional arrangements that actors can choose between. A second related difference deals with the interaction between power and authority: political authority means that certain actors can "impose rules on others," and hence power can beget more power. Alternatively, where power is evenly distributed, initial conflict over rules imposed by one set of actors may lead to the taken-for-granted acceptance of these rules by all parties through coordination effects or adaptive expectations (Pierson 2004, 38).

Finally, Pierson also notes that, unlike markets, in politics there are complex and hard-to-measure goals (for example, the maintenance of resilient and functional ecosystems), and strong mechanisms that induce learning are absent. This is particularly problematic since in politics, links between actions and outcomes are less clear. Because of this looseness, actors may not think to propose an alternative arrangement, and thus existing institutions can persist.

AN EXPLANATORY FRAMEWORK

The discussions of path dependence, mechanisms of reproduction and change, and the distinctions between markets and politics serve as the foundation for the analytic framework developed below. Following Mahoney's (2000) analytical distinction between initiation and reproduction, the framework delineates two stages of analysis. The first stage deals with initiation—the book's first research question—and the second assesses internal consolidation and sector-level processes of copying and competition—the book's second and third research questions (figure 2.1). Following Hacker's (2002) definition of path dependence, the

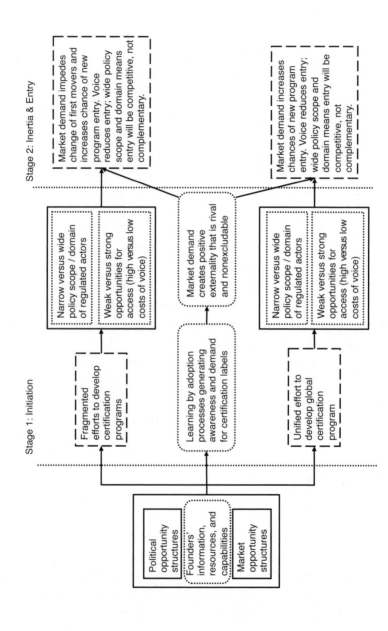

Stage 2: Inertia & Entry

Market demand impedes change of first movers and increases chance of new program entry. Voice reduces entry; wide policy scope and domain means entry will be competitive, not complementary.

Market demand increases chances of new program entry. Voice reduces entry; wide policy scope and domain means entry will be competitive, not complementary.

Narrow versus wide policy scope / domain of regulated actors

Weak versus strong opportunities for access (high versus low costs of voice)

Market demand creates positive externality that is rival and nonexcludable

Narrow versus wide policy scope / domain of regulated actors

Weak versus strong opportunities for access (high versus low costs of voice)

Stage 1: Initiation

Fragmented efforts to develop certification programs

Learning by adoption processes generating awareness and demand for certification labels

Unified effort to develop global certification program

Political opportunity structures

Founders' information, resources, and capabilities

Market opportunity structures

FIGURE 2.1. Analytic framework for explaining the initiation and evolution of certification

argument holds that the causes identified in stage 1 are at least partially independent of the processes of reproduction discussed in stage 2. Once early choices about how to begin certification activities were taken, separate forces emerged to shape the processes of development.

Stage 1: Program Initiation

Two contextual factors are hypothesized to explain variation in four program attributes: whether local certification activities occurred first; the broadness of the policy scope; the extent to which the domain of regulated actors was restricted; and what opportunities for voice existed. The factors are: the market and political opportunity structures and the information available to founders and their resources and capabilities.

Market and Political Opportunity Structures

By-product theory, described by Olson (1971) and further elaborated by others (for example, Hardin 1982), suggests how social context affects the likelihood and form of collective outcomes. Traditional interest groups, such as business associations, succeed in providing collective goods in part because they are organized on the basis of "other, selective (that is, private rather than collective good) incentives" (Hardin 1982, 31). Similarly, social movement scholars conceptualize social context as political opportunity structures, which represent "formal and informal political conditions that encourage, discourage, channel, and otherwise affect movement activity" (Campbell 2005, 44).[10]

Two aspects of these opportunity structures are important for understanding why local certification activities began early in certain sectors and not in others. The first involves the perceived relative openness of political versus market venues, where openness is measured by the influence over decisions available to private actors. The second aspect of these opportunity structures derives from their geographic scale. Market and political venues must exist and be well developed at a particular spatial scale (from local to global) for openness to matter. Companies need to operate in multiple different countries, trade needs to occur, and states need to interact to govern these market activities for any form of transnational NGO mobilization to transpire.

Where political and market venues are weakly developed at the global scale but markets are more open, domestic market strategies are favored.

That is, NGOs will have the greatest successes in achieving their goals if they employ market-based strategies domestically. Likewise, the scale of market and political opportunity structures will also mediate how companies respond to NGO pressures. If an industry is organized to lobby a national government, as opposed to having well-established international ties through an international association, any collective industry response is most likely to occur initially at the national level. Overall, this means that examining the relative openness of different political and market structures at different spatial scales should help explain why local certification activities start first in certain cases and global programs begin first in others.

Of course, the specific type of strategy chosen should depend on the configuration and scale of the market and political opportunities. This general expectation guides the hypotheses that follow; each identifies the expected effects of different components of market and political opportunity structures that, when combined, help explain program initiation.

We turn first to market structures. For NGOs, markets offer at least three opportunities for remedying social and environmental problems associated with economic activities. These are targeting companies to change their behavior, partnering with companies to work on change from within, and constructing model enterprises to lead by example. The structures in a given market will favor one or more of these options over the others. Market structures also shape the options available for companies either in their efforts to act proactively or in their work fending off external pressures, including those coming from NGOs. Considering differences in openness combined with their spatial scale helps identify three hypotheses.

Hypothesis 1: When markets have low barriers to entry, the development of local-first programs is more likely.

The intuition for this hypothesis is that low barriers to entry in a given domestic market greatly facilitate the creation of model enterprises as a means to lead by example. That is, NGOs or individuals can create new companies that operate in a responsible manner and thus serve as an example of best practice (for example, creating a company that deals only in fair-trade products). Entry barriers, such as economies of scale in production, strength of existing brands, switching costs, access to distribution channels, and access to inputs, location, and experience, will condition the utility of this approach (Porter 1998b). This expectation also draws directly from the discussion of spatial scale. Low barriers to entry imply that it will be possible for many of these enterprises to develop, particularly at a local level.

Hypothesis 2: When there are concentrated points of multinational companies in a supply chain, the development of global-first programs is more likely.

Considerable research discusses how large, highly branded companies are most susceptible to NGO shaming (Spar and La Mure 2003; Klein 1999), and that shaming can have spillover effects on more insulated upstream producers (Sasser 2003; Roberts 2003).[11] Work on global commodity value chains (Gereffi, Korzeniewicz, and Korzeniewicz 1994) identifies the critical role of concentrated points in a supply chain in governing the standards of economic transactions.[12] Several works underscore how these can transmit new standards and practices in supply chains (Sasser 2003; Sasser et al. 2006; Daviron and Ponte 2005; Konefal, Mascarenhas, and Hatanaka 2005; Roberts 2003; Vandenbergh 2007; Conroy 2006; Schurman and Munro 2009), although there is no consensus on the progressive benefits of these mechanisms (Klooster 2005; Raynolds 2004).[13] The specific tactics used to push change frequently involve careful control of information to draw attention to disparities between commitments and behavior, and symbolic framing to induce moral outrage and general concern (Keck and Sikkink 1998; Wapner 1995; Schurman and Munro 2009). The utility of this strategy hinges on the brand or public image of the targeted entity and its bargaining power vis-à-vis clients.[14]

A second, increasingly complementary strategy to direct targeting is collaboration: an actor might seek to partner with a company, hoping that direct collaboration will open doors to influence the company's environmental or social policies (Ashman 2001; Berger, Cunningham, and Drumwright 2004; Bendell 2000; Murphy and Bendell 1997). When market opportunities favor these tactics, they also favor the creation of global-first initiatives. This is because larger companies, all else being equal, are more likely to perceive the need for something approaching a global solution. Compared with smaller competitors, these companies are most likely to operate in global markets.

The character of companies at these concentrated points can also matter. Research uncovers important differences in the motives of companies with private reputations (excludable and rival) relative to companies with collective, interdependent reputations (Sasser 2003; Andrew A. King and Lenox 2000). The former are more likely to develop their own individual, internal approach to environmental and social problems, hoping to maintain private control over the benefits. Alternatively, they may see a partnership as most amenable to their interests, given the lessened transaction costs of having to deal with only one NGO. Only when pressures from NGOs are expected to last for some time is it likely that such a company will favor and support a third-party program (Garcia-Johnson 2001). Companies with collective reputations, by contrast, will see benefits from a collective industry response, given that otherwise their individual efforts may be offset by the questionable practices of other companies (Sasser 2003).[15] Since these companies are negatively affected by the actions of their competitors, they will have stronger incentives to seek ways to set industry-wide standards. Thus, if all else is equal, companies with collective reputations are likely to favor global-first initiatives.

Hypothesis 3: With higher levels of international trade, the development of global-first programs is more likely.

The logic of this hypothesis builds from the early work of Bartley (2003), which suggested different expectations for the development of certification based on the extent of intranational versus international trade. Those industries "heavily international in scope" would have incentives to develop overarching certification systems checking industry claims (457). Tarrow's (2005) contentions about the importance of international ties as a key factor facilitating transnational social movement mobilization also undergird this expectation. Without high levels of trade, there would be no need for global certification programs. In a related way, the hypothesis follows in part from the logic that underlies the efficiency effects of global product and technical standards; certification standards have, at least in theory, the potential to smooth the global flow of goods and services (Büthe 2010, 324).

Turning to political structures, NGOs have an equal or greater number of strategic options, such as forming or supporting political parties, supporting individual political candidates, pressing legal suits, lobbying, and undertaking direct protests (Tarrow 1998; Campbell 2005; Kitschelt

1986). Different political systems will provide hospitable conditions for certain strategies and not others. For instance, proportional representation and large k-past-the-post electoral systems (where k indicates the number of representatives selected from a single electoral district) facilitate the development of more political parties and give independent candidates better shots at winning seats. Systems with first-past-the-post, single-member districts favor more party consolidation preelection and hence "more muted and centrist" legislatures as well as fewer elected parties (Shepsle and Bonchek 1997, 191). In other words, in PR and large k-past-the-post systems, forming a Green party or seeking to get officials elected on environmental platforms is a more tenable project. Law pertaining to nonprofit, tax-exempt status is another critical facet of how easily NGOs can gain influence. It is much easier to gain nonprofit status in some countries, such as the United States, than in others, such as Japan (Schreurs 2002). Companies, for their part, also benefit from certain political structures that give them preferential access to and influence over policy decisions (Lindblom 1977; Migdal 2001). Government activity, or the threat of regulations, also motivates firms to take on environmental and social responsibilities. Collective or firm-level activities can operate to preempt or fend off government regulations (Oliver 1991; Gunningham, Kagan, and Thornton 2003; Cashore and Vertinsky 2000). Conversely, there are cases in which firms can use government regulations to increase competitors' operational costs, forcing them to meet higher standards at a higher marginal cost (Reinhardt 2000).

Social movement scholars also explain how the emergence of national social movements occurred concurrently and interdependently with the consolidation of nation-states (Tilly 1984, cited in Tarrow 1998, 18). Tarrow's (2005) recent work unpacks the international expansion of social movements, a phenomenon given extensive attention in the literature (Wapner 1995, 1996; Keck and Sikkink 1998; Florini 2000; Lipschutz 1992). Tarrow hypothesizes that "the openness of the opportunity structure for non-state actors is a function of the institutionalization of interstate ties and of the degree to which they have produced multilateral interactions" (2005, 27). These ties—international institutions, regimes, and practices—are "coral reefs" attracting and supporting the activities of state and nonstate actors in world politics (27). Work on global environmental governance examines the role NGOs play in state-state deliberations over environmental treaties and agreements, and it has identified the different opportunities these processes present for NGO influence (Betsill and Corell 2008). Thus, how these opportunities compare to opportunities for influence domestically and how they feature as sources of information on environmental and social problems are critical (Ronald B. Mitchell 2011). Finally, a perception of openness also includes the output side. Openness flows from the responsiveness of the political system to a particular group's demands, but also involves the ability to effectively implement policies that address these demands (Kitschelt 1986).

These points lead to the following hypotheses.

Hypothesis 4: When international political opportunity structures are more open than domestic ones, the development of global-first programs is more likely.

The logic of this hypothesis draws directly from the above discussion. It implies that there will be incentives to develop strategies that take advantage of the most open political venues. Work on transnational advocacy networks and the specific case of the boomerang effect identified by Keck and Sikkink (1998) follow a similar logic; that is, when there is a domestic blockage that prevents NGOs from gaining political influence, they can take their claims to international audiences in the hopes that pressure will rebound back to change domestic policy.

If domestic opportunities are more open, the scales tip the other way. For instance, the separation of powers system of government in the United States gives Congress incentives to pass action-forcing or nondiscretionary statutes in order to exert control over the implementation of those laws by the executive. This institutional configuration, along with an open and activist judiciary, creates conditions in which the legal challenges of NGOs can be successful (Hoberg 1997). Still, having a legal option does not mean it will be effective: Keck and Sikkink (1998, 25) suggest that the slowness of Brazil's legal system has rendered it less useful for activist ends (see Hochstetler and Keck 2007, 51–57). In contrast, there are countries where the legal option is very rarely available. In Canada's parliamentary system, for instance, where the executive and legislative branches are fused, environmental laws are typically written to leave agencies discretion over implementation, greatly reducing the utility of legal challenges (Hoberg 1997).[16] In those cases where domestic opportunities for influence are relatively closed compared with those available internationally, all else being equal, the likelihood of a global-first program is increased.

Another reason why the scale of political opportunity structures matter relates back to Olson's (1971) by-product theory. Collective action for a separate purpose—lobbying for a global forest convention within intergovernmental fora, for instance—can build organizational capacity and network ties that facilitate the creation of a certification program. This suggests there may be a middle level of openness that facilitates coalition building but stops short of meeting NGO demands. When such levels of openness exist in global political and market structures, an environment ripe for the emergence of a global certification program appears to exist. The coalitional or network ties would exist to garner sufficient mobilization behind a program once efforts to pursue political strategies failed.

Hypothesis 5: Where political opportunity structures are open, they act to legitimize particular ideas of key social and environmental problems.

Political processes that are open to the interests and perspectives of various actors reinforce the legitimacy of the information such processes generate on social and environmental problems. As Keohane and Nye (1998) suggest, "To be credible, [information] must be produced through a process that is in accordance with professional norms and characterized by transparency and procedural fairness" (92). Thus, if an intergovernmental process is open to NGOs, even if it does not adequately act to meet their goals, to the extent it has procedural legitimacy, such a process will likely shape how NGOs and companies perceive the key social and environmental problems in a given sector (see also Clark et al. 2002).

Information, Resources, and Capabilities

The information available to founders and the founders' resources and capabilities are also critical to the initiation of these programs. Initiatives develop at different times, meaning that their founders will have access to distinct information about how best to develop and operate a certification program.

The greater experiential information available to late starters does not mean these programs are more likely to succeed, however. Due to asymmetrical information and uncertainty (Blyth 1997, 2003; Young 1991), actors invariably have incomplete knowledge.[17] In addition, because of the cognitive limitations of actors (North 1991; Jones 1999) and the actors' normative predispositions (Campbell 2005, 2004), what they draw from the information will vary. To the extent that learning by doing is operating, information may also be a specific asset, not readily translated to assist the formation of a new program. Thus, although mimicry may facilitate the creation of similar programs across sectors (Dimaggio and Powell 1983), perfect copying is unlikely (Braithwaite and Drahos 2000, 578–601).[18] Moreover, since information is costly to obtain, it is expected that only a subset of actors—call them leaders—will take it upon themselves to craft solutions to perceived problems (Buchanan and Vanberg 1989).[19]

The following hypothesis builds from this discussion.

Hypothesis 6: Certification's policy scope and regulatory domain will be a reflection of the founders' perceptions of key social and environmental problems and the necessary solutions.

The logic of this hypothesis is that much can be learned about the initiation of certification programs from the organizations and individuals that were involved at their inception. For the reasons just discussed, depending on which organizations and individuals are involved, the types of issues raised and the types of solutions offered are likely to vary. More specifically, the design of a new certification program should reflect the resources and capabilities, perception of the problem, and network ties held by those organizations and individuals instrumental in the early stages of development—in particular, those organizations that channel information across issue areas or networks (Campbell 2005; Granovetter 1985; Dalton, Recchia, and Rohrschneider 2003). This hypothesis is applicable both to the first-mover program in a sector and to those programs that follow. More on this latter process is discussed in the section to follow.

In addition, although not centrally relevant to the initial form programs take, the character of the founders also matters for ensuring the program is able to mobilize sufficient support to transform an idea into an institution. New institutions are not likely to gain support effortlessly; new ideas, enterprises, and organizations are frequently met with indifference or resistance (Aldrich and Fiol 1994). If this is true, mobilizing support should present the biggest challenge to transforming an idea into an actual governance program. From this perspective, although individuals are the source of ideas, it soon becomes a collective endeavor as more and more individuals are won over to a particular cause. Because of this, Garud and Karnoe (2001) explain that boundary spanning and the generation of momentum are crucial features of processes creating novelty. Social entrepreneurs must be able to transform and modify their ideas to give them broader relevance. They must mobilize minds in support of the idea through conviction, but be amenable to friendly feedback on how to make the idea better. In certain cases they will even have to convince others that a problem exists that requires fixing. These actors can be individuals or organizations. How these leaders conceive of the problem and how they work to mobilize the support of a broader coalition of actors should prove crucial for understanding differences in program developments across sectors (Campbell 2004; Young 1991; Andresen and Agrawala 2002; Braithwaite and Drahos 2000, 578–601). The discussion turns to these questions of mobilization below.

Stage 2: Consolidation and Sector-Level Copying and Competition
Once certification activities take form in a sector to address a certain scope of issues and domain of actors, two processes are set in motion: (1) processes affecting how and whether programs consolidate at the global level; and (2) processes affecting the patterns of programs at the sector level. The two processes are closely linked. Programs that find it difficult to change, for instance, will provide opportunities for new entrants as the initial program—paraphrasing Blyth (2002)—becomes part of the problem rather than part of a solution. Despite these links, they are best separated for the purposes of analysis since the outcomes operate at different levels: individual-program consolidation versus sector-level patterns.

Internal Program Consolidation
The proposition that time lags matter suggests that mechanisms of reproduction are, at least in the short run, outweighing mechanisms of change. To assess this, it is necessary to identify both. The trajectory programs track will be the product of these two mechanisms operating concurrently over time. It is also crucial to remember that certification programs are both institutions (sets of rules and procedures) and organizations (with their own interests).

This stage of the analysis draws on Hirschman's (1970) discussion of exit, voice, and loyalty and Tsebelis's (2000) work on veto players.[20] Tsebelis's concept of a veto player—"an individual or collective actor whose agreement is required for a policy decision" (Tsebelis 1995, 293)—helps identify pressure for change but also for reproduction when the status quo is an uncoordinated outcome. His model explains policy stability based on three features of a political system: (1) the number of veto players; (2) the degree of congruence in their political positions; and (3) the degree to which collective actor veto players are internally cohesive. Greater policy stability is associated with more veto players, greater incongruence in their political positions, and greater collective actor cohesion. Put another way, when powerful actors that have influence over certification programs perceive high distributional costs from moving to a new coordinated outcome, the chances of a move occurring will be low. Applying this to certification institutions means that given a program's initial form—what is identified by stage 1—having more veto players with incongruent political positions and collective players that have internal cohesion means programs will be less able to change.

One modification is needed, however. Unlike a consolidated political system in which veto players are institutionalized, certification programs are nascent, and hence a veto player's power should be incomplete and subject to change. This is where Hirschman (1970) is useful. He specifies bargaining tools available to veto players and how these operate through time and together to recuperate the dropping quality of goods and services provided by corporations, organizations, and bureaucracies. Analogously, this can be applied to assessing how veto players seek to influence the choices being made by certification programs and what this means for a program's evolution.

There are two key issues Hirschman (1970) identifies. First, a decision to exit should vary according to an actor's outside options. A company that decides to rescind its support gives up the opportunity to influence a program from within. If, however, a substitute exists or can be developed at a cost less than the perceived cost of seeking to influence the existing program, then exit should become more widespread. Likewise, this outside option matters for NGOs. Perhaps voice from without is perceived to be a better option than voice from within. Or perhaps, like the company, a group sees that creating an alternative program will better serve the group's goals.

Second, the nature of the problem matters. Because certification programs regulate the provision of public goods and matters of social equity, as was discussed in chapter 1, an organization's choice to exit does not mean it will be unhampered by the declining quality of the work performed by the program (Hirschman 1970, 102). Hirschman concludes from this that certain quality-conscious actors may choose to remain in an organization, seeking to improve it, rather than exit, a phenomenon he terms loyalty. Since they will be influenced by the quality of the good, whether having exited or not, some may choose to remain within to put upward pressure on quality, or at least prevent it from further declining.

Another interpretation of loyalty is to think of investments in a program rising steadily over time. There may be some quality attribute that provides positive feedbacks to early supporters (Page 2006); alternatively, these can be conceptualized as relationship-specific assets—things loyalists gain from being involved in a given program that cannot be transferred to other uses (Williamson 1985, 52–54). Adapted expectations can also increase the value of working within the program rather than exiting. This is similar to Pierson's (2004, 147) proposed model of institutional stability; as he explains, "Resilience stems not only from the fact that coordination problems and the presence of veto points may make particular institutional revisions difficult. Even more important, individual and organizational adaptations to existing arrangements may also make reversal unattractive." Unlike political institutions, however, private certification programs face a greater threat of entry and exit. Also, Pierson assumes a centralized authority exists that can enact binding decisions. This is absent with certification programs, since their authority relies more on the evaluations of an external audience (Cashore 2002). Thus, the predicted strength and stability of veto players' power—that is, a decision is past and almost immediately veto players resist change in a time-invariant way—is inappropriate. Rather, a veto player's strength will change over time. Likewise, by framing this in terms of costs, Pierson's model does not directly consider the benefits of change and how these need to be considered when thinking about from whom we can expect pressure for change to emanate (Thelen 2003).

Thus, as a starting point, Tsebelis's (2000) model provides expectations about change and reproduction based on the number and characteristics of veto players. When actors for intentional or unintentional reasons invest energy in creating local certification initiatives before attempting to build a global program, the status quo in Tsebelis's model becomes an uncoordinated world, and efforts to change will likely face resistance. Beyond this, however, Pierson's (2004) analysis of coordination and investments as well as Hirschman's (1970) concept of loyalty are added mechanisms influencing programmatic change. The following makes these ideas concrete by discussing those actors that are likely veto players for certification programs and how the mix of voice, exit, and loyalty should influence the path of programmatic change.

First, let us consider the relevant veto players for certification programs. They usefully follow Büthe's (2012, 33) conceptual model for multistakeholder private regulations, which distinguishes between those that demand the rules (rule demanders), those that supply the rules (rule makers), the targets of the rules (targets), the users of the rules (users), and other general stakeholders. These are not mutually exclusive categories; an actor may be a user, a target, and a rule maker. Still, they are important to separate for the purpose of identifying the kinds of exit threats different types of veto players present.

Two of the veto players are best categorized as rule demanders.[21] The first is the funding community. The Austrian government, for instance, provided very important funding for the FSC early on (Bartley 2003; Elliott 2000; Synnott 2005), and U.S. charitable foundations have made significant contributions to several certification programs (Bartley 2007a; Gulbrandsen 2010). Funders can exert pressure for change or reproduction by threatening to withhold or withdraw contributions, a tactic especially powerful early in a program's formation when it may rely exclusively on these contributions.

The second veto player in this category is the community of NGOs focused on the problems being addressed by a program, what Cashore (2002) and Cashore, Auld, and Newsom (2004) referred to as a program's core audience. These groups can leverage change or support reproduction by threatening to publicly criticize the program and the companies it is certifying, using what Keck and Sikkink (1998) term information and accountability politics. This power should also diminish over time as the program establishes its own credibility (Lawson and Cashore 2001), although if many NGOs exit, the program's credibility is still expected to suffer (Cashore, Auld, and Newsom 2004; Cashore 2002; Boström 2006).

The third veto player is the group of actors the program's rules target —that is, the economic actors to which the program's standards apply (both requirements for production practices and product tracking). These actors may refuse to certify or threaten to revoke their certification if already involved, rendering the program unable to achieve its goals for behavioral change. They also serve as a source of program revenues which, though not as significant as contributions from foundations and governments to date, still gives them influence in most cases. Limited support from these actors is arguably the strongest threat and it should not diminish with increased program credibility, since legitimacy and authority in large measure hinge on the participation of the regulatory target (Cutler, Haufler, and Porter 1999a; Cashore 2002). Given a large enough number of defectors, the credibility of the organization will be significantly compromised, and the program may even cease to have operational relevance.

Different institutional designs have implications for the balance of power among the three general veto players. For instance, programs that have a diversity of funding sources will reduce the veto power of government and foundation donors; moreover, it may be questionable whether certification will continue to be underwritten by these funds in the longer term. However, as noted above, the targets of a certification program are arguably the most significant and powerful veto player.

Institutional differences also create program-specific veto players best captured by Büthe's (2012) rule makers category. Examining three program functions helps identify these: stakeholder engagement/participation, revenue generation, and rule making and implementation. With rule making and implementation, two players matter: auditors and national program affiliates, often called national initiatives. Auditors have important rule-making and implementation powers; typically these are specified by contractual agreements with the certification program. Auditors can be responsible for making local interpretations of a program's global standards; they also hold critical information for a program on issues, including the ease with which a standard can be achieved by participants, on-the-ground change in practices, and experience related to auditing outcomes and learning by doing. Auditors are the analogue to government bureaucracies, presenting similar principle-agent dynamics (Kiewiet and McCubbins 1991), yet auditors can also exert influence by threatening not to accredit with a particular program or threatening exit if they have already accredited. When there is a single auditor, which is true of FLO, the influence of this veto player should, by contrast, be even more akin to a government bureaucracy. Rather than posing a credible exit threat, it will have a monopoly on information related to auditing outcomes and learning by doing. Again, as the program's credibility and recognition grows, the pressure from auditors should diminish. Finally, auditors can be a source of revenue through their payment of accreditation fees.

National program affiliates also perform rule-making and implementation functions for certain programs. They may be responsible for creating nationally specific interpretations of global standards, marketing and outreach strategies, and support services for companies involved in the program. They may also be financially independent, having responsibility to generate their own revenue, and sometimes collect fees for services, such as logo licensing. In certain programs, they are the local representatives of an international office that give policies greater local credibility. Though an individual national initiative may lack power to change the direction of the entire program, sufficient dissenting voices create problems. Finally, some of the programs have members with statutory roles and responsibilities, including electing a board of directors and voting on policy changes. Though individual members are not likely to influence the organization's direction through voting decisions, voting blocks may exert influence.

With these veto players in mind, the following describes specific expectations for how veto players will view changes from the initial arrangement of certification activities. There are three issues to keep in mind. First, the threat of exit is a tactic that can push for change or reinforce stability. All actors can exit, though the relative power of the exit threat varies by actor and through time. Second, the discussion clarifies how market premiums can reduce the willingness of veto players to support globalizing a program. Finally, and by contrast, it also reveals that voice matters and should be inversely related to the likelihood that actors will pursue outside options. When market demand exists, the option to exit will be weighed against the strength of opportunities for voice from within. Stronger demand, therefore, should raise the likelihood of exit. This discussion leads to one hypothesis about the internal development of local-first certification programs.

Hypothesis 7: With local-first certification initiatives, the development of market demand creates resistance to change that can slow efforts to create a global program.

The logic of this hypothesis draws directly from the discussion of relative gains (or losses). There are two different ways in which it can operate. The first instance is when in an early time period more than one local initiative develops to address the same or similar issues, thus creating alternative arrangements that then may globalize. The second is where there are alternative rules being followed by economic actors not eligible to participate in the local program, but that would become targets of the program's rules were the local program to expand to become global. In both cases, just as industry may try to have government regulate entry to protect its profitability (Stigler 1971),[22] when market demand exists for local certification programs, early adopters may see change as threatening their use of certification as a tool for product differentiation (Harrison 1999; Guthman 2004). Because of learning effects and the development of assets specific to certain rules and procedures, these companies may resist change even when a different rule generates the same level of environmental or social performance. If a company's operations meet one set of rules that lead to a certain level of performance, having to meet different rules to achieve the same performance might erode the company's cost advantage vis-à-vis competitors, allowing more competitors to certify.[23]

Where market demand is limited or nonexistent, by contrast, producers that do certify, perhaps for other reasons, will have few incentives to prevent other companies from certifying. They should actually want other companies involved, if this raises their rivals' costs (Bernstein and Cashore 2007; Reinhardt 2000). Critically, the desire to have competitors meet a particular standard will be lessened when an early adopter receives market benefits for meeting the standard. Rather, the company will likely want to protect its differentiation by ensuring the standard and processes do not change. If, by contrast, the company certified and realized no additional market benefits, it will likely seek to foist the program onto its competitors or simply drop out. In this way, market demand should be a key driver of company behavior with respect to a program's expansion.[24]

The influence of market demand extends to other actors as well. Auditors and national labeling initiatives that begin their activities before coordination efforts commence are likely to have their own standard and assessment procedures. Though agreeing to a single standard and auditing approach can create benefits by smoothing economic transactions and opening new market opportunities, such agreement is likely to benefit some of these actors more than others. An auditor like KPMG with operations around the world is better placed to gain from a global program than the Nova Scotia Organic Growers Association, which certifies only in the Canadian province of Nova Scotia. As well, for all auditors and national labeling initiatives, changing standards and assessment procedures involves switching costs, meaning each of these actors will prefer a global approach mirroring their own. They will also likely resist using a new label, especially if their own label is recognized and trusted by customers. With more auditors and labeling initiatives and larger differences among their approaches, forming a global program should become increasingly contested (Snidal 1985b). Those facing higher switching costs and benefiting less from coordination will likely threaten not to participate or eventually drop out if the unfavorable program is adopted.

Finally, much like early-adopting firms that gain from market demand, NGOs may feel a global standard will erode gains attained in the formation of local standards. This is particularly the case if local companies are certifying and receiving benefits in the market; such a situation serves to justify that the program's approach is feasible and possibly even preferable (Bernstein and Cashore 2007). Hence, if supporting a global program changes standards in regions where hard-fought battles were waged, the uncoordinated status quo might be preferable. Certain production practices might be, from the NGO's perspective, unacceptable in a given region. Creating a global standard will, therefore, be pulled and pushed by these localized concerns. NGOs that oppose a global compromise could opt out or vocalize their disappointment and dissent, slowing the consolidation of a global program.

The interests of these individual veto players also interact to create self-reinforcing processes. To the extent that there are companies benefiting from early certification activities, auditors or national labeling initiatives will feel more justified that their approaches are superior and valuable. Likewise, as noted above, NGOs may see this as an indication that the system is working. Hence, taken together, the individual incentives to resist change create a network effect that enhances the individual value of the collective choice. In this way, starting local can build inertia, slowing the consolidation of a global program. However, as the next section reveals, market demand creates an offsetting source of instability, namely, the threat of new entrants.

Sector-Level Patterns of Emergence
Programs do not develop in isolation: information is exchanged and programs compete and learn. There is a considerable amount of literature

that details these processes; however, it remains unclear how the dynamics of internal program development, as discussed above, affect patterns at the sector level. This is the focus of this final section.

Exit and voice were introduced above as strategies actors might employ to influence a certification program. The choice to exit was considered more likely when opportunities for voice were less effective than outside options, which included supporting an existing alternative program or creating a new one more amenable to the interests of the particular group. Put another way, one important outside option is the creation of an alternative program.

Under what conditions will this happen? The decision to develop an alternative hinges on several factors. First, the ability of a program to update its functions to meet changing demands mediates whether actors feel a new solution is needed. As Hirschman (1970) would state, it depends on the declining quality of goods and products being offered by the organization and how costly it will be to recuperate those quality losses relative to other options. This is particularly challenging for certification programs that are seeking to address problems that are contested and in flux. A program developed at time 1 to address the then dominant problem definition may find itself less qualified to address the new problems that emerge by time 2. Organizational inertia, the partial consequence of specific assets a program generates while addressing an initial problem, can then restrict its ability to shift in the future (Mintzberg 1978). Or, alternatively, it may be paralyzed by a deadlock where certain actors prefer the status quo compared with any possible coordinated outcome, as was suggested in the above discussion of veto players.[25] Finally, the program might simply decide that the new issues are outside its core competency, and determine deliberately to allow others to address those needs. This discussion leads to the following hypothesis:

Hypothesis 8: Certification programs that are unable or choose not to respond to external pressures create opportunities for the emergence of new programs.

In this sense, the actions of early programs can complement the development of later programs. However, it is not only that early programs struggle to change, choose not to change, or are unable to change, and hence leave problems unaddressed. Early programs and their supporters also generate positive spillovers by shifting consumer and societal interest in certified products. To the extent that these spillovers are open-access goods—they provide rival but nonexcludable benefits—there will be opportunities for late-moving programs to establish and quickly grow. Indeed, the stronger the market demand, the greater the likelihood that other programs will emerge to serve as either substitutes or complements to the first mover. Some of these may be the result of actors rescinding their support from the first program with the hope that a second attempt will yield a better result. Or entirely new actors might form a new program. Arguably the only advantage the first mover will have over these late starters is information and experience gained via learning by doing and potentially the continued support of loyalists. Again, loyalty will probably reach higher levels in those organizations where effective mechanisms for voice exist. When early programs also choose to leave certain problems unaddressed or actors unregulated, programs that form later can become complements rather than direct competitors. What scope and domain early programs choose as a focus should, therefore, help explain the constellation of programs in different sectors.

This means that NGOs, companies, and auditors, among others, have two options: they can participate in or support an existing program, or they can form a new program to complement or compete with existing programs. This leads to the following hypotheses:

Hypothesis 9: When existing certification programs have a narrow policy scope or regulatory domain, new programs are likely to be complements; when early programs have a broad policy scope or regulatory domain, new programs are more likely to be competitors.

Hypothesis 10: When existing certification programs offer opportunities for influence from within, the likelihood of new programs developing is diminished.

Taken together, these hypotheses propose that it will be challenging for an individual program to dominate. They also suggest that local-first and global-first programs are hypothesized to share many similar challenges. For both, early choices about policy scope, regulatory domain, and provisions for voice all are expected to factor in explaining whether and in what form new entrants will emerge. The endogenous creation of market demand and the positive spillovers it generates should work to increase the likelihood that new entrants of all forms will emerge.

However, market demand has an additional effect only relevant to local-first initiatives: it gives those actors benefiting from a local certification approach reasons to resist moves to make the program global. Thus, and in summary, those programs that start with global structures are expected to face the top-down challenge of courting potential supporters and preventing entry by competitor programs that seek to offer alternative means to the same end. Those programs that start local should face similar threats of competitive entry but also must address the bottom-up challenge of coordinating preexisting standards development and auditing efforts that may be supported by actors hesitant to change.

Beginning with an assessment of current work on the development of private governance and the specific form of social and environmental certification programs, this chapter revealed a key lacuna in the current literature. Limited attention has been paid to finer-grained details of the certification institutional form and how early choices about design might have lasting influence over the way programs evolve and what patterns of programs emerge within a given sector. To develop ideas about how early choices might matter, the chapter turned to theories of path dependence. Out of this emerged a perspective on how existing work grapples with explaining patterns of institutional initiation, stability, and change, which highlighted that path dependence is best conceptualized as a class of models under a larger umbrella of history dependence. The review also underscored a need to better specify mechanisms of reproduction and change rather than noting the probable role of path dependence. Mechanisms will vary by empirical setting, but in all situations one must be clear about what underlies a given history dependence. By drawing out differences between politics and markets, the chapter underscored that with social and environmental certification programs, neither analogy is an outstanding fit. Certification programs occupy a middle ground between the world of political authority, where laws often serve to lock in patterns of choices and outcomes for periods of time, and the world of market exchange, where path dependence forms in situations where the standard assumptions of functioning market systems fall short.

The explanatory framework built from these insights. It identified, first, factors that are expected to explain variation in the emergence of certification programs, particularly in regard to whether they began as local or global initiatives. Second, it outlined mechanisms of reproduction and change expected to shape a program's evolution. Finally, it de-tailed processes expected to influence whether new programs are able to enter and compete with or complement a first-mover program. The discussion emphasized the cost-benefit calculations made by various veto players about their options vis-à-vis how to interact with emerging certification initiatives. One key aspect that was hypothesized to impede the move of local certification activities toward becoming a global program was the relative endowments of actors and hence the benefits (losses) they felt they would face relative to others given a chosen institutional form. In the chapters to come, the value of this framework and the individual hypotheses are assessed against the developments of forest, coffee, and fisheries certification.

CHAPTER THREE

Markets and Politics in the Forest Sector

HUMANKIND HAS EXPLOITED FORESTS for thousands of years. In the last several decades, however, exploitation has intensified. Calls for action to protect forest resources grew in the 1980s, but these were followed by frustration with government-led initiatives. A critical mass of interest in seeking alternative solutions formed, laying fertile ground for the emergence of certification programs designed to identify and reward responsible forest management practices.

The conditions and processes that led to this fertile ground are the focus of this chapter. Guided by the discussion in chapter 2, the analysis reviews how market and political opportunity structures help explain the initiation of certification programs. The sector's market has the following relevant features. First, it has high barriers to entry, which are expected to inhibit the creation of local certification programs. Second, its supply chain has several points of concentration occupied by multinationals; this condition is expected to push toward global programs. Finally, and counter to the last factor, the lower levels of international trade compared with fisheries and coffee, in particular, are expected to dampen interest in a global program.

On the political side, early intergovernmental processes for forests focused on the tropics, yet critically, they were open to NGO participation and even included direct attention to forest ecosystem integrity. The openness helped foster and legitimize a broad understanding of forest

53

problems, allowing social issues to reach the agenda concurrently with ecological ones; this openness also nurtured a community of NGOs that were ready to act on their own when government efforts stalled. Finally and most important, these conditions appeared to tip the scales in favor of faster movement toward a global certification program than otherwise expected. The specific way this evolution unfolded will be examined in detail in chapter 4.

We now turn to a descriptive overview of the forest sector to identify the conditions for the three market opportunity structure hypotheses. The second part of the chapter traces the history of intergovernmental processes on forests, detailing how they have coevolved with NGO activism. In so doing, it highlights differences in opportunities available to NGOs and businesses alike, while identifying changing perceptions of the key social and environmental problems. Chapter 4 picks up the analysis with the beginning of stage 1 of the analytic framework to trace how the conditions reviewed below shaped the initiation and evolution of forest certification.

MARKET STRUCTURES

Around 30 percent of the world's land area, or nearly 4 billion hectares, is forested, with ten countries accounting for two-thirds of the total area (FAO 2007c). Of the total global forested area, around half is considered available for timber production; the other half is economically inaccessible due to physical constraints, including rugged terrain, low productivity, or limited density of commercial species (Bull, Mabee, and Scharpenberg 1998).

Harvested wood is often classified by end use, with around half of global production used for fuelwood and the other half for industrial purposes, a global split that is a long-standing trend.[1] Geographic patterns of industrial production have undergone certain changes since the 1970s. At that time, the USSR, Europe, and the United States all produced around 300 million m³ per year. U.S. production has since risen to just over 400 million m³ per year. After the collapse of the USSR, production from the Russian Federation hovered around 80 million m³ per year for much of the 1990s, but grew to nearly 150 million m³ by 2005. The greatest growth in production has occurred in Latin America and the Caribbean, where in 1970 output was 50 million m³ per year and by 2005 it had reached 186 million m³. Brazil accounted for 63 percent of this growth in 2005 (or 118 million m³). Production in Oceania and Africa also trended upward, but less quickly. Oceania's production occurs mainly in Australia and New Zealand (94 percent in 2005). In Africa, production is spread across more countries. In 2005, South Africa produced 21 million m³, or 30 percent of the continental total. Nigeria was the second-largest producer in 2005, contributing 9.4 million m³, or 13 percent of the total (FAO 2007a).

Industrial round wood is used in three parallel and linked production chains: other industrial round wood (for example, telephone and electricity poles), which accounted for 145 million m³ in 2006; sawlogs and veneer logs, which accounted for 1 billion m³; and pulpwood in round and split form, which accounted for the remaining 539 million m³. The solid wood segment uses sawlogs and veneer logs to produce various construction materials. Veneer serves as an input for both fine furniture and plywood. Also, and increasingly, panels and engineered wood products are manufactured from wood chips. Consequently, this secondary processing sector is large.

Although pulp and paper facilities are often integrated, there is sizable trade in wood pulp. Pulping occurs via chemicals, mechanical grinding, or a combination of the two, and involves breaking down solid wood into its component parts, particularly separating the cellulose fibers from a matrix of lignin and hemicellulose (Haygreen and Bowyer 1996). Chemical methods produce higher-grade fibers but lower yields, and have been implicated in environmental concerns due to toxic effluent releases, particularly dioxins (Harrison 2002).

Production of intermediary products is also unevenly distributed around the world. Saw and veneer log production mostly uses softwood inputs (conifers), a pattern due to the dominance of the United States, Canada, and the Russian Federation (formerly the USSR) as producers. Between 1960 and 1990, the United States, Canada, and the USSR accounted for, on average, over half of the global volume of production in this category. Canada and the United States continued to account for an average of 42 percent (or 197 million m³) of annual global total from 1992 through 2005. For nonconiferous saw and veneer logs, Indonesia and Malaysia ranked as two of the top three producers from the 1970s to 1990s. Their combined contribution rose from 6 percent in 1960 to a high of 27 percent in 1989, dropping back to a low of 14 percent in 2001. From 1970 to 2005, they combined to supply 20 percent of global annual production. Brazil also emerged as an important producer of nonconiferous saw and veneer logs; its peak output came in 1999 and 2000, when it produced 9 percent of the annual total (FAO 2007a). With pulpwood, in 2005, production was more evenly divided between coniferous and nonconiferous tree species. Again, the United States dominates: since 1998 it has accounted for an average of 33 percent of the total annual production (165 million m³). Sweden, Finland, Canada, and the Russian Federation also rank regularly in the top five, with Brazil becoming increasingly important.

The United States has also long dominated wood-based panel production. In the 1960s it accounted for, on average, 39 percent of global production; its output has also grown from 10 million m³ per year in the 1960s to around 45 million in 2005. Germany and Canada, two other top producers, have followed a similar pattern. Indonesia and Japan, by contrast, had peak production of around 10 million m³ per year and have since dropped back to around 5 million m³ per year. Japan's production peaked from the early 1970s through to 1989, whereas Indonesia peaked from 1991 through 1997. Chinese production grew more slowly, but by 2004 and 2005 it had replaced the United States as the top world producer (FAO 2007a).

The descriptive overview above provides a basis for identifying the conditions in the forest sector for the three market opportunity structures hypotheses (table 3.1). These are each reviewed below.

Barriers to Entry
With the first hypothesized factor, the forest sector is similar to the fisheries sector in having high barriers to entry compared with the coffee sector. Capital costs of building a new pulp mill can reach between $300 million and $500 million, with an integrated pulp and paper mill costing over $1 billion (Korutz 2003). Recently built Latin American facilities cost as much as $1.25 billion (*Pulp and Paper Report* 2003). Access to inputs can also be challenging, given that resources are typically fully allocated. Licensing arrangements for logging rights to public lands serve as a significant entry barrier against potential competitors, since these rights are usually fully allocated through long-term concessions. Finally, unlike coffee, which is a well-studied crop, forests comprise thousands of species, for some of which there is very little known about their strength, den-

Table 3.1.

Forestry market opportunity structures and expected effects

CHARACTERISTICS	CONDITIONS	EXPECTATIONS
Barriers to entry (hypothesis 1)	High barriers to entry	Inhibits creation of local-first programs
Concentration in supply chain (hypothesis 2)	Several concentrated points occupied by multinationals	Supports creation of global-first programs
International trade (hypothesis 3)	Lower levels of aggregate international trade	Supports creation of local-first programs

sity, rot resistance, and other product qualities. Building the knowledge necessary to market these species imposes further barriers for would-be entrants.

According to hypothesis 1, all else being equal, the conditions in the forest sector do not support the development of local certification programs.

Multinationals at Concentrated Points in the Supply Chain

Compared with coffee, the forest sector has a more complicated supply chain; the major division is between paper and solid wood products, although many material flows connect the two. Also, unlike sectors in which concentration resides near a single peak, several points of concentration exist that are occupied by multinationals.

The forestland base has both points of concentration and great fragmentation. Forest ownership falls in two broad categories: private and public (FAO 2006, 202–7, table 5). The latter dominates most regions.[2] This pattern hides certain realities, however. First, in many countries, governments claim ownership, yet they exert little authority over activities within forests, particularly those in remote areas (Dauvergne 2001). Second, forests are subject to overlapping claims or even legal rights to their resources. Mining rights, water rights, and rights to harvest trees, for instance, may be licensed to separate companies, communities, or individuals (White and Martin 2002). Many indigenous peoples claim traditional rights to forestlands and continue to contest government ownership (Dauvergne 2001; Keck and Sikkink 1998; Kolk 1996). Finally, when governments do exert control, they often give corporations licenses to log large forest tracts.[3] With outright private ownership, by contrast, holdings are typically smaller, meaning there are millions of small private owners. Consider the United States: in 2003, 71 percent of the commercial timberland was privately owned, with 81 percent of this area owned by small, nonindustrial owners (58 percent of the total area) (Smith et al. 2003). There were over 10 million of these small owners; over half of these (6.2 million) had holdings of between 1 and 9 acres (0.405 and 3.642 hectares) in size (Butler and Leatherberry 2004). Similar ownership patterns exist in some European and Scandinavian countries. Land ownership is also changeable, as illustrated by the recent spate of divestitures in the United States (see, for example, International Paper 2006).

With processing, the pulp and paper supply chain is quite different from the solid wood products chain. Pulp and paper production is highly capital intensive (Callejon et al. 1998, 2–19; Environmental Defense Fund 1995; Ince 1999). Capital expenditures for solid wood facilities are less, ranging from $50 million to $70 million for sawmills to $100 million to $150 million for oriented-strand board facilities (Korutz 2003). Hence, whereas there are innumerable sawmill operations around the world, in 1995 there were fourteen hundred pulp mills outside China and another eight thousand in China, which were all comparatively small facilities. Total capacity of all mills was around 290 million tons per year, with 40 percent of this capacity located in North America, 29 percent in Europe, 23 percent in Asia, 6 percent in Latin America, and the remaining 2 percent split between Africa and Oceania (IIED 1996). Similarly, there were thirteen thousand total paper mills in 1995, with approximately ten thousand of these in China. Capacity figures for the non-Chinese facilities averaged around eight thousand tons per year with a global total of 300 million tons per year. Around a third of the paper facilities were integrated with pulp mills (IIED 1996).[4]

Further concentration exists among the companies that own these facilities. In 1993, the top 150 companies were responsible for 67 percent of the world's total paper production (measured by weight); the top 10 companies accounted for 23 percent (IIED 1996).[5] Consolidation continues and the sector has shifted, with investment in North America declining; capacity expansion has been occurring mainly in Latin America and other emerging markets (PWC 2006). Concentration is not as extensive on the solid wood side, and it varies by country. With countries harvesting mostly conifers, sawmilling production is relatively concentrated.[6] By contrast, in countries harvesting a mix of conifers and deciduous forests, sawmilling is more fragmented.[7]

After the processing stage, solid wood and paper products are sold via many outlets. Some segments are concentrated. The retailer Home Depot's annual wood purchases in the late 1990s were estimated at around 10 million m³ round wood equivalent—approximately 10 percent of the world's lumber market (*Wood Technology* 1999; Howard and Stead 2001). B&Q and OBI are similar big European retailers (Cashore, Auld, and Newsom 2004). It was also a period of rapid growth for the home retail sector. Home Depot began the 1990s with 145 stores in twelve states; by 1995, it operated 423 stores in thirty-one states and three Canadian provinces and had net sales of over $15 billion (Home Depot 1997). Ten years later, in 2005, the company operated over 2,000 stores and had net sales of over $80 billion (Tratensek and Jensen 2006). In fiscal year 2006, Home Depot purchased the Home Way, a Chinese retailer, giving the company 12 stores in six cities and marking its entry into the Chinese market (Home Depot 2007).

Thousands of other outlets also sell wood products. In 1997, the United States had 29,461 furniture stores, 3,997 home centers (such as Home Depot), 71,916 building material and supplies dealers, 43,742 other building material dealers, and 11,046 retail lumberyards (U.S. Census Bureau 2000c).[8] Within the home center category, the four largest firms accounted for over 75 percent of sectorwide sales; the other seller categories are an order of magnitude less concentrated (U.S. Census Bureau 2000c). With paper products, large printing and publishing houses and office supply stores (such as Staples) are the most concentrated; however, many smaller-scale operations, serving individualized markets, also exist. Again, in the United States, there were 36,617 companies with printing operations and the top fifty accounted for only 28.1 percent of the value of shipments for 1997 (U.S. Census Bureau 2001). Office supply stores, by contrast, numbered 6,128, with the four largest firms owning 1,932 of the outlets (32 percent of the total) and accounting for 78 percent of the total sales (U.S. Census Bureau 2000c).

According to hypothesis 2, these conditions, if all else is equal, should favor the creation of global certification programs. The presence of multinationals at concentrated points in supply chains offers NGOs more targets to pressure and gives these companies greater resources and interests to develop and support the creation of global certification programs.

International Trade

For the final market factor, the forest sector ranks lowest compared with the other two sectors. In aggregate, trade in forest products is much lower than in the coffee and fishery sectors, albeit its significance has been rising. With volumes, industrial round wood exports have grown from 4 percent of total production in the 1960s to 7.5 percent (128 million m³) in 2005 (FAO 2007a). Much like production, this trade also varies by region. Before the 1990s, most regions exported less than 10 percent of their industrial round wood production; after this time, the Russian Federation and Oceania began increasing exports. In 2005, the Russian Federation reached a high of nearly 35 percent. The high exports from Oceania are driven by New Zealand, where exports made up 25 percent of production in 2005. Within each of the other regions a few countries account for most exports. Indonesia, Malaysia, and the Philippines have been significant in Asia. From 1976 through the 1980s, Indonesia was the top exporter of industrial round wood, representing around 20 percent of the total (equivalent to 20 million m³). Previously, the Philippines was a dominant exporter (Dauvergne 1997), and throughout—from 1960 to 2005—Malaysia has contributed an average of 14 percent to global industrial round wood exports. For the same period, the United States has been a top exporter, contributing an average of 15 percent to the global total. Within Europe, France and Germany exported sizable volumes from the late 1970s forward; at least one of them has been a top-five exporter almost every year since 1980. Overall, since the 1960s, the top five exporters contributed on average 65 percent of the total annual volume (FAO 2007a).

Among importers, Japan stands out. From 1960 to 2000, it was the world's largest importer of industrial round wood, consuming a high of 49 percent of total imports in 1973, and from 1960 to 1998, 35 percent per year, on average. With China, after its 1998 logging ban, imports grew from 10 percent of the world total in 1998 to 23 percent in 2005. China also surpassed Japan as the largest world importer in 2005, with Finland, Japan, Sweden, and Austria completing the rankings; together they represented 56 percent of global import volumes (see Kozak and Canby 2007). Overall, import intensities are generally highest in Asia. From 1961 to 2005, imports accounted for around 20 percent of Asian industrial round wood production; during this time, they averaged 85 percent of total Japanese production. China, too, relies heavily on imports. Between 1961 and 1998, imports accounted for an average of only 8 percent of China's production. From 1999 onward, they have averaged 20 percent, growing from 12 percent in 1999 to 32 percent in 2005 (FAO 2007a).

Regional patterns underlie the aggregate figures. Canada exports mainly to the United States; from 1997 to 2004, it supplied 94 percent of U.S. imports of particleboard and 67 percent of U.S. paper and paperboard (excluding newsprint) imports. In 1992, China, Japan, Thailand, and Korea imported 80 percent of world exports of tropical industrial round wood; Japan alone accounted for 45 percent (FAO 1995). A considerable amount of this wood is then reexported to the European Union and the United States. Chinese furniture exports are reported to have grown 19 percent per year since 1997, rising from 3.2 million m³ round wood equivalent to 12.7 million. U.S. imports from China have grown by 1,000 percent over the same period; European imports have grown by 800 percent (White et al. 2006).

Based on these conditions, all else being equal, the logic of the third hypothesis implies that local-first programs are more likely in the forest sector. That is, because trade is less prominent, the need for a global program to smooth international commerce should have been less salient.

POLITICAL STRUCTURES

Turning from markets to politics, chapter 2 detailed two hypotheses related to the nature of the political opportunities in a sector; conditions on these two factors are detailed in table 3.2. The discussion to follow reviews the recent history of intergovernmental processes on forests and evolving NGO tactics. In short, it details how tropical forests gained the earliest attention, with several intergovernmental organizations seeking to slow forest degradation and tackle poverty. Out of these efforts in the 1980s, a unique commodity agreement formed—the International Tropical Timber Organization (ITTO)—that was open to NGO participation and even included direct attention to forest ecosystem integrity. Through the ITTO, NGOs were able to expand the problem scope to include social

Table 3.2.

Forestry political opportunity structures and expected effects

CHARACTERISTICS	CONDITIONS	EXPECTATIONS
International political opportunity structure (hypothesis 4)	The ITTO served as an open forum	Supports the creation of global programs
Opportunity structures for legitimizing new ideas (hypothesis 5)	The ITTO helped legitimize particular ideas about the character of global forest problems and the appropriate solution	Affects the character of the problems certification programs seek to address

issues and solidify network ties that helped undergird the development of forest certification. As the chapters to follow document, this role of intergovernmental processes was in contrast to the experiences of both the coffee and fisheries sectors.

The Scope and Domain of Governance Structures

The period before the rise of certification saw a considerable growth in attention to forests and their exploitation. Two notable developments occurred in the 1970s to raise concerns about tropical forest loss. First, analysts from the United Nations' Food and Agriculture Organization (FAO) began noting the absence of good global inventory data (Adrian Sommer 1976); this led the FAO to form a global tropical forest monitoring project in 1978 to assess the status of tropical forests (FAO 1980). Second, at the 1976 meeting of the UN Conference on Trade and Development (UNCTAD) a resolution established the Integrated Programme for Commodities (IPC), which was to work on commodity agreements for eighteen goods, including tropical timber (Khindaria 1982b; Poore 2003; Humphreys 1996).

The first initiative—the FAO's global tropical forest monitoring project—uncovered high levels of forest loss (that is, the conversion of forests to other land uses) in tropical forests of Africa, Asia, and Latin America (FAO 1980, 1981). These losses were only part of the story (which the project's reports explained). Activities that did not completely convert forests also damaged important ecosystem functions, meaning conversion rates provided an incomplete view of actual degradation. The reports were still significant: they improved understandings of the problem and underscored a need for swift action (Guppy 1984; Myers 1984).

Other organizations also drew attention to the issue. In March 1980, the International Union for the Conservation of Nature (IUCN), the World Wildlife Fund (WWF), and the UN Environment Programme (UNEP)· jointly released a report entitled *World Conservation Strategy* (IUCN 1980). The report explained challenges to conserving and sustainably managing tropical forests and recommended international action, in the form of law and assistance, as a solution. Notably, the tropics were the focus of concern; boreal and temperate forests had yet to reach the international agenda.[9] The report was also an ideational antecedent to the 1997 Brundtland report—the outcome of the UN World Commission on the Environment and Development—in advocating a development-environment nexus (Keck and Sikkink 1998, 125; Stevis 2006, 24).

In the years that followed, international attention to tropical forests burgeoned. In 1983, FAO created action programs for tropical forest management. The Tropical Forestry Action Plan (TFAP) was published in October 1985 (Humphreys 1996, 32; FAO 1985). Concurrently, the World Resources Institute (WRI), working with the World Bank and the UN Development Programme (UNDP), organized a task force on tropical forest loss. Also in October 1985, this group published its own report, *Tropical Forests: A Call for Action* (Humphreys 1996, 32), which proposed, inter alia, a doubling of funds dedicated to tropical forest management (Osterlund 1985). The two processes then merged in 1987 (Humphreys 1996).

The TFAP dealt only with tropical forests,[10] yet its emphasis was broader than forestry practices. The first TFAP action program read as follows: "This programme is at the interface between forestry and agriculture and aims at conserving the resource base for agriculture, at integrating forestry into agricultural systems and, in general, at a more rational use of land" (Humphreys 1996, 33). Indeed, at the report's release, Gus Speth, then president of the WRI, explained that the aim was to help countries with tropical forests to meet energy needs, overcome food scarcity, and slow the loss of plant and animal species. It took a broad view of tropical forest loss, highlighting poverty, poor agricultural productivity, and skewed landownership as root problems (Shabecoff 1985b).

The early 1980s was also when negotiation for a tropical timber commodity agreement began as part of the 1976 launch of the IPC. Slow

to begin, progress quickened when Japan—the largest importer of tropical timber at the time—realized a growing potential for timber-supply
shortfalls (Khindaria 1982a). The resulting talks culminated in the UN
Conference on Tropical Timber in March 1983, where final negotiating
points for an agreement were resolved. A second conference in November led to the official text of the first International Tropical Timber Agreement (ITTA) (Humphreys 1996, 56).

Three aspects of the agreement and subsequent meetings of the
ITTO are important in relation to hypotheses 4 and 5. First, the ITTA was
the first intergovernmental agreement to consider tropical forest degradation; it contained an objective about forest ecological health that was
included in the final agreement text thanks to the IUCN and efforts of
the WWF and UNEP to assuage concerns that forest ecology fell outside
the purview and expertise of UNCTAD (Poore 2003, 34; Humphreys
1996, 56). As a consequence, the 1983 ITTA had an objective promoting "national policies aimed at sustainable utilization and conservation of
tropical forests and their genetic resources, and at maintaining the ecological balance in the regions concerned" (Humphreys 1996, 57; Poore 2003,
40). This was significant, especially when compared with other commodity agreements, none of which addressed the ecosystems supplying
the given commodity (Humphreys 2004). The ITTA was also distinct in
not focusing on price regulation through buffer stocks or other supply-
control mechanisms (Gilbert 1996; Tharian 1987). Second, its meetings
became a venue where NGOs could seek changes in the way tropical timber was harvested and traded (Gale 1998; Humphreys 1996).[11] Indeed,
the intervention of the IUCN and the role of the WWF helped ensure
that the ITTA gave attention to tropical forest conservation. Finally, it focused on tropical forests. Although consuming countries were members
with half the voting rights, management of boreal and temperate forests
was not addressed.

With the ITTA entering into force in mid-1985 (John Edwards 1985)
and the TFAP process beginning to develop national plans, attention
shifted to implementation. More on implementation is detailed in the
next section, but two points are important here. First, it was at this time
that social issues reached the agenda. Second, by the turn of the 1990s,
problems with forest management outside the tropics were gaining international attention. At the G-7 meeting in July 1990, President George
H. W. Bush proposed negotiating a forest convention, an idea endorsed

by the entire G-7 (Houston Economic Summit 1990). Several similar proposals were circulating, including ones in the WRI-commissioned and independent reviews of the TFAP (Humphreys 1996, 84–86). The proposals were short lived. The idea of a binding international convention was dropped in the preparatory meetings for the Rio Earth Summit due to strong disagreements among countries over national versus global rights and responsibilities over forests; countries such as Malaysia and Indonesia felt a treaty would restrict their ability to export timber and might impose costly requirements for sustainable forest management (Dimitrov 2006, 102; Poore 2003, 99).

Still, the considerations given to a convention were indicative of a growing interest in a global instrument, a process that would bring attention to forest degradation around the world. Even within the ITTO, overtures were made to include tropical, temperate, and boreal forests. Environmental organizations sided with producing countries to support this move. Consuming countries rebuffed the advances, and the renegotiated 1994 ITTA remained a tropical forest agreement (Humphreys 1996; Gale 1998; Agence France-Presse 1993).

By the beginning of the 1990s, international forest policy had a skewed focus toward the tropics, yet there was a latent interest in a global forest mechanism. The UN Conference on Environment and Development (UNCED) produced the *Non-Legally Binding Authoritative Statement of Principles for a Global Consensus on the Management, Conservation, and Sustainable Development of All Types of Forests* (known as the Statement of Forest Principles) (UNGA 1992), and deforestation received attention in chapter 11 of *Agenda 21* (UNCED 1993). The Convention on Biological Diversity opened for signature at the UNCED; it entered into force in December 1993 and developed a program on forest biodiversity in late 1996 (Humphreys 2006). Thus, intergovernmental processes were ongoing. The next section examines how these initiatives coevolved with NGO activities and perceptions of forest problems.

Coevolution of NGO Tactics and Perceived Problems

The above discussion highlighted NGO involvement in international forest negotiations and the initial optimism some groups had about the potential effectiveness of these processes. This optimism quickly waned. First, frustrations were voiced over slow implementation—it took eight years to negotiate and even a year to decide where to house the ITTO headquarters (Dullforce 1986; *Financial Times* 1986). Even still, many NGOs continued pushing for implementation and remained hopeful that the agreement would be useful.[12] Their optimism was bolstered by the pro-conservation vision outlined by the executive director at the second session in March 1987.[13] Quickly, however, this was stymied by entrenched differences between the producer and consumer countries that Poore (2003, 45) suggests were exacerbated by the commodity-agreement structure, which reinforced rather than lessened differences in producer and consumer interests.

The early stages of the ITTO did have other significance. Much like the FAO reports released in the early 1980s, and following the logic of hypothesis 4, the organization helped legitimatize a particular problem definition. The ITTO commissioned a survey of tropical forest management, and later it created an effort to draft guidelines for appropriate management of these forests. The survey was under way by 1987, led by Duncan Poore of the International Institute for Environment and Development (IIED). Its conclusions, similar to earlier FAO studies, painted a glum picture. The team found that less than 1 percent of the world's tropical forests were, by its assessment, being sustainably managed.[14] When the survey was released in November 1988 at an event—the International Seminar on Sustainable Utilization and Conservation of Tropical Forests—run just prior to the Fifth ITTO Council session, reactions signified its import. According to Poore, "Participants could have heard a pin drop when slides were shown of the area of forest under demonstrated sustainable management for timber production as compared with the total area of tropical forest! But no delegate disputed the findings." From this Poore concluded, "[The] seed was sown. There was a changed perception of the scale of the problem; a sense of urgency was generated" (2003, 62). This view was shared. A WWF official participating in the meetings explained that prior to the report government and industry officials claimed forests were sustainably managed; NGOs just would not accept it. After the report, this argument vanished—the discussion turned to how sustainability might actually be achieved.[15]

The ITTO and TFAP were also focal points for criticism; in this way they nurtured a coalition of groups capable of challenging status quo forestry—for both social and ecological reasons. Just one year after the TFAP was first released, in 1986, Consumer Organizations of Penang and Sahabat Alam Malaysia established the World Rainforest Movement (WRM) to link the efforts of groups in the north and south that were working to defend the world's forests and particularly to highlight the limitations of the TFAP and the ITTO (Keck and Sikkink 1998, 131). From this came the 1989 WRM *Penang Declaration,* which detailed the misgivings that WRM members had with existing intergovernmental and industry policies for tropical forests.[16] By 1990, the criticism had increased.[17] Commentators noted the limited NGO involvement in national project development relative to TFAP commitments (Cabarle 1992; Schoon 1990; Amanda Brown 1990; Madeley 1989), and generally characterized TFAP projects as too focused on timber development (Marshall 1991). After the FAO rebuffed requests for reform from lending countries and conservation organizations (Sullivan 1990), both the WWF and the WRI withdrew their support (Humphreys 1996, 47). The WWF also pressed the World Bank to adopt new guides for its loans to tropical forested countries (U.S. Newswire 1990). In addition, the ITTO was criticized for placing excessive weight on the timber trade (Kolk 1996) and for directing insufficient attention to forest conservation and management given the extent of the problems (Blackwell 1991; Poore 2003, 106). Thus, although NGOs had promoted and participated in these processes, by 1990 questions arose about the value of continued engagement.

Paradoxically, the ITTO also helped increase the prominence of social aspects of forest sustainability—in particular the rights of indigenous and forest-dwelling peoples.[18] The entire international problem of forests was shifting during this period. With countries producing tropical timber feeling unfairly pinpointed and increasingly virulent debates over protection and management of forests in countries like Canada (Wilson 1998; Pralle 2006), a change in focus to social and environmental problems in all forests was not surprising.

Developments in British Columbia, Canada, are illustrative. In several cases, NGOs and First Nations formed coalitions to protest companies with logging licenses for the province's forests. In 1980, for example, the Nuu-chah-nulth Tribal Council submitted a formal land claim for an area of Vancouver Island's west coast, asking that no logging occur on Meares Island during settlement negotiations (Wilson 1998, 195). Just before this, MacMillan Bloedel had announced logging plans for the island, setting the stage for confrontation. With the creation of Friends of Clayoquot Sound—a local group of residents opposing logging—an environmental–First Nations alliance was formed that eventually, with the help of a favorable decision by the British Columbia Court of Appeals, succeeded in temporarily stopping logging on the island. This was the beginning of a widely followed international conflict over forestry practices in Clayoquot Sound and in the province more generally (Bernstein 2000), and it highlights the disquiet about practices in temperate and boreal forests that was growing in the 1980s.

Concurrently, new information that chlorine-bleaching processes were creating toxic pollutants such as dioxins and furans led Greenpeace to launch an international pulp and paper campaign in 1986 (Harrison 2002). Disseminating findings from early studies in Sweden and leaked documents from the U.S. Environmental Protection Agency, the organization pressed for quick and stringent regulations (Harrison 2002) and set in motion protests against chlorine bleaching in many countries (Auld 2009). Although Canadian federal and provincial governments moved to regulate pulp-mill effluent (Harrison 2002; Noble 1989; *Globe and Mail* 1988), the speed of these efforts and eventual backpedaling and delayed implementation (Gibbens 1991) spurred an internationalization of the issue. This venue shift began most concretely around May of 1991 when Greenpeace and the Sierra Club organized a tour of British Columbia for European journalists, politicians, and scientists to expose them to existing forest practices (Stanbury 2000). Before this, Greenpeace Germany had published *Das Plagiat,* a takeoff on *Der Spiegel,* a widely read German newsmagazine, as a way to highlight problems with the province's forestry. What began as a campaign against toxic releases quickly broadened to include a critique of forestry practices. When in 1992 the WWF published *Forests in Trouble: A Review of the Status of the World's Temperate Forests,* which uncovered many shortfalls in forestry management, a shift in framing was solidifying, calling for improvements in forest management worldwide.[19] In 1992, the Taiga Rescue Network was established to address forest protection, forest management, and respect for the needs and rights of indigenous peoples in the boreal forests (Auld 2009).

Well before this, as the creation of the WRM illustrates, NGOs were simultaneously working within and outside the ITTO. Based on research started in 1984 that traced UK tropical timber imports, and motivated by concerns that the ITTA lacked enforcement mechanisms, Friends of the Earth–UK began targeting UK tropical timber importers, pressing them to sign a code of conduct that would require timber supplies to come from responsibly managed forests (Jeanrenaud and Dudley 1997; Dudley, Jeanrenaud, and Sullivan 1995). The group also urged importers to contribute 1 percent of their profits to a Tropical Rainforest Preservation Fund (Gowers 1985a).[20] These campaigns kept developing, with similar efforts emerging in Germany and the Netherlands in the coming years. In 1988, the European Parliament even voted to recommend an EC-wide ban on imports from Malaysia. Though the European Commission overturned the vote, it still had symbolic import (Keck and Sikkink 1998). In the United States, similar campaigns were waged. The Rainforest Action Network (RAN), established in 1985, orchestrated a successful boycott against Burger King in 1987 that persuaded the company to cancel $35 million in contracts with Central American beef suppliers (Rainforest Action Network 1997). This was a foretaste of more RAN campaigns to come, and it illustrates, moreover, the importance of the market opportunity structures discussed in the first part of this chapter.

In sum, even before certification took hold, the forestry problems encompassed social and environmental considerations worldwide. By the turn of the 1990s, as the next chapter makes clearer, the view that a private solution was needed was gaining ground, and there was a sizable interest in it being a global solution. This shift was in part made possible by the character of the intergovernmental processes for forests, and the role they played in legitimating a broader conception of the problems facing global forests.

As we will see in the next chapter, the political and market structures in the forest sector have played an important role in shaping the rise of forest certification. Market conditions pushed in different directions. The sector's high barriers to entry should have made local certification initiatives difficult, and points of concentration occupied by multinationals should have helped to facilitate global initiatives. However, the sector's lower levels of international trade are expected to work against the production of a global program. With political conditions, on the other hand, the expectations point in a clearer direction. The openness of the intergovernmental processes, as detailed above, helped legitimize a particular idea of the key forest problems and it supported the creation of an NGO community with the capacity to act alone in the absence of progress from government-led efforts. These conditions ostensibly favored a faster movement toward a global certification program than otherwise expected.

CHAPTER FOUR

The Rise and Evolution of Forest Certification

THE CHARACTER OF INTERGOVERNMENTAL PROCESSES on forests played a pivotal role in laying the foundation for the growth of forest certification. Rather than an array of separate national initiatives, each addressing a similar problem, a relatively cohesive community coalesced with an interest in creating a global program. The ITTO was critical to this process. It became a focal point for discussions and debates over forest management practices, and although it fell short of expectations, it helped spur interest in a private solution. Had this venue been absent, it is likely that a proliferation of individual auditors would have formed, similar to the pattern in organics.

It is equally apparent that political and market structures shaped the efforts of industry players. Forest companies and landowners were organized to mobilize nationally. Yet the global scope of the community supporting the FSC idea, particularly buyers with global supply networks and NGOs operating transnationally, meant that country-level programs were increasingly seen as second best. Producers tried to scale up their initiatives and eventually were successful in forming a global program. These efforts, in turn, created self-reinforcing processes spurring more attempts to foster support for the FSC. Investments in one program by one side of supporters led to equal or greater investments in the other program by its supporters. In particular, efforts to build support for the FSC in the marketplace created positive spillovers, increasing the value of outside options for producers. It was reasonable for producers to expect it would be easier to convince buyers that they were offering a reasonable substitute program compared with the challenges of trying to work within the FSC. Investments by producers worked to legitimize the certification idea, creating a positive feedback loop reinforcing the overall pattern of competition. The presence of producer-backed programs meant, moreover, that NGOs tentatively supporting the FSC were left having to offer more support, given the possibility of market penetration by the competitor programs.

Why did this two-program competition emerge, unlike the fragmentation seen in coffee and fisheries? In closing, the chapter outlines how careful attention to the strategic dynamics that follow from the institutional design of the FSC (particularly membership rules and the discretion given to accredited certifiers) helps explain why producers created programs as substitutes and why we have not seen the successful entry of other programs to date. Finally, the unique structure of the FSC's governance and its attention to social and environmental issues proved influential within and beyond the forest sector. The FSC changed understandings of what was possible and, consequently, became an important model for the construction of future efforts.

STAGE 1: PROGRAM INITIATION

The initiation of forest certification efforts illustrates the influence of existing opportunity structures, in particular the openness and geographic scope of intergovernmental processes for forests. The ITTO and TFAP were moderately open to NGO participation and pressure, but they stopped short of sufficiently addressing the problems these groups felt warranted urgent attention. Meetings of the ITTO itself were also critical for building the connections, or community, from which certification emerged. A WWF official, recalling the processes, explained: "[There] were like fifty observers from NGOs at each [ITTO] meeting, and they were networking and exchanging views, sitting in lobbies waiting for things to happen and coming up with all sorts of ideas. . . . I think ITTO, whether it intended to or not, played a role as a kind of forum where lots of people came together, and quite a number of those same people ended up being involved in FSC."[1] Hence, having some access was important.

Ultimately, it was the ITTO's unwillingness to champion labeling that led NGOs to consider other options. The issue came to a head in 1989 during the fifth meeting of the ITTO committees; the UK delegation, led by the Overseas Development Agency and backed by Friends of the Earth, put forward a preproject proposal: *Labelling Systems for the Promotion of Sustainably-Produced Tropical Timber*. Because the proposal came after Friends of the Earth and other groups had initiated campaigns against tropical imports in Europe, major exporters, particularly Malaysia and Indonesia, felt it was a boycott in disguise (Humphreys 1996, 72). A modified proposal on incentives for sustainable development of tropical forests went forward, but lost the support of Friends of the Earth. For the time, certification dropped from the ITTO agenda.

Simultaneously, the idea filtered into the deliberations of groups and individuals coalescing to develop the FSC. After attending the two meetings mentioned above, the Rainforest Alliance launched its SmartWood program in 1989, the first-ever forest certification initiative. Almost concurrently, in August of 1989, the WWF announced a target of 1995 by when, it argued, all tropical timber should come from sustainable sources (Humphreys 1996). A similar desire to address tropical forest problems led others to get involved. For instance, certain North American woodworkers were becoming aware of the environmental implications of wood they used for musical instruments, boats, and fine furniture. Those using exotic woods were particularly vulnerable to public criticism (Petit 1989). Out of concern and hoping to protect and shore up their reputation (Duffy 1992; Bartley 2007b), they formed the Woodworkers' Alliance for Rainforest Protection (WARP)—an organization that would later become a forum for discussing and launching the FSC.[2]

Before this could happen, however, there was considerable experimentation. Silas Kopf, an early member of WARP and the owner of a custom furniture operation, later explained his worries about the environmental costs of using tropical wood (Cooke 2004). Like others, he struggled to find wood from sustainable sources, and thus chose to add an "ecology surtax" on items made from tropical wood. He explained: "I added the dollar value of the tropical woods used in the piece to the final price, to make the point that the true cost of my materials would have been significantly higher if the market were to account for the cost of conservation" (Kopf 1993). He then donated the surtax to groups working to protect rainforests (Cooke 2004; Shaw 1991).

Other experiments copied the alternative trade model discussed in the next chapter. These woodworkers engaged directly with suppliers, identifying forest operations that were producing tropical hardwoods in socially and ecologically appropriate ways (Duffy 1992; Petit 1989). One prominent example was Hubert Kwisthout's Ecological Trading Company, incorporated in 1989. Having volunteered for Friends of the Earth during the late 1980s, Kwisthout was aware of the tropical wood campaigns. In his work making bagpipes, he confronted the difficulties of sourcing responsible wood and decided there had to be a better way. Seeing the Alternative Trade Shops, he asked: "Why don't we have a third world shop only for timber?"[3] Kwisthout knew one of the developers of Max Havelaar in the Netherlands, which had, by this time, been in operation for two years (chapters 5 and 6). He turned to his friend for advice, while also seeking input from Oxfam, Traidcraft, Twin Trading, and the Oxford Forestry Institute.

Much of the advice warned against a charity model since external donors had short time horizons for funding, meaning their support might not last. Kwisthout explained: "It had to be self-financing. So the only way you could do it really was to do it through a separate trading mechanism, in some form or another, so people buy, like me, from well managed sources, and close the loop." Since there was no such mechanism —as many of WARP's founders had realized—Kwisthout formed his own company, the Ecological Trading Company (Tickell 1994). It soon became clear, however, that he would also need a credible means of communicating his efforts. "I might have been happy with the timber that I bought, but when I tried to sell it to other people, it became very clear you don't have anything to back it up and so you really need endorsement of an independent organization."[4]

Kwisthout was not alone in coming to this realization. By the end of the 1980s, in the United Kingdom and the United States, attention was shifting to retailers, a growing market player in the solid wood segment (chapter 3). Questions were asked about wood sourcing that many companies were unable to answer (Dudley, Jeanrenaud, and Sullivan 1995). Bill Whiting of B&Q, a large UK retailer, admitted to a reporter: "Nobody is in a position to offer a guarantee that their tropical timber comes from sustainable sources" (*Times* 1989). Likewise, in the United States, Home Depot's manager of environmental marketing, Mark Eisen, explained to the press how "information from overseas is not easy to come by," and that many retailers are just as much in the dark on the sustainability of wood sources as are end consumers (Stark 1992). B&Q and Home Depot were not alone: UK retailers, including Marks & Spencer, and importers such as Charles Barr were also underlining the lack of good information about where imported tropical hardwoods came from (*Times* 1989).

These events coincided with the November ITTO meeting when the UK delegation submitted its labeling proposal. From this point forward, Kwisthout's thoughts on certification quickly evolved. In December he and a colleague, Chris Cox, paid a visit to the Oxford Forestry Institute to discuss next steps (Synnott 2005). Only a few months later, in May 1990, Kwisthout approached B&Q's Alan Knight to seek funding for a proposed International Forest Monitoring Agency (IFMA), which he had been contemplating in the intervening period. Knight is reported to have decided, based on the idea, to remove all labels from wood products in B&Q stores in anticipation that a single logo would soon exist (Synnott 2005; Alan Knight 2000). The timing was good for B&Q, given that Bill Whiting had just publicly admitted the company had little knowledge of its timber sources.[5]

After this point, a coalition of supporters united around the certification idea. WARP's founding meeting in November 1990 brought members of the wood artisan trade together to hear forest specialists discuss the problems of tropical forest loss and degradation (Cumpiano 2007). The meeting had three main outcomes: the participants agreed that education was critical and that boycotts were not the solution; they decided on immediate next steps that would foster awareness; and they committed to sourcing more wood from well-managed tropical forests and avoiding endangered species such as mahogany, rosewood, teak, and ebony (Delaney 1990). To realize these aims, WARP began compiling a list of companies supplying wood from well-managed or recycled sources and began organizing a fine-furniture exhibition aimed at building awareness about the use of tropical wood and the conservation of forests (Landis 1993). Finally, the group discussed Kwisthout's IFMA proposal, which, various accounts indicate, led to the formation of the Certification Working Group (CWG).[6] The CWG immediately began drafting standards, procedures for monitoring and certification, and an organizational structure for the future FSC (Synnott 2005). Around the same time, the Rainforest Alliance's SmartWood program announced the first-ever forest management certification, which it had awarded to a teak plantation operation, Perum Perhutani, in Indonesia (Elliott and Donovan 1996; Donovan 2001).

Certification was taking root. The initial pattern was similar to that occurring in organics (chapters 6 and 8), with individual certifiers, such as SmartWood, developing standards and inspecting forest operations. Others would soon follow. However, unique and important to the forestry case was how the WWF, Friends of the Earth, and others were involved and aimed to establish an organization beyond the scope of a single certifier. B&Q's early involvement, in particular, signaled an interest in considerable volumes of certified wood.

STAGE 2: CONSOLIDATION AND SECTOR-LEVEL COPYING AND COMPETITION

The Rainforest Alliance's SmartWood initiative was a whitecap on a larger wave poised to break. Two processes were occurring. First, momentum built around work on the FSC. Second, the enthusiasm and extent of the community pushing certification caught the attention of North American and European forest companies and forest landowners that previously felt forest degradation was largely a tropical problem. Chapter 3 explained how the scope of problems expanded to include social considerations, and also how it broadened to encompass all forests. Recall that in 1994 NGOs had lobbied unsuccessfully to have the ITTO expand beyond tropical forests, and before this, initiatives to negotiate a binding forest convention at the 1992 Earth Summit had fallen flat. These early factors helped shape the consolidation of the FSC and the sector-level patterns of competition. In what follows, these two developments are discussed.

Internal Program Consolidation

By 1990, the WWF and other NGOs were no longer supporting the TFAP (Sullivan 1990; Friends of the Earth 1991b) and were voicing increasing alarm about the ITTO's glacial progress in addressing tropical forest degradation and loss (Agence France-Presse 1991). Given this, Kwisthout's research found growing interest. The IFMA proposal received further attention and support at a December 1990 conference, Steps to Sustainability, hosted by WWF-UK (Synnott 2005). By April 1991, Kwisthout secured funding from B&Q and WWF-UK to further develop his idea; in the same month, the CWG met in San Francisco and decided to focus on forming an organization to set standards, not certify forests (Synnott 2005).

The push for oversight coincided with similar discussions in organics (chapter 6). This was not surprising. At a period when considerable interest in consumer-driven campaigns and environmental consumerism existed, other initiatives responded to the demand. Just before the April 1991 meeting, Scientific Certification Systems launched its Forest Conservation program as an initiative for evaluating and certifying "well managed" forest operations (Scientific Certification Systems 1999b; Bryan Evans 1996). Likewise, in May 1991, the Soil Association began talks with the WWF about a UK forest certification program (Wenban-Smith 2001). Groups including RAN and the Natural Resources Defense Council (NRDC) also launched the Green Seal program, which would set standards for the environmental performance of various consumer products in the U.S. market (Wetzstein 1990b). In July, the Société générale de surveillance (SGS) announced its intention to develop forest certification services (Synnott 2005). SmartWood was also continuing certification activities; it assessed the first "group" operation in 1991 in Honduras (Donovan 2001).

Concurrently, more questions about the validity of UK marketing claims were prompted by a WWF-commissioned report (Schoon 1991). In truth, the report simply underlined the earlier realization that buyers had no idea where their wood products came from, but it did also sustain attention to the issue. Change was becoming more and more likely, since industry leaders were acting. In September 1991, B&Q announced its commitment to the WWF 1995 target of no longer selling tropical wood from unsustainable sources and of only selling wood from known sources by the end of 1993 (PR Newswire 1991). Across the Atlantic, the retailer Home Depot was also acting. In October 1991, the company announced a partnership with Green Cross Certification (a nonprofit subsidiary of SCS) to assess the environmental claims made by suppliers of building and home improvement materials (*New Hampshire Business Review* 1991). The U.S. National Retail Hardware Association and the Home Center Institute adopted Home Depot's approach, extending the initiative and the partnership with Green Cross industry-wide (PR Newswire 1992; Lober and Eisen 1995; Troy 1992). Retailers in the United States were acting in parallel to UK retailers, addressing sourcing practices and the environmental claims made on products. Notably, the U.S. move was partly preemptive. There was a mounting threat that either the National Association of Attorney Generals or the Federal Trade Commission would clamp down on false claims if the industry did not do so itself (Petty 1992; Troy 1992). In the United Kingdom, the main incentive came from NGO pressure. In November 1991 Friends of the Earth–UK launched a campaign against the six largest home retail stores in the United Kingdom—B&Q, Do-It-All, Great Mills, Sainsbury's Homebase, Texas, and Wickes—calling consumers to boycott all of the stores' timber products (Friends of the Earth 1991a). Although B&Q's announcement predated the campaign, other retailers had not taken public positions. This changed in December 1991, when WWF-UK launched a UK wood buyers and retailers group (later known as the 1995 Group) that committed to phasing out purchases of tropical hardwoods from unsustainable sources by 1995 (Hunt 1991). The group included B&Q, Texas Homecare, Sainsbury's Homebase, Richard Burbidge, Milland Fine Timber, and the Ecological Trading Company, among others (Hunt 1991). The announcement also made direct mention of the FSC, which the WWF believed would replace the unreliable labels coloring the market.[7] Indeed, by this time, work on a first draft of the FSC charter and forest management standards had begun (Synnott 2005).[8]

Friends of the Earth–UK remained skeptical and continued calling for a boycott. Early in 1992, Simon Counsell of Friends of the Earth explained: "Given the rate the rainforests are disappearing we don't think you can justify stalling at all" (Katz 1992).[9] Even members of the nascent WWF buyer group were raising questions. Don Dennis, director of Milland Fine Timber, publicly annulled his organization's involvement in the group in early 1992, charging that the WWF and the participating companies were not committed to preserving forest biodiversity (Pearce 1992). Although the standards were not yet written, these debates underscored tensions among NGOs over the value of boycotts versus a more business-friendly certification approach and, even more important, what a business-friendly approach ought to look like. Groups such as the WWF, the Rainforest Alliance, and SCS were, not surprisingly, backing the certification approach, whereas Friends of the Earth–UK placed greater emphasis on boycotts (Wille 1991).[10]

Nonetheless, certification efforts gathered steam. The SCS issued its first certificate in February 1992 to the U.S. Menominee Tribal Enterprise in Wisconsin (Scientific Certification Systems 1999a). WWF-UK and its partners were working on a UK certification program that could credibly oversee the claims of its newly launched WWF 95 Group (Peter Knight 1991). In March 1992, the CWG met to discuss drafts of the FSC charter and statutes, a manual for accrediting certifiers, and the FSC forest management standards (Synnott 2005). The meeting also appointed an Interim Board that included representatives from the WWF, B&Q, SCS, Cultural Survival, and WARP (Synnott 2005). The mixture of perspectives illustrates the diverse community interested in certification. Partly because of this, disagreements over what the FSC ought to accomplish were already ripe. A recap of the meeting noted how Friends of the Earth's "bottom line" was an end to "large-scale logging in virgin forests (which have never been logged)," and that any company "trading in or [buying] wood from these virgin forests—which still represent the bulk of surviving tropical woodlands—should not receive any endorsement or encouragement" (Schoon 1992). Friends of the Earth exempted only "small scale, sustainable logging by forest tribespeople" (Schoon 1992). These challenges would punctuate the development of standards, the FSC structure, and implementation.

In the ensuing year, the Interim Board worked to coordinate various activities all surrounding the soon-to-happen launch of the FSC. Foremost was work on the standards, which by this time were being termed the Principles & Criteria (P&C). Drafts were informed by the just-released ITTO (1992) *Guidelines for the Sustainable Management of Natural Tropical Forests* (Synnott 2005), but the scope of the standards was the management of all forests. Richard Donovan, head of SmartWood, made a few further revisions, and five thousand copies were distributed for review. More revisions and eleven country-specific field assessments took place in 1993 (Synnott 2005; Viana et al. 1996).[11]

From the start, social issues were deemed important. Kwisthout later noted the influence of the 1987 Brundtland report on his ideas of what the standards should contain—specifically, that they needed social and environmental facets.[12] After the initial draft, Donovan added a special section on plantations (Synnott 2005), and by August 1993, two months before the founding meeting, a seventh draft of the P&C was under way. Results from the eleven country consultations were done by this time and were considered for the final drafts. A principle on indigenous peoples and one focused on the relationship between natural forests and plantations instead of plantations alone were added to the final draft (Synnott 2005). Notably, plantations received attention from the beginning.[13] They would then require greater work after the founding meeting and before the membership endorsed their inclusion in the P&C.

Alongside this work, the Interim Board considered how the future FSC should be structured. In April 1993 the board received legal advice that, above all else, the governance structure should ensure no one interest could dominate, and that a foundation with a self-perpetuating board rather than a membership association could well serve this aim (Synnott 2005). Yet members of the Interim Board also felt that the IFOAM and the IUCN, both membership organizations, were useful models.[14] As such, one idea was to have members representing interest-based chambers that together would form a General Assembly. The assembly's members would have ultimate authority but would delegate decision-making power to a board. In the end, the Interim Board chose to raise both options at the Founding Assembly. However, the draft statutes that were to be presented proposed the former option—a foundation with a self-perpetuating board—and explained the Interim Board's concerns about the challenges and costs membership could pose.[15]

The Founding Assembly was held in Toronto on October 1–3, 1993. Invitees totaled 130 from twenty-four countries, chosen with an aim to balance geographic and interest representation (Synnott 2005). Several decisions were made. With the question of membership, participants voted for a voice. A WWF official explained: "I guess, you have a room full of people and you ask, 'Do you want to have a voice in the future of this organization or no voice?' it is pretty obvious what they are going to say."[16] However, how to structure membership was controversial. Certain participants felt industry should not be members, seeing this as a conflict of interest that would undermine the FSC's watchdog capabilities. Over the objections of representatives from Friends of the Earth and Greenpeace (Peter Knight 1993b; Dudley, Jeanrenaud, and Sullivan 1995, 147), the final decision was a chamber structure giving 75 percent of the voting rights to environmental and social interests and 25 percent to economic interests (Upton and Bass 1996; Synnott 2005; Ghazali and Simula 1996; Scrase 1995). Each chamber was then split between northern members (high-income countries, according to UN criteria) and southern members (upper-middle-, middle-, and low-income countries), with each getting an equal share of the chamber's votes (FSC 1999a).

The vocal opposition of Friends of the Earth and Greenpeace foreshadowed ongoing wariness over the direction of the nascent FSC. While both groups became FSC members, Simon Counsell, with Friends of the Earth at the time, would become an important outside critic, later taking a position with the Rainforest Foundation. Nevertheless, the opportunity to work within the FSC, having a voice to shape the organization's growth, appealed.[17] There were certain actors that exited immediately—producers in particular. Their efforts are discussed more below. First, however, the steps taken by the FSC to become a full-fledged global certification program are reviewed.

The FSC formalized quickly. A working group that met in May 1994 further refined the P&C. The group proposed a structural definition of plantations and a ban on genetically modified organisms (Synnott 2005), then submitted the final P&C to the board and membership for formal endorsement. All but principle 10, concerning plantations, received endorsement by June 1994 (FSC 1994); principle 10 was endorsed in February 1996 (FSC 1996). The FSC also decided to limit its label to products with 100 percent FSC content (Upton and Bass 1996).

Attention then turned to accrediting the existing certifiers, the list of which was growing. It included the Soil Association, SGS, SCS, and SmartWood, as well as the Rogue Institute for Ecology and Economy, the Institute for Sustainable Forestry, the Eco-Forestry Institute Society, and the Silva Forest Foundation, all based in North America (Landis 1993, 155); TRADA Certification in the United Kingdom; and Skal in the Netherlands (Viana et al. 1996, 8–9). The FSC conducted its first accreditation field visits in late 1995. By this time, the four initial certifiers had audited seventeen operations in ten countries, covering a total area of over 4.2 million hectares. SmartWood accounted for nearly 73 percent of the total area; its original assessment of Perum Perhutani remained the largest certified operation, covering 2.8·million hectares, or 67 percent of the total certified area. SGS and SCS followed in the rankings, each having certified around 13 percent of the total (Upton and Bass 1996, 201–10).

No formal accreditation manual existed at this point; the first manual was published in 1998. The FSC was learning by doing, making judgments about what would be appropriate through interaction with the initial certifiers. Final accreditation contracts were signed in early 1996, allowing four certifiers to conduct forest management audits under the endorsement of the FSC. The FSC logo was also trademarked in 1996 (Synnott 2005; WWF 1996). Ten years later, the FSC created Accreditation Services International (ASI) as an external body to conduct its accreditation work.

A related but separate process was the establishment of FSC national affiliates, which would adapt the P&C to local sociopolitical and ecological conditions. Nothing had been formalized yet. Many organizations, some of which were members of the FSC, served as local representatives. This was particularly the case for the eleven countries where workshops were held in 1992 and 1993 to review the draft P&C. In Sweden, the WWF, later joined by the Swedish Society for Nature Conservation, began work on a national standard in 1993 (Ervin 1996; Elliott 2000, 187). In North America there were several regional standards-setting processes already under way. Operating in southern Oregon, the Rogue Institute for Ecology and Economy formed in 1990 and began drafting standards, subsequently certifying forest practices as early as 1993 (Rogue Institute for Ecology and Economy 2000, 1997, 1999). The Institute for Sustainable Forestry worked on standards in California, and the Sigurd Olson Environmental Institute did so for midwestern states near the Great Lakes, such as Wisconsin, as early as 1994 (Mark Sommer 1993; Ervin 1996, 16).[18] Germany provides another example. Starting in 1995, Greenpeace, the German Association for Nature Conservation, and Robin Wood worked with Naturland to develop a program for ecological forest management that would be based on organic principles (Cashore, Auld, and Newsom 2004, 171). Rather than continue with this program, in 1996, Naturland became a founding member of a group striving to develop FSC standards in Germany (Auld 2009).

Many of these organizations had been involved with the FSC from the start, having even attended the Founding Assembly. As such, they were a local presence for the organization, helping to promote the FSC as a different model for forest management. Starting in 1995, the FSC Board and Secretariat moved to formalize ties by endorsing national representatives. The first contact person was endorsed for the United Kingdom in August 1995, and by February 1996 it had been upgraded to a national working group. Also in 1996, the United States, Sweden, the Netherlands, Mexico, and Ireland each had a contact person endorsed (FSC 1999c).

However, because the relationships were not formalized under contract, ambiguity about responsibilities fomented conflict. Indeed, the original FSC statutes made no reference to national branches, mentioning only members, the accreditation process for certifiers, and the board and officers (FSC 1995). On this very point, the first executive director, Tim Synnott (2005, 31), later explained: "By 1997, some of the better established working group members felt strongly that they should be taking the decisions in the endorsement of national standards, accreditation of certification bodies in their countries, and approval of new FSC members. It was understood that all these items were initially decided by the board of directors and staff, because initially there were no national initiatives, but many people felt that these tasks should be devolved." The issue was resolved through a clarification of governance roles and responsibilities going forward (FSC 1999e) and by 1998 the FSC began signing formal contracts with existing and future contact persons and working groups (FSC 1998b). Nevertheless, the debate was telling of how local groups were already pushing for autonomy to direct FSC activities in their jurisdictions, a dynamic consistent with the expectations laid out in chapter 2.

By contrast, little resistance to globalizing was coming from those companies already certified. It is critical at this point to note that there were different dynamics operating in North America and Europe. Recall that both Home Depot and B&Q had announced commitments to forest certification in 1991. Indeed, in October 1993, the month of the FSC Founding Assembly, Home Depot announced it would stock SCS-labeled wood from Collins Pine in eleven Arizona stores (Pelline 1993). In 1996, this initiative won a President's Sustainable Development Award for work encouraging better production practices and sustainable design through a credible eco label (Home Depot 1996; Greenwire 1996). The relationship had been quite useful for Collins. The company reported a 15 percent premium from the Home Depot for pine shelving sold in six of the retailer's San Francisco–area stores.

However, just after the President's Award was granted, Home Depot dropped the shelving product (Hansen and Punches 1998, 1999). One interpretation explained this as a matter of strategy: Home Depot saw no evidence of a green premium and hence was unwilling to continue paying more to FSC suppliers (McNichol 2002, 269–71). Yet another problem was a mismatch between what the FSC offered and what Home Depot needed. The Home Depot and other retailers were investing in SCS as the one on-product green claim (McAlexander and Hansen 1998; PR Newswire 1994). In 1994, SCS's new environmental report card provided an "eco-profile" for all sorts of products, not just wood. B&Q, by contrast, quickly invested in the FSC. The company reported having sent a catalogue that explained the FSC to over 8 million UK households; by 1997, it was confident it would sell only FSC wood by the end of 1999

(*DIY Week* 1997). Recall that B&Q also gave funds to help establish the FSC, and a company representative, Alan Knight, had been a member of the Interim Board (PR Newswire Europe 1991). By September 1996, the entire WWF 1995 Plus Group included around seventy members and was reported by the WWF to account for approximately 20 percent of the UK wood and wood products market (Peter Knight 1996).

FSC outreach in the United States, by contrast, was minimal. Although WARP had done awareness campaigns—Scott Landis had engagements to speak about the problem in various venues, for instance (Duffy 1992)—and eventually WARP cosponsored an art exhibit to draw attention to conservation issues surrounding wood craft (Landis 1993), these were minor events with minimal impact, given paltry public understanding of the problem. Plus, it took until 1996 for the Forest Products Buyers Group, an outgrowth of WARP and the Good Wood Alliance, to emerge in the United States. An aggressive campaign to promote FSC certification in the United States did not take shape until 1997, when the Certified Forest Products Council (CFPC) was formed (McNichol 2002; Cashore, Auld, and Newsom 2004) and U.S. foundations began a coordinated effort to promote the FSC, including financing the CFPC, the FSC-US initiative, and other NGOs including the WRI, the National Wildlife Federation, and the NRDC (Bartley 2007a).

Thus, there were pockets of interest in certification.[19] However, the logistical challenges posed significant problems for those trying to increase market penetration. As a result, there were few reasons for early-adopting companies to resist further entry by competitors. Collins later argued that without more companies involved, market demand was very unlikely to develop.[20] This was particularly the case for the larger-volume producers and given the 100 percent FSC-content rule for labeled products (Alpine 1998).

Thus, by 1996, the FSC had all the working parts of a global program (figure 4.1). Consistent with hypothesis 7, it had faced little resistance because the time needed to build resistance was too short and the benefits of threatening exit by those beginning to develop investments in local approaches were small. By mid-1997, a total of over 3 million hectares had been certified in seventeen countries. In terms of area, Poland accounted for 50 percent, and the United States, the United Kingdom, the Czech Republic, the Netherlands, and Sweden accounted for another 33 percent, meaning only the remaining 17 percent were areas certified in tropical forests. Five auditors were accredited by this time (*Timber Trades Journal* 1997a), with the SGS accounting for the lion's share of area certified—nearly 70 percent. SCS was a distant second with 20 percent of the total; the SmartWood program contributed only slightly less than 8 percent. Skal and the Soil Association had each certified less than 1 percent of the total area.

There is more to the story, though. The FSC's consolidation was quick partly because of its ambiguous aims: it meant different things to different people. During implementation, this ambiguity was lifted and conflict emerged as a consequence, although devolving discretion to the certifiers averted some of the tensions. They had power to determine the interpretations of the P&C in jurisdictions with no local standard, and they were still able to continue their own certification services in addition to those now endorsed by the FSC. Moreover, not all auditors were immediately required to accredit with the FSC. Yet, giving this authority to certifiers stoked the concerns of others. Soon disagreements over what FSC certification meant in practice grew, especially as the pressure for more certified area intensified. The discussion returns to these disagreements in offering an explanation for the sector-level pattern. Before this, what follows examines the development of producer-backed programs and their efforts to quickly become a global substitute for the FSC.

Producer-backed programs also have connections to intergovernmental fora. However, the FSC and the boycott campaigns noted in chapter 3 made certification almost unavoidable for the forest industry around the world, though especially in export-dependent countries selling to Europe (Auld, Gulbrandsen, and McDermott 2008). Analysts note how the FSC's initial decision to allocate only 25 percent of voting rights to economic interests gave these actors further reason to exit. That the economic chamber housed all organizations or individuals deriving a livelihood from forestry—consultants, certifiers, retailers, and book publishers, among others—made matters worse (Cashore, Auld, and Newsom 2004, 12; Ghazali and Simula 1996, annexes 7.1, 7.2). Put another way, the opportunities for voice within the FSC, including invitations to the Founding Assembly, were insufficient to outweigh the value of outside options such as creating a substitute program.

Producers responded to the perceived threat with national-level sustainable forest management (SFM) certification programs in part because this was where they were organized to mobilize. Although the World Busi-

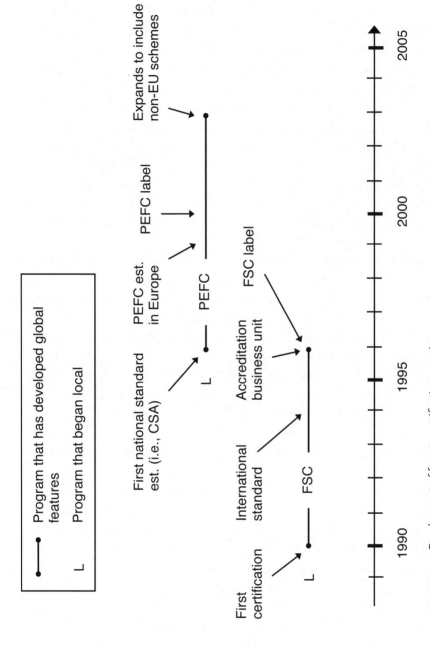

FIGURE 4.1. Development of forestry certification over time

ness Council for Sustainable Development (WBCSD) and other international business organizations participated in the Rio Earth Summit and even helped spur the emphasis on voluntary self-regulatory tools (Chatterjee and Finger 1994), for most of the 1990s, attempts by producers to form a global program failed. The structure of the forest sector supply chain also mattered. It meant forest product producers and downstream retailers were responding concurrently, and sometimes at cross-purposes. Recall how B&Q was closely involved in the creation of the FSC and Home Depot was launching its own initiative. Likewise, paper purchasers were responding independently. Publishers in Europe were addressing concerns over chlorine-bleached paper and later harvesting in old-growth forests (Stanbury 2000), and in the United States, paper purchasers (for example, McDonalds, Time, Inc.) were working with the Environmental Defense Fund on a Paper Task Force in the hopes of improving their collective environmental practices (Paper Task Force 1995; Environmental Defense Fund 1993). However, primary producers also had an interest and capacity to respond. So with action from Home Depot and B&Q on the solid wood side and Time, Inc., Alex Springer, and others on the paper side, primary producers took notice.

How they responded was strongly influenced by existing associational structures, which, by and large, were organized along national lines and less so regionally, for instance, the Confederation of European Paper Industries. It took until 1994 for producers to form the International Forest Industry Roundtable (IFIR) (Greig-Gran 2004, 3n2), a group that would later become a proponent of mutual recognition within the sector (Griffiths 2000). However, for the time, the nationally focused nature of industry interests constrained producer responses.

To understand the impetus for these efforts, we need to return to the ITTO and the broader intergovernmental processes around forests. Although the ITTO blocked the initial calls for labeling, the idea did not disappear. Rather, the London Environmental Economics Council (a group within the IIED) was commissioned to write a report on the feasibility of incentives for improved forest management. The report concluded that trade was actually a relatively insignificant concern. It also promoted country-level certification schemes (Gale 1998, 71). Both these arguments countered the coalition working to form the FSC and raised the possibility that an alternative certification arrangement was conceivable and perhaps even preferable. A WWF representative remarked,

"People have gone from arguing about whether [labeling] should happen to how it should be [organized]" (Peter Knight 1993a).

Thus, just prior to the launch of the FSC, the ITTO and its member countries were seriously discussing certification and labeling (Makabenta 1993), which engendered a series of country-level initiatives to verify SFM practices. This was also bolstered by the emphasis placed on national SFM guidelines by the Statement of Forest Principles and chapter 11 of Agenda 21 (Humphreys 1996, 38; Elliott 2000, 50). The ITTO guidelines (ITTO 1992) were a precursor to similar regional processes, which occurred in the years following. From 1993 to 1998, governments negotiated sets of Criteria and Indicators (C&I) for measuring sustainable forest management in different regional forests, such as the Amazon Basin, European forests, and temperate and boreal forests outside Europe, and they established national programs to implement and monitor them (Humphreys 1996, 139–41).

Thus, producers' national orientation and governments' C&I work stacked the deck in favor of country-level responses to the FSC's advances. As a result, producer-backed programs formed separately in several countries throughout the early 1990s. The emergence pattern was multifaceted. Discussions in Malaysia began in 1994 and were formalized in 1995, creating the Malaysian Timber Certification Council (MTCC) (H.O. 2005). With Indonesia, interest in certification formed due to the ITTO process and the 1992 decision of the Austrian Parliament to restrict imports of tropical timber unless labeled as coming from a sustainable source (Bartley 2003). An Indonesian program formed near the end of 1992; allying with the FSC was debated, yet the ultimate choice was to form a separate program known as LEI (Indonesian Ecolabel Institute) (Muhtaman and Prasetyo 2006; Elliott 2000). The Brazilian Silviculture Society, along with other organizations, began discussing certification around 1991. These discussions fed the formation of Cerflor (ITS Global 2005).

North America and Europe saw similar competitive responses. Days after the FSC held its Founding Assembly in Toronto, the Canadian Pulp and Paper Association (CPPA), announced it would work to create a domestic certification program (*Financial Post* 1993). The Canadian Standards Association (CSA) led the initiative, which was released in 1996. In the United States, the American Forest and Paper Association (AFPA) transformed its Sustainable Forestry Initiative (SFI) from an industry code of conduct mostly designed to head off government regulation and respond to public concern over forest practices into a certification program meant to undercut FSC advances (Sasser 2003; Overdevest 2004).

This patchwork of producer programs meant that the FSC initially faced no unified global competitor. One WWF official noted: "FSC had quite a few years where it was the only show in town."[21] This was not due to lack of effort; on several occasions producers sought to scale up their initiatives or build new efforts via international standard-setting bodies. For instance, there were attempts to apply ISO 14001 standards directly to forestry. The 14000 series had originally been advocated by the WBCSD following from the UNCED, encouragement that led the ISO to form Technical Committee 207 Environmental Management for the task (Elliott 2000, 13). Industry, particularly in export-oriented countries —Canada, Sweden, and New Zealand, for instance—liked the ISO option because it gave companies discretion to set their own targets and had acceptance from the WTO (Bass 1997; Vertinsky and Zhou 1999). Given this, lobbying for a forestry-specific ISO standard began. Starting in 1995, Canadian officials proposed using their CSA-sponsored program as a starting point (Elliott 2000, 16; Zarocostas 1995), and, in June 1996, a meeting of the Technical Committee voted to form a forestry working group to determine the feasibility of applying the generic ISO 14001 standard to forestry (*Printing World* 1997). Although at first WWF International supported this work and was involved in the talks (Business Wire 1995), this soon changed (WWF et al. 1998). A WWF representative explained: "WWF is deeply concerned that certain sections of the international timber industry will try to use ISO's good name to develop a 'quasi-eco label' as an alternative to independent certification" (*Printing World* 1997). In the end, the idea faltered. Still, the ISO was a critical early option for internationally oriented companies—Canadian companies quickly sought ISO certification and worked to ensure the CSA program was complementary to ISO requirements (Timber & Wood Products 1999a; Cashore et al. 2005).

The next push for a global producer program took form in Europe. In June 1999, the Pan European Forest Certification (PEFC) program (now the Program for the Endorsement of Forest Certification) was officially launched, with the support of European forest landowners (Timber & Wood Products 1999b; PEFC 2008). Forming as an umbrella organization, it began endorsing national certification schemes in 2000. It recognized programs from five countries (Finland, Germany, Norway, Sweden, and Austria) and licensed the use of its logo in this first year (PEFC 2008). Before this, forest owners had also worked to have government intervene in their favor, lobbying the European Commission to develop a certification approach amenable to small-forest owners. With no government action and with the growing interest in the FSC, they moved on their own (Humphreys 2006, 127). A meeting in October 1998 of a small Steering Group led to the June 1999 launch. The group had explicit motives: a new program was needed because, among other things, existing certification systems were inappropriate for smaller-forest owners (PEFC 1998).

At first, the PEFC remained a European initiative, as the list of founding countries illustrates. However, interest in consolidating a global producer program remained high. Pushes in this direction then came from the IFIR—a group comprising national industry associations from around the world (Humphreys 2006, 131). The IFIR began efforts to coordinate producers in 1996 when it obtained commitments from members to a vision statement on SFM (Griffiths 2001). In 1999, the IFIR established a working group to explore how to accomplish international agreement among different certification programs. The working group's proposal was endorsed at an IFIR meeting in October 2000 (APP Newsfeed 2000). They hoped that mutual recognition would "provide a critical mass of credibly certified wood products by recognizing that different certification systems can provide substantively equivalent standards of sustainable forest management" (Griffiths 2001). Yet for those groups supporting the FSC, this appeared as a threat. Depending on what schemes were accepted, a low-bar standard might emerge, creating little or no incentive for future improvements (Humphreys 2006, 131). An official from the Global Forest Policy Project, a group representing a coalition of NGOs, explained: "As soon as a mutual recognition system embraces all certification schemes in the world, the competition stops. . . . There's no incentive anymore" (Reese 2001; see also WWF 2001b).

With mutual recognition faltering, attention returned to the programs that were becoming dominant: the FSC, the PEFC, and the host of national-level programs, including the CSA, SFI, LEI, and MTCC. The PEFC, designed as an umbrella program, was well suited to slowly take the lead as the producer-backed global initiative. Moves to include Chile, Australia, Canada, the United States, and other non-European countries would expand the PEFC beyond its regional origins, a shift that began around 2003 after it adopted guidelines for endorsing national schemes that were more inclusive than the pan-European guidelines the program had started with (PEFC 2002). In addition, the PEFC produced accreditation processes, which it released in 2002. Thus, by 2003, PEFC had successfully globalized (figure 4.1).

By 2003, PEFC had certified 52.3 million hectares in thirteen countries. A total of twenty-seven national schemes were members, indicating that the program still had much potential to grow. Indeed, by the end of 2005, eighteen countries had endorsed schemes, including the CSA program in Canada (Auld 2009). Additional organizations supportive of the PEFC's aims could enroll as extraordinary members; nine groups were involved in this capacity by the end of 2003. Still, reflecting the concerns with the FSC structure noted above, only national schemes had voting rights, weighted according to the member country's volume of annual harvest. Each national scheme could have its own provisions for membership, but these were not standardized (Auld 2009).

To recap, the FSC was a pivotal force behind producers' efforts to globalize a program. Their attempts were slowed by the absence of well-developed connections across political boundaries compared with the strength of their domestic and regional organizational capacity. In the next section, the analysis focuses specifically on the interplay between the FSC and the PEFC and examines why a two-program competition has been resilient to date.

Sector-Level Patterns of Emergence

After the initial accreditation contracts were signed and national contact persons and working groups began receiving FSC approval for their work on national standards, uncertainty surrounding the FSC lessened. By this time, it had successfully gained the support (sometimes tentative) from a wide range of actors. From the beginning, NGOs were an important block of members; chapters of Friends of the Earth and the WWF, respectively, held three and six membership spots of all one hundred FSC members in 1996 (Ghazali and Simula 1996). General support was also growing: by 1997 membership had expanded to two hundred (Elliott 2000).[22] Remember, however, that preceding years featured debates about what the scope and domain of the FSC ought to be. Debate about the standard was central, but attention also focused on whether the domain of operators should be constrained and even whether certification could effectively address forest loss. Those NGOs favoring boycotts were especially persistent, pointing to illegal logging and destruction of intact primary forests as critical concerns. Those in the WWF 1995 Plus Group, particularly B&Q, envisioned a system for mitigating supply chain management risks and simply communicating the company's activities to customers (Alan Knight 2000). When these actors learned what FSC certification would mean for on-the-ground practices, would it meet their expectations? Furthermore, if they were unhappy, would they vocalize these concerns from within, or exit to pursue outside options?

Two facets of FSC's implementation are pertinent to these questions: the development of national specifications of the P&C and the work of FSC-accredited certifiers. Certification was especially important because accredited certifiers could use generic FSC standards in places where a nationally endorsed FSC standard was not in place. Eventually, FSC-endorsed working groups were to develop these localized standards to increase buy-in and legitimacy. Drafting the P&C had taken time, and developing local interpretations would take more time. The first contact person was endorsed for the United Kingdom in 1995—imagining a network of endorsed FSC affiliates developing standards in any short time horizon was far-fetched. Recall that by September 1997 over 3 million hectares of forests in seventeen countries had been FSC certified. Sweden had the first FSC-endorsed national standard and this only happened in January 1998 (FSC 1998a). Understandably, groups keen to steer the FSC were aware of the precedent initial audits would set.

Hence, some early assessments were contested, with criticism typically pointing to problems with how the P&C were interpreted on the ground. SmartWood's certification of Flor y Fauna in 1995 was questioned over concerns with the operation's financial performance forecasts.[23] This was followed in 1996 and 1997 by disquiet surrounding an SGS assessment of Leroy Gabon. A group of Gabonese NGOs maintained that Leroy's practices near a forest reserve violated FSC standards; there were also complaints about limited stakeholder consultation and an insufficient management plan (Ngangoue 1997). The claims were backed by NGOs including Rettet den Regenwald, Friends of the Earth, and the RAN (Atyi 2006; Danielle Knight 1997; FSC 2000b), and eventually led the FSC to undertake a formal enquiry (*Timber Trades Journal* 1997b).

The decision initially supported Leroy (Tickell 1997b) but was then re-versed. The FSC also suspended SGS's accreditation for forest manage-ment certification activities pending certain reforms, and it requested that all accredited certifiers respect a six-month moratorium on certifica-tion activities in primary forests (Tickell 1997a).

These controversies highlighted the sensitivity around how auditors were interpreting the P&C in practice and whether they would align with what NGOs felt the FSC was meant to accomplish. On the Leroy Gabon incident, Simon Counsell (by this time with the Rainforest Foundation) noted, "It points to a need for much more rigorous assessments by the FSC and far more strict application of its principles and criteria by the certifier" (Tickell 1997a). This was also Friends of the Earth's perspec-tive: the FSC had potential but would require careful attention and scru-tiny, especially its certification procedures (Friends of the Earth 1997b). Nevertheless, it seemed NGO members had weighed the benefits of exit versus voice—a Friends of the Earth representative noted how they had been unhappy with the initial FSC decision, but chose not to withdraw support (Tickell 1997b). Working within still had value; it helped shift the FSC in a direction favorable to these NGOs' interests.

Far from isolated examples, these incidents illustrate broad tensions that surrounded what forestry problems the FSC planned to tackle, and furthermore, what needed to happen to ensure it did not indirectly coun-teract issues it was not designed to address. These were not static con-cerns. Once in place, the FSC was undergoing changes that themselves were also issues for NGOs to assess. For instance, though illegal log-ging was a serious concern in the early 1990s—Friends of the Earth was campaigning against the trade in mahogany throughout the early 1990s (Friends of the Earth 1994, 1995a, 1995b)—the FSC's 100 percent con-tent requirements meant illegal wood should not be a concern. Yet, as of January 1997, the FSC Board was beginning to consider a percentage-based policy for labeled products (FSC 1999d).[24] Hence, even illegal log-ging became relevant in the FSC's future.

Logging in primary forests was immediately controversial. Recall from chapter 3 that in the early 1990s, Greenpeace, Friends of the Earth, and the Taiga Rescue Network were pressing for greater protection of temperate and boreal forests in Scandinavia, Russia, and Canada (Green-peace 1994a, 1995b). That the FSC requested a six-month moratorium on certification activities in primary forests after the Leroy controversy was telling of this concern. Disquiet was actually intensifying, partly fueled by a WRI report released in 1997 that found greatly diminished areas of large intact forests: Canada, Russia, and Brazil accounted for up to 70 percent of what was left (Bryant, Nielsen, and Tangley 1997). These tensions had also been growing in the United States. Although protests against old-growth harvesting were regular events in the late 1980s and early 1990s (Diringer 1990; Simons 1990; Pralle 2006), in 1997 RAN, Greenpeace, and the Sierra Club launched a campaign calling for a boycott of products made from California redwood (*Pittsburgh Post-Gazette* 1997). Many companies acquiesced, with Home Depot joining the ranks by May 1997 (Kay 1997). Building from the momentum, the campaigns continued while emphasizing a larger aim: stopping the sale of all old-growth products, particularly those from Canada (Hettena 1998).

The old-growth issue was one reason the Leroy controversy emerged, but underlying how it unfolded was distrust of the certifier. A similar dynamic permeated the early development of FSC certification in British Columbia, Canada (McDermott 2003). A focus on Canadian operations, and particularly those in British Columbia, had a longer history in Europe, dating back to the mid-1980s with concern about pollution releases from pulp facilities (Harrison 2002) and the early 1990s with opposition to clear-cut logging old-growth forests (Lush 1991; Stanbury 2000).[25] In the mid-1990s, this was leading Greenpeace Canada to promote the FSC as a mechanism to certify small-scale, eco-friendly suppliers. The group even posted ads seeking out this kind of producer in the hopes of having model operators to champion (Matas 1996; Greenpeace 1994b). At the time, a lumberyard with thirty hectares of forest in the British Columbia interior had achieved what Greenpeace considered FSC-equivalent certification and was being touted as the right model for the province's forestry (Lush 1995; Greenpeace n.d.), a marked contrast to the operations of forest products companies holding sizable public forest tenures—but this was exactly the point. In reference to the certificate, a Greenpeace representative was quoted stating: "The forest industry has said we would never be happy with any kind of logging in B.C. but we are happy with this" (Hamilton 1995).

Although the audit was not endorsed by the FSC, it had been conducted by Silva Forest Foundation, a British Columbia–based nonprofit and FSC member. Silva had been working with the Institute for Sustainable Forestry, the Rogue Institute for Ecology and Economy, and the Eco-

Forestry Institute Society to develop eco-forestry standards for the western forests of North America. Because the FSC had no official presence in Canada at the time—the first contact person was endorsed in January 1997 and a Canadian working group was endorsed in May 1998 (FSC 1999c)—Silva was serving as a proxy for the FSC in British Columbia, without having official accreditation (Hammond 2003).

With Silva as an ally, groups felt confident they knew what the FSC would mean in British Columbia. This strategy worked while Canadian producers continued supporting the CSA program. However, with a series of announcements by British Columbian companies to pursue FSC certification and to undertake changes in their practices, including ending the use of clear-cuts (MacMillan Bloedel, Ltd. 1998), the groups had to specify priorities. Efforts by Western Forest Products (WFP) to obtain FSC certification—announced in June 1998 but having already been under way for eighteen months prior (Western Forest Products 1998)—were particularly troubling in this regard. To make matters worse, WFP contracted SGS to perform the assessment rather than Silva Forest Foundation.

This was a case where the discretion the FSC gave to certifiers led to tension with NGOs focused on British Columbia forestry (McDermott 2003). The problem was that Silva had not yet been FSC accredited. It submitted an application in 1998 (Hammond 2003). (Although the exact dates are a little uncertain, it appears this happened soon after the WFP announcement.) Those concerned with the WFP announcement also took actions. The Heiltsuk First Nation, with claims to an area where WFP operated, submitted a complaint to the FSC about the possibility of WFP obtaining endorsement; British Columbia NGOs including Sierra Club and the Forest Action Network also issued strong criticism of the move (Hamilton 1998c, 1998b). By September 1998, months after the announcement, Greenpeace released a damning report assessing WFP's practices against P&C and concluded that the company would not make the grade (Zammuto et al. 1998; Canada Newswire 1998). The emphasis of the demands also shifted, with an opposition to any certification taking place in British Columbia's Central Coast, what was coined the Great Bear Rainforest (Greenpeace Canada 1997). A representative from the NRDC added that organization's support, highlighting how old-growth protection, in this case, trumped support for the FSC. An official with the group stated: "We think no logging is appropriate in the Great Bear Rainforest until they set aside much more of the area for preservation"

(Nesmith 1998). Greenpeace, joined by groups such as RAN, continued actions against U.S. companies that were selling wood from British Columbia. Despite Home Depot's efforts to find and sell FSC products, which had begun even before the FSC launched (Tice 1998) and its commitment to stop selling old-growth redwood (Kay 1997), Greenpeace and RAN were still protesting at the company's stores throughout the fall of 1998, demanding an end to purchases of British Columbia old-growth wood (Associated Press 1998b; Hettena 1998).

In the lead-up to this conflict, it might have appeared that one objective was being pursued. Members of the UK 1995 Plus Group were pressing British Columbia companies to seek FSC certification; Richard Burbidge, Ltd., a leading supplier of the UK home retail sector that had contracts for British Columbia wood worth $3.5 million, insisted that commitments to certification would need to be in place by June 1998 for the company to continue buying from the province (Hamilton 1998a). Greenpeace supported this pressure and noted FSC supply from other parts of the world; the campaign had also secured some level of support in the United States by this time (Hamilton 1998a). The press coverage invariably indicated that NGO campaigns in the United States and Europe were pressing companies to favor FSC supplies. Yet the same articles also noted the importance placed on "old-growth free" and alternatives to wood (Tice 1998; Associated Press 1998b; Nesmith 1998; Danielle Knight 1998). A clear example is a *New York Times* print ad issued by the Coastal Rainforest Coalition (later to become ForestEthics), Greenpeace, the NRDC, and the RAN that was published on December 8, 1998. It praised twenty-seven Fortune 500 companies that were supporting efforts to save ancient (old-growth) forests and pinpointed Interfor, Doman (the parent company of WFP), and West Fraser as the key British Columbia companies that needed to change. It did mention independent certification, but not the FSC specifically, and the preponderance of the ad focused on old-growth loss, including how many British Columbia coastal valleys remained pristine—69 of 357—but how the majority of these were slated for logging (*New York Times* 1998). Table 4.1 details the commitments of companies as reported by ForestEthics and confirmed with further archival research. Notably, the number of companies making "no old-growth" and "ancient forest friendly" commitments outnumbers those for the FSC or for independent third-party certification.

Table 4.1.

Forest product purchasing commitments

COMPANIES	NO WOOD PRODUCTS FROM:			STATED PREFERENCE FOR:			
	BRITISH COLUMBIA GREAT BEAR RAINFOREST	OLD-GROWTH/ ANCIENT FORESTS	ENDANGERED FORESTS	FSC CERTIFIED	THIRD-PARTY CERTIFIED	RECYCLED PRODUCTS	PERIODIC AUDITS
1996							
The Body Shop	✓	✓		✓	✓	✓	
The Body Shop, Canada	✓	✓		✓	✓		
1998							
Bristol-Myers Squibb	✓	✓			✓	✓	✓
Dell Computer Corp.	✓	✓				✓	
Estée Lauder	✓	✓				✓	
Hallmark Cards, Inc.	✓	✓				✓	
IBM Corp.	✓	✓				✓	
Johnson & Johnson	✓	✓		✓		✓	✓
Kinko's, Inc.	✓	✓				✓	
Levi Strauss & Co.	✓	✓					
Liz Claiborne	✓	✓			✓		✓
Lockheed Martin Corp.	✓	✓				✓	✓
McGraw-Hill	✓	✓				✓	✓

Mitsubishi Electric Corp.	✓		✓		✓	
Mitsubishi Motors, North America, Inc.	✓		✓		✓	
Mother Jones Magazine	✓	✓	✓		✓	
Mutual of Omaha	✓				✓	
National Geographic Society	✓				✓	
New Leaf Recycled Paper	✓		✓	✓	✓	
Nike, Inc.	✓		✓		✓	
Pacific Gas & Electric Co.	✓	✓	✓		✓	
Patagonia	✓		✓		✓	✓
Quantum Corp.	✓		✓		✓	✓
Seventh Generation	✓		✓		✓	✓
Starbucks Coffee Co.	✓	✓	✓		✓	
3M Corp.	✓		✓	✓	✓	
United Stationers Supply Co.	✓		✓		✓	✓
Utne Reader	✓		✓		✓	✓
1999						
The Home Depot	✓	✓	✓	✓	✓	
IKEA	✓	✓	✓	✓	✓	
Wickes Lumber		✓	✓	✓		

Source: Modified from Auld 2006, 2009

It is not then surprising that, when WFP committed to FSC certification, the two objectives—promote the FSC versus save old growth—were placed at odds. The company made clear it was not going to end clear-cutting in old-growth forests, noting how the FSC had permitted such practices in Africa and South America (Hogben 1998). The FSC had also begun a review of principle 9—the principle stating that "primary forests, well-developed secondary forests and sites of major environmental significance shall be conserved" (FSC 1994)—meaning a policy change that helped WFP's chances was possible.

Given the great emphasis placed on the FSC, especially in Europe and particularly within the 1995 Group, both WFP and Richard Burbidge—which had been subject to continued Greenpeace campaigns against its purchases of WFP old-growth wood—expressed annoyance with the apparent Greenpeace flip. Bill Dumont, vice president of WFP, was quoted stating: "Environmentalists demanded we get certified yet the minute we applied, they began to attack us" (Hamilton 1998c). A press release expressed Richard Burbidge's similar frustrations: "We completely reject Greenpeace's claims and we are surprised and disappointed that they have singled out the company for attack in this way. . . . The criticism of Canada is completely misplaced. Western Forest Products is currently working with independent certifiers to define standards for FSC certification which it hopes to achieve next year. . . . We have been at the forefront of British timber buyers encouraging the Canadian industry to embrace the FSC standards and this criticism from Greenpeace really is a 'stab in the back'" (Richard Burbidge 1999). A representative from SGS, the certifier contracted by WFP, also spoke critically. SGS rebuked Greenpeace for misusing the FSC name and not following proper FSC procedures for undertaking the assessment of WFP operations (Timber & Wood Products 1998b).[26]

Concerns over harvesting endangered species and forests continued, in many situations, to supersede support for the FSC. In Friends of the Earth's explanation for its *Good Wood Guide,* for instance, the ranking of aims were as follows. First, "to discourage the unnecessary overconsumption of timber products," and second, "[where] wood resources have to be used, to encourage the use of, for example, reclaimed timbers (i.e., secondary sources) or timbers from local, environmentally positive origins (i.e., primary sources in your area)" (Friends of the Earth 1997a). The organization's Web site expanded this advice by ranking harvested

timbers as follows: (1) FSC certified, locally grown wood; (2) FSC certified wood from overseas; (3) local wood; and (4) overseas wood from
plantations (Friends of the Earth 1997b, 1998).

Thus, in this early stage, key FSC founders offered tentative support
to the program. Where the FSC did not counter other goals, especially
protecting old growth and stopping illegal trade in endangered species,
it was seen as part of the solution. Otherwise, it could actually be a problem, condoning logging in places where groups really wanted outright
protection. In the FSC's 1999 annual report, a Greenpeace official suc-
cinctly outlined the group's views: "We in Greenpeace see ourselves as one
of the NGOs, who are key stakeholders without a vested economic interest
in the success of FSC certification. We have a clear mandate as a watchdog
to keep the FSC system honest and credible within the scope of what we
can do" (FSC 2000a, 39). Greenpeace forest campaigners also met annually for a planning meeting in which they would discuss their level of
engagement with the FSC system and decide whether the resources and
time needed were merited given Greenpeace's own priorities.[27]

The WWF played a different role. As one FSC official later remarked,
it was "FSC's only true supporter."[28] The WWF did take heat from other
NGOs, which felt that it was too friendly to business interests and was
thus promoting a watered-down direction for the FSC. Early controversies reinforced this impression (see Timber & Wood Products 1998c;
Dixon 1997). However, the point to take from this is that the WWF invested differently in the FSC project. Unlike many other groups, the
WWF began building programs and actions around certification, creating relationship-specific assets. These steps were strengthened with the
launch of its Forests for Life campaign in 1995, which had five objectives: increase the area of representative forest protection, ensure appropriate forest management, restore degraded forests, mitigate effects of
global change, and reduce consumption (Dudley, Jeanrenaud, and Sullivan 1995, 157–59). With the second objective—ensure appropriate management—independent certification was considered key, with the FSC
being the de facto program of choice. The campaign received considerable attention from the WWF and, given that certification was a central
pillar of its aims, the investment relative to other groups was high.

Consider a few illustrations. With UK public awareness, the WWF
campaign had ten articles dedicated to it in a supplemental section of the
Observer published on September 29, 1996. Each article focused on the

global forest challenges and many highlighted the FSC as a possible solution. From 1991 through 2007, the WWF was also referenced in more
FSC-related news releases than any of the other NGO founders (figure
4.2). Before 2000, the WWF and the FSC had been mentioned together
thirty-five times; Greenpeace, RAN, and Friends of the Earth were noted
with the FSC only twenty-seven times altogether. The WWF cited the FSC
in its press releases, noting and lauding the progress made toward various WWF targets (see WWF 1998, 1999a). Also, up to the end of 1999,
the WWF was the only NGO that gave the FSC a donation over $50,000;
WWF Netherlands contributed $237,236. In contrast, for the six years
(1994 through 1999) membership fees comprised only $138,782 and ac-
creditation fees $443,974 (FSC 2000a). Most contributions came from
governments ($2,047,282) and philanthropic foundations ($1,038,774).
(FSC 2000a; Bartley 2007a). Still, compared with financial support from
other NGOs, it illustrates the WWF's early commitment to the FSC. Finally, the FSC had endorsed fifteen national contact persons by 1999,
four of these WWF employees (FSC 1999c). When a WWF official did
not take on this principal role, the organization still often helped draft
national or subnational standards.

Unlike in any other case, the WWF also took a strong role in coordinating market support for certification. Beginning with the UK 1995
Group, the FSC was seen as a credible means to oversee the sustainable procurement commitments of buyer-group members (Hunt 1991).
Buyer groups quickly spread. One was established in the Netherlands in
1992, followed by one in Belgium in 1994, Austria in 1996, and Switzerland, North America, and Germany in 1997 (Hansen and Juslin 1999).
Not all were run by the WWF, but it was clearly the driving force behind the overall strategy, having launched the Global Forest and Trade
Network (GFTN) in 1998 to coordinate these groups (WWF 1999b). By
2000, there were GFTN activities in eighteen countries and the network
was composed of around 635 companies (Vilhinen et al. 2001; WWF
2001c). The WWF also integrated certification into its other forestry initiatives. Having leveled criticism at the World Bank over the TFAP and
the bank's forestry policies in the early 1990s (chapter 3), the two organizations later created the World Bank–WWF Alliance for Forest Conservation and Sustainable Use in 1998. One of the alliance's goals was to
bring 200 million hectares of forest under independent certification by
2005, half in tropical forests and the other half in temperate and boreal

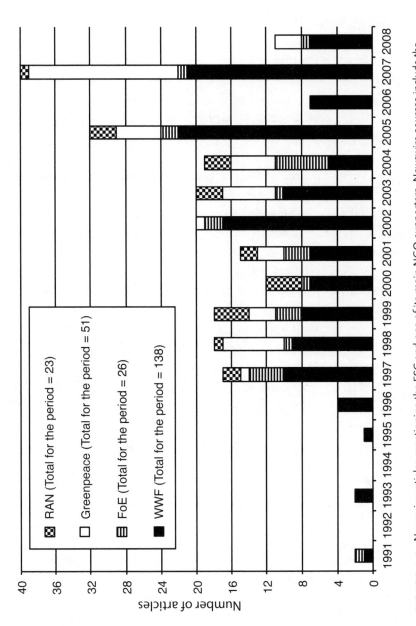

FIGURE 4.2. Newswire articles mentioning the FSC and one of its main NGO supporters. Newswire sources include the Associated Press, Business Wire, Canada Newswire, PR Newswire, PR Newswire Europe, M2 Presswire, Agence France-Presse, U.S. Newswire, and IPS–Inter Press Service (www.lexis-nexis.com).

forests (Humphreys 2006, 174; WWF 1997). Although the FSC was not explicitly named as the preferred program, the guidelines for what constituted acceptable certification mirrored the FSC's P&C. Importantly, this was not an initiative of the FSC, nor was it a product of the larger NGO community that supported the FSC (Aslam 1997). Soon after the WWF–World Bank launched their cooperative efforts, FSC certification hit 10 million hectares, with 115 forest operations certified in twenty-five countries. Having met its 10 million target by June 1998, the WWF refocused its energy, pushing the bar to 25 million hectares by 2001 (WWF 1998).

Behind these investments was a clear understanding within the WWF that the FSC was the program most open to their influence. One WWF official noted, "We have always come to the conclusion that even if the FSC was doing things that we didn't like, we felt that there were ways to influence the organization from the inside that were just not available with any other certification system."[29] What consequences did these developments have for forest products companies and landowners? The developing market interest from large buyers, coordinated by the WWF in particular, meant it was hard to avoid doing something. By mid- to late 1998, the UK 1995 Plus Group (formerly the 1995 Group)—comprising nearly ninety members that held a reported 15–25 percent share of the UK wood and paper products market (Tice 1998; Forestry & British Timber 1998; Hansen and Juslin 1999)—and the expanding GFTN network were gaining prominence. Bill Dumont of WFP explained it clearly when the company announced its pursuit of FSC certification: "The most important aspect of certification is its acceptability in the market. Our European customers have made it clear that FSC is the most credible system at present. In the future they may come to accept other mechanisms, but for now FSC is the most acceptable" (Western Forest Products 1998). Major producers in Sweden were also supporting the FSC by this time—due to interest from European buyers in the United Kingdom and Germany —and were having their land certified (Elliott 2000, 188). By mid-1998, AssiDomän had successfully certified all of its holdings, covering 3.3 million hectares—the largest area certified under the FSC since its launch (AssiDomän 1998; WWF 1998).

Thus, even if there were headaches involved, those companies under pressure had to act. Canadian companies, recall, had exited the FSC process early, pushing the CSA program and the idea of a forestry-specific

ISO standard as alternatives. One reading of this turnaround was that the costs of building a credible alternative program no longer seemed low enough. Some industry representatives were indeed questioning whether the CSA would be all that easy to achieve given its requirements for stakeholder engagement (Lush 1998). Moreover, the FSC was actually open to their voice. Having SGS perform an FSC certification might well have given WFP some influence over the direction the FSC took in British Columbia, precisely the outcome feared by certain NGOs. After the initial rancorous back and forth over the announcement and responses, British Columbia industry associations and companies actually sought FSC membership.[30] Companies such as AssiDomän in Sweden had followed a very similar logic, feeling that being involved in the FSC would offer influence over the eventual standard (Price 1997). For the same reasons, Greenpeace and Friends of the Earth were wary of industry involvement from the beginning, and British Columbia groups worried about the industry's participation in the British Columbia standards development process post-1998 (McDermott 2003). The concerns led many groups to invest new energy in the FSC process with the aim of ensuring the FSC standard was as high as possible. The Good Wood Watch was formed as a coalition of British Columbia–focused NGOs (Greenpeace, Sierra Club of British Columbia, the Friends of Clayoquot Sound, West Coast Environmental Law, the David Suzuki Foundation, and the Rainforest Conservation Society) that aimed to ensure the British Columbia standard set a high bar (Good Wood Watch 2001; Cashore, Auld, and Newsom 2004, 82). Many British Columbia groups also became members of the FSC in an effort to shape how the FSC would be interpreted in the province. In July 2000 there were 86 Canadian members, or 21 percent of the 414 worldwide FSC members; a year later, in June 2001, Canadian membership had risen to 129 of 488, or 26 percent (FSC 2000b, 2001).

Stepping away from British Columbia, for other companies in the situation where NGOs raised challenges to their audits, the value of engaging was less clear. In the Leroy case, Atyi (2006) explained: "The impact of the Leroy Gabon withdrawal was significant in dousing the interest of other companies in pursuing FSC-style forest certification. For example, the forest company Thanry Gabon, which had been preparing for FSC certification, gave up its efforts after learning of the Leroy Gabon case" (460). J. D. Irving in the Canadian Maritimes had a similar reaction to challenges over its certificate in New Brunswick (Cashore and Lawson 2003). All these situations gave the impression that the FSC would not be enough to prevent further scrutiny and criticism from NGOs, and it might actually spur more (Auld 2006). It reminded industry that although the FSC had an economic chamber, gaining influence would not be straightforward.

As well, not all companies were equally sensitive to growing demand for the FSC from European buyers. British Columbia was particularly vulnerable because of the concurrent timing of the Asian financial crisis that reduced export demand from the region just as the European campaigns picked up steam (Cashore, Auld, and Newsom 2004). Scandinavian countries were all major exporters to the European countries where the FSC was becoming a requirement (Cashore, Auld, and Newsom 2004; Cashore et al. 2007; Gulbrandsen 2005). As noted above, this was a general pattern: export dependence increased vulnerability to certification demands.

Patterns of trade and production, in this way, were influential in opening opportunities for later emerging producer-backed programs. Cashore, Auld, and Newsom (2004) explain how only the existence of large, vertically integrated forest products firms made the United States a friendly environment in which to foster support for the FSC. Another factor highlighted by Bartley's (2007a) work was the late attention the United States received as a marketplace wherein to advocate for sectorwide adoption of the FSC. The Certified Forest Products Council, the GFTN group in the United States, formed only in 1997, and the campaigns targeting Home Depot and others gained momentum only from that point forward (Bartley 2007a). Thus, although Cashore, Auld, and Newsom (2004) are correct that the United States was not as susceptible to European market pressure, had the WWF launched a buyers group in 1991, things may have unfolded differently.

That the FSC received limited early attention as a sectorwide tool to improve management practices in the United States meant companies had time to watch and learn what happened in other countries. A similar process occurred in Finland, where attention, even among NGOs, was initially directed to public forest policy developments; efforts to draft FSC standards came later (Cashore et al. 2007). In both cases, this gave producers that were not being targeted time to build substitutes that they could later mobilize to fend off the FSC. Also, since the FSC was designed to certify forest operations of all sizes, in all forests, and cover social and ecological considerations, there was little room in which to make an argument for a complementary approach.

The limited opportunities for voice seen to be available within the FSC meant producers closed ranks in a collective front against the FSC. Industries' reaction meant NGOs that had been initially critical of the FSC realized that the program was better than the alternative. Wagon circling occurred on both sides. The discussion to follow explores this dynamic to assess its potential resilience going forward.

We learned above that from 1996 to 1999 NGO support for the FSC was muted and sometimes inconsistent. There was, however, a degree of irreversibility in the rhetorical demands. Once certification was put on the table, even if sometimes weakly backed, buyers began committing to increasing certified supplies and producers realized they had to have some way to meet the demands. By what means was an open question. Though the wagon-circling phenomenon on the part of forest companies and landowners has been examined in other analyses (Cashore, Auld, and Newsom 2004; Sasser 2003), a key insight from the above discussion is that the existence of a viable alternative changed the calculations for NGOs. Although there were many producer-backed programs that developed in the early part of the 1990s, none were global.[31] What changed around 1998 and 1999 was that viable industry alternatives emerged that had enough collective power to stand toe-to-toe against buyer demands.

Recall that PEFC was launched in 1999 and had endorsed national schemes in five European countries by the end of 2000, giving the program a total certified area of 23.5 million hectares (Auld 2009) (figure 4.3). The program grew by almost 100 percent in the following year, having 41.6 million hectares certified by December 2001 and adding four new endorsed national schemes (PEFC 2008). By this time, the U.S. SFI program had also expanded to include members from Canada (AFPA 2000b) and had signed a mutual understanding agreement with the American Tree Farm System concerning its approach to small U.S. landowners (AFPA 2000c). The AFPA also announced that CSA would be considered "functionally equivalent to the SFI program," meaning Canadian companies could use the program to meet their AFPA membership obligations (AFPA 2000a). As well, by 2000 the IFIR had initiated efforts pushing mutual recognition.

In addition, as pressure on U.S. buyers grew with announcements by Home Depot and others in the fall of 1999, B&Q, one of the FSC's strongest and longest supporters, voiced frustration with the program's inability to evolve. That fall B&Q chose to accept the Finnish Forest Certification Scheme and LEI from Indonesia. It would not use the programs' labels (opting instead for a truth statement on products endorsed by the programs); truth statements were also used on products with more than 82.5 percent recycled content. Still, this marked the end of B&Q's long-standing "FSC only" policy. There were several reasons for the change, including the FSC's slowness in adopting a recycled content policy and its inability to work with other schemes, all of which B&Q's Alan Knight outlined in a report on the company's new approach released in 2000. The report praised the FSC, yet noted how an "FSC only" policy was no longer workable, explaining, "B&Q's supply chain is too diverse and the FSC finds it difficult to adapt to this diversity and to future demands" (Knight 2000, 15).

As a consequence, unlike in the early stages, when the support of buyers was relatively secure, making this case for supporting only the FSC became harder as producer-backed programs began evolving into third-party certification schemes (Overdevest 2005; Cashore, Auld, and Newsom 2004). What is interesting is that by around 2000 and 2001, the way the FSC was being discussed by certain NGOs had changed. Take Friends of the Earth as an example. By 2000, a Friends of the Earth campaigner, Matt Phillips, was encouraging suppliers to "only sell wood that has been independently certified to come from forests with the highest social and environmental standards—that means choosing the FSC label" (Amanda Brown 2000). A year later, Phillips wrote a piece for the *Observer* of London in which he stated: "Corporations can contribute to solutions rather than cause problems. B&Q, for instance, has played a key role in the Forest Stewardship Council, the world's best—and most credible—scheme promoting well managed forestry" (Phillips 2001). Finally, to announce the 2002 version of its *Good Wood Guide*, another Friends of the Earth campaigner explained: "This new easy-to-use guide is a must-buy for the discerning shopper. By checking out where wooden products come from and insisting they are FSC-certified, we can make sure that having beautiful wooden things does not damage the forests— or destroy the wildlife that lives in them" (Friends of the Earth 2002). In

2000, the Brazilian branch of Friends of the Earth also established the country's first pro-FSC buyer group and secured support from forty local companies that were committed to seeking FSC supply and helping to reduce illegal logging (WWF 2000; Lehman 2000).

Numerous reports were also written at the time that compared programs on a host of characteristics, often for strategic ends. Overdevest (2005) examined twenty-one written comparisons of the FSC and its competitor programs between 1995 and 2001, fifteen of which were written by NGOs in favor of the FSC and two of which were written from the counter position. Consistent with the chapter's argument, all but one report was published in 2000, 2001, or 2002, and those written by NGOs championed the FSC over the SFI (a few also included the PEFC and CSA). Notions of procedural (input) legitimacy were strong with groups emphasizing how the FSC's standards were developed, giving equal say to social, environmental, and economic interests (Ozinga 2001). Recall that the Global Forest Policy Project director had issued a strong rebuke of the IFIR mutual recognition framework by this time. WWF and Greenpeace issued their own press release to this effect (WWF 2001b, 2001a). Efforts to highlight the differences between the FSC and producer-backed programs took center stage and pushed aside some of the vocal criticism of the FSC by NGOs early on.

This is not to say that there was a miraculous transformation and that once a global competitive threat emerged, NGOs did nothing but champion the FSC. Rather, it illustrates a shift that made working from within more important and hence lessened the power of the exit threat. Exit still did occur, as was most clearly demonstrated by the publication of *Trading in Credibility* in November 2002 and the much more recent creation, circa November 2006, of FSC-Watch (www.fsc-watch.org), a Web site dedicated to shedding light on the many problems with the FSC, particularly the limited transparency concerning complaints against certificate holders and certifiers (FSC-watch.org 2008). Yet the tight feedbacks between the FSC and the producer-backed programs were reasonably entrenched by this point.

Finally, the competition also appears responsible for the extent to which certification has spread. Figure 4.3 provides data for certified forests. The total area certified under the two programs was over 400 million hectares by the fall of 2012, around 10 percent of the world's forest cover, 5.9 percent and 4 percent for the PEFC and FSC respectively. With forests allocated for production, the proportion certified totals 33 percent.

The initiation and growth of certification in the forest sector took shape in a way probably envisioned by very few original founders. Although the speed and pace of change has been criticized for being too fast for some and too slow for others, it is hard to look back on the twenty-year history and not find the development impressive. Chapters to follow discuss cases where experiences in the forest sector informed the emergence of other programs. The FSC in particular has been a significant model spurring both emulation and competition. To close, the discussion relates the narrative back to the explanatory framework presented in chapter 2.

With initiation, there were factors that favored global-first and local-first initiatives. As suggested by hypothesis 3—*With higher levels of international trade, the development of global-first programs is more likely*—the lower levels of forest products trade favored the development of local-first initiatives. The power of this factor is supported by the early efforts of certifiers such as the Soil Association, the SGS, and SCS, and subnational standard setters such as the Rogue Institute. It was a pattern very similar to the emergence of organics (chapter 6). By contrast, with hypothesis 1—*When markets have low barriers to entry, the development of local-first programs is more likely*—Kwisthout's Ecological Trading Company and Greenpeace's attempts to find a model small-scale operation to champion in their British Columbia campaigns are exceptions that prove the rule. These attempts faced challenges due to the barriers to entry in the forest sector. Likewise, for hypothesis 2—*When there are concentrated points of multinational companies in a supply chain, the development of global-first programs is more likely*—conditions in the forest sector also favored a global-first initiative. For instance, given that companies such as B&Q were easy targets for boycotts and that they quickly became involved in the development of certification, it was clear early on that there would be a need for considerable volumes of certified wood and for a system that could monitor global supply networks.

Also concerning hypothesis 2, forest product companies did indeed struggle from a collective reputation and this did lead them to favor a global response. However, this push was offset by the limited extent of global trade (hypothesis 3) and the resources and capabilities companies had developed in lobbying for domestic policy. This speaks to

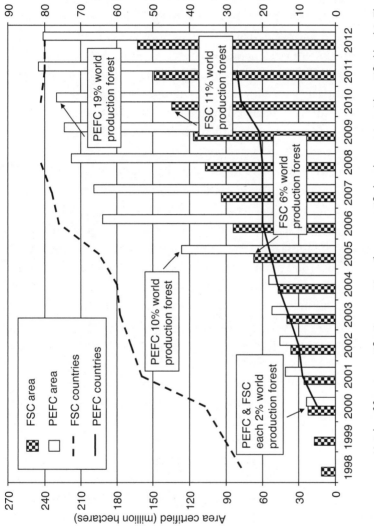

FIGURE 4.3. Uptake of forestry certification over time (by area certified and countries with certified lands). The data are from archival Web searches (via www.webarchive.net) and FSC and PEFC annual reports. The percentages of production forests are calculated based on FAO data on the proportion of the world's forests allocated for production.

the broader lesson from the forestry sector in relation to hypothesis 4—
*When international political opportunity structures are more open than domes-
tic ones, the development of global-first programs is more likely*—and hypothesis 5—*Where political opportunity structures are open, they act to legitimize
particular ideas of key social and environmental problems.* Early interest in
certification was helped by the relative openness of the ITTO and its attention to social and environmental issues. Network ties built through lobbying for strong intergovernmental action solidified an NGO community
ready to support alternative solutions. Producers responded to similar
and separate concerns, yet they were best equipped to mobilize domestically (and sometimes regionally). This tendency was reinforced by the intergovernmental processes emerging from the UNCED that emphasized
national action supported by a network of regional C&I processes. Consequently, producer-backed programs began as country-level initiatives.

On the issue of program design, as predicted by hypothesis 6—
*Certification's policy scope and regulatory domain will be a reflection of the
founders' perceptions of key social and environmental problems and the necessary solutions*—the immediate involvement of the WWF, Friends of the
Earth, Greenpeace, and other groups helped to ensure that the program
had a broad policy focus and regulatory domain. The chapter also revealed how FSC founders drew lessons from other sectors. Knowledge of
the Dutch Max Havelaar experience informed Kwisthout's early thinking
on certification; likewise, the IFOAM and IUCN membership structures
informed the FSC's governance design. However, at that stage, it was
less clear that these initiatives were a direct analogue to what the founders had in mind, which is in contrast to what happened in fisheries. Still,
the founders' use of the ISO, IUCN, and IFOAM as models for aspects of
the FSC's structures lends some support to the hypothesis.

Early on, both those supporting the FSC and producer-backed programs
faced challenges in becoming global programs. FSC supporters got started
on this earlier and were greatly assisted by their global representation.
Thus, although several certifiers were operational before the FSC formally
launched, it appears there was insufficient time for resistance to emerge.
Furthermore, and offering support to hypothesis 10—*When existing certification programs offer opportunities for influence from within, the likelihood of
new programs developing is diminished*—the FSC was able to assuage possible
resistance from the certifiers by giving them discretion over implementation early on. The WWF's commitment to the FSC is also consistent with

this hypothesis and the expectations about the role of loyalty; more than any other NGO, the WWF developed relationship-specific assets in its work with the FSC. However, the early choice of the FSC to limit voice for economic actors tipped the scales in favor of exit for some of these actors.

Nevertheless, resistance to the FSC among other actors lurked under the surface. The FSC was able to build the apparatus of a global program by early 1996, but then it spent several years negotiating disputes over its goals and who should have power to determine its local application. Criticisms of certain early certificates and the tension between the FSC's informal, national affiliates and FSC International were indicative. The reaction of NGOs to the FSC's certification activities in certain localities aligns with expectations about resistance to change identified in chapter 2. As suggested by the discussion of hypothesis 7—*With local-first certification initiatives, the development of market demand creates resistance to change that can slow efforts to create a global program*—had there been more demand for the FSC early on (for example, a market niche for ecologically friendly timber from British Columbia), resistance from NGOs supporting a local alternative could easily have developed. However, while certain early-certified companies did receive benefits, even in the form of premiums, these were erratic.

Consistent with hypothesis 9—*When early programs have a broad policy scope or regulatory domain, new programs are more likely to be competitors*—at the sector level, the defining theme in the forest sector was competition. Key here was the early choice of the FSC to have a broad policy focus and regulatory domain. At first the FSC stood alone, but eventually producers created a global program. This induced self-reinforcing processes sparking greater attempts to foster support for the FSC. That the FSC was not able to successfully use its first-mover status to prevent the entry of competitors underlines the learning by adoption processes that were at play. Unlike a pure coordination effect, where a network externality can make one choice rational over alternatives, increased market interest had an open-access quality. Thus, efforts to build support for the FSC created positive spillovers, increasing the value of outside options for producers. The perceived cost of creating alternatives and convincing buyers that they were suitable substitutes was apparently less than the perceived cost of working from within the FSC. Investments by producers then worked to legitimize the certification idea, creating a positive feedback loop reinforcing the overall pattern of competition.

CHAPTER FIVE

Markets and Politics in the Coffee Sector

FROM COFFEE'S SIMPLE ORIGINS as a species endemic to the African continent, its production now drives economies, spurs political contests within and between countries, and has become central to millions of peoples' daily lives. Coffee production and trade also present social and environmental challenges. Forests have long been cleared to create coffee plantations, and cyclical overproduction and associated price drops along with political corruption and power imbalances in supply chains have engendered social challenges in many coffee-producing regions. Certification programs are recent mechanisms that seek to address some or all of these problems.

To understand the move to certification as an instrument to address governance challenges in the coffee sector, this chapter reviews the market and political conditions in the sector that have shaped the rise and evolution of certification. The analysis is guided by the framework set out in chapter 2 that identifies the expected effects of different market and political opportunity structures. On the market side, the coffee sector's first characteristic is its low barriers to entry—lower than either the forest or the fisheries sectors. This feature is expected to facilitate the rise of local-first certification programs. The second condition, by contrast, is the extensive points of concentration in the sector's global supply chain occupied by multinationals, which is expected to point in the opposition direction, favoring global, not local, certification. Finally, and also supporting global certification, coffee is the most globally traded of the three sectors' products.

On the political side, the intergovernmental processes for coffee began much earlier than in the forest sector and were less open to non-state actors and later-developing social and environmental concerns. Indeed, the central intergovernmental process remained focused on rent flow and distribution. Without an open venue in which to build ties and champion new understandings of problems, the coffee sector was less amenable to the development of a global-first initiative. As chapter 6 will reveal, this condition along with the low barriers to entry in the coffee market appeared important for the early initiation of multiple local certification initiatives.

To commence, the chapter describes production in the coffee sector to elucidate the market conditions expected to affect the rise of certification. It then traces the history of intergovernmental processes for coffee, detailing how they have coevolved with NGO activism and clarifying both the opportunities for influence available to NGOs and businesses and the changing perceptions of social and environmental problems in the sector. Chapter 6 picks up the analysis with the beginning of stage 1 of the analytic framework to trace the specific way the conditions reviewed below shaped the initiation and evolution of coffee certification.

MARKET STRUCTURES

Two species of coffee are grown commercially: *Coffea arabica* and *Coffea canephora*. Both require high seasonal rain (more than fifteen hundred millimeters a year), a warm climate with little temperature variation (eighteen to twenty-six degrees Celsius), and no frost (ICO 1997). *Coffea arabica*, or arabica, grows at high elevations in the tropics, whereas *Coffea canephora*, or robusta, can grow from sea level to approximately eight hundred meters in tropical regions. Robusta is also more resistant to disease and pests than arabica (Daviron and Ponte 2005), and its beans contain more caffeine, making them popular in mass-market and instant-coffee blends. For both species, it takes two to four years for a coffee tree to produce an initial crop and five years to reach optimal production (Daviron and Ponte 2005). Once in production, a coffee tree can be harvested economically for around twenty to thirty years (ICO 1997).

Coffee production occurs only in countries near the equator. From 2001 to 2006, an average of 30 percent of production came from countries growing only arabica; around 16 percent came from countries producing only robusta. The remaining 50 percent or so came from countries producing both. Arabica-only countries are located in Central America, the Caribbean, the northern portion of South America, and eastern Africa. Robusta-only countries are in western parts of Africa, Asia, and parts of South and Central America as well as the Caribbean (ICO 2012). Countries producing a mixture are scattered around these two regions in places where geography and climate meet the separate needs of the two species. At the close of the twentieth century, around 70 percent of world production was arabica, of which approximately 80 percent grew in Latin America (Rice and McLean 1999).

The geography of production reveals several notable patterns. First, South American countries, particularly Brazil and Colombia, are major coffee producers, a dominance that has actually waned since the turn of the twentieth century. Between 1900 and 1920, Brazil accounted for 70–85 percent of the world's total annual green coffee exports (Bates 1997). Since the 1960s, Brazil's annual production accounted for, on average, 28 percent of world production. It started the 1960s producing around 50 percent and ended 2003 producing only 28 percent. Nonetheless, from 1961 through 2003, South America produced an average of 45 percent of global green coffee output.

Growing Asian coffee production is a second notable trend. In 1961, countries in Asia and Oceania contributed only 5 percent to global production annually; by 2003, this had grown to almost 30 percent. Most of this increase comes from investments in robusta production in Vietnam and Indonesia (Gresser and Tickell 2002; Lewin, Giovannucci, and Varangis 2004). In 2003, these two countries ranked second and third after Brazil based on production of green coffee, replacing Colombia, which had ranked second since the turn of the twentieth century (Bates 1997).

The production process varies regionally. Highly mechanized harvesting and processing occur in parts of countries such as Brazil, and labor-intensive approaches are used on the majority of smallholdings around the world. Before being shipped for export or sale domestically, beans are graded. Grading varies by country, but generally considers the coffee species, processing method, existence of defects, size of bean, and bean density, shape, and color (Daviron and Ponte 2005). Graded beans are then shipped to ports in Europe and North America, where storage facilities hold green beans before distribution and roasting. Unlike certain other tropical commodities, green coffee beans can be stored for quite a long period before degrading (Daviron and Ponte 2005), though the storage conditions are critical (Mabbett 2007).

Roasting typically occurs in the consuming country since, once roasted, bean quality quickly degrades. Even with the invention of vacuum-sealed containers and bags with one-way valves for transporting roasted whole beans, coffee consumption is recommended within weeks, preferably days, of roasting (Pendergrast 2001). Nevertheless, the improvement of storage techniques does permit greater transport of roasted coffee.

Blending—the mixing of various beans—is also standard practice for roasters (Pendergrast 2001). Only recently, with the upswing of the specialty market, have roasters begun to more widely market the variation in bean taste. Technological improvements have also given roasters greater flexibility in the possible green coffee inputs. Steam processing can now reduce the harsh flavor of robusta and limit the acidity of certain arabica beans, making the final product friendlier to the general consumer (Lewin, Giovannucci, and Varangis 2004). These technological changes also mean roasters are less vulnerable to supply shortfalls in coffee from any particular production region since they are able to substitute across inputs with relative ease (Lewin, Giovannucci, and Varangis 2004).

The decaffeination process is probably the most capital-intensive part of coffee production. There are a number of methods, all of which follow a similar overall approach: the beans are heated with either steam or hot water and then some agent (for example, methylene chloride or ethyl acetate) is used to separate the caffeine from other water-soluble compounds (Norr 2007; Beckman 2004).

This descriptive overview provides a basis for identifying the conditions in the coffee sector for the three market opportunity hypotheses (table 5.1). These are each reviewed below.

Barriers to Entry

With the first hypothesized factor, the coffee sector, arguably, has the lowest barriers to entry throughout its global supply chain. Although there are only a handful of large industrial roasters and traders, capital costs for establishing a small roasting facility to compete in a local market are not large. Thus, setting up a small coffee roasting/retail operation

Table 5.1.

Coffee market opportunity structures and expected effects

CHARACTERISTICS	CONDITIONS	EXPECTATIONS
Barriers to entry (hypothesis 1)	Low barriers to entry	Supports creation of local-first programs
Concentration in supply chain (hypothesis 2)	Points of concentration in supply chain occupied by limited number of multinationals	Supports creation of global-first programs
International trade (hypothesis 3)	High levels of international trade	Supports creation of global-first programs

is feasible in certain markets, especially given the recent rise in specialty coffees. Indeed, there are numerous single-location coffeehouses in the United States that roast on their own premises and sell to a small local market. The history of new growing regions entering coffee production also illustrates how the production end does not present large barriers to new entrants.

Given these conditions, according to hypothesis 1, all else being equal, the coffee sector should facilitate the creation of local-first programs.

Multinationals at Concentrated Points in the Supply Chain

The coffee supply chain is by far the simplest and exhibits the highest levels of concentration occupied by multinationals. It is much like an hourglass. Coffee trees are planted, cultivated, and picked on small-holdings in around seventy countries, with some 20–25 million families involved in this stage of production (Rice and McLean 1999; Lewin, Giovannucci, and Varangis 2004). More than 50 percent of the world's production is estimated to come from smallholders with fewer than five hectares of farmland (Rice and McLean 1999).[1] At the other end, millions of consumers enjoy a daily cup of coffee. In Europe, the average per capita consumption of coffee exceeded five kilograms a year between 1995 and 2002. The highest consumption rates are commonly found in Scandinavia; in Finland per capita consumption exceeded eleven kilograms a year in 2002 (Lewin, Giovannucci, and Varangis 2004). Still, only 17 percent of the world's population consumes around 65 percent of the world's coffee production (Lewin, Giovannucci, and Varangis 2004).

Between these extremes, the hourglass narrows considerably. With traders, consolidation has led to ever-increasing concentration. Neumann and Volcafe held 29 percent of the market for green coffee in 1998 (Ponte 2004). Further mergers have increased this dominance (Daviron and Ponte 2005); as of 2010, the Neumann Gruppe, Volcafe, and ECOM traded 50 percent of the world's green coffee (Tropical Commodity Coalition 2012). The hourglass is narrowest with the roasting sector. Back in 1998, Philip Morris, Nestlé, Sara Lee, Procter & Gamble, and Tchibo captured 69 percent of the instant and roasted coffee market (Ponte 2004; Daviron and Ponte 2005). Other estimates note how the five main roasters purchased approximately 50 percent of the world's annual green coffee production (Gresser and Tickell 2002). As of 2010, the main players are Nestlé, Kraft, and Sara Lee (Tropical Commodity Coalition 2012). Whereas large roasters remain dominant, since the 1980s, the United States has developed a vibrant specialty coffee industry that has opened up a large segment of smaller café and roasting operations.

At the end of the chain, coffee is sold by retail outlets such as grocery stores, or as a prepared beverage at coffeehouses or restaurants. The typical means of buying and consuming coffee varies. In the United States, as an example, in 1997 there were 6,843 coffee shops owned by 4,852 independent firms; the 4 largest firms owned 1,458 of these establishments and another 46 firms owned the next 380 (U.S. Census Bureau 2000b). Coffee shops have been growing in numbers. Between 1992 and 2002, the number in the United States grew from 2,250 to 13,700 (Lewin, Giovannucci, and Varangis 2004); this includes companies such as Starbucks, which operated over 7,000 coffee shops by the beginning of 2007 (Starbucks 2007). In 2006, around 57 percent of all U.S. coffeehouses were independents (that is, owning 1–3 units) (SCAA 2007). Also, in 2006, there were around 1,900 retail operations that roasted on their premises; as a segment they constituted $1.76 billion in sales of the $11.78 billion for the whole U.S. café segment (SCAA 2007). With grocery stores, there were 96,542 establishments in 1997, with 4 firms owning 4,352, and another 12,181 owned by 46 additional firms (U.S. Census Bureau 2000c). Finally, restaurants and other eating establishments numbered at 580,123 in 1997, with little concentration in the hands of a few companies (U.S. Census Bureau 2000a).

Based on hypothesis 2, these conditions, all else being equal, should facilitate the creation of global certification programs.

International Trade
Coffee is by far the most heavily traded on the global market; the majority of coffee is grown for export.[2] Although there are certain exceptions (for example, Brazil has a large domestic market), most coffee is exported from producing countries in its green form.[3] It is either exported directly to a consuming market or reexported from consuming country to consuming country. Excluding trade among consuming countries, exports accounted for nearly 80 percent of total production in 2003. Reexporting has been on the rise, however.

South America accounted for an average of 41 percent of annual global exports from 1961 to 2003. Until around the mid-1970s, African producers contributed 20–25 percent of global exports, mostly of robusta, with Ivory Coast, Angola, and Uganda ranking as the third-, fourth-, and fifth-largest exports, not necessarily in that order. After the mid-1970s, however, African exports slowed, dropping from 28 percent of world exports in 1977 to 9 percent in 2003. They were replaced by growing production in Central America, Brazil and, most recently, Asia. Vietnam was the second-largest exporter after Brazil in 2003, accounting for 10 percent of world exports.

Import data also uncover significant trends in the market for coffee. Germany now rivals the United States for top importer, and all together, European countries now import more green coffee than the United States. In 1961 the United States imported around 50 percent of all green coffee exports; by 2003 this had dropped to 23 percent. Taken as a group, Germany, France, and Italy (the top three European importers) accounted for 29 percent of all imports in 2003. Notably, Japan has also increased its coffee imports: from 1961 to 2003, imports rose from 1 to 7 percent of the world's annual total.

The sources of U.S. and European imports do differ. Most U.S. imports come from Central America, the Caribbean, and South America; from 1986 to 2005, these regions accounted for an average of 78 percent of U.S. annual imports (FAO 2007a). In Germany, 60 percent of imports over this period came from these regions; another 17 percent of annual imports came from Africa, a region that contributed only an average of 5 percent to U.S. imports.

Table 5.2.

Coffee political opportunity structures and expected effects

CHARACTERISTICS	CONDITIONS	EXPECTATIONS
International political opportunity structure (hypothesis 4)	Lacked an international forum open to NGO participation	Inhibits creation of global-first certification
Opportunity structures for legitimizing new ideas (hypothesis 5)	Lacked an international forum wherein to legitimize broad understanding of the coffee problem	Inhibits early creation of certification with a broad policy focus

According to hypothesis 3, this is another facet of the coffee sector that should facilitate the creation of global certification programs, all else being equal.

POLITICAL STRUCTURES

Turning to the political opportunity structures, chapter 2 detailed two conditions expected to affect the spatial scale of initial certification efforts and the policy focus of programs. Table 5.2 details the character of these conditions in the coffee sector.

What follows reviews the history of intergovernmental processes addressing the coffee sector and the evolution of NGO tactics. In contrast to the forest case, intergovernmental processes for coffee started sooner and were less open to the later-developing social and environmental concerns. The coffee commodity agreement also remained focused on rent distribution. When other issues arose, particularly concerns over the environmental and human health consequences of extensive pesticide applications on farms, there was no amenable intergovernmental venue wherein to press for change. Without an open venue for building ties and legitimizing new understandings of coffee problems, the formation of certification was pushed toward fragmentation.

The Scope and Domain of Governance Structures

The north-south pattern of production and trade in the coffee sector was the initial focus for international cooperation. Under the 1948 Havana Charter (UN 1948) countries established, inter alia, procedures for negotiating international commodity control agreements. These agreements were deemed appropriate when a study group and a commodity conference found surplus commodity production existed, or could develop, that would threaten the livelihoods of small producers, or when widespread unemployment was linked to changing production of a given commodity (UN 1948, 51–58; Hemmi 1964). In both cases, the charter advocated multilateral intervention to regulate prices, production, or exports and imports of a given commodity. Notably, the focus of these efforts was economic. The interwar period had illustrated the destructive results of protectionism and domestic economic crises and hence led to an interest in international market regulation to foster more lasting stability (Hemmi 1964; Bilder 1963). Environmental concerns were far from the agenda and negotiations remained a state-state affair, with certain provisions for the participation of intergovernmental organizations (UN 1948, 57).

The problem, in this sense, concerned rent flow and distribution. Coffee producers faced ever-increasing competition that pushed down prices. Coffee's climatic requirements made production on the margins of its range susceptible to weather-related losses. Frost, drought, and pathogens were the major causes of crop losses (Pendergrast 2001). Frosts, for instance, periodically decimated Brazil's southern production regions, precipitating large price spikes for green coffee. Price volatility ensued due to relatively inelastic demand. Small changes in the quantity supplied raised prices, which in turn greatly encouraged increased production (through either replanting or the entry of new producers). Because of the fixed costs of establishing new plantations (purchasing land, clearing it, and planting trees), the long gestation period (it takes about three years for a tree to bear fruit), and low variable costs (picking coffee cherries and processing them is either mechanized or relies on low-cost labor), once new plantations are established in periods of peak prices, they create long-lasting and lagged oversupply (Bilder 1963). Even without another shock, a cycle of high and low prices can persist for years as producers come in and out of the market (Lewin, Giovannucci, and Varangis 2004).

Efforts to address these problems have been driven by more than the concerns of small producers, unemployment, and international stability. Producing countries see coffee as a critical national development tool. Of the more than thirty countries producing coffee in the late 1950s, thirteen relied on coffee exports for 30–80 percent of their foreign exchange earnings; a 1 percent decline in coffee price meant a $45 million loss of foreign exchange for Latin American producers at the time (Bilder 1963, 333). Not surprisingly, then, countries have long attempted to control supply in order to raise prices. In the twentieth century, this aim was first pursued unilaterally by Brazil, which supplied 70 percent or more of the world export market (Pendergrast 2001). Despite its strong market position, Brazil failed to influence price for all but short periods of time. The success it did have worsened the situation by lowering entry barriers for competitor producers. From 1900 to 1940, Colombia's share of world exports grew from around 2 percent to closer to 12 percent (Bates 1997). Other producers also began to compete with Brazil, slowly eroding its dominance.

World War II broke the normal pattern. Postwar rearrangements in Colombian and Brazilian politics mattered in particular; they freed the countries' central governments to seek greater influence over coffee prices (Bates 1997). As well, immediately after World War II, Brazil's neglected coffee plantations predicated a supply shortfall, driving prices to a peak in 1954. Thus, when work on commodity agreements began, coffee was not under direct consideration. This changed after 1954 when prices fell precipitously. A meeting of the Inter-American Economic and Social Council of the Organization of American States led to calls for a multilateral agreement to restrict coffee exports (Bates 1997, 106; Bilder 1963). Although nothing concrete resulted from these discussions, by 1957 the situation had deteriorated. Latin American producers responded by agreeing to export restrictions set out in El convenio de Mexico, negotiated in October of that year (Bilder 1963).

These efforts failed. Increased supplies from African producers left Colombia and Brazil unable to sanction free riding on their significant efforts to withhold supplies from the international markets (Bates 1997). It was then clear that without the help of consuming countries, continued export controls were unlikely to succeed (Hemmi 1964). This meant overcoming significant and continued resistance from the primary consuming country—the United States.[4] Its opposition only began to wane in the late 1950s as it recognized the negative consequences price declines had for Latin American economies (Talbot 2004, 57). With the United States helping to form a Coffee Study Group in 1958, steps began toward the first International Coffee Agreement (ICA). A short-term agreement was signed in 1959 and then extended in 1960, during which time the participation of non–Latin American producers and importers began to increase. Nevertheless, these efforts remained ineffective for several reasons, including the lack of committed U.S. participation, particularly in terms of enforcing export controls (Bilder 1963).

The U.S. position changed with President Kennedy's March 1961 speech "Alliance for Progress," in which he announced a policy of a case-by-case interest in negotiating commodity agreements (Bilder 1963). The standard assessment underscores the move's political motives: the United States was willing to redistribute wealth from its consumers to coffee producers in Latin America as part of broader U.S. efforts to stave off a Communist expansion in the region (Bates 1997; Pendergrast 2001; Talbot 2004; Fridell 2007).[5] The agreement also benefited from the acquiescence of large U.S. roasters. The agreement actually proved in their interests; as Bates (1997) explains, they were able to negotiate bulk contracts with coffee producers that reduced their costs below the quota-driven price, meaning they were able to use the ICA to increase the costs of their smaller competitors.

The first ICA, signed in 1962, opened a period of thirty or so years in which international coffee trade was regulated. Commodity agreements of the era concerned rent flow and distribution and gave no attention to the environmental impacts of a given crop's production. National delegations did include private actors, but most were business interests. The U.S. delegation, as an example, included eight representatives from the coffee industry (Bilder 1963). There were delegates from fifty-eight countries, observers from another thirteen, and representatives from three intergovernmental organizations: the FAO, the International Bank for Reconstruction and Development, and the International Monetary Fund (Bilder 1963).

The agreement's basic provisions set a target price for coffee, which was used to set export quotas; later changes introduced separate indicator prices for the four main coffee grades: robusta, mild Colombia, other milds, and natural arabica (Bates 1997). The International Coffee Organization (ICO) was in charge of calculating indicator prices that dictated when the ICA restrictions were imposed. If an indicator price exceeded the target price, quotas were relaxed; when it fell, quotas were tightened (Ponte 2004). Membership included the main producing and consuming countries. The producer countries that negotiated the original agreement represented around 95 percent of the world's green coffee production in 1962. The twenty-five consuming nations that signed up as members imported around 92 percent of the world's total exports.[6] Similar to the ITTO, voting rights in the ICO were divided among producers and consumers mostly based on their significance to the coffee trade (Bates 1997).

The ICA went through four iterations between 1962 and the suspension of its export quotas and other economic provisions in 1989. Although subsequent agreements were adopted in 1994, 2001, and 2007, none contained the export-control provisions.[7] The eventual breakdown of the regulatory provisions of the ICA was driven by external changes in market and in political conditions. Market problems included quotas not aligned with changing consumer demand for higher-quality mild arabica and increasing problems with "Tourist coffee," a term describing how nonquota coffee was initially sold to non-ICO members and then resold to a member but outside the quota system (Lewin, Giovannucci, and Varangis 2004). Nonmember markets were also becoming more significant coffee consumers, creating further strains on the ICA price controls. Politically, U.S. support changed under the Reagan administration. It no longer felt the benefits of staving off Communism outweighed the costs to U.S. consumers (Bates 1997). There were also ideational changes—particularly the "Washington Consensus"—that made international commodity agreements a less appealing intervention (Fridell 2007, 43). Indeed, the 1980s and 1990s saw the collapse of nearly all existing commodity agreements (Gilbert 1996). The agreement for sugar lapsed in 1983; the one for tin collapsed in 1985; and the one for cocoa was suspended in 1988 (Gilbert 1996). An agreement for natural rubber began in 1980 (Gilbert 1996) and was ended in September 1999.[8] The ITTA, discussed in chapter 3, was an exception; it was coming into force just as these other commodity agreements dissolved.

Finally, the perceived nature of the problem was changing. Most analyses had concluded that the ICA price controls worked to raise prices and reduce volatility (Talbot 2004; Bates 1997). However, it no longer seemed sufficient to redistribute wealth to producer countries without also considering how that money was spent. Small farmers were not necessarily the beneficiaries of the higher and more stable coffee prices. Concerns over industrial practices in agriculture and particularly the use of pesticides were also on the rise; the publication of Rachel Carson's *Silent Spring* had set the tone for growing disquiet on this issue (Gottlieb

1993, 81–86). These environmental concerns began to reach the international agenda late in the 1960s with the UN Educational, Scientific and Cultural Organization's (UNESCO) Biosphere Conference in 1968 and calls from Sweden for a global conference on the environment (Betsill and Corell 2008). Both were important precursors to the UN Conference on the Human Environment (UNCHE), which took place in Stockholm in 1972 (Bernstein 2002, 31–32). In Stockholm, environmental NGOs, including Friends of the Earth and WWF, also gained a more prominent role in international negotiations, both as observers in the formal UNCHE event (Feraru 1974) and in a parallel, officially sanctioned Environment Forum that involved hundreds of NGOs (Bernstein 2002, 32; Ungeheuer 1972).

Bernstein (2002, 31–32) explained the controversy over what the Stockholm conference ought to address, noting how the UN General Assembly's 1968 call for the conference stressed environmental problems more salient for developed countries—issues such as biocides, soil deterioration, waste, and water and air pollution—problems connected explicitly to processes of urbanization and population growth (UNGA 1968). Developing countries, he argued, sought to place development center stage, making it an explicit precondition to environmental protection efforts (Bernstein 2002, 36; see also UNGA 1971). Moreover, the discussions at the time also highlighted the trade-distorting consequences of growing environmental concerns among developed countries, warning that these could construct nontariff trade barriers. *The Founex Report*—reputed to have been a pivotal framing document orchestrated by Maurice Strong in advance of Stockholm to reconcile environmental concerns of the North and development concerns of the South—foreshadowed what would become a fulcrum of international debate. It stated: "The major danger that both developing and developed countries have to guard against is that the argument for better environment may be turned into an argument for greater protection by vested interests. When the concern spreads from the quality of a product to the environment in which such a product was produced, the alarm bells should ring all over the world, for it would be the beginning of the worst form of protectionism" (*Development and Environment* 1971).

A de-emphasis of the environmental concerns that motivated the call for the Stockholm conference meant this venue was less amenable to the concerns, such as pesticide use and industrial agriculture, that were motivating increasing interest in organic practices. The absence of a susceptible international venue proves significant for how organics developed, which by extension shaped the development of organic coffee certification. Indeed, although *The Founex Report* clearly outlined that developing countries would face the challenge of ensuring that the industrialization path did not create the environmental challenges experienced by developed countries, these challenges did in fact transpire and became an important part of the problem definition in the coffee sector.

Coevolution of NGO Tactics and Perceived Problems

Although the ICA's regulatory features ended in 1989, support for coffee regulation had begun to falter earlier, and there were growing concerns about other aspects of coffee production not covered by the ICA pricing mechanism. Environmental problems were being attributed to industrial forms of coffee production (Rice and Ward 1996). Intensive forms of production were linked to negative impacts on forest ecosystems and forest-dependent species (Dicum and Luttinger 1999; Greenwire 1991; Kinnaird et al. 2003) and, as analysts foresaw, intensive application of chemicals created human health problems for small farmers and farm workers (Rama and Jaga 1992; Wesseling et al. 1999). Coffee price volatility, moreover, created challenges for poor and marginalized coffee growers. Unlike exporters or roasters that were able to stockpile coffee or seek alternative sources of supply when coffee crops failed in a given country, farmers might rely entirely on coffee for revenue. Recall that an estimated 20–25 million families depend on coffee production and often face prices below their production costs (Lewin, Giovannucci, and Varangis 2004); many countries also depend on coffee as a source of foreign exchange. Thus, the link between coffee prices and rural poverty in coffee-producing regions was palpable. Yet the ICA pricing mechanism alone did not guarantee that individual farmers would benefit from the price gains or reduced volatility. The health effects associated with increased use of pesticides exacerbated these challenges.

The late 1970s and 1980s were politically tough for the sector. Coffee was being linked to problems of corruption, brutality, and human rights violations by repressive regimes (Tarmann 2002). In Uganda—where 93 percent of the country's export earning came from coffee (Morgan 1977)—it was easy for observers to see the revenues as partly facilitating

President Idi Amin's human rights abuses (Ullman 1978). Most of these revenues came from sales to Europe (approximately two-thirds) and the United States (approximately one-third). In the first six months of 1977, for instance, U.S. companies were estimated to have imported $150 million worth of green coffee from Uganda (Morgan 1977).[9]

Latin America was another hotbed of unrest. Civil war was occurring in Nicaragua, Guatemala, and El Salvador. The victory by the Sandinistas over the Somoza regime in Nicaragua led to the nationalization of coffee holdings and the establishment of a leftist government, a development viewed unfavorably by the U.S. administration (Tarmann 2002). Fearing the further spread of leftist guerrillas in the region, the U.S. government provided military and economic aid to El Salvador's conservative government of President Álvaro Magaña.[10] The United States also provided military and economic aid to the Contras, a guerrilla force working to usurp power from the Sandinista government of Daniel Ortega in Nicaragua. The costs were high. Staving off the Communist threat had serious human rights implications, which led to claims that the U.S. government was funding genocide (*Financial Times* 1983; Manuel 1985).

Turning the situation on its head, in 1989, labor activists and a select group of U.S. politicians called for a boycott of Salvadoran coffee, as a direct attack on U.S. aid to the country's right-wing government (*Boston Globe* 1989). The boycott took aim at the big U.S. coffee brands. Although certain companies acquiesced, Procter & Gamble (P&G), the owner of the largest U.S. brand—Folgers—resisted. Over the next two years, P&G and Neighbor-to-Neighbor (the U.S.-based organization pushing the boycott) were deep in battle.[11] Similar consumer activism occurred over U.S. policy toward Nicaragua. In 1985 the Reagan administration imposed an embargo on Nicaragua.[12] A year later Equal Exchange was founded as the first U.S.-based for-profit fair-trade company dealing in coffee, beginning by importing Nicaraguan coffee in defiance of the embargo (Rice and McLean 1999).[13] Even before this, in 1985, Thanksgiving Coffee, a California-based company, began importing coffee from Nicaragua, also in opposition to the embargo (Thanksgiving Coffee 2008). Paul Katzeff, the owner, had the company's slogan changed to "Not just a cup, but a just cup"; fifty cents on the sale of each pound of coffee was donated to the Sandinistas (Pendergrast 2001, 353).

Concerns about government actions were also focusing on failures of development aid. The Ethiopian famine of the mid-1980s uncovered concern with UK aid policies, especially how they failed to offer long-term solutions for rural poverty (Steele 1985; Bovard 1989). Many African countries in the business of coffee were struggling throughout the 1980s. Recall that Uganda, Ivory Coast, and Angola had ranked among the top five exporters through to the mid-1970s, after which they were typically surpassed in the yearly rankings by countries in Latin America and Asia. Africa's share of world coffee exports fell from 30 percent in 1976 to 9 percent by 2003 (FAO 2007a). Although commitments to assist African nations had been ambitious in the early part of the 1980s, by the 1990s situations had not improved, leading many to refer to the 1980s as the "lost decade" (Brittain 1991).

There was an important regional difference here. Relative to Latin America, the United States had less direct interest in Africa, with fewer economic ties and less at stake from a security perspective (Michaels 1993).[14] It was also open about having other priorities for aid dollars at the time (Connors 1990). This is not meant to imply that there was no U.S. interest in or attention to the plight of African coffee growers. Rather, it simply illustrates that the sphere of concern among governments was not exactly the same in Europe and North America.[15]

The U.S. administration's focus on Central America was significant for several reasons. First, it provided a focal point for NGOs that sought ways to speak in opposition to official policy and in turn fostered alliances between coffee growers and U.S. consumers. Organizations such as Nicaragua Exchange coordinated groups of senior citizens called "the Elders Brigades" that traveled to Nicaragua and worked on coffee farms. It was a way to show allegiance with Nicaraguans in opposition to official U.S. foreign policy (Galen 1985). And although seemingly insignificant in its effects, it served as one small development that helped spur alternative solutions to the ongoing poverty and environmental problems attributed to coffee production (Pendergrast 2001).[16] Second, although P&G never yielded to the pressure from Neighbor-to-Neighbor, and a peace treaty was eventually signed by El Salvador's government and the Farabundo Martí National Liberation Front (*Philadelphia Inquirer* 1992; *Adweek* 1992), the episode illustrated the growing consumer activism of the time (Ramirez 1990). Yet in these cases, the campaigns were shaped by the central role of the U.S. administration and efforts to support peace over continued conflict and violence in the Americas.

In Europe, although the conflicts in Central America were salient and similar solidarity initiatives did occur, the precursors to fair trade were also influenced by an emphasis on "trade, not aid" as a development strategy. The foreign aid debacles of the 1980s left groups and individuals disenchanted with state intervention, feeling that aid to help producers develop was less useful if there were not markets readily accessible for their products (Pendergrast 2001). In chapter 6 we will see how this emphasis was critical to the launch and advocacy behind fair-trade labeling and commercial brands.

In all situations, though, the episodes underlined the limits of the ICA regulatory approach and became aspects of the problem definition of the period. By not paying attention to domestic political issues, it gave increased revenues to powerful elites without guarantees that higher prices would trickle down to the coffee growers (see Ullman 1978).[17] In addition, and linked to debates over the UNCHE agenda, environmental problems with coffee production did not merge immediately with social equity and justice issues surrounding fair prices, market access, and political corruption. Environmental problems were becoming an increasing concern, especially the intensive use of pesticides and the transformation from extensive to intensive forms of production. Yet, notably, the community concerned about coffee growers was fragmented between those attending to social justice issues and those focused on the environmental implications of agricultural production. Unlike forestry, there was no international venue where these issues intermingled.

The review of market and political opportunity structures in the coffee sector has revealed important conditions expected to affect the rise of certification. The balance of market conditions supports the creation of global certification. The sector is characterized by a global supply chain that has extensive concentration occupied by multinationals and by its high levels of international trade. Only its low barriers to entry—lower than fisheries and forestry—are expected to support the creation of local certification. However, with the political opportunity structures, the sector lacked intergovernmental fora wherein to develop network ties and develop a broad, encompassing understanding of the global social and environmental problems arising from coffee production. As chapter 6 shows, this condition, along with the low barriers to entry in the coffee market, appeared important for the early initiation of multiple local certification initiatives that focused on social and environmental issues separately.

CHAPTER SIX

The Rise and Evolution of Coffee Certification

COFFEE CERTIFICATION HAD MORE DIVERSE ROOTS than its forestry counterparts. Building from chapter 5, the analysis to follow traces how developments in the intergovernmental arena since the 1960s affected the formation of certification programs. Unlike the forestry sector, in which the ITTO was a forum where NGOs connected to share ideas and devise a new path for governance, with coffee such a forum was absent. Certification activities emerged in the largely separate communities of actors involved in organic agriculture and those facilitating alternative trade with small, developing-world villages through a network of third world shops and alternative trade organizations. Both had erected parallel markets, mostly outside the practices of mainstream commerce. The independence of the U.S. and European coffee markets and lessons from the forestry sector supported the formation of additional certification. The separate markets provided unique testing grounds where groups were able to experiment with coffee labeling. The lessons from forestry were channeled to coffee by the Rainforest Alliance.

The above factors combined to support three separate streams of certification: organics, dealing with farm environmental conditions; fair trade, emphasizing equitable terms of trade and social development; and sustainable production, aimed at lessening the impacts of coffee cultivation on tropical forests. Their relatively quick development was helped by the low barriers to entry throughout the coffee production chain, a feature not true of the majority of fishery and forestry production.

That these processes were fragmented initially created hard-to-overcome inertia shaping the development of individual programs and sector-level patterns. Unlike in forestry, where the two-program dynamic created feedbacks reinforcing the competition, with coffee, small choices about program design and when these choices were made relative to changing market interest in certification and perceptions of sectoral problems help explain the sector-level constellation of coffee programs. Thus, the time it took fair trade and organics to consolidate facilitated the entry of other programs—an outcome the chapter argues fits the explanation proposed in chapter 2.

STAGE 1: PROGRAM INITIATION

Intergovernmental processes for coffee were under way early and were less open to later-developing social and environmental concerns. The ICA, which was operational on and off from 1962 to 1989, also remained focused on rent flow and distribution. When other issues arose, particularly concerns over farm-level environmental and human health consequences of pesticide applications, an amenable intergovernmental venue wherein to build ties and legitimize new problem definitions did not exist. Consequently, the processes of emergence remained fragmented. Regional trade patterns and connections among countries gave different issues salience, which also amplified fragmentation.

The coffee supply chain's low barriers to entry also facilitated the development of private initiatives. Unlike in forestry, the initiation of certification for coffee developed along three parallel and largely separate tracks, each producing its own first-mover programs and building momentum around them. These tracks—one for organic certification, one for fair trade, and a third for sustainable coffee—are discussed below.

The first process in the coffee sector arose from the organic movement, which began expanding certification in the mid-1970s. Organic practices had been around long before this. The Soil Association—an early UK advocate for organic husbandry—was established in 1946 (Reed 2001). Organic practices were also motivated by alternative, back-to-the-land lifestyle ideas and health benefits (Guthman 2004); the latter received more attention, particularly in the United States, after the publication of Rachel Carson's *Silent Spring* in 1962 (Dankers and Liu 2003).

International connections among the disparate efforts emerged in the 1970s. The International Federation of Organic Agriculture Movements —formed in 1972 to coordinate the organic movement—initially focused on refining the basic understanding of what defined "organic" agriculture practices (Geier 1999; Langman 1992). The five founders comprised organic movement organizations from the United States, France, the United Kingdom, Sweden, and South Africa, which all saw benefits from information exchange on the principles and practices of organic agriculture (Langman 1992). The founders decided to have an inclusive membership policy that allowed any organization or individual espousing support for organic agricultural principles to join (Langman 1992). Membership grew immediately, reaching fifty groups from seventeen countries by 1975, more than one hundred from fifty countries by the mid-1980s, and up to five hundred from seventy-five countries by the turn of the 1990s (Geier 1999; IFOAM 2001).

Work on the first standard began in 1978 (Guthman 2004, 139) and was released in 1980; it has since been revised biennially (Dankers and Liu 2003). Certification was not a central concern early on; farmers were learning as they went, writing down standards based on their personal experiences (Geier 1999). Organic associations first used internal inspections to offer members technical assistance and improve practices. Only later, as the number of consumers grew, did independent certification gain ground, reportedly as a means to avoid conflicts of interest and protect against fraud (Dankers and Liu 2003).

With coffee, the first organic farm—Finca Irlanda in Chiapas, Mexico —began using biodynamic practices in 1928; the operation was certified in 1967 by the German organic organization Demeter (Giovannucci and Koekoek 2003, 5). It would take until the 1980s, however, for organic coffee practices to gain wider support, with Demeter remaining an important auditor. These early certified coffees were imported to the U.S. market by Clean Foods under the brand Café Altura (Ramaswami 1992). By 1984, the Organic Crop Improvement Association (OCIA) was also involved, having certified farmers in Guatemala and Mexico, allowing Coffee Bean International to offer a second line of organic coffee to the North American market (Pendergrast 2001). Naturland began certifying organic coffee in the mid-1980s; it even assessed the Union of Indigenous Communities of the Isthmus Region (UCIRI), the coffee cooperative in Mexico noted below as a partner that helped launch the

Max Havelaar label (UCIRI 2005). Although coffee was now just one of many commodities certified according to organic rules, it became part of the process and would thus be connected with efforts to globalize organic certification over the coming years. Most important, certification work was being undertaken by individual organic organizations, such as Demeter and the OCIA. Even though the IFOAM had been in place since 1972, attempts to coordinate auditing practices were yet to form.

The second process in the coffee sector had roots in earlier alternative trade initiatives, which were a precursor that nurtured market awareness and built organizational capacity foundational for labeling initiatives. World shops—such as Ten Thousand Villages, formerly SELFHELP —emerged as early as the 1950s in Europe and the United States (Kochen 2003; Fridell 2007, 62). Starting with handicrafts and other artisan products made in small, developing-world villages, commodity food products were incrementally added to the shelves. In 1973, the Dutch Fair Trade Organization began selling "fairly traded" coffee from a Guatemala cooperative. Then in 1979, Traidcraft established as a UK-based, fair-trade mail order business (Hockerts 2005); coffee and tea were first included in its catalogue in 1980 (Auld 2009); and, as mentioned in chapter 5, Equal Exchange was founded in 1986 (Equal Exchange 2008).[1] Not unlike the forestry case, this was a period of experimentation. Recall that Thanksgiving Coffee in the United States developed a scheme in the mid-1980s whereby proceeds from the company's coffee sales supported the Sandinistas; this was similar to what Silas Kopf had thought of doing with his ecology surtax (chapter 4). Another example from the time was Coffee Kids, a nonprofit organization established by the owner of Coffee Exchange, a roaster based in Providence, Rhode Island. With the support of other coffee companies, Coffee Kids channeled funds to coffee communities to assist in locally run and developed projects to improve, inter alia, health care and education services (Coffee Kids 2008).

The opportunity to develop these alternative market outlets was facilitated by limited barriers to entry. The growth and primary processing of coffee beans is possible at relatively low capital cost. Mechanized operations are prevalent, yet great quantities of coffee were and continue to be grown on small farms and require lower levels of capital for primary processing. Likewise, although a few large roasters dominate coffee sales to the mass market, roasting equipment is relatively inexpensive. Hence, buying green coffee directly from farmers, roasting it close to a local market, and selling it to ethically minded consumers was a tenable strategy.

There was another appeal to this shift. The villages where alternative trade organizations sourced their handicrafts were producers of commodities such as coffee. An official from Traidcraft later explained: "I remember someone saying how ironic it is that we've all supported these handicraft supplies, and this income generation project is in a community or village where the people are farmers, you know, or in the middle of a farming community. We must think what drives them to look for income generation and perhaps it should come from farming."[2]

Even with this redirected focus, the alternative trade shops were still able to capture only a small sliver of the market (Giovannucci and Koekoek 2003). Partly for this reason, advocates of fair trade in Europe began to consider how to achieve greater market penetration. The European Fair Trade Association (EFAT) formed in 1987 in an attempt to foster cooperation and information exchange among national fair-trade associations and organizations.[3] Yet certain members of the movement also saw a need for a new tool—one that they could use to "exert pressure on commercial companies to change their procurement practices" (Bird and Hughes 1997, 162). They wanted a system that minimized free riding by developing a method to verify that products sold by non-fair-trade-committed shops were in fact fair-trade products. Bird and Hughes (1997) explained: "There was a fear that manufacturers would capitalize on the marketing advantage (provided by the fair-trade proposition) without altering their trading methods, encouraging damaging consumer skepticism" (162). Other accounts emphasize the interest of southern fair-trade producers who were eager to broaden their own market access (Fridell 2004).

In truth, these separate accounts partly explain different emergence dynamics occurring within individual countries and trading relations. The first initiative to develop was the Max Havelaar label, which began to take form in 1986 as the brainchild of Franz van der hoff Boersma, a priest working with the UCIRI coffee cooperative in Oaxaca, Mexico, which connected with Solidaridad, a church-based development-aid nonprofit located in the Netherlands (Kochen 2003; Jaffee 2007, 13; UCIRI 2005).[4] The label (and the Max Havelaar Foundation) formed to offer the UCIRI cooperative an alternative market channel that circumvented coffee middlemen (*coyotes*) and that ensured more coffee could be exported under "fair-trade" terms than was possible through existing alternative trade organizations (Jaffee 2007, 13). On the Dutch side, the foundation committed to finding an alternative market outlet if and when the

UCIRI obtained permits for direct export of the cooperative's green coffee. Max Havelaar chose to first ask Douwe Egbert, the largest roaster in
the Netherlands, to buy the Mexican farmers' coffee at a fair price. After
a year and a half of stalling, the company refused. With this first option
closed off, Max Havelaar's founders considered two alternative models.
One was creating a commercial company similar to Equal Exchange. The
challenge here was financial; they estimated start-up costs of 10 million
guilders. The second, less expensive approach, estimated to cost only 1.5
million guilders, was to form a "fair-trade" label, an idea that was reportedly advocated by supermarkets that sought to frustrate Douwe Egbert.[5]
Under the program, companies that wanted to use the label would need
to buy coffee from farmers at a fair-trade price and also guarantee them
credit for 60 percent of their harvest value before the harvest had begun
(Carpio 1993). Originally focused on providing market access and cir-
cumventing political corruption, the initiative took for granted the ICA
price controls. It was an understood part of the market at the time.

In a few years, Max Havelaar coffee had greatly increased its share
of the Dutch market (Kochen 2003).[6] Indeed, while the supermarkets
backed down from supporting the initiative after the launch, the interest
was too large for them to resist. Notice that with fair trade, the immediate emphasis was on the consumer end of the system. Although it was
critical to determine that the price being paid for the green coffee was
up to standard, questions about the certification process at the farm end
of the chain would not come until later. Also, although the ICA was in
place when Max Havelaar formed, recall from chapter 5 that its regulatory measures were dropped in 1989, precipitating a landmark decrease
in world coffee prices (Bates 1997). Thus, a desire to use fair trade as
a solution to this problem migrated to the center and would shape the
consolidation of fair-trade certification, which is discussed further below.

As fair-trade labeling grew in Europe, a final process was occurring in Latin and South America that would eventually connect with the
North American market. Although U.S. fair trade had taken a step beyond world shops with the creation of Equal Exchange in 1986, it would
take another ten years before fair-trade labeling formed. Moreover, the
United States was experiencing a massive growth in the specialty coffee
industry at the time, which influenced the campaigning tactics of U.S.
advocacy groups (Pendergrast 2001; Dicum and Luttinger 1999).

The significant developments in Latin America had to do with the

increasing recognition that coffee farms had ecological importance beyond the farm-level environmental considerations associated with organic agriculture. This led to several efforts to raise awareness about
and set standards for sustainable coffee production that related to the
concerns with tropical forest loss salient in the 1980s (chapters 3 and 4).
The first initiative in this vein originated in 1987, when the Fundacíon
interamericana de investigacíon tropical (FIIT) began developing criteria
for shade-grown coffee production (Rice and McLean 1999). At the time,
a U.S.-based nonprofit, the Rainforest Alliance, had just formed with
the aim of conserving tropical forests. Its cofounders secured a $40,000
grant to begin work on a certification program for rainforests (Taylor
and Scharlin 2004). Recall that its early efforts focused on responsible
management of forests, including its work to create standards for "well-
managed tropical wood" and its certification in 1990 of a teak plantation
in Indonesia. Two years later, in 1991, the group partnered with Latin
American NGOs, including the FIIT, to create the Eco-OK program for
the purposes of certifying products whose normal means of extraction
harmed tropical forest ecosystems (EPA 1998). This began a two-year
consultation process to develop "principles of sustainable agriculture"
and an associated standard (Wille 2004b), and led to work on the Better
Banana Project (Taylor and Scharlin 2004; Rainforest Alliance 2005).
The first banana plantations were certified in 1993 (Wille 2004b).

Attention to coffee followed. Starting in 1994, the Rainforest Alliance began promoting the value of shade coffee (Schapiro 1994); concurrently, it worked with its partners to develop a program for certifying
responsible coffee production that included attention to shade as well as
ecological, social, and environmental considerations in farm management practices (Rice and McLean 1999; Sustainable Agriculture Network 2002). The intention was to set standards for responsible or sustainable coffee production, much like the standards for its Better Banana
Project and its SmartWood program (Taylor and Scharlin 2004). The
first coffee plantation was certified in 1996 (Wille 2004a). This was one
clear illustration of how the experiences in forestry were being applied to
other sectors, carried there by key organizations such as the Rainforest
Alliance (Auld et al. 2007).

With a similar focus but developing independently, in November
1990, the U.S. Congress established the Smithsonian Migratory Bird
Center as an effort to address the conservation of neotropical migratory

birds (Luxner 1996). Its director, Russell Greenberg, had a track record researching the declining populations of these migrants (see, for example, Robbins et al. 1989), and would continue this research after joining the SMBC. The concerns through this period were understandable. In the mid-1970s, coffee production in northern Latin America began to change. A leaf rust that had devastated coffee plantations in the East Indies at the close of the 1800s (Pendergrast 2001; Dicum and Luttinger 1999) made landfall on the eastern coast of Brazil in 1970; it reached Central America around 1976 (Rice and Ward 1996). One response was to accelerate the transformation of traditional coffee plantations (where shade was prevalent) into intensive sun plantations. The theory was that drier conditions on coffee farms would halt the leaf rust's spread (Rice and Ward 1996). Many farms were transformed in the coming years; for instance, by the mid-1990s around 68 percent of Colombia's coffee area (about 1.1 million hectares) had been converted to sun plantations (Rice and Ward 1996). Other Latin American countries exhibited similar patterns (Dicum and Luttinger 1999). This proved, in the longer term, detrimental to birds that used trees growing on traditional coffee farms as wintering habitat. In the early 1990s, the work of Greenberg and colleagues documented this problem (Perfecto et al. 1996; Greenberg et al. 1997), and the SMBC began to communicate the issue to the coffee sector and the wider public (Jamieson 1994).

In 1996, the focus on sustainable coffee production culminated in a conference—the Sustainable Coffee Congress—organized by the SMBC (Luxner 1996; SMBC 2001). It brought biologists, coffee industry officials, and other experts together to discuss the environmental and social consequences of the trend toward sun coffee in the Americas. It highlighted a perceived gap in the existing coffee certification programs: the lack of adequate and integrated attention to ecosystem-level consequences of coffee production (Rice and Ward 1996). One of the meeting's outcomes was further work by the SMBC to create a set of shade standards for coffee production that could be audited and hence allow "bird-friendly" coffee sales in the U.S. market. Russ Greenberg, director of the SMBC, explained in an interview after the meeting that 61 million Americans are self-identified birders. This, in his view, was a perfect market segment in which to gain support for a bird-friendly label (Luxner 1996). The first SMBC bird-friendly coffee was certified in 1997 (Rice and McLean 1999).

To recap, there were three strands that generated coffee certification initiatives. The first came from the alternative trade movements that had formerly focused on handicrafts but increasingly realized the value of working on commodity production and trade. Low barriers to entry throughout the commodity chain meant that creating alternative trading channels was feasible. These efforts also benefited from the history of experiences in bringing handicrafts to market and the established clientele amenable to fair-trade products. Second, organic agriculture was expanding, and rather than starting as an effort to coordinate one approach globally, the IFOAM served as a means for information exchange. Coffee was added to the list of organic crops in the mid-1980s, just before it became apparent that coordination would be required. Finally, the efforts of the Rainforest Alliance and the SMBC developed in the U.S. market, where fair-trade labeling was slow to emerge. Likewise, they sought to tackle a broader set of environmental issues than organics, where on-farm effects were the principal focus.

These developments can, in part, be explained by the lack of a unified global community concerned about the social and environmental implications of coffee production. The fragmented first stage in the coffee sector appeared much more likely, given the absence of an ITTO-like venue wherein to build closer network ties. As well, the independence of the U.S. and European markets created two largely separate testing grounds in which proponents were able to develop labeling experiments. This environment-social split in the policy scope would become a defining feature of coffee certification early on.

STAGE 2: CONSOLIDATION AND SECTOR-LEVEL COPYING AND COMPETITION

The first stage in coffee certification produced initiatives in three tracks. Below, we turn to what happened next, examining how these separate tracks began to globalize. There are two processes to examine: program-level consolidation and sector-level patterns of emergence. The discussion turns to these processes sequentially.

Internal Program Consolidation

Efforts to consolidate organic certification took form very soon after Demeter, Naturland, and the OCIA certified their first coffee operation in the mid-1980s. At the time, organic agriculture was expanding, and concern about consistency emerged (MHR 1999; Raynolds 2000). Recall that the IFOAM had formed in 1972 and that much of its early efforts were directed to information exchange and enhancing and broadening the understanding of organic practices. It had become a network of over four hundred members and affiliates by the turn of the 1990s.

For these years, the certification process had been left to individual certifiers. These organizations built reputations around their own standards and labels (Commins 2004). For example, when Irish organic farmers realized the threat of false organic claims in the marketplace, they turned to the UK Soil Association for advice on how to develop an organic certification process for Ireland.[7] A similar pattern of dissemination occurred elsewhere and led to a very dynamic period of growth. An early participant explained: "You had standards being developed all over the place. And people copying each other's standards, and there was amazing growth as a result."[8] It was this proliferation, however, that spurred calls for greater harmonization. Certifiers feared that, if left unchecked, rapid expansion could foster a race to the bottom. This was particularly the case as more specialized organizations became involved in certification (Westermayer and Geier 2003); questions arose about the trustworthiness of the new entrants in maintaining the principles of organic agriculture. There were also economic concerns for growers, who at the time were frequently members of the organizations conducting the certification assessments—organizations such as the California Certified Organic Farmers (CCOF) (Guthman 2004). With the growing interest in organics, efforts to erect barriers to entry emerged.

As well, with the increased expansion of organic production, differing private and public standards made the costs of fragmentation increasingly palpable. Attention to this challenge formed in Europe and North America through largely independent processes. In North America, although these debates had already happened at the state level, with "organic" label laws having passed in Oregon (1974) and California (1979) (Guthman 2004; Dankers and Liu 2003), the Organic Food Production Association of North America (OFPANA), formed in 1984, began coordinating work to delineate rules and procedures for a verifiable certification system (Cohlmeyer 1985). Practically speaking, it formed to lobby for a national organic labeling law in the United States as a way to overcome discrepancies between differing state laws (Guthman 2004, 115). Although the organic industry had some success in self-governing, partly facilitated by the OFPANA, by the late 1980s, the interest in government intervention had grown (Elizabeth A. Brown 1989). The Organic Farmers Association Council, the Organic Food Alliance, and some twenty-seven other NGOs joined the OFPANA to lobby for a specific definition of organics to be included in federal legislation (Vaupel 1999; PR Newswire 1990). Though the U.S. Department of Agriculture (USDA) was initially resistant, the broad coalition eventually won out and helped pave the way for the Organic Food Protection Act of 1990 (Guthman 2004, 115).

In Europe, similar interest in consistency emerged in the late 1980s. The dynamic development of standards and certification organizations mentioned above raised interest in creating a system to better monitor consistency. Similar to the U.S. government, the European Union (EU) moved to regulate the meaning of organic claims. Previously, individual European countries had developed their own label regulations; France passed the first organic regulations in 1985, with others not far behind (Dankers and Liu 2003). Then, in 1991, the passage of EU Regulation 2092/91 established a common standard for organic plant production EU-wide (Michelsen 2001). It also mandated inspection for organic practices within the EU or for imported products, and it offered a voluntary logo for on-product use (Scharpe 2003).

These developments were important for two reasons. First, they impeded any efforts to develop international accreditation procedures that the IFOAM was just initiating. Second, in the U.S. case, the choice illustrates how organic producers were seeking ways to regulate competitor entry and protect against fraud. The legislated definition of organics was at least partly a barrier against further entry to the organic market. Guthman (2004, 152) explained: "The disallowances of efficacious inputs acted as a powerful disincentive to organic production, as did processes intrinsic to certification (and state registration), including fees and compliance costs, bureaucratic hassles, and unusual levels of surveillance. Growers of all sorts were keenly aware of these barriers, and many supplements and additions to the regulations were inventions of those already in the fray, including the phasing out of several materials."

Governments' involvement did not dissuade those in the organic movement from taking their own steps as well. The IFOAM basic standard had been around since 1980; in the late 1980s IFOAM's Technical

Committee started examining the practices of organic certifiers (IOAS 2006; Herrmann 2003). There were no formal requirements at this point—rather, a report was written and the certifiers were invited to fix issues that were raised as concerns before the report was published. Remedied concerns were then not reported and the final report was circulated to the other participants. In this sense participants considered it a "trust-building exercise."[9] By this time, around 40 certifiers were in operation (Rundgren 2007).

Nearer the end of the 1980s, the IFOAM recognized that a committee dedicated to accreditation would be valuable. This precipitated the reorganization of the IFOAM's Technical Committee: it was broken in three creating a Standards Committee, Program Evaluation Committee, and Accreditation Committee (IOAS 2006). By the 1990 meeting of the General Assembly, the membership was ready to approve the development of a full-fledged accreditation program. Even though this was also when the EU and the U.S. governments had begun pursuing a legislated "organic" definition and sanctioned inspection systems, those involved in the IFOAM efforts felt a private alternative was still valuable. For one, they felt a responsibility to self-regulate and also recognized that neither the EU nor the U.S. processes would be global.[10] Over the next two years, with input from the Program Evaluation Committee, the Accreditation Committee developed a program that was unanimously endorsed by the membership in 1992. This led to the creation of the IFOAM Accreditation Programme Board (IAPB). It completed the first accreditation in March 1993, and by December 1994 three certifiers were officially accredited (IOAS 2006). By 1997, twelve certifiers had accredited under the program and six had pending applications. Involved certifiers included Naturland, the Soil Association, Oregon Tilth, Bio-Gro, and CCOF, among others (IOAS 2006).

With coffee, the IFOAM released its first generic basic standard covering the crop in 1995 (Linton 2004), more than ten years after coffee certification had taken off. Consequently, by 1995, the OCIA had certified over a million hectares of coffee production farmed by around thirty thousand coffee producers worldwide (Rice and Ward 1996). Naturland, Demeter, and Institut für Marktökologie, three German-based certifiers, were also significant players in coffee at this point (Rice and Ward 1996; ICO 1997).[11] By country, Peru led, with around 44,000 certified hectares; Mexico, in second place, had around 26,000 hectares; and then

Guatemala (7,000 hectares), El Salvador (4,900 hectares), Nicaragua (1,400 hectares), and Costa Rica (550 hectares) also had certified reasonable areas of organic coffee production (Rice and Ward 1996). In each of these cases, however, certifiers continued to use their own labels; they did so even in situations where they had been accredited by the IAPB.

Finally, in 1997, the IFOAM created the International Organic Accreditation Service (IOAS) as an independent company and gave it responsibility for conducting IFOAM accreditation (IOAS 2006). By this time, there were thirty-three associations in the United States performing organic assessments (ICO 1997). By 2001, seventeen organizations were accredited by the IOAS, and another twelve were under review (Commins 2003), and by 2003, thirty organizations were in the system, conducting an estimated 50–60 percent of the world's organic certifications (Herrmann 2003). Overall, this indicates that the IFOAM's control over the certification of organic practices was far from complete. Moreover, at the time, these certifiers were using their own labels for on-product claims. An IFOAM label stating "IFOAM Accredited" was released in 1999 and was to be used concurrently with an accredited certifier's own label (Commins 2003). It was only at this point that organics had consolidated as a global program that could oversee the certification of organic coffee.

Surrounding the IFOAM's efforts to consolidate, the market for organics in general and coffee specifically continued to grow. The estimate for organic consumption in 2002–3 totaled 38,320 tons, of which 12,000 were consumed in the United States and 6,600 in Germany, where organics held a 1.1 percent and 1.6 percent market share respectively (Ponte 2004). The market was also growing in this period; in Europe, for instance, market growth varied from a low of 2 percent from 1999 to 2001 in Norway to a high of 60 percent for the same period in Italy (Lewin, Giovannucci, and Varangis 2004). Overall, by 2005, an estimated 324,000 hectares of coffee farms around the world were grown as organic, with nearly half of this area in Mexico (around 150,000 hectares), and organic coffee's share of the world market had reached approximately 1.2 percent (Baraibar and Willer 2006).

By 2006, there were 395 organizations reporting that they offered certification services; only 32 of these were IFOAM accredited (Rundgren 2007). Moreover, many of these certifiers were still using their own labels for on-product claims. An IFOAM survey in 2004 found that only

566 operators from a total of 67,354 (or 0.84 percent) had been licensed to use the IFOAM label (IFOAM 2005). Thus, there were still issues of harmonization that confronted the organic facet of coffee certification, a set of issues that has been the focus of considerable discussion within the organic movement (Westermayer and Geier 2003) and that has become more difficult with the entry of government regulations.

The manner in which organic coffee developed meant that market demand, rather than facilitating the consolidation of the IFOAM as a global program to oversee certification, pushed outcomes in favor of the initially uncoordinated structure. Unlike fair trade, the main sources of resistance to change were organic farmers and certification organizations, although these sources of resistance were not directly attributable to coffee production. Nevertheless, because coffee had become part of organics, it was implicated in these processes.

Turning to fair trade, while Max Havelaar was taking form, the fair-trade community in other countries watched with interest. The model quickly spread. In 1991, Belgium set up a Max Havelaar Foundation office. Concurrently, in the United Kingdom, the Catholic Agency for Overseas Development (formerly the Catholic Fund for Overseas Development, or CAFOD), Christian Aid, New Consumer, Oxfam, Traidcraft, and the World Development Movement copied Max Havelaar with their own UK Fairtrade Foundation (Auld 2009). Discussions within Oxfam about how better to harness consumer demand for development-friendly products in the UK market had begun in 1987 (Oxfam GB Archive 1989–98a). In 1989, a number of UK charity organizations heard of the Max Havelaar project, which led them to fund a two-year study to assess whether a UK equivalent would work (Oxfam GB Archive 1989–98b). The timing coincided with the launch of the *Green Consumer Guide,* which Oxfam even supported with a £5,000 grant, and which gave credibility to the idea that an "ethical" label could gain market traction (Oxfam GB Archive 1989–98a). A year later, Switzerland created a Max Havelaar office and by 1994 France, Luxembourg, and Denmark were also part of the network (Bird and Hughes 1997; Auld 2009).

There was a strong belief that this initiative had real potential, especially since coffee prices had plummeted following the 1989 end to the ICA's regulatory controls. In 1990, reports from the United Kingdom about the development of a Fair Trade Mark cited a 1989 Gallup poll that found 79 percent of respondents would pay premiums for products they knew gave producers higher wages (Andrew Jack 1990). Other reports from the time quoted similar survey results, with more than 70 percent of respondents willing to pay more (Schwarz 1992). These estimates spurred confidence in the instrument's potential.

The old model of "fair-trade brands" was not abandoned (Tallontire 2001). In 1991, Oxfam, Twin Trading, Equal Exchange, and Traidcraft formed Cafédirect, a move directly linked to the ICA collapse. It was formed to ensure that farmers received more than the world market price for their coffee (Cafédirect 2006a). In the coming years, Cafédirect was a pivotal tool for fair-trade advocates. Rather than immediately campaigning for the adoption of fair-trade labeling, groups like Oxfam, Christian Aid, and CAFOD pressured retailers to sell Cafédirect brand coffee (Oxfam 1994). Safeway and Co-op trialed these coffees in 1992 in their Scottish stores (Simpson 1992), and by July 1993, Sainsbury's agreed to stock them as well (Bain 1993). Only in 1994 did the UK Fairtrade Foundation launch its fair-trade mark, at which time Cafédirect became the first coffee to carry the logo (Cafédirect 2006b). Sainsbury's was selling Cafédirect in 150 of its stores by this point (Oxfam 1994).

Between 1988 and 1994, the period when fair-trade labeling quickly spread, the degree of cooperation among the national labeling initiatives was mixed. Certain countries, such as Belgium and Switzerland, created Max Havelaar offices and hence were more closely connected to the original Dutch experiment. For instance, they adopted similar labels. Others, such as the United Kingdom, borrowed the idea but maintained more autonomy. Nevertheless, all the initiatives agreed to create one International Coffee Registry to ensure that producers certified by any national initiative would be recognized by all others. Formalizing ties began in 1993. An official with Max Havelaar explained: "We started this relationship sometime in 1993 or 1994; we already had split some work . . . , for instance, like here in the Netherlands we had a relationship with producers in African countries, especially regarding coffee. In Switzerland, they had the relationship with the banana producers. Germany did the tea. We spread it throughout. Worked with those we were most interested in. And in the meantime we had all kind of meetings to bring this sort of information together, to decide on all common issues regarding producers."[12]

Yet early on there were differences of opinion that kept the national labeling initiatives from committing to a more formalized coordination arrangement. Some argued that experimentation through a diverse array of national approaches was a critical part of an initial stage. Others were concerned about different overall goals and thus hoped to retain autonomy. Bill Yates, from Oxfam UK, a founder and key member of the UK Fairtrade Foundation, wrote in 1993 about the challenges of coordination: "Although the Fairtrade Foundation has been enormously encouraged by the Dutch experience, and gratefully are willing to adopt their criteria for coffee from small producers, there has been a distinct difference of approach from the outset. Havelaar has been more strongly motivated by considerations of solidarity and a concern to support democratic cooperative structures. By contrast, FTF [Fairtrade Foundation] has been equally concerned to develop mechanisms that would achieve benefits for a wider target population of waged workers, and influence the practices of the commercial enterprises that employ them" (Oxfam GB Archive 1989–98b).

The tension between an aim of helping small producers versus one of helping hired workers and ending child labor heightened when labeling expanded to other products. Both tea and bananas, two products quickly following coffee's lead, were more extensively grown on plantations (U.S. Department of Labor 1997, 128). Although coffee plantations are not atypical, the large role of small farmers meant that focusing only on cooperatives was tenable, which made it easier to ensure that the farmers got the extra benefits of fair trade. With tea plantations, or plantations of any sort, the ultimate aim was to help hired labor and end child labor (U.S. Department of Labor 1997). This meant devising a contract with the plantation owner to ensure that benefits were given to workers, good labor practices were being maintained, and also that the extra benefits were helping social development objectives.[13]

Although there was a commitment to greater coordination, the process took time. Each national labeling initiative was able to work independently on many functions and hence waiting was not costly. Early events also exacerbated the perceived struggle for control. For example, the European Fair Trade Association had been important in backing the creation of Transfair International, formed with its initial base in Germany (Bruin 1992). For the UK Fairtrade Foundation, it was unsettling that Transfair International registered its logo and name in the United Kingdom without consulting the foundation. This move, which happened in 1993, pushed the foundation to develop its own label for the purposes of controlling how fair-trade labeling would operate in the United Kingdom (Oxfam GB Archive 1989–98b).

By 1997, there were fourteen national fair-trade labeling initiatives (Linton, Liou, and Shaw 2004) and something over 286 coffee-producing cooperatives (comprising approximately five hundred thousand growers) listed on the International Coffee Register (Rice and Ward 1996). There were also seven fair-trade labels, three of which were variants of the original Max Havelaar label. These variants were in use in the Netherlands, Belgium, Denmark, Switzerland, and France. The Fair Trade Mark was used in the United Kingdom and Ireland. And Transfair had been adopted in Germany, Austria, Luxemburg, Canada, Italy, and Japan (U.S. Department of Labor 1997). The United States had a Transfair initiative as well but had not yet secured sufficient funding to commence operations (TransFair USA 2000a).

It was clear by this time that an international body would be useful to better coordinate the existing labeling initiatives, and thus in the spring of 1997 the Fairtrade Labeling Organizations International (FLO)—now Fairtrade International—was formed (Raynolds 2000). The intent was to create a consistent standard and label for fair-trade products and to ensure the credibility of fair-trade certification processes (Krier 2005). Harmonizing, however, has remained challenging, with different visions of · appropriate governance being one issue of debate. Initially, for instance, the FLO did not offer voting rights to producer groups; rather, they were able to express their views through the Fair Trade Producers' Assembly, a move reportedly done to preserve the independence and objectivity of the certification process (Rice and McLean 1999). By 1999, the Producers' Assembly was lobbying to have voting status within the FLO (Rice and McLean 1999), but it would take another eight or so years before it realized this goal. In May 2007, the FLO granted membership rights to three producer networks—Coordinadora Latinoamericana y del Caribe de comercio justo, African Fairtrade Network, and Network of Asian Producers —after having changed its constitution in late 2006 (FLO 2007).

Thus, for many years, the principal players in the FLO were the national labeling initiatives; they were the only group with formal membership and voting rights. Notably, though, producers did have a voice through the Producers' Assembly and through their involvement in committees, and with individual national initiatives. In addition, after the 2002 restructuring, producers were able to elect four of the twelve board members. National labeling initiatives elected six and certified traders elected two (Slob and Oldenziel 2003; Zonneveld 2003). There was still a feeling among producers that the FLO was not entirely open to their voice (UCIRI 2005).

Inspection, or certification, was an additional aspect of the FLO that changed after the program's launch. Compared with forestry, inspections received less early attention. They were initially done in house and frequently occurred as a joint support and monitoring activity (Slob and Oldenziel 2003; Courville 2003).[14] Fair trade emphasized the development aspect of its standards and thus saw the farm-level visit as a chance to observe problems and offer advice on how to improve. Although very valuable as a system of assistance for producers, with the growth of the initiative a need to change became increasingly apparent. Consistency was one concern; credibility to outside observers was another. In 2002, the FLO created an independent Certification Committee for making certification decisions (these were previously made by the board). The committee included representatives of producers, traders, and national initiatives (Zonneveld 2003). Then, in September 2003, the FLO made its certification department an independent legal entity—FLO-Cert GmbH (Ltd) (FLO 2003)—explaining how the move would increase the FLO's credibility and protect it from liabilities associated with the commercial activities of certification. The program did consider creating an accreditation program similar to the IOAS, discussed above, and the recently formed Accreditation Services International, the company conducting accreditation for the FSC and MSC (chapters 4 and 8). However, it opted for a single certification service, in part because of its mission to include the world's most marginalized producers. Officials with the FLO explain that this meant few commercial certifiers would be interested in accrediting with the program, since the market remained small.[15]

The FLO was also challenged to keep pace with the adapting concerns within the coffee sector. Two issues in particular arose: developing environmental requirements and the certification of plantations or estate coffee. With the former, the FLO chose to expand its standard to address certain basic environmental considerations. Still, the standards continued to focus on social development issues, as this was an area the FLO was more competent addressing. With the latter, it decided to continue certifying only coffee from small-farmer producers. This decision was taken even though the FLO had standards for addressing hired labor, ones it had developed for other products, including tea and bananas (Rice and McLean 1999).[16] The still-sizable pool of uncertified small coffee farmers in part rationalized the restriction. These growers were seen as abundant enough to provide a sufficient supply of fair-trade-labeled coffee for some time to come (Fairtrade Foundation 2008). However, this did leave the door open to other initiatives that saw the plight of coffee workers as a key concern. The regulatory domain of the coffee standard also had implications for the FLO's relations with its member initiatives. Indeed, and as is discussed further below, it was ultimately one of the main reasons why Fair Trade USA decided to end its FLO membership starting January 2012 (Fair Trade USA 2012).

There are two aspects of these coordination challenges that are important to note. First, they occurred while demand for fair-trade coffee was growing. Certified green coffee grew from seven thousand metric tons in 1992 to thirteen thousand in 1996 (FLO 1999). In 1998, reports indicated as much as fourteen thousand metric tons of coffee worth $40 million were being produced under fair-trade labels (Beekman 1998). Reports at the time also indicated fair-trade-labeled coffee had 5 percent of the Swiss market, 2.6 percent of the Dutch market, and 2 percent of the Danish market (Martinelli 1998). The uptake continued, particularly in Europe. By 2003, nearly twenty thousand metric tons of coffee production had been FLO certified, a growth of 26 percent over 2002 (FLO 2003). The list of producer organizations had expanded to 422 in forty-nine countries, of which over half produced coffee. The number of traders stood at 154 in the coffee sector (FLO 2003). Reports also indicated that fair-trade coffee had a 20 percent share of the UK market, and there was growing awareness of fair trade and the fair-trade label among consumers (Krier 2005).

Second, all of this growth occurred during the transition to the FLO's increased oversight of certification, logo licensing, and standards development. Yet considerable investments had already been made in national market recognition for different labels (Thomson 1995). When the FLO formed, there were four unique labels and several variants in use; even after the FLO introduced a single label in 2003, the United States and Canada continued to use the original Transfair logo, and Switzerland began to switch only in January 2008 (Max Havelaar 2008).[17] Adopting

the new label meant spending money to redesign packaging and promotional materials and also required time and resources for informing
consumers of the change so as not to lose their trust.

Thus, in this case, the development of national labeling initiatives
in advance of a coordination effort slowed the development of a global
program, consistent with the expectations of hypothesis 7. The new label
was not without benefits. The UK Fairtrade Foundation, for instance,
noted how the new label was an opportunity to adopt a "more contemporary and eye-catching presentation" (Fairtrade Foundation 2003). Similarly, larger commercial companies were likely to benefit since it would
be costly to label different bags of roasted coffee with separate labels for
each of the different European markets.[18] Despite these benefits, there
were costs, and it was these costs of switching that were partly responsible for slowing down the process of change. Early on, the FLO also
suffered from limited funding, which only made things worse. Its limited resources constrained its ability to effectively carry out the functions
the national labeling initiatives had agreed it would oversee. This under-
mined their trust and made them leery of handing over more power and
resources to the FLO without some confidence that the situation would
improve.[19]

Nevertheless, by 2003, with the introduction of FLO-Cert and the
implementation of a global fair-trade mark, the FLO had the features of
a global program (Auld 2009). It had undergone several changes since
launching and more were to come. Importantly, though, it was the time
the program took to consolidate and the decisions it made about the regulatory domain of its activities that would facilitate the later entry and
quick growth of other programs.

Turning now to the Rainforest Alliance and the SMBC, the late 1990s
was also a period when environmental concerns beyond organics gained
central attention in the United States. The above-discussed Rainforest
Alliance program and the SMBC bird-friendly initiative continued to
develop. The latter quickly developed a set of criteria for shade-grown
coffee and began figuring out how to verify practices on the ground. As
the next section discusses, the SMBC's work on shade standards did not
happen in isolation. With the question of what conservation coffee was
going to accomplish still in the open, there were deliberations as to how
the bird-friendly program should be pitched. In a paper written after the
Sustainable Coffee Congress, Greenberg outlined two options for the ini-

tiative: develop a stand-alone program or work with either fair trade or organics. Greenberg reasoned that because "the infrastructure and markets were in place for organics, it made most sense to broaden organics' scope to include considerations for shade" (Greenberg 2000, 4). Thus, the bird-friendly program formed as an add-on for organics in an effort to adapt the existing system to the changing problem definition. The SMBC standards required all bird-friendly certification to occur concurrent with an organic one (SMBC 2002). SMBC staff trained assessors from accredited certifiers in how to apply the bird-friendly standards.

Despite the expected support from the 61 million U.S. birders, the program remained fairly small. By April 2000 there were thirteen roasters and retailers in the United States and Canada selling bird-friendly coffee, and eight brokers and importers were endorsed. Four years later, only nineteen farms covering around twenty-seven hundred hectares in seven Latin American countries had certified (Ponte 2004); by mid-2007, twenty-eight farmer cooperatives (with around seven thousand hectares of production) were certified, representing 2,341 producers from eight countries. Production totaled 6.6 million pounds of green coffee. There were fourteen importers dealing in bird-friendly coffee and more than fifty-four roasters located in Canada, the United States, and Japan (SMBC 2008). At this point, only coffee farms in the Americas were eligible, but expansion to Asia and Africa was under way (SMBC 2008). Two farms were certified in Ethiopia in 2011.

The Rainforest Alliance charted its own course. The program continued as a partnership between the Rainforest Alliance and a network of NGOs in Latin America. This network formalized as the Sustainable Agriculture Network (SAN) in 1997 (Wille 2004a; Sustainable Agriculture Network 2012a) and included eight "practitioner groups" based in various Latin American countries that both certified farms and took part in SAN decision making. An additional member served as a watchdog group. It was given access to the information on the certifications and worked as an internal critic to flag issues that might cause problems with external credibility (Vallejo and Hauselmann 2004).

Unlike the SMBC, the Rainforest Alliance sought to encompass the spectrum of social and environmental considerations, setting a reasonable standard that could potentially impact a larger landscape. Shade was given consideration, but not to the extent it was highlighted in the SMBC criteria. At the farm level, the standard advocated integrated pest management approaches and conservation of water and soil rather than organics' stricter requirements. Finally, worker rights, community interests, and local development received attention, but farmers were not guaranteed a set price, nor were only small cooperatives able to participate. In 2002, the SAN partners formalized a chain of custody process and in 2003 they adopted a unified "Rainforest Alliance"–certified label that replaced existing ones for bananas and coffee. Following this, the network began to formalize other aspects of its work, including creating an international standards committee in 2007 (Sustainable Agriculture Network 2012a). Moves to create independent certification and accreditation also began. Similar to the MSC, RA-SAN chose to employ an already existing accreditation organization to oversee its certifiers. Work began in 2008, and in 2012, the program publicly launched a new accreditation program in partnership with the IOAS, the accreditation service established in 1997 by the IFOAM (Sustainable Agriculture Network 2012b) (figure 6.1).

Although it took until 1996 for the first Rainforest Alliance coffee certification to occur, the program grew quickly. By 1999, nine farms were certified, covering around twenty-three hundred hectares and producing 780,000 kilograms of green coffee (Rice and McLean 1999). In 2004, more than twenty-eight thousand hectares were certified in nine countries (Wille 2004a), and by 2006, more than two hundred farms were certified in eleven countries, producing almost 120 million kilograms of green coffee annually.[20] The growth in certified production has been matched by increasing interest from significant coffee buyers. In January 2007, for instance, McDonald's UK announced it would source all its coffee from Rainforest Alliance–certified farms. The commitment meant the company's twelve hundred stores would begin buying Kenco, a Kraft-brand coffee containing 100 percent Rainforest Alliance–certified coffee (Rainforest Alliance 2007), an undoubtedly significant boost for the Alliance, giving the program a toehold in the European market.[21] McDonald's indicated it would expand its sourcing policy to other European countries during 2007. The move was possible only because Kraft had made an earlier commitment to the Rainforest Alliance program. Since its 2003 commitment, Kraft has bought increasing quantities of Rainforest Alliance coffee: 2.28 million kilograms in 2004, 6.35 million in 2005, and 13.15 million in 2006 (Rainforest Alliance 2007). Kraft is now considered the largest buyer of Rainforest Alliance coffee; in 2010 it purchased 50 million kilograms (Tropical Commodity Coalition 2012).

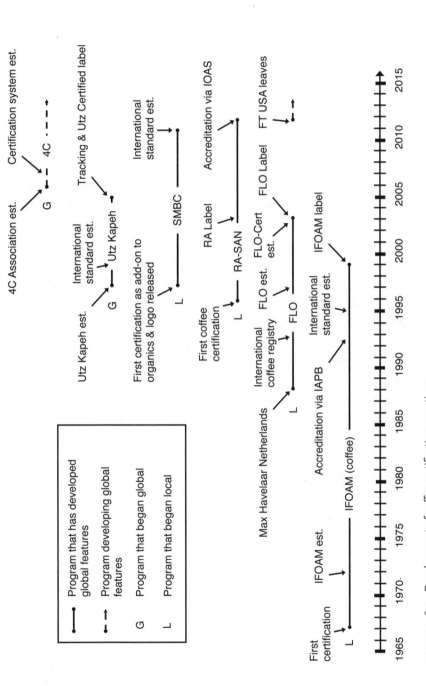

FIGURE 6.1. Development of coffee certification over time

Other significant commitments include KLM Royal Dutch Airlines' commitment to obtaining around 30 percent of its coffee as Rainforest Alliance–certified sources; Lavazza's launch of iTierra in 2006, another 100 percent Rainforest Alliance–certified coffee; the commitment of Caribou Coffee Company to sell Rainforest Alliance–certified coffee as half of its products by the end of 2008; and Costa Coffee's decision in mid-2008 to include a cut of Rainforest Alliance coffee in one of its drinks (Auld 2009).

There are a few critical conclusions to draw from the consolidation of coffee certification. First, market demand was a feature in the coffee sector that facilitated the growth of labeling. However, with fair trade and organics, the development of market demand impeded attempts to quickly consolidate a global program when these efforts took form. With fair trade, market demand meant that individual national labeling initiatives were more financially independent. They were able to license their own respective fair-trade logos in the market, generating revenue sufficient —in certain cases—to make them less inclined to centralize. When combined with differences in how they viewed the aims of fair trade and how best to achieve them, an uncoordinated status quo gained further support.

In organics, timing and the atomized efforts of national organic movements worked against attempts by the IFOAM to better coordinate the certification side of organic production. Starting at the state level in the United States and with countries in the EU, organic producers and certifiers turned to government to define and oversee the standardization and inspection facets of organic certification. Although done to protect the integrity of the "organic" claim, turning to government also served to erect entrance barriers that helped protect incumbent producers (Guthman 2004). Coffee was not the focus of concern, yet because it is one product in the organic mix, it has been implicated in the consolidation of organic certification practices writ large.

With sustainable coffee, two separate outcomes merit discussion. First, with the Rainforest Alliance we get a glimpse of what might have developed in forestry had it not been for the interest of the WWF and of other certifiers, such as SGS and SCS. The Rainforest Alliance and its partners in the SAN have maintained a streamlined organization. For much of its development, there have been no national initiatives or individual certifiers that were able to develop an interest in slowing the development of the program. In fact, measured against the features of a certification and labeling program outlined in chapter 1, the RA-SAN program began a global program only in 2012. Nevertheless, it is gaining significant market penetration, arguably because of its streamlined design. Agricultural producers were not given a voice in the organization in a way that would have enabled them to resist the expansion of the program; rather, the SAN members were all groups that were ultimately motivated to address improving practices affecting tropical forests.

Second, the SMBC's move to connect the bird-friendly label with organic certification hints at a growing trend at the end of the 1990s: discussions of harmonization and coordination. Both organics and fair trade undertook changes to their standards to bring them in line with emerging notions of sustainable development that encompassed social, environmental, and economic responsibility. Yet the speed at which this happened was not sufficient to meet the changing demands. This dimension of change is discussed more in the next section, where the analysis untangles the sector-level patterns.

Sector-Level Patterns of Emergence

After the mid-1990s, the direction and nature of coffee certification shifted. For one, it became evident that fair trade and organics did not cover the full scope of issues relevant in what was becoming a field of "sustainable" or "responsible" coffee initiatives. Although fair trade and organics continued to grow and develop, decisions the two programs had made around the scope and domain of their activities meant other actors observed opportunities to develop new initiatives better suited to address their perceptions of the key coffee-sector problems. These other alternatives were partly facilitated by the fewer opportunities to work from within to change existing programs in these new directions. Largely separate markets in Europe and the United States also provided testing grounds in which labeling programs could begin before expanding more broadly. Hence, in spite of growing market shares—in fact, partly because of them—the field of coffee certification remained fragmented.

To begin, recall from chapter 5 that although around 80 percent of coffee production enters international trade—levels far higher than trade in fisheries and forestry—there remain important regional patterns. In addition, the U.S. specialty market, with the growth of café chains such

as Starbucks, was not mirrored by an equally vibrant growth in continental Europe, where coffee consumers were already favoring their perception of higher-quality coffees. The U.S. specialty market ended up
playing an important role as an incubator for numerous smaller coffee
companies that often prided themselves on the direct connections they
had with coffee growers. Thanksgiving Coffee, for instance, had a line
of coffee in the mid-1980s that supported the Sandinistas in Nicaragua.
The company then became an innovator in responding to the need for
shade (Greenberg 2000). Bill Fishbein, owner of Coffee Exchange, had
also cofounded Coffee Kids in 1988.

Yet the specialty sector also became a campaign target. Recall that
in the United Kingdom, campaigns around coffee immediately focused
on supermarket retailers: Safeway, Sainsbury's, and Tesco, among others
(Bain 1993). In the United States, the specialty roasters and café chains
became the target. Although Starbucks was founded in 1971 as a single
café in Seattle, by 1993 the company owned 275 outlets, which jumped
to 1,000 by 1996 (Klein 1999, 132). This newfound success brought increased scrutiny both at home and abroad. Starting in 1994, the U.S./
Guatemala Labor Education Project (US/GLEP) pushed Starbucks to
adopt a code of conduct that would commit the company to improve
working conditions on coffee plantations (Tarmann 2002). This followed on the boycotts and protests directed at the mainstream roasting
companies, such as P&G, that had been led by Neighbor-to-Neighbor
in the late 1980s. Neighbor-to-Neighbor and Oxfam had also connected
with Equal Exchange in late 1992 to begin importing coffee from El Salvador on fair-trade terms with the aim of supporting the peace process
(Sibaja 1993).[22]

There were important differences, however, between what developed
in the United Kingdom and in the United States which, from the perspective of the emergence of certification programs, facilitated further
entrants. Recall that Cafédirect launched in the United Kingdom in 1991
with the help of Equal Exchange and had become a useful ally for the
Fairtrade Foundation's labeling efforts. Christian Aid and Oxfam linked
their campaigns to Cafédirect, urging consumers to buy its coffee. Christian Aid was calling its campaign "trade for change" (Gourlay 1992). The
United Kingdom was also a somewhat late entrant; it launched its fair-
trade mark only in 1994. For this reason, Cafédirect had been a critical
public face for the movement.

In the United States, things took even longer to form (figure 6.2). Indeed, alternative trade organizations based in the United States formalized relations only in 1994 by establishing the North American Alternative Trade Organization (a year later it became the Fair Trade Federation) (Fair Trade Federation 2007). Buoyed by the growing specialty coffee market, Equal Exchange did well in the early 1990s, surpassing a million in sales in 1992 (Feder 1992). Oxfam America and Equal Exchange began discussing the idea of labeling when a representative from Transfair International visited in 1994. Yet struggles for turf among existing interests in fair trade along with debates among those concerned with coffee's environmental impacts, which concentrated on shade and organic production practices, and those concerned with social justice reportedly slowed progress (Chip Mitchell 1998). Without a label developing concurrently, the linkages solidified in the United Kingdom did not form. Instead, pressure on the coffee industry remained fragmented.

Thus, while Equal Exchange and other members of the Fair Trade Federation continued importing coffee and other goods and products under fair-trade terms, other groups were pressuring the coffee industry somewhat separately. As noted above, US/GLEP, and particularly its U.S.-based group, the U.S. Labor Education in the Americas Project (USLEAP), began campaigning against Starbucks in 1994, pushing for the adoption of a code of conduct to guarantee workers' rights and welfare throughout the company's supply chain. Starbucks quickly responded with a code of conduct in 1995 (Tarmann 2002; USLEAP 1995), yet limited implementation led to continued criticism. Notably, the complaints were aimed specifically at the poor working conditions of coffee plantation workers, not small farmers; the group even noted how small coffee farmers represented around 15 percent of Guatemala coffee production and hence the real problem was the plight of coffee workers on the plantations producing the other 85 percent (USLEAP 1997). This made the debate within the fair-trade labeling community over whether to extend the program to cover coffee plantations particularly significant. With the FLO's choice to eschew this issue, there was a gap left unaddressed by existing certification programs. The discussion returns to this point below.

The campaigns against Starbucks were not isolated events. Recall that concerns over shade-grown coffee were on the rise. However, this early pressure appeared to have been important in propelling Starbucks

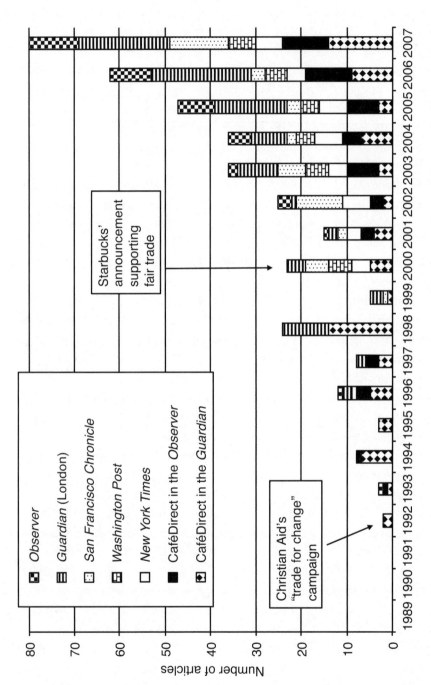

FIGURE 6.2 Keyword search (www.lexis-nexis.com) in select U.S. and UK newspapers for (1) "Fairtrade coffee" or "Fair trade coffee," and (2) "CaféDirect" or "Café Direct"

to focus on its own solution rather than considering programs such as fair trade or organics to be means for addressing its responsibility, at least initially. Indeed, Starbucks began investing in its code and soon partnered with Conservation International (CI) to address environmental concerns with sourcing. In February 1999, CI and Starbucks announced a partnership to encourage coffee farmers in the buffer zone around El Triunfo Biosphere Reserve in Chiapas, Mexico, to produce shade-grown coffee and hence reduce deforestation pressures (Business Wire 1999b). By August 1999, Starbucks began selling shade-grown Mexican coffee (Business Wire 1999a). All this meant Starbucks began charting its own course, taking on the responsibility for addressing social and environmental issues in coffee production and doing so in-house or in partnership with select environmental organizations. Recall that although organics was well established in the U.S. market, and the Rainforest Alliance and the SMBC were in the process of getting programs under way to address broad ecological concerns surrounding coffee production, no program was in place to address working conditions on plantations, the exact demands laid out in the US/GLEP campaigns. It took until April 1999, months after the CI-Starbucks partnership was announced, for the campaign against Starbucks, launched at this time by Global Exchange, to support fair trade specifically (Tarmann 2002). A year before this, TransFair USA (now Fair Trade USA) had officially begun work, after sitting dormant for two years due to lack of seed money.[23] The plan behind the launch of TransFair was clear. The founders felt the U.S. specialty industry was the best place in which to build momentum around a fair-trade label. In the organization's *Market Opportunity Assessment* report posted to its Web site, TransFair explained:

> Unlike the commercial coffee industry, the specialty coffee
> segment is extremely attractive and promising for new en-
> trants. . . . In relation to the overall coffee industry, the specialty
> segment offers the most favorable conditions for TransFair's
> entry. Furthermore, as high quality becomes the new standard
> in specialty coffee, the industry is becoming more competitive.
> Soon, it will no longer be enough to offer great-tasting coffee
> because consumers will expect more. Roasters and retailers will
> increasingly seek new ways to differentiate themselves from
> their competitors. Because of consumers' increasing demands

regarding corporate social responsibility, the conditions for social
responsibility as a differentiator are attractive. This is precisely
the strategic window that is opening for TransFair: the opportunity to offer specialty industry players a new, significant point of
differentiation from their competitors. (TransFair USA 2000b)

The report even mentioned Peet's and Starbucks as logical points of
initial entry. The strategy appeared to work. Global Exchange, the "bad
cop" in this scenario, waged a campaign against Starbucks that mobi-
lized student activists across the United States to demand that the company sell fair-trade coffee. In April 2000, Starbucks acquiesced and soon
would be the largest roaster of fair-trade coffee beans in the U.S. market.

Yet targeting the specialty industry appeared to alienate a potential
ally when campaigns against the mass-market brands later took hold.[24]
Moreover, not unlike the different goals that were apparent in the forestry case, the work of activists in the coffee sector sometimes provided
mixed messages. Deborah James of Global Exchange wrote about the
Starbucks campaign, explaining the decision facing consumers as one
between "coffee produced under sweatshop conditions, and a product
based on principles of fair trade" (James 2000, 11). From an outsider's
perspective it could appear that fair trade was the solution to poor conditions for coffee plantation workers. Yet fair trade still focused only on
small farmers, as just discussed. And although Global Exchange linked
its efforts to what US/GLEP had been advocating in its campaign and
took advantage of a child-labor scandal that, by coincidence, hit the press
in February 2000 (James 2000), fair trade did not tackle concerns for
coffee plantation workers. Indeed, USLEAP had tempered its criticisms
of Starbucks. After Global Exchange began its fair-trade campaign, US-
LEAP was careful to point out the difference between what it desired and
the aims of the new initiative. In a press release, the group noted:

> While a code of conduct for coffee companies is intended to
> benefit workers on medium and large-scale plantations, "fair
> trade" coffee is intended to benefit small farmers and coopera-
> tives by ensuring that they are paid an acceptable minimum
> price for their coffee, sufficient to maintain an adequate standard
> of living. USLEAP supports the goals of "fair trade," which ben-
> efits small farmers and sees the fair trade initiative as comple-
> mentary to its initiatives that would benefit workers. USLEAP

also strongly agrees with Global Exchange's position that Starbucks has moved far too slowly in implementing its code of conduct. However, there are currently new discussions with Starbucks underway regarding what steps it can and should take in Guatemala, and *at this time USLEAP itself is not campaigning against Starbucks.* (USLEAP 2000; emphasis added)

Thus, as much as TransFair USA might have wanted to solve the problems of labor conditions on coffee plantations, its hands were tied. USLEAP supported the fair-trade cause, but conditions of workers on coffee plantations remained its central concern. This meant that even with Starbucks announcing it would stock fair-trade coffee and that the company had signed a contract with TransFair USA to source from the appropriate farmers, the plight of plantation workers remained on the table. Moreover, the interest in environmental concerns remained high. In addition to Starbucks' initiatives noted above, the Specialty Coffee Association of America even convened a committee to draft standards for shade coffee production as part of the association's overall response to increasing concerns about the environmental impacts of coffee production (Rice and McLean 1999). The delay in campaigners connecting fair trade to their demands against companies and their choice to target the specialty industry as opposed to retailers or mass-market roasters meant two things. First, for specialty companies that had to respond, unlike with forestry, a single program ready for support did not exist. Starbucks' initiative was one outcome, but other, smaller specialty roasters also chose to act alone (Ponte 2004). Second, the delayed attention to the mass-market roasters gave them time to evaluate the situation. This gave the Rainforest Alliance an opportunity to position itself as a middle-of-the-road program that addressed the panoply of coffee-related social and environmental concerns.

Returning to Europe, it is notable that the absence of attention to labor rights and welfare was also an issue. Recall that the founders of the UK Fairtrade Foundation had expressed some unhappiness about the solitary focus on small cooperatives by fair trade. However, unlike the TransFair USA initiative, the UK initiative was part of discussions founding the FLO and hence had some stake in the final outcome, probably moderating its willingness to exit. Furthermore, the focus on small farmers remained confined to coffee. Nevertheless, as expected, in the United Kingdom there was the creation of the Ethical Trading Initiative (ETI)—a coalition of trade unions, nonprofits, businesses, and other agencies, with funding from the UK Department for International Development, that sought to create codes for retailers, manufacturers, and suppliers that addressed social and environmental aspects of production (Senter 1998). The ETI founders explained that the initiative was meant to broaden the reach of fair trade: "The fair trade movement has traditionally sought to help small producer groups and farmers in the developing world to fight exploitation and to trade on more advantageous terms. Now the Ethical Trading Initiative wants to bring some of these principles into the mainstream, aiming at the bigger businesses which supply UK retailers" (Senter 1998).

Similar to the Specialty Coffee Association of America's (SCAA) work on standards for shade-grown coffee, a group of European supermarket companies launched EurepGAP in 1997 (now Global GAP). The initiative was designed to delineate broadly accepted Good Agricultural Practices (GAP), mostly in response to food safety scares that developed in the mid-1990s (EurepGAP 2006). Concurrently, Ahold (a Dutch-based supermarket and food service conglomerate), in collaboration with a Guatemalan coffee producer, launched a sustainable coffee program, Utz Kapeh (Dicum and Luttinger 1999). Two years later, in 1999, Utz Kapeh officially formed, creating an office in Guatemala and using the EurepGAP code as a benchmark for its own coffee-production code of conduct (Rosenberg 2003).

That fair trade focused on the challenges facing small coffee farmers and thus restricted participation to this set of operators proved critical to Utz Kapeh's initiation and subsequent growth. It was a key reason the Guatemalan producer took an interest in a new program; he wanted a tool to differentiate his "responsible" practices from those of his neighbors, which he felt were not meeting existing government regulations. Being excluded from fair trade led him to seek alternatives, and hence he helped launch Utz Kapeh.[25] Fair trade's focus also motivated other supporters of the Utz Kapeh model. In fact, by 2002, Solidaridad, and in particular its director, Nico Roozen (a founder of the Dutch Max Havelaar), became interested in Utz Kapeh. The program was seen as a tool to tap the growing interest of large coffee companies in supply-chain sustainability. In a later report, Solidaridad explained its vision for the program: "Sustainability must also be 'precompetitive': with Utz Kapeh, Solidaridad wants to introduce a system that all the coffee companies will accept as standard business procedure, regardless of the extra costs it may involve" (Solidaridad 2006, 24). That is, it hoped to create an industry standard. The first board included a representative from Solidaridad, Hans Perk (Utz Kapeh 2004), and Solidaridad has remained an important supporter: Nico Roozen was in fact appointed as the interim board director of Utz Certified in April 2007 (Utz Certified 2007).

Also around this time, a group of Dutch NGOs (including Oxfam Novib and Hivos) created the Dutch Coffee Coalition. The group intended to pressure large supermarkets and producers to take responsibility for the conditions of coffee workers up their supply chains. In addition, it explained how fair trade focused on small farmers, but that many problems also occurred for plantation workers, a clear indication of how Utz Kapeh and these other initiatives were potential complements.[26] The effort was not simply about a label and certification, however. Solidaridad and partners created the Coffee Support Network in 2004 as a means to assist producers in bettering their management and eventually complying with the Utz Kapeh code. This program reached eighteen thousand producers in eight countries that in total exported 11.22 million kilograms in 2005 (Solidaridad 2006).

From the first Utz Kapeh certifications in 2002, the program immediately grew. By 2004, forty-two farms and cooperatives in twelve countries had been certified, with a potential production of nearly thirty-eight thousand metric tons of green coffee (Ponte 2004). By the fall of 2007, over two hundred producers were certified, with holdings of around 125,000 hectares in eighteen countries (Auld 2009). Ahold remained a critical supporter, having originally committed to sourcing 100 percent of its coffee from the program. It accomplished this by 2003, and by 2005 had the Utz Kapeh logo on 90 percent of its private brand coffee (Auld 2009).[27] In 2006, ninety-three roasters from eighteen countries were registered with Utz Kapeh to roast and sell labeled coffee (Auld 2009). Many significant international coffee traders had also signed on, including Volcafe. Finally, according to the Dutch Coffee Coalition, by 2006 Utz Kapeh supplied over twenty-seven thousand metric tons to the Dutch market, capturing a 25 percent market share (Panhuysen and Weiligmann 2006).

Still, this was a tiny dent in the coffee market. In 2005, the five main roasters (Nestlé, Sara Lee, Kraft, P&G, and Tchibo) roasted around 2.562 million metric tons of coffee, of which Nestlé had 1,500 metric tons certified; Kraft, 11,300 metric tons; Sara Lee, 12,000 metric tons; P&G 1,500 metric tons; and Tchibo, 1,500 metric tons (Panhuysen and Weiligmann 2006). Together, their sustainable coffees represented around 1 percent of their combined market share. Clearly, sustainable coffee had a great deal of room for growth—no reason, according to the Dutch Coffee Co-alition, for concern about competition among the programs.

Following a similar idea, one additional initiative emerged in an ef-fort to lift the performance of the entire coffee supply chain. Starting in 2002, the parliamentary secretary of state for Germany proposed a sectorwide initiative at an ICO meeting in London (Auld 2009). The resulting process would be named the Common Code for the Coffee Community, or 4C, and began its work as a collaboration of the German Coffee Association and the German Development Corporation (GTZ) (Ponte 2004; SCAA 2005) along with cooperation of farmers, industry, trade unions, and NGOs (Luttinger and Dicum 2006, 204). It aimed to develop a code of conduct for coffee production, processing, and mar-keting to ensure their environmental and social appropriateness. From its start it has consulted widely and drawn on the experiences of other initiatives to develop a unique program designed to set a baseline for the entire industry. Formally launched in December 2006 as an association, its membership includes producers, roasters, and civil society groups.[28] At the time, the industry participants were estimated to account for as much as 60 percent of the world's coffee production, giving the initiative a great deal of potential. Verification is conducted by 4C units, which are defined as a quantity of coffee needed to fill a shipping container. Any individual or group of operators can be assessed as a unit.

How successful the implementation will be is now one of the big questions; indeed, TransFair Germany was an early critic, calling the code too lenient, especially in regard to supporting better prices for small farmers (Hoobanoff 2004). Other NGO participants dropped their support for various reasons. Greenpeace, while feeling the initiative had merit, was disappointed that the code did not ban genetically modified organisms (*Down to Earth* 2006; Tallontire and Greenhalgh 2005). The organic certifier, Naturland, outlined its own set of concerns over the lenience of the standard (Naturland 2006).

Nevertheless, the initiative itself represents the progression toward a new problem definition: sustainable coffee and corporate social respon-sibility. It also took care to position itself aside from the labeling programs within the sector. Participants are not allowed to make on-product claims with the 4C Association logo, and the rules for participants explicitly state that the program is meant to be precompetitive. Members are required not to use the "4C Code of Conduct to benefit directly the company they represent or to disadvantage other stakeholders" (4C Association 2006). As of October 2011, the initiative also prohibits coffee grown with the use of GMOs, acquiescing in the near term to the concerns of groups such as Greenpeace, and it now is working directly with the Rainforest Alliance, Utz Kapeh, and, more recently, the FLO, to encourage continual improvement of coffee production beyond the baseline standard set by the 4C Code of Conduct (4C Association 2012).

In summary, the initiation of coffee certification in three largely separate streams set in motion a development path supporting persistent fragmentation. Differences in how and when certification gained attention in the United States and Europe meant there were many opportunities for entrants. Given that markets were amenable to coffee labeling and that early programs, while having opportunities for stakeholder involvement and membership, proved hard to change from within, the possibility of further entry grew (figure 6.3).

Three final points further illustrate the link between market demand and fragmentation. First, there has been splintering within the fair-trade movement. The advent of fair-trade labeling brought to the fore a debate about the nature of fair trade. For a company such as Equal Exchange, the concept extends beyond sourcing goods from democratically run cooperatives that receive fair prices for their labors. As a consequence, in 2004, the International Fair Trade Association (IFAT, what became the WFTO, or World Fair Trade Organization, in 2009) launched the Fair Trade Organization (FTO) mark at the World Social Forum in Mumbai. Initially the mark was not to be used for on-product claims. To use the label in promotional materials, an IFAT member had to undergo a self-evaluation with the addition of peer review and the possibility that its operations will be subject to external evaluation (some 5–10 percent of the organizations are randomly audited) (IFAT 2008). The standard covers social and environmental criteria, and focuses on giving credit to fair-trade organizations, not companies that carry fair-trade labeled products. The IFAT Web site explains: "The FTO Mark gives Fair Trade Organizations definable recognition amongst consumers, existing and new business partners, governments and donors who would like to support Fair

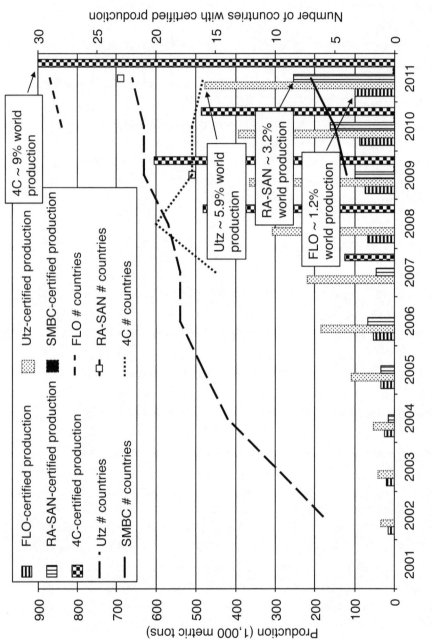

FIGURE 6.3. Uptake of coffee certification over time (for certified production and countries in which certifications have occurred). Data come from Auld 2009 and from program annual reports. Total production in 2010–11 equaled 134,386,000 bags times 60 kilos per bag, or 8,063,160 metric tons (www.ico.org/historical/2010–19/PDF/TOTPRODUCTION.pdf).

Trade activities—providing wider market opportunities for producers." Moreover, "The FTO mark is a means of identification. It sets organizations apart from other commercial businesses, making [recognizable] mission driven organizations whose core activity is Fair Trade."[29] In September 2013, WFTO extend the initiative to allow on-product use of the label.

Second, the limits of fair trade were an ongoing point of discussion within the specialty coffee market. Recall how several companies chose to pursue their own corporate initiatives, independent of or sometimes in complement to institutionalized programs such as fair trade, shade grown, or organics (Courville 2008). Companies such as Rogers Family Company publicize how their practices exceed those required by fair trade, organics, and shade coffee standards. Instead of undergoing certification, they contracted a consultant to conduct independent assessments of their operations and posted the reports on the company Web site (Auld 2010). These companies have chosen to differentiate themselves by pursuing their own corporate responsibility initiatives and communicating these directly to consumers. Other initiatives, as discussed by Jaffe and Bacon (2008), seek to reintroduce the core principles of the fair-trade movement through more direct interactions between coffee farmers and coffee consumers.

Third, in the fall of 2011, Fair Trade USA announced it would end its FLO membership as of January 2012 (FLO 2011a). The challenges discussed above were central to this decision. First, the initiative made clear that it was going to begin working on certifying coffee estates, arguing that coffee cooperatives accounted for only 10 percent of the world's production, justifying the need for a broader approach. Second, it also made clear that its increased membership fees to the FLO were a growing concern that eventually led to an impasse between itself and the FLO, highlighting the points about control and finances made above (Fair Trade USA 2011a, 2011b). The FLO has since moved to establish a new national initiative in the United States, but still much remains to be seen as to how the two initiatives will interact going forward (FLO 2012). Nevertheless, it further underscores, as with the other points, that the development of certification in the coffee sector remains fragmented, a pattern consistent with the argument in chapter 2.

This chapter assessed the development of coffee certification programs, untangling their origins and the factors influencing consolidation and sector-level patterns of emergence. With initiation—stage 1—conditions were not favorable to the quick consolidation of a global program. Intergovernmental processes dealt with environmental concerns separately from social concerns. Discussions of an agreement attending to these problems, something like a forestry convention or a modified ICA that would have woven in environmental concerns, were not under consideration. As suggested by hypothesis 4—*When international political opportunity structures are more open than domestic ones, the development of global-first programs is more likely*—and hypothesis 5—*Where political opportunity structures are open, they act to legitimize particular ideas of key social and environmental problems*—the intergovernmental processes in coffee did not help propel the initial development of a global-first initiative, nor did they serve as a venue wherein the idea of combining social and environmental considerations could be legitimized.

Rather, in support of hypothesis 1—*When markets have low barriers to entry, the development of local-first programs is more likely*—the coffee sector facilitated the early entry of model enterprises, which in turn enabled fair-trade and organic farm advocates to populate coffee with initiatives designed to help the lot of individual farmers and their communities. It was from these foundations that two coffee initiatives emerged. A final development—also helped by low barriers to entry—took insights from the forestry sector, where concerns over tropical forest loss had led the Rainforest Alliance to develop several agricultural initiatives directed at arresting the degradation of tropical forests. There were two initiatives, each of which had a design supporting the logic of hypothesis 6 —*Certification's policy scope and regulatory domain will be a reflection of the founders' perception of key social and environmental problems and the necessary solutions*. The Rainforest Alliance was clearly concerned about crops that were produced in and around tropical forests, and its initiative, eventually including the partnership with the Sustainable Agriculture Network, reflected these concerns. The SMBC, for its part, also developed a program tailored to its aims: protecting habitat for neotropical migrants.

That the developments in the coffee sector began with local initiatives provides important conclusions in relation to hypothesis 2—*When there are concentrated points of multinational companies in a supply chain, the development of global-first programs is more likely*—and hypothesis 3—*With higher levels of international trade, the development of global-first programs is more likely*—since chapter 5 revealed that, of the three sectors, coffee has the most extensive international trade and has considerable concentration in the trading and roasting stages of the supply chain. There appear to be three reasons why the findings contradict these hypotheses. First, although coffee is highly traded, the separation between markets in Europe and the United States allowed greater experimentation in the development of certification. Second, it appears that the low barriers to entry were significant and, to some extent, outweighed the other options made available by the sector's market opportunity structures. Finally, and related, the absence of an intergovernmental venue in which to develop a coalition supporting the development of a global-first initiative also tipped the scales to favor local-first initiatives. What this case critically reveals, therefore, is that having globalized trade does not appear sufficient to propel the initial development of global certification initiatives.

In the second stage, efforts by fair trade and organics to globalize offer the strongest support for hypothesis 7—*With local-first certification initiatives, the development of market demand creates resistance to change that can slow efforts to create a global program.* The FLO's attempts to consolidate were shaped by disagreements among the different national labeling initiatives. With organics, the challenges involved coordinating different certifiers and national organic legislation. Part of this was a product of clashes over strategy, with different initiatives having in mind different goals for fair trade to tackle. Aspects of power and functionality also mattered. National initiatives worried that ceding control to a centralized office too quickly might undermine the trust they had built with clients and producers, especially if the centralized office was not able to perform to expectations. Furthermore, considerable resources had been invested in local marketing efforts around initiatives' aims. Switching costs were one stumbling block. With organics, challenges to consolidate were not a coffee-specific process, and yet being tied to the organic system meant environmental certification for coffee farms was highly fragmented well into the late 1990s.

The challenges faced by fair trade and organics also provide support for hypothesis 8—*Certification programs that are unable or choose not to respond to external pressures create opportunities for the emergence of new programs.* The slowness to consolidate offered a window of opportunity for later-developing programs. Additionally, since fair trade decided to remain focused on small farm cooperatives and since organics was initially about farm-level environmental considerations and fair trade dealt with social development issues, the types of new programs that emerged offer strong support to hypothesis 9—*When existing certification programs have a narrow policy scope or regulatory domain, new programs are likely to be complements.* The restricted domain of fair trade and the initial social-environment split between organics and fair trade meant there were still spaces for other programs. Indeed, the campaigns against the U.S. specialty sector highlighted how labor practices were a central concern, and yet they fell outside the self-chosen domain of fair-trade coffee. Because of this, characterizing Utz Kapeh as a competitor to fair trade is slightly misleading. Rather, the entrance of Utz Kapeh, the individual initiatives of Starbucks and other specialty coffee roasters, and the 4C process all illustrate how the combination of growing demand for responsible coffee along with fair trade's institutional design led to further fragmentation. Add to this the slowness of fair trade to include producers as formal members, the decision of Fair Trade USA to leave the FLO, and the creation of the FTO mark, and the high degree and continuation of fragmentation seems almost certain.

CHAPTER SEVEN

Markets and Politics in the Fisheries Sector

OCEANS AND FRESHWATER LAKES, rivers, and streams provide a
wealth of food and other resources for human populations, supplying
billions of people with essential sustenance. The diversity of resources is
astounding, and our efforts to extract and utilize them are extensive. With
the growth of human demand, however, negative environmental and social
problems are mounting. Government-led processes—international and
regional—have been the center of past and ongoing attempts to ameliorate these problems. Recently, certification programs have emerged as
additional governance tools.

To understand the rise of fisheries certification, this chapter reviews
the market and political conditions in the sector that are relevant to the
opportunity structures discussed in chapter 2. On the markets side, the
sector has high barriers to entry, numerous points of concentration, and
levels of trade that are intermediate to those in coffee and forestry. On
balance, these conditions are expected to favor global versus local certification initiatives. On the political side, there were more extensive opportunities for influence at the domestic level than in either coffee or forestry.
U.S. laws were critical early on for upward pressure on practices around
the world. As this lever lost strength by the late 1980s, intergovernmental
efforts gained prominence and gave the impression that fisheries problems might be successfully resolved. While success remains elusive, the
time taken meant that a shift in NGO attention to private alternatives

took longer to form and, when it did, a community of interests akin to what developed in forestry was absent. These developments, in a different way from coffee, nonetheless meant that the political opportunity structures in fisheries did not favor a global-first initiative early on. The specific way these counteracting conditions affected the rise of certification is taken up in the next chapter.

What follows presents a descriptive overview of the fisheries sector to clarify the market opportunity structures hypothesized to influence the rise of certification. It then traces the history of fisheries governance processes to elucidate opportunities available to NGOs and businesses alike and the changing perceptions of the key social and environmental problems. Chapter 8 turns to stage 1 of the analytic framework to examine the specific way the conditions reviewed below shaped the initiation and evolution of fisheries certification.

MARKET STRUCTURES

Fisheries target many different parts of the world's oceans and freshwater bodies that comprise habitats, including coral reefs, mangroves, the ocean floor of continental shelves and sea mounts (the benthic zone), and the open oceans (the pelagic zone). Across these different habitats, approximately seven thousand species are captured and tended or threatened by habitat degradation (Froese, Palomares, and Pauly 2000). These species yield thousands of seafood products. In 2004, reported world fisheries production in all waters from both aquaculture and capture production totaled around 140 million metric tons. Of this, 34.8 million metric tons (25 percent) was used for nonfood products such as fish oil and meal. The other 105.6 million metric tons (75 percent) went for human consumption, with approximately half of this (51 million metric tons) undergoing some form of processing and the other half (54.6 million) being sold in whole-fish form (FAO 2007b).

Capture fisheries have risen dramatically since the 1950s, when around 16 million metric tons were landed. This reached around 80 million metric tons by the end of the 1980s, after which production has leveled off, although overreporting by China is purported to have masked a decline in landings of 0.7 million metric tons per year (Watson and Pauly 2001).[1] Pelagic species (such as herrings, sardines, anchovies) and demersal species, those living on the ocean floor (for example, cods, hakes, haddocks), make up the lion's share of ocean production. In the 1950s, these two types accounted for approximately 80 percent of total capture; by 2004 this had dropped only slightly, to 72 percent.[2] A regional breakdown also illustrates the increased pelagic-fishing intensity of Asia relative to North America. Asia's growing takes are evident across species, and especially with aquaculture.

Global production from aquaculture has risen from 2.7 percent of total fisheries production in 1970 to 32.4 percent in 2004 (FAO 2007b). Asia accounts for the largest growth, and specifically China. For mollusks (for example, clams, abalones, mussels, scallops), the growth of aquaculture has been even more pronounced. Over 12 million metric tons were produced in Asian marine waters in 2005, up from only 73,000 metric tons in 1950. Between 1981 and 1997, China sustained a thirteen-fold increase in per capita consumption of mollusks (Delgado et al. 2003).

Fishing methods can be categorized as active or passive (Kura et al. 2004; see also Chuenpagdee et al. 2003). Active gear is pulled through the ocean to trap target species. For instance, trawls are large nets that have one open and one closed end; they are dragged either through ocean waters or along the ocean floor. Passive gear is set in one place to catch target species. Long-lines, for instance, place multiple hooks into the water at regular intervals off a main line that rests on the surface. Passing fish or other marine life that take the bait are then pulled in after the line has been out for hours, sometimes days (Kura et al. 2004). Although designed to capture certain species, all of these gear types are imperfect: annually they capture millions of tons of nontarget species, or bycatch (Chuenpagdee et al. 2003).

Once caught, fish and other marine life undergo some form of processing. Since seafood is perishable, the catch must be frozen, chilled, cured, treated, or processed quickly after being hauled onboard (FAO 2005). In 1996, a little over 32 percent of the world catch was sold fresh; another 23 percent was sold frozen (Bhattacharya 2002, 64). How processing occurs depends on the species and the size of the vessel—for instance, with oily fish such as salmon, processing onboard is kept to a minimum to keep the flesh quality high (Jespersen, Christiansen, and Hummelmose 2000). With other species, processing may occur entirely onboard. A developing trend in processing has come with the advent of factory trawlers, a form of fishing vessel adapted from whaling ships that have massive trawling capacity, complete onboard processing facilities, and sizable storage space. These boats can stay at sea for months at

Table 7.1.

Fisheries market opportunity structures and expected effects

CHARACTERISTICS	CONDITIONS	EXPECTATIONS
Barriers to entry (hypothesis 1)	High barriers to entry for many segments of the sector	Inhibits creation of local-first programs
Concentration in supply chain (hypothesis 2)	Points of concentration in supply chain occupied by limited number of multinationals	Supports creation of global-first programs
International trade (hypothesis 3)	Intermediate levels of international trade	No clear support for global versus local certification programs

a time and return to port with completely processed seafood, ready for market (Ken Stump and Batker 1996). Processing tends to occur on-shore, however. Fresh or frozen fish are delivered to port and go through de-icing and washing in preparation for filleting and trimming (or other methods of extracting the edible parts of the marine organism). The seafood is then kept in chilled or frozen storage before being distributed to market (Jespersen, Christiansen, and Hummelmose 2000).

With canning, fish arrive at a processing facility where their nonedible parts (heads, tails, fins, and sometimes skins) are removed and discarded. Small fish tend to be cooked in the can after it has been filled with oil or brine; medium and large fish are precooked before brine or oil is added (Jespersen, Christiansen, and Hummelmose 2000). All cans are sealed, sterilized, and stored ready for subsequent transport to market.

This overview provides a basis for identifying the conditions in the fisheries sector for the three market opportunity hypotheses (table 7.1). These are each reviewed below.

Barriers to Entry

The fisheries sector has, in general, high barriers to entry. Similar to forestry, processing is capital intensive in the fishery sector (Zugarramurdi, Parin, and Lupin 1995), and access to the resources can be a constraint.

Licensing arrangements to public waters can serve as a significant entry barrier against potential competitors, since these rights are usually fully allocated through long-term access or quota rights.

According to hypothesis 1, all else being equal, the fisheries sector is less likely to see the development of local certification programs compared with the coffee sector.

Multinationals at Concentrated Points in the Supply Chain

With fisheries, it is hard to identify a single supply chain (Wilkinson 2006). Nonetheless, there are certain points of concentration and fragmentation. For starters, production is highly diverse and employs many millions of people. In 2004, 41 million people worked as fishers or fish farmers worldwide (FAO 2007b). The majority of them work in aquaculture, and most of these workers and fishers are small-scale operators, as many as 90 percent in coastal fisheries. The international fisheries fleet is also vast. In 2004, the FAO estimated it at 4 million strong (FAO 2007b).

Rights to fish also vary. Coastal waters, the area to the outer reaches of the continental shelf with water typically less than two hundred meters deep, are generally contained within the two-hundred-nautical-mile Exclusive Economic Zone (EEZ) that gives the coastal state fishing and management rights (Kura et al. 2004). The open oceans, where water depths exceed two hundred meters, are generally outside the EEZs of coastal nations and hence can be fished by any vessel from any nation; waters outside the EEZs are legally defined as the high seas (Kura et al. 2004). Rights to fish these waters are licensed to fishing vessels, and controls of total catches have, historically, been done through annual quotas. Shifts toward individual quota systems designed to correct overcapitalization developing from competition for limited aggregate quotas have gained recent interest in many fisheries (FAO 2007b).

Within processing and retail sectors, the supply chains of various species narrow, but the pattern varies geographically. There were 152 seafood-canning companies in the United States in 1997, the top 4 of which contributed 25.9 percent of the annual value of shipments. The top 50 companies contributed 93.4 percent (U.S. Census Bureau 2001). Fresh and frozen seafood processors were less concentrated. A total of 586 companies operated in this sector in the United States in 1997, with the 4 largest accounting for only 13.6 percent of the annual value of shipments; the top 50 companies contributed just 65.8 percent (U.S. Census Bureau 2001). With the U.S. retail sector, in addition to grocery stores and restaurants, there were also 1,634 fish and seafood markets, where the 4 largest companies accounted for 4 establishments and only 8.9 percent of total 1997 sales (U.S. Census Bureau 2000c). Concentration in the supermarket sector is more notable, but varies by country. In the United Kingdom, where more concentration exists (Schurman and Munro 2009), figures for 2005 indicate that over 85 percent of retail sales of chilled and frozen seafood occurred through supermarkets. Combined, Tesco and Sainsbury accounted for over 40 percent and 30 percent of the UK chilled and frozen seafood market, respectively (Greenpeace 2005). Thus, although concentration exists, many smaller companies sell seafood to end consumers. Moreover, these outlets do not capture the large quantities of seafood not consumed in developed-country markets.

Consumption patterns have indeed shifted over the past few decades. In 2004, excluding China, apparent global per capita consumption of fish products was 13.5 kilograms; including China, the figure jumps to 16.6 kilograms (FAO 2007a). Worldwide, fish provided about 2.6 billion people with approximately 20 percent of their annual animal protein intake (FAO 2007a), and demand continues to grow, mostly driven by developing countries. Whereas in 1973, developed countries accounted for 55 percent of the global fish consumption, by 1997, this had fallen to 31 percent. China's contribution, in contrast, had grown to 36 percent and other developing countries to 33 percent (Delgado et al. 2003). The pattern of increasing consumption is not uniform: in Latin America and sub-Saharan Africa it fell, whereas in Southeast Asia, India, and China, it rose (Delgado et al. 2003).

According to hypothesis 2, these conditions should support the creation of global certification efforts, all else being equal.

International Trade
Compared with the other two sectors, the fisheries sector has intermediate levels of global trade. In 2004, over one-third of world fish production (by weight) was traded internationally (FAO 2007b). A regional breakdown, however, shows that most production is consumed region-

ally. This is particularly the case when mollusks are excluded. In only some cases do export quantities exceed 20 percent of a region's total production; even less frequent are proportions higher than 30 percent.[3] Overall, import and export quantities as a proportion of total annual production are highest in Europe, although even here, they rarely exceed 30 percent. Still, export proportions have steadily grown in Europe since the 1960s, with the greatest increase in freshwater diadromous species: only 10 percent of production was exported in 1960, whereas nearly 35 percent was in 2000.

With imports, Europe again has the highest level relative to apparent consumption (production minus exports). Imports closely match exports, indicating that much of the import-export activity is occurring within Europe.[4] In Asia, by contrast, imports comprise no more than 1 percent of apparent consumption for all species groups. Likewise, the proportion of imports is also limited in South America across all species and in Africa, with the exception of other marine fish species (FAO's category for unclassified species). North America is more intermediate, exhibiting growth in imports but not yet to the level seen in Europe (FAO 2007b).

Based on these conditions, hypothesis 3 leads to unclear predictions for the sector, implying that other factors are more likely to affect whether certification begins as a local- or global-first process.

POLITICAL STRUCTURES

With the political opportunity structures, the fisheries sector had a notable difference from the other two sectors (table 7.2). Most important, opportunities for influence were quite different owing to the character of U.S. laws that offered leverage to potentially affect international practices on certain fisheries through to the end of the 1980s. Attention to international processes then took hold, as governments began to seek agreements on several shared challenges in fisheries management. While these processes remain ongoing, their later initiation helped delay certification, and they also did not provide the same community-building environment as was the case in forestry. These developments, in a different way than coffee, pushed fisheries toward fragmentation.

To provide further details on these conditions, what follows reviews intergovernmental attention to fisheries and the evolution of NGO tactics. Chapter 8, the final empirical chapter, then examines how both the

Table 7.2.

Fisheries political opportunity structures and expected effects

CHARACTERISTICS	CONDITIONS	EXPECTATIONS
International political opportunity structure (hypothesis 4)	Not as open to influence early as domestic opportunities (particularly in the U.S.)	Inhibits creation of global-first certification
Opportunity structures for legitimizing new ideas (hypothesis 5)	Lack of open intergovernmental fora wherein to develop broad understanding of fisheries problems	Inhibits early creation of certification with a broad policy focus

market and political conditions in the fisheries sectors affected the rise and evolution of certification programs.

The Scope and Domain of Governance Structures

The period following World War II moved ocean governance away from the freedom-of-the-seas doctrine, according to which states controlled just a three-nautical-mile strip of ocean along their territorial shores, toward a system of expanded territorial jurisdictions and improved efforts to coordinate management among nations. Before this, most of the oceans were open to exploitation by fishing fleets from any country. Japanese, U.S., and European vessels were the most active in the postwar period, fishing around the globe and increasing competition for dwindling resources (Garcia 1992). Consequently, the freedom-of-the-seas doctrine lost favor. In 1945, the United States moved to exert sovereignty over its continental shelves (DeSombre 2000, 108; Caron 1989). South American countries followed suit: Argentina claimed sovereignty over its continental shelf in 1946; Peru and Chile made similar claims in 1947 (UN 1998). Joined by Ecuador, they then signed the Santiago Declaration in 1952 to buttress their new maritime claims (Garcia 1992).

These were both grabs for control and conservation efforts to better regulate marine resources. Indeed, stocks in the Northern Hemisphere were strained, a point highlighted by the London International Conference on Overfishing, convened in 1946, that examined bottom-fish stocks (Garcia 1992). At the time, management interventions mainly entailed technology standards—gear and mesh-size restrictions for nets, as examples—and largely neglected the continuing growth of fishing activity (Garcia 1992). Pressure on the oceans steadily rose, with countries such as China and Peru joining the United States, Japan, and the EU as significant contributors to global fishing. The FAO was the hub of international governance, yet overall, decision making and management were decentralized. Regional Fisheries Management Organizations (RFMOs)—such as the Asia-Pacific Fisheries Commission and the General Fisheries Council for the Mediterranean—were formed by the end of the 1940s; others followed and regional fisheries organizations still remain central to ocean governance, with eighteen bodies holding management responsibilities and twenty-four playing advisory roles (DeSombre 2000, 109–10).[5]

During the postwar growth in extraction, the problems of open access gained wider recognition (see Anthony Scott 1955; Gordon 1954), furthering support for a change to the freedom-of-the-seas doctrine. These issues were taken up by the first, second, and third Conferences on the Law of the Sea held in 1958, 1960, and 1973. The first of these negotiated the Convention on Fishing and Conservation of the Living Resources of the High Seas, which came into force in 1966 (Garcia 1992). A definition of "high seas" and the extended territorial claims remained in dispute. Nothing further was resolved at the second conference, and even the third conference produced only a draft framework for extending territorial sovereignty to twelve nautical miles and providing coastal states with a two-hundred-nautical-mile EEZ in which they would control fishing and mining rights (deFontaubert 1995). Implementation of these provisions happened during the 1970s and then, in 1982, the UN Convention on the Law of the Sea (UNCLOS) was formally opened for signatures (UN 1998); it entered into force in 1994 (Cochrane and Doulman 2005). The agreement also required collaborative, joint management of stocks outside countries' EEZs by distant states and coastal states (deFontaubert 1995).

Establishing the EEZs addressed only part of the problem. It did not resolve management issues with fisheries; it only redistributed fishing rights to coastal states over distant water fishing nations. Overfishing continued and worsened (Delgado et al. 2003), largely because of a growing mismatch between global fishing infrastructure—both in terms of overall capacity (David W. Evans 2001) and in terms of methods for locating, capturing, processing, storing, and transporting fish (Caddy and Seij 2005; Wilkinson 2006)—and governments' capacities and willingness to regulate these activities. In developing countries, for instance, a strong economic imperative works counter to effective regulation, since licensing fees charged of foreign fleets for access to a country's EEZ provide foreign currency exchange (Caddy and Seij 2005; Petersen 2006, 115). Even in developed countries, where government scientists and managers track and monitor fishing activity, significant stock depletions and even crashes have occurred (Finlayson 1994).[6] The discussion below reveals that, in spite of these real concerns, an oceanwide focus on overfishing would not emerge until the 1990s and even then, the role of RFMOs and individual coastal states remained critical.

Outside of the UNCLOS, there were other developments important to the evolution of NGO strategies and the eventual formation of fisheries certification. One of the most significant initiatives focused on whaling. At the UNCHE, the parties supported a resolution for a ten-year moratorium on whaling. This was formalized in 1982 when members of the International Whaling Commission (IWC) agreed by a twenty-five to seven vote that a commercial whaling moratorium would be implemented by 1986 (Skodvin and Andresen 2003; Shabecoff 1982). This was a coup for environmental groups that were part of efforts successful in overcoming the resistance of pro-whaling countries led by Japan (Skodvin and Andresen 2003; DeSombre 2000; Wapner 1996). The U.S. government was also critical. The 1979 Packwood-Magnuson Amendments to the 1976 U.S. Fishery Conservation and Management Act required the secretary of commerce to assess whether countries holding quotas to U.S. waters were undermining the effectiveness of the IWC. If any were, the secretary of state had to reduce the defiant country's quota by 50 percent. The earlier Pelly Amendment, added in 1971 to the Fisherman's Protection Act of 1962, gave the U.S. president discretion to ban fish product imports from violating countries (DeSombre 2000; Caron 1989). These two laws empowered the United States to make concerted efforts supporting the IWC, which it did both before and after the 1982 decision to ban whaling (Caron 1989).

Before the UNCLOS entered into force, and partly because it was taking time, fisheries reached the Rio Earth Summit agenda (Cochrane and Doulman 2005). In May 1992, Mexico and the FAO convened a conference in Cancun addressing "responsible fishing," which clarified what the term meant and the obligations it placed on states. The conference also charged the FAO with developing a code of conduct for responsible fisheries (Caddy and Griffiths 1995). Chapter 17 of the Rio Earth Summit's agenda 21 further directed the fisheries policy agenda. It called for greater cooperation regarding high seas fisheries regulation and better management of coastal regions under national jurisdiction, including greater protection for critical marine ecosystems (Caddy and Griffiths 1995). Though the summit stopped short of resolving the ongoing challenge of straddling and highly migratory stocks, the parties did agree that a post-Rio conference should be dedicated to this end; talks commenced in April 1993 and led to the approval of the UN Fish Stocks Agreement in August 1995 (deFontaubert 1995; Doulman 1995). A total of seventy-two NGOs held observer status for the negotiations of the Fish Stocks Agreement, including Greenpeace International, Friends of the Earth International, and the WWF. Certain business groups, such as the Bering Sea Fisherman's Association, and unions, such as the Food and Allied Workers, were also involved (Doulman 1995).

Concurrently, in October 1995, the FAO Code of Conduct for Responsible Fisheries Practices was adopted by the twenty-eighth session of the FAO Conference (Caddy 1999). Here again, NGOs were involved in the negotiations, but have taken an even greater role in implementation.[7] The concurrent development of these instruments also meant that the code actually included provisions from the Fish Stocks Agreement. There was a great deal of harmony in wording and phraseology across these agreements (Caddy 1999). Consequently, although the Fish Stocks Agreement entered into force only in November 2001, many of its provisions were inserted in domestic laws earlier through voluntary adoption of the FAO Code (Richards and Maguire 1998). The Fish Stocks Agreement reinforced the governance role of RFMOs; it held that states' fishing stocks covered by an RFMO should become members or, if an RFMO did not exist, states should cooperate to establish one (Cochrane and Doulman 2005). Nevertheless, the Fish Stocks Agreement covered only an estimated 10 percent of the world's capture fisheries; the other 90 percent is caught within the EEZs of coastal states.

Through the FAO, two other instruments have emerged. First, the FAO Compliance Agreement was adopted in 1993 and entered into force in 2003. It includes provisions that require flag states to ensure vessels that are under their jurisdiction are not violating fisheries conservation and management measures, and it requires record keeping for vessels given rights to fish on the high seas (Edeson 2005). Second, in 2009, the Port State Measures Agreement was adopted as a tool to govern fishing activities through the power of port states to oversee the activities of foreign fishing vessels with a particular aim of helping address the problem of illegal, unreported, and unregulated (IUU) fishing (Skonhoft 2012). This agreement followed on the FAO's work developing and promoting its International Plan of Action (IPOA) to Prevent, Deter and Eliminate IUU fishing, which was adopted and endorsed by FAO member states in 2001.[8]

Taken together, improvements made to the international governance of ocean resources have been generally recognized. Yet because implementation has been challenging and taxing, scrutiny of the sector has not waned.[9]

Coevolution of NGO Tactics and Perceived Problems

Across the board, information on stocks is unsettling. Nearly 30 percent of global fish stocks are overexploited, with another 57.4 percent of stocks fully exploited, meaning they have little if any room for further production (FAO 2012). The impacts of overexploitation, moreover, extend beyond direct effects on individual fish stocks. Fishing for a target species, as explained above, can take significant quantities of nontarget species, or bycatch (Chuenpagdee et al. 2003).[10] Although some is sold, in 2004 bycatch was estimated at 20 million metric tons, nearly one-fourth of global reported catch. Habitats destroyed or degraded by bottom trawling and dredging further exacerbate the ecosystem-wide effects of heavy fishing.

The beginnings of NGO activities on global ocean issues focused on whaling. Recall that a resolution at the UNCHE meeting in 1972 proposed a ten-year moratorium on commercial whaling. This immediately became the focus of the IWC's annual meetings. Countries, including the United States, began pressing to formalize the moratorium; resistance came from Japan and the Soviet Union, which at the time accounted for approximately 83 percent of the world's annual catch, or thirty-two thousand whales (Pearlstine 1974). The issue ignited wide popular concern, with various NGOs taking up the cause. Greenpeace, a group founded to protest nuclear testing in the Aleutian Islands, formalized its first anti-whaling campaign in April 1975 (Weyler 2004). After Japan and the Soviet Union blocked efforts to impose an IWC moratorium, the National Wildlife Federation, the Fund for Animals, Friends of the Earth, and the Animal Welfare Institute, among others, were calling for a U.S. consumer boycott of Japanese products (*New York Times* 1974). Later in the 1970s and through the 1980s, whaling captured global media attention and facilitated the 1982 decision of the IWC to place a moratorium on commercial whaling. This was also when Greenpeace and other groups voiced outrage over the long-practiced commercial hunt of baby harp seals (Raloff 1979). Other groups founded at the time built from Greenpeace's direct intervention tactics to champion the defense of marine life. The Sea Shepherd Conservation Society (or Sea Shepherd) formed in 1977 (officially incorporating in 1981) and used direct-action tactics with the aim of ending the seal pup hunt and exposing and stopping illegal whaling (Sea Shepherd Conservation Society 2008).[11] Greenpeace and Sea Shepherd actions against Japan, Norway, and Iceland occurred throughout the late 1980s and even into the 1990s (Wapner 1996). Indeed, since 1985, there has not been a year where "whaling" and "Greenpeace" have not been mentioned in either London's *Guardian* or the *New York Times*.[12] Boycotts and name-and-shame tactics used by groups such as Greenpeace and Friends of the Earth operated in concert with continued threats of U.S. economic sanctions against Iceland and Norway (Andresen and Skodvin 2008, 137).

Alongside the whaling disputes, the UNCLOS was under negotiation. Although it included attention to conservation, urging states to cooperate to manage joint stocks, the main thrust of debate was territorial rights over resources. For instance, the U.S. government voiced strong opposition to the UNCLOS because of its deep seabed mining provisions (Malone 1983) and restrictions on fishing in the two-hundred-nautical-mile EEZs of other coastal countries (Nossiter 1983). In 1983, the Reagan administration announced that it would recognize all but the seabed mining provisions of the UNCLOS as customary international law. The seabed mining disputes captured attention for much of the 1980s and led many industrialized countries, such as the United States, the United Kingdom, Germany, and Italy, to withhold their support (*New York Times* 1989). Because of this, other provisions in the UNCLOS received less attention. Rather, the core debate remained between developing and developed countries over whether the high seas and ocean floor were the "common heritage of mankind," distracting the international agenda away from marine conservation (Pitt 1993).

Thus, following whaling, similar actions developed for concerns over dolphins, with U.S. involvement and NGO campaigns being key. The dispute centered on incidental killing of dolphins associated with purse seine netting techniques used by commercial tuna fishers in the eastern Pacific (Vogel 1995). Although the rates of incidental kills had fallen dramatically (Shabecoff 1988), in 1988 the issue grabbed media attention when video footage from a Panamanian tuna-fishing boat caught drowning dolphins entangled in nets (Nix 1988; Associated Press 1998a). Groups such as Earth First and the Earth Island Institute began calling for an end to dolphin deaths linked to tuna fishing. Similar to the case with whaling, U.S. domestic laws made internationalization almost inevitable. The 1984 amendments to the Marine Mammal Protection Act required the administration to take action against foreign tuna fisheries that did not make efforts to reduce dolphin kills through such measures as boat observers (Shabecoff 1988). This legislative change gave NGOs an opportunity to force these actions through legal suits (MacLean 1989).

Unlike the whaling issue, which garnered similar attention in Europe and North America, the tuna-dolphin dispute was mainly a U.S. concern. This elucidates important facets of the coevolution of the fisheries governance institutions and the actions taken by NGOs. First, the regional and species-specific structure of ocean management channeled the NGO activism. Whereas the IWC addressed whaling around the globe, other fisheries management organizations were focused on regional waters or single species and hence did not provide an international forum wherein to legitimize a set of concerns. Thus, although overfishing remained an issue of discussion for much of the postwar period, with the exceptions of whaling and the seal hunt, it would take until later in the 1990s for oceanwide campaigns to emerge.

This facet of fisheries was also conditioned by the openness of domestic regulatory venues, particularly those in the United States. The Pelly and Packwood-Magnuson Amendments discussed above enabled the U.S. government to sanction countries that condoned commercial practice antithetical to IWC provisions on whale conservation. Even when the U.S. administration was not willing to take such measures, the nondiscretionary character of these laws meant NGOs could and did use legal suits to force action (Shabecoff 1985a; Franklin 1985). The legal institutions in the United States, and particularly the court system, married with the "action-forcing" form of legislation, meant court challenges have and remain a central arrow in the NGO quiver. Additionally, De-Sombre (2000) and Vogel (1995) show how these U.S. environmental laws became the foundation for Bootlegger-Baptist coalitions seeking to regulate the activities of foreign fishing interests.

While the whaling case was a relative success—the IWC moratorium remains in place—with the dolphin-tuna and shrimp-turtle disputes, U.S. efforts to internationalize domestic rules were mired by the absence of an international agreement protecting turtles and dolphins. Nevertheless, in spite of General Agreement on Tariffs and Trade (GATT) and World Trade Organization (WTO) rulings against U.S. laws designed to protect dolphins and turtles (DeSombre 2000; Rotherham 2005), efforts to internationalize domestic legislation have been reasonably successful. This is important since it meant government rules could be used to press for change. This openness did not prevent groups from using other tactics. The stalled efforts to internationalize dolphin-friendly tuna-fishing practices facilitated the emergence of the well-known "dolphin-safe" label, a version of which was legally enshrined under the 1990 Dolphin Protection Consumer Information Act (DeSombre 2000; Percival et al. 2003). Later efforts to create a "turtle-safe" label for shrimp began to build consumer awareness about the environmental impacts of seafood consumption, and the Earth Island Institute has continued to advance its "dolphin-safe" label to all tuna fisheries, requiring no use of drift netting, a provision that goes beyond the U.S. rules (Baird and Quastel 2011).

These patterns also highlight the species and regional focus of NGO actions. Although this was true in the forestry sector (groups targeted forest practices in parts of the world or championed efforts to protect individual tree species), the forestry campaigns by the early 1990s were connecting via a burgeoning community concerned with worldwide forestry practices. Greenpeace began a comprehensive oceans campaign in 1996 that targeted industrial fishing in the North Sea and that led Unilever and Sainsbury's to commit to stop using fish oils and meals from North Sea fisheries (Jackie Brown 1996). However, what is particularly important is how Greenpeace continued to focus on government action. Though happy with the companies' commitments, a Greenpeace representative told a reporter: "We have to get more Government regulation, the only way you can be really safe is when it is made illegal" (*Herald* 1996).

The growth of aquaculture production represents a final important development for evolving fisheries problems. Despite centuries of aquaculture practice in parts of the world, from the 1960s, and particularly in the 1980s, the intensity of production rose markedly (Quarto, Cissna, and Taylor 1996; Stonich and Bailey 2000; Wilkinson 2006). The environmental and social impacts of the intensification awoke certain concerns. First, habitat destruction raised concerns since wetland forests, such as mangroves, were regularly cleared to make way for aquaculture pens (Quarto, Cissna, and Taylor 1996). Shrimp farms, for instance, were associated with the destruction of coastal mangrove forests. Salmon farms also created negative spillover effects through higher concentrations of fecal matter in the vicinity of coastal pens (Hume et al. 2004).

Second, although aquaculture can offset pressure on wild stocks, this is not true for all species. With herbivores or filter feeders, Naylor et al. (2000) explain, aquaculture can have a positive effect on the total fishery supply. When carnivorous species are farmed, such as salmon, fish meal from ocean-capture fisheries is needed to sustain the farmed species. It has taken as much as two to five kilograms of fish meal protein to create a single kilogram of farmed-fish protein (Naylor et al. 2000). Thus, farming carnivores actually amplifies fishing effort aimed at lower trophic level stocks, a trend that itself has been occurring independently as large, easier-to-catch high trophic-level species are heavily depleted (Pauly and Palomares 2005). Third, due to high stocking densities, intensive production creates conditions ripe for parasites, diseases, and other pathogens,[13] and also creates concerns about escapes. Escaped farmed salmon, for instance, can compete with wild salmon, threatening the stability of wild populations. This is particularly concerning when nonnative species of salmon are farmed.

The speed with which this industry developed also meant regulators were largely playing catch-up.[14] Although NGOs did quickly raise questions about fish farming and efforts to regulate the industry's environmental harms developed, these were location specific and species specific, and hence they did not help form a community from which a global certification initiative could arise. In sum, when combined with the availability and success of U.S. court action, the single-species and region-specific approaches taken by NGOs and the late development of concerns around aquaculture had a lasting influence on certification developments in the later 1990s. They appear to have impeded the quick development of a sectorwide approach early on.

This chapter has detailed the character of the market and political opportunity structures in the fisheries sector to identify the background conditions wherein certification arose. The sector's high barriers to entry are expected to limit the possibility of local certification initiatives, whereas intermediate levels of international trade and the presence of concentration in the global supply chain occupied by multinationals should favor global certification. Unlike coffee or forestry, the political opportunity structures were most open within the U.S. domestic political process, where U.S. laws offered some leverage for putting upward pressure on global fisheries practices. Then, as this opportunity waned in strength, intergovernmental efforts gained momentum and served to delay broadbased attention to certification from NGOs. In the next chapter, the specifics of these effects are traced.

CHAPTER EIGHT

The Rise and Evolution of Fisheries Certification

RELATIVE TO FORESTRY AND COFFEE, certification came to the fisheries sector late. Even though by the end of the 1980s, organic certifiers were responding to interest from producers that hoped to differentiate their practices from the commercial mainstream, these activities remained confined to the expanding aquaculture segment of the sector. Single-species initiatives, such as dolphin-safe tuna, also emerged at this time, yet certification for a variety of wild-capture fisheries would rise only in the mid-1990s. This meant those creating fisheries certification programs had more existing programs to emulate, which they did. Similar to the Rainforest Alliance carrying its forestry and banana experiences to the coffee sector, and organic certifiers diversifying into coffee and aquaculture, the emergence of fisheries certification was facilitated by the entrepreneurship of the WWF.

Because the MSC emerged as a global program structured to offer certification services for ocean-caught fisheries worldwide, the pattern at the sector level has been shaped not by a slowness in its ability to consolidate, but by the issues it chose not to address or that were viewed by outside actors as insufficiently addressed. The MSC's institutional design conditioned this process since—unlike in forestry, where groups could become FSC members and participate in standards-setting processes—the same opportunities for voice were not immediately available. The institutional design choices of the MSC, thus, led to certain successes, while also driving outside actors to create new initiatives rather than working within the MSC to steer the program in new directions.

Producers did attempt to form their own initiatives, but these were not solely counterpoints to the MSC. Since NGOs other than the WWF were themselves outside the MSC and did not adopt it as a cause célèbre, producers were responding to several independent campaigns. Again, unlike in forestry, where the FSC took center stage in debates over forestry practices, the MSC remained peripheral early on. As the program gained momentum, however, it received more attention and gave rise to competitors and attempts by certain actors to gain access to the program's decision-making processes. These forces have compelled the MSC to undergo adaptations to assuage outside concerns.

Beyond the struggles over MSC governance, and the changes that have ensued, the fisheries certification field remains in flux. The MSC has faced a few potential challengers. So far, the most notable has been the Friend of the Sea, which certifies ocean capture and aquaculture. On the aquaculture side, organics has been followed by several other initiatives, including the recently created Aquaculture Stewardship Council. Before this, the GAA and Global GAP were both active on the aquaculture side. With organics, Naturland, an IFOAM-accredited organic certifier, has developed a program for ocean-capture fisheries, potentially setting on track future IFOAM work on fish. Hence, the possibility of even more fragmentation seems clear.

STAGE 1: PROGRAM INITIATION

The later development of fisheries certification and labeling meant information features more prominently in the explanation for how events unfolded. The transmission of information occurred through at least three separate paths: first, organic certifiers spread to the sector, applying the ideas of organic husbandry to the burgeoning fish-farming industry; second, the WWF took its specific experience with the FSC and sought to replicate it in fisheries; and third, producers in North America responded to building campaigns directed at fisheries by creating industry codes of conduct and eventually a certification program.

The market and political structures outlined in chapter 7 also matter. Intergovernmental processes for fisheries were unfolding later, which meant a perceived government failure was not present to motivate a certification alternative. Nor did these processes work as a community-forming venue similar to the ITTO. Finally, in many fisheries, governance decisions were made at the regional level by the global network of RFMOs. This governance pattern focused attention toward specific fisheries in specific waters, and away from broader ocean concerns. With markets, the pattern was equally fragmented. While trade levels were intermediate to coffee and forestry, regional patterns are important. Nevertheless, there are certain points of concentration, among them supermarkets in certain countries and large food-processing companies. The interest in responding to societal pressure and direct targeting focused on these companies was critical for the emergence and evolution of fisheries certification.

As a result of these conditions, two forms of fisheries certification formed, one preceding the other. Producers then responded, but in a less cohesive and energetic manner than in the forest sector. The discussion turns to this history in sequence.

The process of creating a global organic certification and labeling program was well under way when interest in aquaculture gained attention. Recall from chapter 5 that by the end of the 1980s, the IFOAM had released multiple iterations of its basic organic standard. It had also begun to address consistency problems across certifiers with work on an accreditation program. In 1992, the membership approved the creation of the IAPB; in 1997, it was broken from the IFOAM to create a separate legal entity, the IOAS, which from that point forward would oversee IFOAM accreditation (chapter 6).

At this time, certain organic certifiers were expanding their services to offer assessments for fish-farming operations, a process that had happened approximately ten years earlier with coffee. Starting in 1989, the UK-based Soil Association began work on a draft standard for certified organic farmed salmon and trout (Auld 2009). They had been approached by certain small salmon farm operations in Scotland that were eager to have their practices recognized in the marketplace as distinct from the intensive, industrial practices of their larger competitors (Soil Association 2004).[1] Naturland soon followed; it released standards for organic pond farming in 1995, and a year later certified a salmon farm off the west coast of Ireland (Auld 2009). Interest in Germany originated from organic farmers who ran carp ponds on their properties and were eager to have these certified (Bergleiter 2008). Interest outside Europe was also developing: Bio-Gro, a New Zealand–based organic certification organization, assessed a salmon farm in 1994; its production was targeting the European market (Tacon and Brister 2002). By 1996, as a consequence of this growing interest, the Soil Association reinitiated its standards drafting process, and it released an "interim" standard in 1998 (Soil Association 2004). A year later, Naturland published shrimp-farming standards, opening its services to an increasing number of developing countries (Scialabba and Hattam 2002). Attempts by the IFOAM to consolidate these efforts under a single standard soon followed. The discussion returns to this process after introducing concurrent efforts to create an ocean-capture certification program.

The same conditions fostering interest in organic aquaculture engendered a certification program for ocean-capture fisheries. The situation for marine resources was distinct, however. It held more in common with developments in the forest sector, since the WWF served as an organizational carrier modeling a new initiative after the FSC experience. Yet, unlike in the forestry sector, the intergovernmental processes for oceans did not help build an international community ready to support a certification effort. In this sense, the later emergence of fisheries certification was significant: there were more working models to emulate when designing new initiatives.

To understand the MSC's formation, three separate developments are significant. First, in 1994, Unilever sought scientific advice on stock levels in the North Sea based on its concern about the security of the company's long-term supplies (Hamprecht 2005, 100). The timing was salient, given that only a few years earlier, the cod stocks off the Newfoundland coast had collapsed. Second, by this time, Greenpeace had also begun ocean advocacy much beyond whaling. It began a campaign against industrial fisheries in the North Sea, particularly those focused on sand eel and other low trophic-level species. These species were being heavily fished to supply demand for fish meal and fish oils used for animal feed and in some food products (such as biscuits). Unfortunately, this meant ocean species higher up the food chain, including seals, cod, sea birds, and dolphins, were being deprived of their food source (Aikman 1997). Companies, including Unilever, were pressed to stop selling products containing or derived from fish oil. Third, in 1995, WWF International launched its Endangered Seas Campaign to advance marine protection and appropriate fisheries management. The initiative was a striking parallel to the WWF's forestry work. It fit the idea of a fisheries eco-labeling initiative into a three-pronged strategy for improving the conditions of the world's oceans. Like the organization's global two hundred ecoregion "hot spots," the WWF first delineated a parallel set of marine hot spots. The WWF then, as in forestry with its promotion of protected areas and FSC certification, began promoting marine protected areas along with fisheries certification (Flanders 1998).

It was not just the WWF's efforts that mattered, however. The creation of certification was the consequence of how these three developments converged. A key player on the WWF side was Mike Sutton from WWF-US; he took the lead role for WWF International's efforts early in 1995 (Hamprecht 2005). Sutton had an interest in finding major industry partners with which to create a market approach similar to the FSC. The WWF had already begun examining what it would take to create a "marine" version of the FSC; a member of the WWF forest team was contracted to examine the logistics of this undertaking (Fowler and Heap 2000, 137). Murphy and Bendell (1997) later explained how the close connections between the WWF's forestry and fisheries work facilitated the diffusion of the certification idea: "Located next to the Forest Unit, the ESC [Endangered Seas Campaign] staff were able to learn informally about the 1995 Group and FSC initiatives" (169).

Over the course of 1995 and early 1996, the efforts of Unilever and the developing interest of the WWF in a seafood-labeling program started to entwine. Sutton communicated the interest in finding an industry partner to Simon Bryceson at Burson-Marstellar, a large public relations company. Only a week later, Bryceson was having a very similar conversation with Unilever officials, who were themselves seeking advice on talks with Greenpeace, which was, by this time, demanding that Unilever carry a point-of-origin label for all its Iglo products (Hamprecht 2005). Bryceson saw the potential for a connection between WWF and Unilever interests, given that he felt Greenpeace would be a less amenable partner than the WWF (Hamprecht 2005). Officials from the WWF and Unilever also met at a conference in January 1996 set up to assess the progress being made by the 1995 Group (Murphy and Bendell 1997, 170).

These informal communications were the foundation for creating the Marine Stewardship Council. Talks between Sutton, Whitfield (an employee with Unilever), Bryceson, and others in the respective organizations began in the fall of 1995 (Hamprecht 2005). The official partnership between the WWF and Unilever was formalized in early 1996 with a joint announcement about the new initiative to create an eco label for responsible fisheries management (Hernes and Mikalsen 2002). The partners' motivations were clear: they wanted to adapt the FSC model to the fisheries case. As Antony Burgmans, the director of Unilever's frozen fish and ice cream division (later to become Unilever's CEO), wrote about this period: "I and my colleagues were impressed with the work that the international conservation organization WWF had done to establish the now independent Forest Stewardship Council (FSC). . . . Our initial discussions with WWF confirmed that we had different motives, but a common purpose: the need to assure the long-term sustainability of global fish stocks and the marine ecosystem" (Burgmans 2003).[2]

To proceed, the partners sought advice about what they could learn from the FSC; they commissioned Coopers & Lybrand to study the FSC's governance procedures. This included sending the team to the FSC's first General Assembly in 1996 to "learn from their successes and mistakes" (Michael Sutton and Whitfield 1996; see also Synnott 2005). One lesson they took from the analysis was that a membership-based organization would constrain any fisheries certification program, leaving it unable to quickly adapt and act (Auld et al. 2007). The choice was also partly rationalized by the possibility of including members later, whereas, they thought, rescinding membership would prove burdensome and potentially impossible (Fowler and Heap 2000, 144). Principally, the idea was to create a streamlined organization, with little bureaucracy but high competency, to operate strategically early on to get the program running. Hence, the eventual MSC was officially launched as an independent nonprofit organization in February 1997 without provisions for membership (Michael Sutton 1998; Schmidt 1999).[3] Instead, in addition to a Board of Trustees and a chair serving as the organization's public face, the MSC would be run by a secretariat that coordinated the activities of a Standards Council, Advisory Board, and National Working Groups (Fowler and Heap 2000, 141). The Advisory Board was the closest analogue to a membership body; according to the MSC's original Web site, it "[was] open to any individual with an interest in fisheries and their certification irrespective of their own background" (MSC 1999b). The Advisory Board was partitioned into three chambers: one for those making an economic living from fisheries; a second for environmental groups and government bodies (domestic and international); and a third for educational, social, and consumer interests (MSC 2000e). Participants, nevertheless, served only an advisory role, rather than holding voting rights, as was the case in the FSC or the IFOAM.[4]

Another aspect of its early work was creating a standard for assessing appropriate fisheries management. With this aim, the MSC began a two-year consultative process that worked off standards detailed in the FAO's Code of Conduct for Responsible Fisheries, the UN Fish Stocks Agreement, and the Principles for the Conservation of Wild Living Resources (OECD 2005; Michael Sutton 1996). This began with a meeting in September 1996 in which twenty experts were invited to participate in the first drafting process (OECD 2005). From there, eight workshops were held around the world, in Massachusetts, British Columbia, Germany, South Africa, Australia, New Zealand, Scotland, and Greece (Constance and Bonanno 1999; Fowler and Heap 2000). International experts were invited to a concluding workshop held in Washington, DC, in December 1997 to debate a final draft of the Principles and Criteria, a document that was then presented to the MSC Board and chair (OECD 2005). Over the next year, further workshops in Ecuador, Chile, Argentina, and Peru (MSC 1999a; Schmidt 1999) both refined the P&C and served as a partial effort to respond to criticisms of the MSC's limited understanding of, or attention to, the issues of developing-world fisheries (Michael Sutton 1998).

Nevertheless, these issues remained a concern, particularly how to grapple with the social side of fisheries management in developing countries. Given the many millions of small-scale fishers and their limited management capacity, many questions were raised about whether certification could serve their interests. A series of debates occurred in *Samudra,* a periodical published by the International Collective in Support of Fishworkers (ICSF), focusing on the development of the MSC and what it meant for smaller artisanal fishers.[5] Many expressed concern that the program would likely favor industrial fishing operations over smaller, inshore fishers (Belliveau 1996), an issue debated after the cod-stock collapse off the east coast of Canada (Finlayson 1994). One commentator explained the challenge facing the MSC: "As the process of developing the MSC Principles and Criteria advances, boundaries will need to be drawn around what the MSC includes and what it excludes. This may mean that environmental and technical factors will be the main determining criteria for accreditation, while social factors may be pushed into the background" (O'Riordan 1997, 11). In essence, the developers had to determine the scope and domain of the program. What issues did they want to address and what fishery operations would be eligible?

The MSC developers recognized this dynamic in terms of both the standards and the governance of the organization. For instance, Michael Sutton (1998) explained to *Samudra*'s readers that although they had originally been advised to stick with a nonmember organizational format, the issue of governance was still under debate, having been raised frequently at regional workshops. This comment foreshadowed ongoing adaptations and reforms, mainly designed to correct what some observers termed the MSC's "democratic deficit." The first governance review was due for completion in December 2001, and others followed (MSC 2001d, 2000c).

With standards, the MSC chose to keep them streamlined, excluding more direct attention to social or development issues and not addressing the issue of fish farming. It made these decisions though conscious of the significance of both for the sustainability of fish stocks (May et al. 2003). Indeed, in early iterations there were five principles, one of which addressed social issues directly. However, this was dropped from the final standard. The P&C were also kept general; they would be made specific in the context of a single fishery, a task given to MSC-accredited certification bodies.

During the development of the MSC, there were a number of other NGOs—in the United States groups like NRDC, the National Audubon Society, and SeaWeb—that were focused on the oceans and marine environments (Helvarg 2001). Recall that Greenpeace was also waging a campaign directed at industrial fishing in the North Sea, which continued concurrent to the WWF-Unilever partnership. In the United States, rather than focus on industrial fishing for fish oil and meals, NRDC, the Pew Charitable Trusts, and SeaWeb initiated a campaign in January 1998 with the catchy refrain "Give Swordfish a Break" (SeaWeb 2008). Responding to declining swordfish populations in the North Atlantic and the declining average-catch size, the groups collaborated with several high-end restaurants that agreed to take swordfish off their menus for one year (Burros 1998). Later in 1998, a number of U.S. groups took this one step further by developing "buyer guides" that identified and ranked fisheries as okay (green light), intermediate (yellow light), and not all right (red light) (Audubon Society 1998).[6] Different organizations issued various rankings, starting in 1998 in the United States (Roheim and Sutinen 2006) and then shortly after in Europe.[7] Groups creating these guides included the Monterey Bay Aquarium, Blue Ocean Institute, and the Environmental Defense Fund in the United States, and the Marine Conservation Society and North Sea Foundation in Europe (Roheim and Sutinen 2006).

More than with forestry, in the late 1990s, these efforts were largely detached from the MSC's work. Of course, the MSC had yet to become a functioning program, and unlike in forestry, there was not a cadre of certifiers already working under the assumption that they would soon be MSC accredited. In the short term, this probably helped the MSC. Just as its founders had hoped, forming a streamlined, quickly operational program did avoid some of the internal strife evident in the first few years of the FSC's activities. Yet, in the longer term, these conflicts would reemerge as issues for the MSC to grapple with. We come back to these issues below.

By the beginning of 2000, the MSC comprised all the features of a global certification program; it had successfully navigated the first few years and was now independent of its founders: the WWF and Unilever. Although debate remained over governance, and early fisheries certification would prove controversial, the MSC had the potential to be a leader in the eco-labeling field. Indeed, in spite of the internal challenges, interest in the program was immediate. By 1997, in the United Kingdom, the major supermarkets Sainsbury's and Tesco indicated they would seek MSC-labeled seafood when available (Boulton 1997); Unilever itself committed to selling only MSC-labeled products by 2005 (Hill 1997). Early adoption of the MSC began in 2000. The first-ever MSC certification was awarded to the Western Australian rock lobster fishery, which was closely followed by the Essex-based Thames herring fishery in the United Kingdom (MSC 2000e) and the Alaska salmon fishery later in the year (MSC 2000b).

Turning now to other initiatives—those focused on single species and those backed by producers—the split between the MSC's work on ocean capture and organics' attention to aquaculture plus the continued campaigns of U.S.-based organizations on shrimp farming and other single-species campaigns, such as the "Give Swordfish a Break" initiative, were an important backdrop to the continued bifurcation of fisheries certification initiatives. Although the MSC's focus was becoming clearer, the fragmentation of organic certification, in terms of both variation in government requirements and the individual certifiers, meant organics was still a possible player for ocean-capture certification. There were also differences between Europe and North America indicative of the separate industries operating in these regions. Certain initiatives were more clearly responding to the MSC, while others were vying against the burgeoning organic aquaculture initiatives and the campaigns launched by NGOs directed at single species such as shrimp and salmon.

European governments took a central role in reacting to the MSC. In August 1996, around when the Unilever-WWF partnership was announced, the Nordic Council of Ministers established a Nordic project group charged with assessing standards for sustainable fish production (FAO 2000, 82). The Nordic Council then became a central proponent of an FAO-led eco-labeling scheme (O'Riordan 1998), owing to a perception that the MSC was undermining countries' regulatory jurisdiction over marine resources (Stokke 2004). It vocalized this position at an October 1998 FAO technical consultation convened to explore the creation of "Non-discriminatory Technical Guidelines for Ecolabelling of Products from Marine Capture Fisheries." The International Coalition of Fisheries Associations (ICFA) expressed similar views. Press releases issued in December 1996 and September 1997 explained the ICFA's concerns about the MSC; it noted apprehension about the program's potential to undermine legitimate government management and its general impracticality (ICFA 1997, 1996). Unfortunately for the Nordic Council and the ICFA, the discussions were mired by the dispute at the WTO over U.S. laws intended to protect dolphins and turtles. Another eco label, such as the MSC, was considered a potential barrier to trade, designed to limit market access for developing-world fisheries, and hence it was not received favorably by certain countries (O'Riordan 1998).[8]

Across the Atlantic in the United States, two separate industry-led initiatives formed: one from the ocean-capture industry and another from aquaculture. With the ocean-capture industry, an initiative began in March 1997 when a coalition of seafood companies, organized by the National Fisheries Institute (NFI), announced the launch of Principles for Responsible Fisheries, a program for guiding industry practices from extraction through to marketing (NFI 1997b). These principles were approved by the NFI Board in April of the same year (NFI 1997a); similar to the MSC, they built from the FAO Code of Conduct for Responsible

Fisheries (NFI 1997b). In June 1998, the NFI chose to create a separate organization—the Responsible Fisheries Society—to facilitate the implementation of the principles (NFI 1998). Note that by this time the "Give Swordfish a Break" boycott was under way and the National Audubon Society had just published its first guide to seafood. As well, the Magnuson-Stevens Fishery Conservation and Management Act had been reauthorized in 1996 (Rue 1997). In this respect, government regulation and pressure from NGO campaigns were reasons for the fishing industry to attempt self-regulation.

Within aquaculture, the development of other programs followed species lines. For shrimp, the focus of concern was the intensification of production and the controversial clearing of mangrove forests for shrimp farm facilities and the local negative social and environmental impacts of these practices. Efforts against industrial shrimp farm expansion had been coordinated by the Mangrove Action Project (MAP) since 1992 (Stonich and Bailey 2000).[9] In 1996, the MAP helped organize a strategy meeting involving international environmental and social nonprofits along with local groups based in the countries where shrimp farming was expanding.[10] The first meeting was held in April 1996 concurrent with the UN Commission on Sustainable Development and sought to highlight problems and demand changes. This included presenting a declaration to the UN General Assembly on the unsustainable character of aquaculture practices (Stonich and Bailey 2000) and was followed by press releases and awareness-raising efforts by U.S.-based NGOs (NRDC 1996). WWF staff in the United States also hoped to convene a working group to define responsible shrimp farming, but did not link this effort to their work on the MSC.[11]

In response to these controversies, in March 1997, the Global Aquaculture Alliance was established at a meeting of the World Aquaculture Society (an international association representing aquaculture industry and scientists) that was held in Seattle, Washington. Newspaper coverage of the event explained how the shrimp industry saw the development as a way "to do what environmental groups are doing, but in our own name" (Christensen 1997).[12] The alliance was initially constituted by fifty-six individuals from twelve countries (GAA 1998b); its first order of business was to commission a report that would propose a "code of practices for mangrove protection" (Bene 2005, 591).

At the time, pressure from NGOs on the issue of shrimp aquaculture continued to grow. In October 1997, groups from fourteen nations created the Industrial Shrimp Action Network during World Food Day (Ramsar 1997). Likewise, the Earth Island Institute had been pressing for government action on turtle protection through its Sea Turtle Restoration Project (later to become a separate initiative run by the Turtle Island Restoration Network). In 1994, the initiative launched an eco label for shrimp trawlers using turtle-exclusion devices (Sea Turtle Restoration Project 1999) and by 1995 was working with Georgia and Florida shrimp fishers to promote their "turtle-safe" trawling practices (Allen 1995).

Those sympathetic to industry noted how such NGO collaborative efforts were a mounting threat given the ongoing fragmentation of fishing interests (IFCNR 2001).[13] Facing these pressures, the GAA continued developing standards; in 1998 a technical committee completed the first review of all the code of practices' nine principles (GAA 1998a). It was also working to form a global coalition. For instance, in 1998, the GAA wrote in its newsletter how the Ecuadorian Chamber of Aquaculture had been exploring a partnership with Fundación natura in order to address sustainability issues in shrimp aquaculture practices. The GAA did not oppose the initiative but emphasized how it hoped to "develop a single comprehensive industry plan for sustainability" (GAA 1998a). A year later, the GAA was one step closer to realizing this objective when it released the first completed version of the code of practices and indicated that farms meeting the code would have access to a yet-to-be-developed eco label (GAA 1999). Shortly after, the RFS and the GAA announced joint work on an eco label for the entire fisheries sector, aquaculture and wild-capture fisheries alike.[14] For the time, the program remained a first-party initiative open to the entire industry (FAO 2000).[15] Also important was how the NFI had given control of the RFS to the Ocean Trust, an organization formed in 1992 to promote marine conservation. The Ocean Trust was an important broker of the alliance between the RFS and the GAA (Ocean Trust 2000), and it would serve as a voice countering the NGO advocacy work in the United States that was promoting seafood buyers' guides and consumer boycotts (see, for example, Ocean Trust 2001).

Thus, during the time the MSC initiated and organics began working with aquaculture, industry, government, and NGOs continued with other efforts to address fisheries problems. Most of these initiatives lacked all the features of a global certification program. Nevertheless, they were embryonic competitors with the potential to become full-fledged certification programs in the future.[16] The next section discusses the market's response and describes the ongoing creation of new certification initiatives and the termination of others.

STAGE 2: CONSOLIDATION AND SECTOR-LEVEL
COPYING AND COMPETITION

The developments in fishery certification diverged from those occurring in the coffee and forestry sectors. The MSC took lessons from the FSC in the mid-1990s and was able to quickly establish a global program. No certifications were undertaken until the MSC had all of its component parts in place. Thus, rather than folding in the efforts of existing certifiers, as had occurred with the FSC or the IFOAM, or developing to coordinate the activities of existing national labeling initiatives, as with the FLO, the MSC built the architecture of a global program before on-the-water assessments occurred. Aquaculture certification, by contrast, remained the purview of existing organic certifiers. As with coffee, organics took a longer time to consolidate, even in spite of the later start of aquaculture efforts. To trace what happened during this period, the following discussion reviews the internal consolidation of organics and then moves to the sector-level patterns.

The tensions surrounding MSC governance and implementation emerged as a key issue in the coming years; these processes were mediated by the MSC's early decision to form without members. Similar to fair trade's concentration on small farmer cooperatives, the choice to focus on capture fisheries and limit attention to social issues meant a set of operators and issues remained unaddressed. Organics and the developing GAA initiative aimed to address aquaculture. However, with organics, not unlike coffee, it would take time for the IFOAM to establish oversight. Plus, concerns within the organic movement, particularly about whether it was logical to consider marine systems as analogous to terrestrial systems and hence appropriate for organic principles, slowed expansion into this area. Additionally, the entry of governments, with the establishment of varying legislated definitions of organic practices, further complicated the global consolidation of organics. With the GAA, its strong drive to address shrimp standards and certification procedures was not immediately transferred to other species, but this changed with the development of standards for species including tilapia and catfish. Thus, there were still good opportunities for entry, leaving the field of certification programs in flux.

Internal Program Consolidation

While the Soil Association, Naturland, and a few other organic certifi- ers were working on aquaculture standards and offering initial certifica- tions, the IFOAM continued refining its accreditation service. In 1997, it finally created the International Organic Accreditation Service as an independent company and gave it responsibility for IFOAM accredita- tion services (IOAS 2006). Recognizing a need to harmonize the core principles of organic aquaculture practice, the IFOAM began drafting a "Basic Standards for Organic Aquaculture Production" in 1998 (Tacon and Brister 2002). An IFOAM label stating "IFOAM Accredited" was re- leased in 1999 and was to be used concurrently with the accredited certi- fier's own label (Commins 2003). Only a year later, the IFOAM "Basic Standards for Organic Aquaculture Production" were accepted by the membership at the General Assembly in 2000 as a draft standard for further refinement (Tacon and Brister 2002).

The consequence of all these developments was the introduction of organic seafood to a number of markets. The first Naturland-certified organic mussels reached the market in 1999.[17] After Naturland's certifi- cation of an Irish salmon farm and with the earlier New Zealand organic salmon certifications, both mentioned above, Scottish producers were spurred to follow. By 1998, the Soil Association was involved and had endorsed salmon farms under its "interim" standard, allowing super- markets to begin stocking organic salmon products (*Aberdeen Press and Journal* 1998; Binnie 1998). Yet many felt applying organic principles to fish farming was highly problematic, riddled with inconsistencies when compared with the original intention of organic agriculture. Officials from the Soil Association recognized the interest in organics but also were astutely aware of a need to proceed with caution. One official was quoted: "We were treading on very sensitive ground but there was a lot of demand from consumers for a better quality product produced in a better way" (Gillian Harris 1999).

Debate erupted. Claims were made that the Soil Association's stan- dard was not truly organic given it lacked government endorsement. And, more generally, activists questioned whether fish farming could ever be considered organic. A campaigner from the Friends of the Earth–UK remarked: "Cramming a migratory species, cooped up in cages, fed on a high-energy diet of fast-diminishing resources is hardly in tune with nature" (Rob Edwards 2000).

Similar debates were being waged in the United States regarding how organic labeling laws should handle fisheries. Here the question was whether capture fisheries could be considered organic. It was, at least in theory, conceivable, and this is what the Alaskan salmon fishers pursued at the end of the 1990s, in part because organic farmed salmon was being sold in UK supermarkets (Gillian Harris 1999; Kennedy 1999). The Alaskan capture fisheries wanted their own mark of environmental quality. They pressed the U.S. National Organic Standards Board (NOSB) to accept capture fisheries as certifiable against organic standards. In 1999, two pilot projects occurred in Alaska to judge whether this was appropriate (Joling 1999). In the end, the decision was against the Alaskan producers. Without the ability to ensure that no prohibited substances were ingested during a salmon's ocean life, the U.S. NOSB concluded that ocean-caught salmon could not be organic (Wessells et al. 2001).[18]

These two examples illustrate how organics were not able, for different reasons, to address the new fishery problems groups were highlighting. In both instances, the existence of government organic rules were constraints; the rules raised questions about the legitimacy of organic certifiers' choices to develop standards for aquaculture practices. The outcomes also signaled an opening for new fisheries certification programs. The market interest was there. A group would need only to develop a credible program to fill the demand. And although government action on fisheries problems gained momentum during this period, there was a perceived shortfall in the implementation of the agreements and rules.

In 2005, the IFOAM accepted the interim "Basic Standards for Organic Aquaculture Production" as a final standard. By this point, the program was in the position to serve as a global program for aquaculture certification (figure 8.1). In spite of the challenges noted above, individual certifiers such as Naturland and the Soil Association have carried on certifying aquaculture operations. By 2000, organic aquaculture production was estimated at five thousand metric tons (Tacon and Brister 2002). Organic aquaculture operations now produce a wide

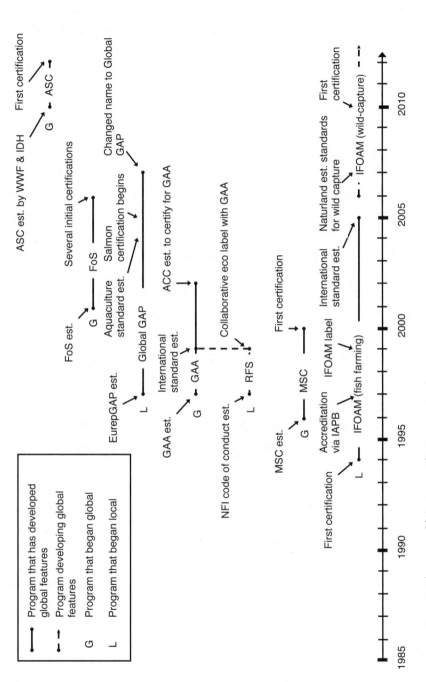

FIGURE 8.1. Development of fisheries certification over time

range of species beyond shrimp and salmon, with centers of production in Europe, Latin America, Asia, and Oceania (Bergleiter 2008). Reports from 2005 estimate global organic aquaculture production at twenty-five thousand metric tons, around fourteen thousand metric tons of which are produced in Europe, eight thousand in Asia, and the remaining three thousand tons in the Americas (Hilge 2005).

Sector-Level Patterns of Emergence

The pattern that emerged at the sector level was partially the product of the initial fragmentation among organics, ocean capture, and the fishery-specific efforts that developed in several countries, including the United States (figure 8.1). Two separate dynamics were occurring. First, the GAA was developing standards and certification procedures for shrimp, which were being closely scrutinized by the Industrial Shrimp Action Network. Meanwhile, organics continued to develop aquaculture standards for shrimp, catfish, and tilapia, among other species. The WWF, for its part, began a series of aquaculture dialogues, starting first with shrimp and then extending to other high-value farmed species such as salmon, mollusks, and tilapia (Auld and McKee 2012). This meant that, at the time, there was no stand-alone aquaculture certification program that NGOs had developed.

Second, the MSC had emerged quickly. Although the RFS formed as a possible competitor, nothing much came of it. Indeed, after the merger with the GAA, the initiative slipped to the background and its promoters exerted more attention to the boycott and seafood buyer guides that were emerging as central tools for U.S.-focused NGOs (Ocean Trust 2001). This left the MSC alone on the ocean-capture side. This could be seen as a success; however, the early process of implementation was a probationary period for the MSC, as it had been for the FSC. NGOs were eager to see what an assessment would mean in practice. Yet the MSC did not have the same openness to outside influence by design. Given the more muted opportunities for voice, when the MSC resisted certain outside pressures, the push to build alternatives grew.

In this final section, the discussion shows how opportunities for voice, the policy scope and domain of early programs, and the development of market demand were all important in shaping opportunities for later-developing programs. Akin to coffee, here it is necessary to also account for certain facets of the U.S. context that shed light on the patterns of programs that have emerged. The discussion begins by examining what happened when the MSC-accredited certifiers began assessing fisheries.

The Western Australian rock lobster fishery and Alaska salmon fishery were two of the three first MSC-certified operations. The Alaskan certification also led to an expanded MSC presence in the U.S. market. NorQuest, a processor based in Alaska, served as the intermediary for the certified fishery, providing labeled products to the U.S. market. At the same time, Trader Joe's, Whole Foods, Legal Seafood, and Shaw's were reported to have committed to sell MSC products (MSC 2000d). Finally, in November of 2000, the MSC announced that Migros—a supermarket chain in continental Europe—would begin selling the program's certified products (MSC 2000a).

In 2001, another three fisheries achieved MSC certification—New Zealand hoki, Burry Cockle fishery in the United Kingdom, and the South West mackerel handline fishery in the United Kingdom (Auld 2009). Market interest also continued expanding, with thirty-one processors and four distributors achieving chain of custody certifications to sell MSC-labeled salmon in the U.S. market; Whole Foods offered the first such products to consumers (MSC 2001a). Unilever also reported having sourced 5 percent of all its seafood products from MSC-certified producers by the end of 2001 (Unilever 2002).

Similar to the wariness surrounding the first wave of FSC certificates, these early MSC activities were colored by persistent apprehension about the program, especially among conservation organizations. There were two separate but related points of dispute. The first had to do with the practices of specific fisheries in relation to the goals of sustainability.[19] These concerns centered on how MSC-certified fisheries could receive endorsement based on a commitment to improving their practices, rather than a requirement that sustainable practices be in place before a fishery could pass an assessment (Pearce 2003; Short 2003).[20] Criteria 1 and 2 under principle 2 of the MSC standard were particular sticking points. The wording of each implied that a fishery must meet certain conditions before being considered certifiable, and yet this was not the process that was undertaken in the assessment. Noncompliance with a single criterion did not mean a failed assessment; an operation just had to receive 80 percent for each principle to pass (David Sutton 2003).

Another set of concerns had to do with marine protection. These are aptly illustrated by the controversy surrounding the Western Australia rock lobster fishery. After negotiations for the Earth Summit and the Convention on Biological Diversity, attention to marine protection rose.[21] Several countries, including Australia, were tackling the issue by this time (Agardy 1999), and it was within Australia where concerns for marine protection gave the MSC some problems.

The Australian governments (commonwealth, state, and territory) had been collaborating to establish marine protected areas, a process strongly resisted by fishing interests (Lunn 1999; Lienert 1999; Faye 1999).[22] In Western Australia, provisions of the 1984 Conservation and Land Management (CALM) Act established the legal authority for designating marine protected areas.[23] Two years later, the Ministry of Environment formed the Marine Parks and Reserves Selection Working Group to identify marine areas in Western Australia that merited conservation (DCLM 2003). In January 1997, the environment minister announced that Jurien Bay—a coastal area with adjoining islands two hundred miles north along the coast from Perth—was under consideration for park status (DCLM 1997).

Jurien Bay happened to be located in the coastal area used by the Western Australia rock lobster fishery (Scientific Certification Systems 2000); hence, the specifics of the park proposal were rather important for the soon-to-develop MSC assessment undergone by the fishery. Commercial interests in rock lobster fishing were opposing efforts to establish marine conservation areas, especially "no-take" zones (marine nature reserves as defined by the CALM Act) (David Sutton 2003). At the time, there was still ambiguity over what the Jurien Bay Park would look like, since the public announcement mentioned "multiple uses," and yet the Marine Reserve Protection Authority (MPRA) reports were discussing a marine reserve (Marine Parks and Reserves Authority 1999). In the planning process for the park, disagreements emerged. In the MPRA's 2000 annual report, Chairman Barry Wilson explains: "The Authority advised the Minister that three aspects that remain especially contentious are the area of the proposed sanctuary ('no take') zones, the ecological impacts of rock lobster fishing and perceived inequities in the treatment of recreational and commercial fishing, notably rock lobster fishing" (Marine Parks and Reserves Authority 2000).

Jurien Bay Park received official status in August 2003 and did include "no-take" zones (DCLM 2003). However, in the interim, the Western Australian rock lobster fishery achieved MSC certification, leaving a bad taste in the mouths of certain members of the local conservation community. These concerns linked back to unhappiness about the wording of the MSC P&C in relation to fisheries passing with an average 80 percent score across criteria and how certification appeared to deflect pressure for marine reserves. David Sutton, from the Australian Marine Conservation Society, explained: "Why should industry, fishery managers or politicians support the establishment of areas closed to fishing activities when they can say the activity concerned is certified sustainable, having no impact on biodiversity or on marine structure, function or integrity?" (2003, 117–18).

Disquiet about the MSC's approach to governance also emerged during debates over implementation. This stemmed from a frustration with the nascent organization's lack of responsiveness to the above controversies and a perception that it was not open to NGO concerns (David Sutton 2003). Recall that in 2000 the MSC launched a governance review. A document posted to the MSC Web site discussing the review reiterated the logic behind the MSC's original decision about structure. "When the Marine Stewardship Council was formed in 1997, many funders and NGOs in particular raised the question of a 'democratic deficit' in the organisation's structure. Comparisons were made with the seemingly more open Forest Stewardship Council (FSC). Some felt that in order for the MSC to be truly accountable to all its stakeholders, the organisation should be membership based. This was, rightly in the view of many, rejected and some argue that the FSC's experience has vindicated that decision" (MSC 2001c).

The document went on to note how the MSC's original governance structure, with the Advisory Board's open membership designed to ensure accountability, proved "cumbersome, expensive to operate, and [left] the MSC open to potential capture by particular interest groups or sectors" (MSC 2001c). At the time, the MSC Board was chaired by John Gummer, former UK secretary of state for the environment, and had eight other members: three represented the fishing and seafood industry, four were former or extant government officials, and one was a former chairman of WWF-UK (MSC 2001b). Conspicuously absent were any major NGOs, including any of those that had been active in the United States or involved in fisheries issues in Australia. Based on the review, the MSC introduced more representation to its board and developed a Technical Advisory Board to give advice on standards, chain of custody, and logo licensing issues. This replaced the former Standards Council. Finally, the Advisory Board was replaced by a Stakeholder Council of thirty members who would meet annually to guide the board. Two members from the council would hold seats on the board (MSC 2001d). This change opened a spot for a representative of Blue Ocean Institute (who had formerly been with the Audubon's Living Oceans Program) and a representative from Whole Foods (MSC 2003).

In spite of these changes, the concerns over governance continued and were expressed most forcibly in two reports commissioned by U.S. foundations released in 2004. The Bridgespan Group wrote a report for the Packard, Oak, and Fairbairn Foundations; Wildhavens wrote a report for the Homeland Foundation, the Oak Foundation, and the Pew Charitable Trusts. The Wildhavens report (Highleyman, Amos, and Cauley 2004) examined the MSC's certification work in four case studies: the Alaskan salmon fishery, the New Zealand hoki fishery, the South Georgian toothfish, and the Aleutian Islands pollock fishery. In certain respects it simply amplified the already public concerns over early certificates, compiling the evidence in a single report and pressing the MSC to tighten its certification procedures. Without changes, the report suggested, there was a real threat that conservation groups would not support the MSC going forward (Paul Brown 2004). In rebuttal, the then chief executive of the MSC, Brendan May, explained in a news report: "The MSC gives incentives and maintains pressure to improve conditions; we're not about certifying perfection" (Schwarz 2004). The report did, nevertheless, spur changes that have been ongoing, with the MSC placing greater attention on stakeholder engagement and improved consistency across certifiers (Auld and Gulbrandsen 2010).

Yet it was still taking time for the MSC to build relations with the broader conservation community. Although the MSC Board now included a representative from Ocean Blue Institute, by 2005 the MSC Stakeholder Council still had representation only from the WWF-US, the David Suzuki Foundation, and the Industrial Shrimp Action Network (MSC 2005b). The commissioning and release of the Wildhavens report also showed how groups working on marine conservation in the areas covered by the four certificates were finding the MSC's processes closed to their concerns. Alaska Oceans Program, a group unhappy with the pollock fishery, offered a link to the Wildhavens' report on their Web site and explained: "We have been disappointed with the slow pace of MSC's reforms and will no longer participate in certification efforts. We have asked the MSC to suspend all certifications until it makes the much needed reforms, but they have declined. Although we are interested in using market-based incentives to improve fisheries management and protect ocean ecosystems, we cannot support the MSC until we are confident that its certification system provides conservation benefits to the ecosystem and rewards fisheries that are truly sustainable" (Alaska Oceans Program 2007).

Greenpeace U.S. had also been campaigning against the Alaska pollock fishery since the mid-1990s in work paralleling its campaign against industrial fishing in the North Sea (Ken Stump and Batker 1996). The MSC certifying an operation that local groups were strongly criticizing closely resembles what happened with WFP in British Columbia. In this case, however, the MSC was unable to form a local standards-setting process where the debates could play out. Rather, the MSC's decision was challenged through a formal dispute-resolution process begun in 2004 that agreed to reevaluate one of the Alaska pollock certification assessments: the Gulf of Alaska certificate. Complaints against the Bering Sea Aleutian Islands certificate were dismissed as not warranting attention (MSC 2004). The dispute process was concluded in 2005, with the independent review panel upholding the certification decision (MSC 2005a), but this was not a resolution for groups unhappy with the decision. The limited voice within the MSC led groups to express concerns from outside. In 2008, Greenpeace vocally criticized the Alaskan pollock fishery and went as far as placing it on its "red list" as an unsustainably harvested fishery (Bernton 2008; Greenpeace 2008).

This is a notable comparator to the forest case and the FSC specifically. NGOs in the fishery case were also sending mixed signals about what behavioral changes they wanted (Auld and Cashore 2013). The Greenpeace supermarket reports illustrate these different demands. Starting in 2005, Greenpeace UK released a series of reports on the performance of supermarkets, a particularly concentrated and competitive part of the seafood supply chain. In its first report (released in October 2005), the group used a simple metric to rank supermarkets on their efforts to source sustainable seafood. The report gave Marks & Spencer the highest grade, whereas ASDA (the UK subsidiary of Wal-Mart) fared the poorest (Greenpeace 2005). Just three months later, in January 2006, ASDA had announced an ambitious commitment to the MSC—it sought to sell only products from MSC-certified fisheries within five years—and it added efforts on depleted stocks, including removing North Sea cod from its shelves (Hickman 2006). Greenpeace took note of this transformation in its next supermarket report, upgrading ASDA from dead last to a respectable fifth with a grade of "pass" (Greenpeace 2006).

The success of supermarket reviews in the United Kingdom led to the spread of the practice among national Greenpeace offices. Even before the U.S. Greenpeace office released its first review, Wal-Mart announced its commitment—equivalent to ASDA's—to sourcing MSC-certified fresh and frozen seafood for its thirty-eight hundred North American stores by 2011. This added to the commitment the company had made in late 2005 to source farmed shrimp certified according to the GAA standard (PR Newswire 2005). Tellingly, though, Wal-Mart placed only fifth on the first U.S. Greenpeace ranking, coming after Whole Foods, Ahold, Harris Teeter, and Wegmans. It had fallen to ninth place by the release of the 2010 ranking report (Trenor 2010). Commitments to source certification by Wal-Mart and ASDA were not enough to place them atop of the Greenpeace rankings.

British Columbia, Canada, offers further illustration of the implications of these mixed signals and the concerns groups had with the implementation of the MSC. Just as the salmon industry in British Columbia was considering MSC certification, Greenpeace Canada noted in its supermarket report serious concerns about the MSC certifying Canadian fisheries, including the Atlantic scallop dredge fishery and the British Columbia Fraser River Sockeye fishery (Hunter and King 2008). There are also interesting parallels between the efforts of the Fraser River Sockeye fishery to be MSC certified and WFP's attempts to be certified by the FSC. In each case, other concerns of NGOs turned the processes into protracted and costly affairs. The Fraser River Sockeye fishery currently stands as the longest MSC certification assessment, lasting from June 2003 to July 2010, or just over seven years.

Three important implications flow from these events. First, unlike in the forestry sector, where debates over FSC implementation focused on the standards development process, with the MSC these debates were waged within the organization's dispute-resolution mechanism, and ultimately outside the MSC, as groups voiced their ongoing disappoint-

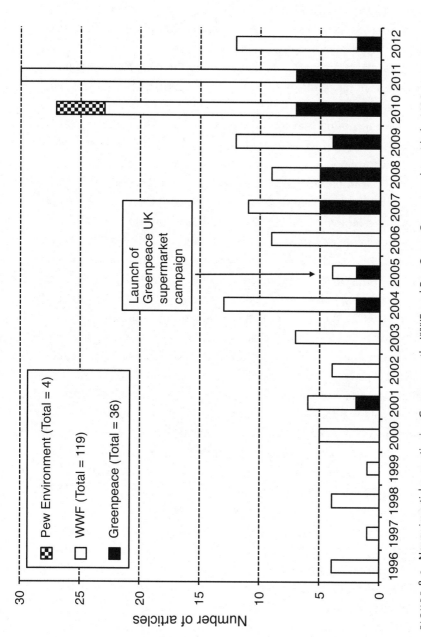

FIGURE 8.2. Newswire articles mentioning Greenpeace, the WWF, and Pew Ocean Group together with the MSC. Newswire sources include the Associated Press, Business Wire, Canada Newswire, PR Newswire, PR Newswire Europe, M2 Presswire, Agence France-Presse, U.S. Newswire, and IPS–Inter Press Service (www.lexis-nexis.com).

ment with the program's work. Second, environmental groups that were concerned about the implementation of certification at the time did not have the same incentives to circle the wagon around the MSC, as there was little threat a competitor program would gain traction in the market. Third, the timing of these disputes and the costs they entailed for operators seeking certification had implications for the ability of other programs to form and gain support. The discussion below returns to this third point in noting that the Friend of the Sea certification by British Columbia salmon fisheries in 2007 in part flowed from the high costs of MSC certification.

The final important point to make about the MSC's early choices concerns its decision to remain focused on ocean capture and environmental considerations. On the former, although the MSC signaled early that it might consider including aquaculture in the future, this has not happened. Indeed, at the close of 2006, the MSC Board issued a statement indicating that, having given the issues considerable thought, the MSC would remain focused on its core competency in capture fisheries (MSC 2006). On the latter, recall the exchange that occurred in *Samudra* in which the benefits of the MSC for small-scale fishers and fish workers were questioned. This has remained a key concern because it means some fisheries can be systematically excluded from markets demanding certification and because it has left social issues of fisheries management largely unaddressed. The MSC has been working on this issue, having launched a pilot project to provide data-deficient and small-scale fisheries better access to the program (MSC 2007a). Still, both of these restrictions have left open space for the entry of other programs.

Several processes have sought to fill the gaps left open by the MSC. Before discussing these, it is important to note that the market interest in certification was growing. Even though Greenpeace was not endorsing a specific certification program, retailers saw these programs as one means by which to respond to the pressure. The commitments by Wal-Mart and others were boosting the profile of seafood labeling, and this was helping increase the MSC's market penetration. By the end of 2006, 332 seafood products in twenty-five countries were carrying the MSC logo (MSC 2007a). By April 2007, approximately 6 percent of the world's edible capture fisheries were engaged in the program. With salmon, MSC fisheries represented 42 percent of total world production; 32 percent with prime white fish catch (cod, pollock, hake, haddock, ling, and saithe); and 18 percent with spiny lobster. The number of labeled products had also jumped to 668 (MSC 2007b).

Thus, in spite of the criticisms, the MSC remained the only comprehensive fisheries certification program. The RFS and GAA collaboration continued, but mainly through the GAA's work to eco label shrimp; this meant the competition was directed more toward organics than to the MSC's work on capture fisheries. In 2002, the Aquaculture Certification Council (ACC) was formed to operate as an external auditor for the GAA program.[24] This was just in time for the program to fill demand from the wave of retail commitments that began around 2005. Indeed, in late 2005, Wal-Mart announced a partnership with the GAA and the ACC to certify that its foreign suppliers are in line with the GAA Best Aquaculture Practices standards (PR Newswire 2005). The announcement was even lauded by Conservation International; the group supported critical changes to the GAA standards that had improved mangrove and wetland conservation. Yet the MAP, the group that had spearheaded early action against shrimp farms, remained critical (Mangrove Action Project 2005). Wal-Mart, nevertheless, stayed committed to the GAA program, and by 2007 there were forty-four shrimp farms certified in ten countries, twenty certified hatcheries, sixty certified processing plants, and twenty-five licensed buyers with sales in the United Kingdom, Canada, and the United States (Auld 2009). Buoyed by this late success, the program has expanded into tilapia—first certified in 2007—and will also soon offer catfish assessments (Market Wire 2007).

Thus, by around 2005 the market signal for certification had begun to solidify, and the MSC and the GAA were the programs benefiting the most from uptake. But as chapter 2 argued, the presence of market demand meant the dominance of these two programs was far from solidified. Indeed, similar to the work of Starbucks and Home Depot on their own standards, certain supermarkets followed suit. Whole Foods, for instance, developed a comprehensive strategy in 2006 that went beyond requiring certification (Mui 2008). Marks & Spencer and Waitrose had received earlier kudos for their comprehensive seafood policies by Greenpeace UK in the group's 2006 supermarket report (Greenpeace 2006). Entry of new certification programs was another consequence of the rising market interest; it occurred on two fronts. Programs that developed in other sectors considered expanding to address fisheries or aquaculture practices, while entirely new programs formed with the support of groups that felt existing certification initiatives were insufficient. The discussion addresses these in turn.

The first program to expand was an agricultural program—Eurep-GAP, now Global GAP—which had launched in Europe in 1997. It had developed a number of standards for agricultural practices since forming, and in 2004, it released an Integrated Aquaculture Assurance standard covering safety, quality, environment, and labor issues for farmed fish (EurepGAP 2004). A year later, an updated standard was released that had been developed through a broader consultative process (Eurep-GAP 2005).

On the fisheries side, organics was the next to move. Although the IFOAM still addressed only aquaculture, since individual certifiers, such as the Soil Association and Naturland, are not controlled by the IFOAM in terms of what they choose to certify, organic capture fisheries was still an open possibility. KRAV, a Swedish-based certifier, was the first to enter this sector.[25] The process began in 2000 when the Nordic countries were still skeptical of the MSC, leading KRAV to believe its own initiative could gain acceptance in Scandinavia (KRAV 2002). However, it remains a project limited to developing standards for "Swedish and possibly Norwegian fisheries" (KRAV 2002). Naturland was next. In 2007, it announced its intentions to develop wild-capture fisheries standards designed to better the livelihoods of fishers, an aspect of the MSC that had long been debated. In a press release, Naturland's spokesperson explained: "Through our work in many developing countries, we felt it would not be justified to certify a fishery which does not offer fair and decent working or living conditions for the fishermen employed in [the fishery]" (Organic Consumers Association 2007). The streamlined approach the MSC had taken to addressing the social side of fisheries sustainability gave Naturland the opportunity to develop an alternative approach that it suggests will be more attuned to these issues. As of 2011, Naturland had pilot tested its standard in Tanzania and a number of fisheries were undergoing certification.

The FLO was the final program to consider expanding to fisheries. This idea had roots in a German Fair Trade initiative to link with the South Indian Federation of Fishermen Societies to develop a fair-trade fish and seafood initiative (Mathew 2004; Kurien 2000). The project was announced at a Seafood Fair in Bremen, Germany, in March 2000. It was then not until early 2011 that the FLO announced work on fair-trade standards for shrimp; the organization justified the need for the standard, noting: "Many smallholder shrimp farmers face difficulties in gaining access to market and in maintaining sustainable development of their livelihoods. This project seeks to develop standards for Fairtrade certification of smallholder shrimp farming and organizations which will enable them to maintain livelihoods and produce in a more socially and environmentally responsible manner" (FLO 2011b). The FLO has undertaken two rounds of consultation on a draft standard, but no final program is operational. Even though it took over ten years for the idea to stick, it was indicative of latent interest in alternatives friendlier to the interests and needs of small-scale fisheries.

On the second track, two entirely new programs also formed. The first, Friend of the Sea, is unique as the only fishery program to address both aquaculture and wild capture. Its roots extend back to the early 2000s. Led by a European representative of Earth Island Institute, Paolo Bray, the program claimed to have undertaken a preliminary assessment of the Azorean Tuna Fishery by the summer of 2001 (Friend of the Sea 2001b) and reported having the support of the retailer COOP Italia (Friend of the Sea 2001a). For the time, however, it remained largely dormant. It gained attention around 2006, which is now considered the year of its official launch (Kalfagianni and Pattberg 2013). It now claims to have assessed 10 million metric tons, 500,000 of which are from fish-farming operations (Washington and Ababouch 2011; Boyd and Mc-Nevin 2012).

The final and most recent initiative is the Aquaculture Stewardship Council. Launched in 2010 as a partnership of the WWF and the Dutch Sustainable Trade Initiative (IDH), it has roots in the WWF's aquaculture dialogues. Similar to the GAA, the WWF began with an interest in shrimp farming, given the sector's prominent growth in the early 1990s (Auld and McKee 2012). This led to further WWF aquaculture dialogues on a number of different species. For instance, in 2004, it hosted a Salmon Aquaculture Dialogue, which included sixty individuals from nine countries (WWF 2007). A series of meetings, technical reports, and draft standards were generated, culminating in the release of the final draft standard in February 2012 (WWF 2012). This process aimed to develop standards for appropriate salmon farming practices, and it fit with the WWF's overall hope to develop "BMP [Better Management Practices] based aquaculture certification programs for key species," an initiative with funding support from the David and Lucile Packard Foundation.[26] The WWF explained that although there are many other existing schemes, none "have met WWF's goal of creating concise, measurable standards that will lead to effective reduction of the most important environmental and social impacts of aquaculture."[27] The ASC was the culmination of this work. The WWF hopes it will serve as a new credible certification program within aquaculture.

Thus, as of 2012, the certification of seafood had changed considerably. The MSC remained central for capture fisheries, yet its early decisions to give little specific attention to the social side of fisheries practices and to not address aquaculture have enabled additional initiatives to enter. Indeed, according to Friend of the Sea's numbers, it has surpassed the tonnage of fisheries certified by the MSC (figure 8.3). Characterizing the Friend of the Sea as a producer-backed initiative akin to the PEFC in the forest sector, however, is tricky. On the one hand, it has served as an alternative for producers that felt the MSC was too costly or controversial. For instance, the British Columbian salmon fishery received endorsement from Friend of the Sea in October 2007. In the press release on the assessment, the general manager of the British Columbian Salmon Marketing Council made clear that the program was preferred over others due to its more lenient standards on discards and seabed impacts (Friend of the Sea 2007). On the other hand, the program adapted its standards in 2008 to incorporate Greenpeace Criteria for Sustainable Fisheries in an attempt to increase the program's legitimacy, yet Greenpeace still does not endorse any certification programs and, when assessing the Friend of the Sea program, noted numerous shortfalls in its procedures and rules that undermine the credibility of the program, even if the paper standards are reasonably high (Greenpeace 2009a). Importantly, however, Greenpeace has been equally critical of the MSC; and, as this chapter has shown, the group continues to express these apprehensions (Greenpeace 2009b; Trenor 2012).

On the aquaculture side, organics has continued to expand, but its influence over the sector has been dwarfed by the GAA, Friend of the Sea, and Global GAP. For 2011, Global GAP and Friend of the Sea were both estimated to have certified 500,000 metric tons of fish-farming production, with the GAA program covering another 304,798 metric tons (Boyd and McNevin 2012). In September 2012, the first-ever ASC certificate was awarded to Vinh Hoan's Tan Hoa farm in Vietnam, which

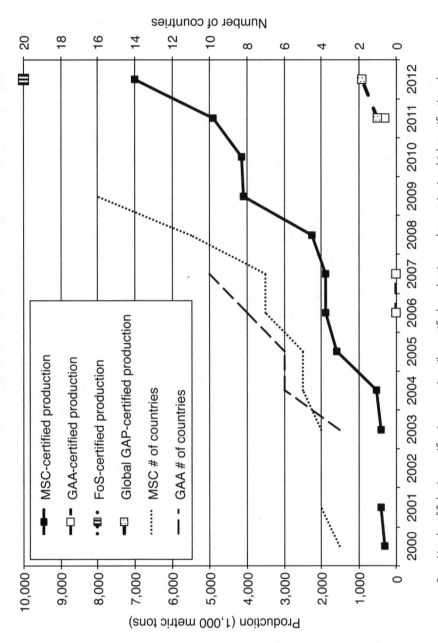

FIGURE 8.3. Uptake of fisheries certification over time (by certified production and countries in which certifications have occurred). The data are from the annual reports and Web sites for the various certification programs as well as Washington and Ababouch 2011; Boyd and McNevin 2012.

produces pangasius (ASC 2012). With the launch of the ASC and this early certificate, much remains uncertain about the future direction of aquaculture certification and, by extension, fisheries certification.

The fisheries sector posed a puzzle in and of itself. While a "dolphin-safe" label for canned tuna emerged in the early 1990s, it would take until the mid-1990s for the idea of fisheries certification to take form. Organic certifiers began developing standards for aquaculture in the late 1980s and early 1990s, and were followed by the launch of the MSC in 1996. Thus, rather than a progressive development of fisheries certification programs, the early promotion of single-species labels and campaigns actually slowed the sectorwide adoption of certification as an idea or a practice. This pattern reinforces the overall argument that early local-first certification initiatives tend to impede rather than assist the quick adoption of a global program. In addition to the sector's political and market structures, the later timing of initiation and consolidation meant there was a larger body of collective knowledge on certification from which to model new initiatives. To conclude this chapter, the discussion reviews how these developments played out in light of the explanatory framework offered in chapter 2.

With initiation, an ITTO-like venue was not available in which groups could collect and collaborate around the idea of a certification initiative. Although the intergovernmental processes discussed in chapter 3 were open to NGO participation, the existing devolution of management and decision-making authority to RFMOs meant fisheries governance was regionalized much more than forestry at the time when it mattered for the initiation of certification. Moreover, most attention focused on single species rather than oceans as a whole. This further fragmented the community, and was reinforced by U.S. laws that had facilitated the reasonably successful internationalization of conservation policies addressing key issues such as whaling and the protection of dolphins and sea turtles. Hence, NGOs were going where the levers for change were most well developed, and in the United States these were federal legislation and boycott campaigns. In line with hypothesis 4—*When international political opportunity structures are more open than domestic ones, the development of global-first programs is more likely*—these features of the fishery sector stalled what might have otherwise been early interest in the creation of an overarching certification program. Rather, it took modeling efforts within organics and the role of the WWF and Unilever to get fisheries certification started. The partnership between the WWF and Unilever is revealing when contrasted with the coalition involved in forming the FSC. The FSC had the early backing of groups such as Friends of the Earth and Greenpeace; auditors such as SCS and the nascent SmartWood program; the WWF; and buyers, particularly B&Q. In taking the ideas of the FSC to the fisheries sector, the WWF sought to avoid the controversies that the FSC faced given the diverse perspectives of its founders. This conscious modeling effort was reflected in the MSC's initial design and offers support to hypothesis 6—*Certification's policy scope and regulatory domain will be a reflection of the founders' perceptions of key social and environmental problems and the necessary solutions.* With the FSC, the founders had concerns for the social aspects of forest management that were not central to the WWF's perspective, and partly as a consequence, the MSC emerged with a narrower purview than its forestry counterpart. In addition, the fact that the MSC formed without a similar membership structure to the FSC also illustrates the normative power of the FSC's open approach. MSC founders spent a considerable amount of energy justifying their decision.

To move to stage 2, the contrast between the MSC and IFOAM's efforts in aquaculture illustrates the mechanisms of reproduction perpetuating initial choices. While the MSC's choice to be streamlined in its governance and standards helped facilitate a speedy launch, the program then faced the challenge of convincing outside actors that it was worth supporting. This decision and the results illustrate the logic of hypothesis 10—*When existing certification programs offer opportunities for influence from within, the likelihood of new programs developing is diminished.* Although the MSC has made progress in gaining outside support, the limited openness to outside stakeholders tipped the scales in favor of outside options for many actors. With organics, much as with coffee, aquaculture was trapped in a pattern of development set in motion for organics as a whole, and hence this feature of fisheries also lends support to the logic of hypothesis 8—*Certification programs that are unable or choose not to respond to external pressures create opportunities for the emergence of new programs.*

That organics struggled to consolidate quickly and the MSC was working to convince the conservation community that its program was legitimate meant there were many more opportunities for entry than in forestry. And though it may have appeared that a two-program competition was poised to emerge when the RFS-GAA collaboration formed, both of these initiatives were not as much reactions to the MSC as they were reactions to other NGO campaigns. Recall that the Ocean Trust was expending energy fighting the boycott campaigns and seafood buyer guides developed by Blue Ocean Institute and others. To complicate matters, the MSC remained focused on ocean capture, meaning that even if NGOs were willing to back the program, it was only a partial solution. Indeed, Wal-Mart ended up supporting the GAA program for its shrimp purchases and the MSC for capture fisheries. These facets of the fishery sector offer support to hypothesis 9—*When existing certification programs have a narrow policy scope or regulatory domain, new programs are likely to be complements; when early programs have a broad policy scope or regulatory domain, new programs are more likely to be competitors.* Had the MSC made the early choice to focus on aquaculture and ocean-capture facets of the fisheries sector, later-developing programs would have more likely been competitors.

As the situation currently stands, it appears that more fragmentation is due before there will be any consolidation. Organic certifiers have begun creating ocean-capture programs; the ASC stands poised to develop as an MSC equivalent for aquaculture; and even the ISO is entering the arena with work on a standard for ocean-capture and aquaculture production. It is clear, nonetheless, that early choices of the MSC and the IFOAM were pivotal in shaping the direction certification developments have taken in the fisheries sector, and these results will have reverberations for some time to come.

CHAPTER NINE

Certification Emergence and
Growth Across Sectors

THE DEVELOPMENT OF CERTIFICATION programs in the forestry, coffee, and fisheries sectors posed a puzzle for current thinking on the potential of these initiatives as global governors. At their core, these certification systems attempt to promote business practices that provide collective benefits, such as improved environmental conditions or equitable terms of economic exchange. Since they are voluntary, a simple economic model predicts a higher supply of these collective benefits when market demand rises—that is, when either businesses or individuals pay more for certified products. With higher demand, by this logic, more companies and auditors would rush to the market to supply these valued goods up to the point where their marginal cost of production equaled the per-unit price. This logic underlies efforts to increase interest in labeled products through outreach and marketing.

Examining the history of forest, coffee, and fisheries certification programs reveals a more complicated pattern. The simple economic model is not wrong, but it is incomplete: it does not tell us which institutions will provide the information and trust necessary to make these economic transactions possible. As the empirical chapters revealed, it was around these issues that disagreement and contestation revolved. And this insight means—most important—that focusing only on incentives to get participants involved and preventing them from shirking their responsibilities to implement fails to recognize that the institutions themselves may be the locus of controversy. Simply put, different types of benefits accruing from certification programs generate incentives to protect relative gains (or protect against relative losses) and hence stoke the fire of political contest.

By examining the initiation and growth of certification within and across the sectors, this book revealed important historical legacies that existing literature does not adequately recognize. Overlooked aspects of the institutional form affected the internal development of programs and the patterns of emergence at the sector level. The unintentional or intentional choice to begin with local and fragmented certification efforts generated important differences in the challenges facing programs. Those programs that started global faced the top-down challenge of courting potential supporters and preventing entry by competitor programs that aimed to offer alternative means to the same end. Those programs that started locally faced similar threats of competitive entry but also faced the bottom-up challenge of finding means to coordinate preexisting standards development and auditing efforts. Identifying and accounting for these differences serves to make sense of otherwise puzzling disparities in the patterns of development across the analyzed sectors and programs.

Several implications flow from these insights. First, program initiation matters. Early decisions that give favor to one set of actors will create inertia by generating a coalition supporting the status quo over change. As the analysis revealed, the emergence of fair trade and organics illustrates how beginning with fragmented, localized certification standards and labels led to contestation when the later efforts to globally coordinate developed. Whether local or global efforts were the point of departure hinged on the political and market structures in the sector, the information available to the founders, and the founders' resources and capabilities. Once in place, however, early choices set in motion processes of reproduction, constraining the opportunities for future adaptation.

Also critical were early decisions about what issues to address (policy scope), which actors to regulate (policy domain), and what opportunities for voice should be given to interested stakeholders. With opportunities for voice, programs made different choices about membership rules which, in turn, shaped the value of actors' outside options. Greater opportunities for voice diminished the value of outside options, all else being equal. With the first two issues, the world is replete with social and environmental problems; any given sector has numerous production processes with the potential to create negative social or environmental impacts. Hence, there is no reason to expect that a program will take on a policy scope and domain that addresses all the possible problems relevant to a given economic sector (see, for example, Visseren-Hamakers and Glasbergen 2007; Auld 2014a). To the extent that a collective action effort, in this case a certification program, is narrow in focus, such as the FLO's and its predecessors' attention to small coffee producer cooperatives, a window is left open for the development of new complementary programs. The reverse is equally true: when programs choose to regulate a broad range of issues and many diverse actors, such as the FSC's attention to the social and environmental facets of any and all forest product producers, new entrants are more likely to be competitors.

Second, although it might appear that first movers enjoy advantages and leave late adopters to pay switching costs, voluntary certification programs do not benefit from the lock-in effects of public authority akin to the nonmarket private standards discussed by Büthe and Mattli (2011). Certification programs occupy the middle ground between political authority and market exchange; they give more options for exit than the former and more options for voice than the latter. Hence, it is critical to consider against what outside options a choice to participate is weighed. As evidence from each of the sectors demonstrates, invariably actors did have other options, which they regularly exercised. This is particularly important given that benefits from certification have the quality of open-access goods—they are depleted by more consumption (rival), but restricting higher consumption is hard or even impossible (nonexcludable). Rising demand for these benefits will therefore create positive spillovers that make it less likely that only one collective action response will emerge.

Given these points, the simple model in which rising demand leads to higher supply may be true; however, this does not mean that more demand creates more success for individual certification programs. To realize such success, a program must do two things simultaneously: (1) increase the demand for its services, and (2) prevent new entrants. Essentially, a program would like to provide benefits only to those that are participating, eliminating the positive spillovers mentioned above. Yet this approach faces two powerful instabilities. First, there is an internal instability derived from differences in the costs and benefits accruing to those participating and supporting a certification program. When the shadow of the future is long, these differences, or relative losses and gains, give those on the losing end incentives to find ways to renegotiate the terms of the institution sometime in the future. Second, there is an external instability. As the benefits from being a participant rise, those actors that are excluded will have growing incentives to build alternative collective action responses that can serve as substitutes for the claims of the program from which they are excluded. These insights, moreover, give needed attention to the institutional design of certification programs. When programs are amenable to change and are open to influence (that is, they provide opportunities for voice), external actors may also choose to join a program to influence it from within rather than create a new program.

This final chapter begins by reviewing the three research questions and offering a synopsis of the findings to elucidate lessons for the initiation of different forms of certification. It then details the common and different challenges global-first and local-first programs faced as they evolved and the lessons from the sector-level patterns across forestry, coffee, and fisheries. Finally, it closes by discussing the conceptual and theoretical issues introduced in chapters 1 and 2 and the implications of the analysis for work on private governance and dynamics of institutional change.

INITIATION OF DIFFERENT CERTIFICATION FORMS

Social and environmental certification programs are composed of four general features: governance structures; monitoring and inspection procedures; standards for production practices and traceability; and on-product logos. The empirical chapters detailed how programs developed these features over time, a task that served three analytical foci: (1) explaining the observed differences across the programs, (2) assessing whether different origins affected the internal processes of programmatic change, and (3) assessing whether different origins affected the patterns of program development within each sector. The findings related to the first are reviewed here; sections to follow analyze the second and third.

Programs varied across four attributes: (1) whether local certification activities occurred first, (2) the broadness of the policy scope, (3) the extent to which the domain of regulated actors was restricted, and (4) what opportunities for voice existed (table 9.1). With the exceptions of the MSC, RFS-GAA, Utz Kapeh, FoS, and ACS, all of the certification programs began with local activities. In terms of policy scope, the programs were

Table 9.1.

Variation in the initial form of certification programs

PROGRAM	PROGRAM ATTRIBUTES			
	LOCAL CERTIFICATION ACTIVITIES FIRST	BROAD SCOPE OF POLICY ISSUES CONSIDERED	UNRESTRICTED DOMAIN OF REGULATED ACTORS	OPPORTUNITIES FOR VOICE (LOW-HIGH)
Forestry				
FSC	Yes	Yes	Yes	Moderate/high
PEFC	Yes	Yes	Yes	Moderate
Coffee				
IFOAM (coffee)	Yes	No	Yes	Moderate/high
FLO	Yes	No	No	Low
RA-SAN	Yes	Yes	Yes	Low
Utz Kapeh	No	Yes	Yes	Moderate
SMBC	Yes	No	No	Low
Fisheries				
IFOAM (fish)	Yes	Yes	No	Moderate/high
MSC	No	No	No	Low
RFS-GAA	No	Yes	Yes/no[a]	Low
Global GAP	Yes	Yes	No	Low/moderate
FoS	No	Yes	Yes	Low
ASC	No	Yes	No	Moderate

[a]When the RFS was operational, the program focused on ocean capture and aquaculture; the GAA now deals only with aquaculture.

more evenly split. The MSC, FLO, IFOAM for coffee, and the SMBC bird-friendly program each focused on a narrower set of policy issues; the FLO initially attended to social development issues whereas the other three concentrated on environmental issues. The nine other programs—the FSC, PEFC, IFOAM for aquaculture, RFS-GAA partnership, FoS, Global GAP, ASC, Utz Kapeh, and RA-SAN—took on social and environmental considerations with varying degrees of detail and emphasis. By this measure, their policy foci were broader. Rules about which actors were eligible to certify—a program's domain—were also split evenly. The FSC, PEFC, IFOAM for coffee, Utz Kapeh, FoS, and RA-SAN had no formal restrictions on which operators could participate. By contrast, the FLO, SMBC, MSC, Global GAP, ASC, and IFOAM for aquaculture had explicit eligibility restrictions. In the case of the FLO, only small farmer cooperatives could enroll. The MSC restricted its attention to ocean-capture fisheries. The SMBC developed its program for coffee farmers in Latin America where tree-shaded farms provided critical bird habitat for neotropical migrants. The IFOAM, Global GAP, and ASC each focused on aquaculture. The RFS-GAA program is anomalous. When the two programs combined, any operator was eligible in principle. However, work on standards and certification processes has since been led by the GAA, which tilted the efforts toward an aquaculture-only initiative. Finally, regarding opportunities for voice, the FSC and IFOAM were the most accessible organizations for actors wishing to seek influence from within; they both had broadly open membership rules. The FLO, RA-SAN, SMBC, MSC, and RFS-GAA partnership were structured with less open channels for influence. Utz Kapeh and the PEFC occupy the middle.[1]

Chapter 2 outlined two factors and associated hypotheses that were expected to shape initiation: founders' information, resources, and capabilities, and political and market opportunity structures (table 9.2). The discussion that follows reviews these factors and their subcomponents, helping to explain the differences noted above (table 9.3).

Market and Political Opportunity Structures

Hypothesis 1: When markets have low barriers to entry, the development of local-first programs is more likely.

Hypothesis 2: When there are concentrated points of multinational companies in a supply chain, the development of global-first programs is more likely.

Hypothesis 3: With higher levels of international trade, the development of global-first programs is more likely.

The events in each sector offer support to the above hypotheses. With low barriers to entry, the coffee sector was the most open to new entrants and, as expected, many individual initiatives formed. This began with alternative trade organizations that formed parallel distribution and sales channels within the sector, and it continues today with budding initiatives

Table 9.2.

Summary of factors shaping the initial form programs adopt

SECTOR	OPPORTUNITY STRUCTURES		FOUNDERS' INFORMATION, RESOURCES, AND CAPABILITIES	
	POLITICAL	MARKET	RESOURCES AND CAPABILITIES	INFORMATION
Forestry	Early timing; relatively open intergovernmental process with attention to broad forest problems	High barriers to entry; complex supply chain; multiple points of concentration; regional trade	Diverse and global	IFOAM, Max Havelaar, fair-trade organizations (e.g., Traidcraft)
Coffee	Very early timing; relatively closed intergovernmental process with narrow attention to coffee problems	Low barriers to entry; simple supply chain; globalized, bilateral trade	Focused and bilateral	IFOAM, eco labels generally, other fair-trade initiatives
Fisheries	U.S. laws help push up global rules; later timing of intergovernmental process	High barriers to entry; complex, but partly separable supply chain; diverse points of concentration; moderately globalized trade, with regionalism	Focused and global	FSC, IFOAM

Table 9.3.

Evidence supporting the hypotheses for the initiation of certification programs

| | SECTORS | | |
HYPOTHESIZED FACTORS	FORESTRY	COFFEE	FISHERIES
Barriers to entry (hypothesis 1)	Mixed	Yes	Mixed
Concentration in supply chain (hypothesis 2)	Yes	Mixed	Yes
International trade (hypothesis 3)	Mixed	Mixed	Mixed
International political opportunity structure (hypothesis 4)	Yes	Yes	Yes
Opportunity structures for legitimizing new ideas (hypothesis 5)	Yes	Yes	Mixed
Founders' perceptions of problems and needed solutions (hypothesis 6)	Yes	Yes	Yes

in the U.S. specialty market, such as the Community Agriculture Network discussed by Jaffe and Bacon (2008), which seeks to work directly with farmers in a manner that returns to the roots of fair-trade ideals.

Critically, however, low or high barriers serve as opportunities or constraints; they do not prescribe how actors will behave. Indeed, the forestry sector's Ecological Trading Company was something akin to Traidcraft or Equal Exchange in the coffee sector. However, as the hypothesis suggests, in the forestry sector, this was a harder model to make stick. The issues surrounding WFP's efforts to become FSC certified are another example. Greenpeace had been actively searching for small-scale forestry operations that it could champion as an alternative model. Because virtually all harvesting rights in British Columbia are allocated to large licensees, the province was not the place for such a search. Barriers to entry, in this case, restricted Greenpeace's ability to support an alternative commercial model.

The empirical chapters also revealed the importance of looking at the combined effects of factors, since the conditions of one might be offset by the conditions of another. This is apparent in looking at the levels of trade across the sectors. Coffee trade far surpasses levels for either fisheries or forestry, implying that global-first initiatives ought to be strongly favored. Likewise, concentration within the roasting and trading segments of the coffee supply chain created favorable conditions for a global-first initiative. Yet local-first initiatives dominated in coffee more so than for either fisheries or forestry. In this case, the limited barriers to entry, regional trade flows, and the lack of open intergovernmental process tipped the scales in favor of local-first processes.

A similar push-pull between the factors is apparent in forestry. The open intergovernmental process (discussed below) along with concentration in the supply chain favored global-first efforts. Yet the limited international trade appeared to be significant in favoring the quick launch of many smaller local certification efforts. Indeed, reflecting this, SCS, the Soil Association, the Rainforest Alliance, and others all had functional certification programs early in the 1990s. Without the open intergovernmental process, efforts such as those of the Rainforest Alliance might have gained greater momentum before interest in a global program formed. With B&Q involved early on, however, pushes toward a global program were hard to avoid.

Hypothesis 4: When international political opportunity structures are more open than domestic ones, the development of global-first programs is more likely.

Hypothesis 5: Where political opportunity structures are open, they act to legitimize particular ideas of key social and environmental problems.

Differences across the sectors underscore the influence of political opportunity structures on the initiation of certification. Within the forestry sector, intergovernmental processes played a pivotal role in motivating a search for alternatives to government intervention. The ITTO served as a venue wherein to build community ties that helped ensure that a coalition of actors participated in the certification efforts that soon followed. The relative openness of international political opportunity structures was, however, better at empowering NGOs to mobilize around a global certification effort. Producers were, by contrast, organizationally constrained to respond at national scales. Recall that a key international forestry association representing the interests of forest producers formed only in 1994, after discussions about certification had already taken hold.

Intergovernmental processes in the fisheries sector offered a mixed signal. They were open to the participation of NGOs, yet they unfolded later. For the purposes of developing a certification initiative, this meant they did not serve as a community-forming function as intergovernmen-tal processes had done in the forestry sector. In addition, many fisheries governance decisions were made at the regional level via the applicable RFMOs. This governance pattern focused attention toward specific fish-eries in specific waters, rather than the oceans overall, and it further frag-mented the community. Opportunities for leveraging U.S. laws to push the internationalization of conservation policies helped to reinforce this fragmented pattern. Overall, these conditions meant that NGOs did not turn to certification as a solution as early in the fishery sector.

With coffee, intergovernmental processes began much earlier and were less open to NGOs' concerns. The ICA, which was operational on and off from 1962 to 1989, also remained focused on rent flow and dis-tribution through its efforts to control international coffee prices. When other issues arose, particularly concerns over farm-level environmental and human health consequences of pesticide applications, the ICA—not any other intergovernmental process—served as a venue in which to build network ties and champion a new approach to addressing the emerging concerns about the environmental and health effects of coffee production. In this sense, the coffee sector was more amenable to local-first certification processes.

Beyond the question of program scale, the story elucidated how inter-governmental processes relevant to forests legitimized the link between social and environmental facets of forest management. Indeed, the FSC built its standard from the ITTO guidelines, and from the first draft it was apparent that social considerations would be included. In terms of the specific standards, moreover, the drafters of the FSC P&C and those involved in developing standards for the very many producer-backed pro-grams, and ultimately the PEFC, all drew on existing intergovernmen-tal C&I processes. Fisheries also provided evidence for this legitimation role. The MSC and the RFS both based their standards off the FAO *Code of Conduct for Responsible Fisheries,* signaling that this process was widely viewed as legitimate.

Information, Resources, and Capabilities

Hypothesis 6: Certification's policy scope and regulatory domain will be a reflection of the founders' perceptions of key social and environmental problems and the necessary solutions.

There are two important facets of this hypothesis to review. First, across the sectors, programs were partly shaped by the organizations centrally involved in their formations. The FSC benefited from a diverse and global set of perspectives. In the mid-1990s, the WWF had twenty-six national offices, Greenpeace had twenty-seven, and Friends of the Earth national affiliates and offices numbered over fifty (Wapner 1996, 77, 121; Greenpeace 1995a). In addition, forest product buyers were more globally networked than many producers. It was critical that the community established around the FSC had global resources and competencies; this tipped the balance toward a structure that could accommodate certification worldwide. For this reason, the competencies of the actors in the coalition supporting the FSC also conditioned the program's direction. The combined organizational capacities of the WWF and the early certifiers were significant. Together, they helped address the demand and the supply sides needed to support the new initiative. Importantly, however, this also set in motion certain differences between countries that had lasting results for the FSC. In the United Kingdom, the WWF took the lead in coordinating market interest in certification, building its efforts during the early 1990s. It then expanded this model throughout Europe. In the United States, by contrast, the WWF played a smaller role; the Rainforest Alliance, SCS, and members of WARP were key players. This difference is discussed further below.

The founders' imprint is also evident with organics and fair trade. In the former, the early work of developing standards fell on groups of organic farmers and land conservation organizations. Fair trade built from the strong network of alternative trade organizations and development NGOs that had long sought means to improve conditions for developing-world farmers. In addition, the Max Havelaar program started partly as a means for Mexican farmers to secure better market access; these beginnings created hurdles for later efforts that aimed to construct global programs. Interviewees speculated that had Douwe Egbert not rebuffed Max Havelaar's approaches, the initial development of fair trade would have charted a markedly different path. In this scenario, like B&Q for the FSC, Ahold for Utz Kapeh, and Unilever for the MSC, fair trade would have had a large corporate supporter at the demand side of the business-to-business chain.

The second facet of this hypothesis bridges into stage 2 of the analysis; it identifies how the designs of later programs were informed by the first-mover initiatives. The chapters revealed how early-forming programs were used as models for later-forming initiatives, and how the organizations carrying the information shaped the lessons being transmitted. The information drawn on for the creation of certification programs was multifaceted. With early programs, there were fewer specific models to emulate and hence the sources of information were more diffuse. In the case of forestry, debates over the UK delegation's labeling proposal was one key source, given that the Rainforest Alliance attended the meeting and Kwisthout was volunteering for Friends of the Earth at the time. The FSC also benefited from Kwisthout's research into the Max Havelaar model and the Interim Board's examination of the membership models offered by the IUCN and IFOAM. With fair trade, the seeming successes of eco labels were a source of inspiration for the founders, particularly in the United Kingdom. Founders of the UK Fairtrade Foundation were aware of the heightened consumer enthusiasm in ethical products and saw a label as a means to capitalize on this interest. Max Havelaar, by contrast, was weighing the label idea against a model akin to Equal Exchange in the United States, but opted for the label due to resource constraints.

With the later-developing programs in the coffee and fishery sectors, the flows of information were clearer. This timing meant that information, and who was carrying it, figures prominently in an explanation of how things unfolded. In fisheries, the transmission happened through at least three paths. First, organic certifiers entered the sector, applying the ideas of organic husbandry to the burgeoning fish-farming industry. Second, the WWF took its specific experience with the FSC and sought to replicate it in fisheries. Third, producers in North America responded to growing campaigns directed at fisheries by creating industry codes of conduct and eventually eco labels; they mimicked NGO tactics, but did so in their own name.

In discussing the role of information, chapter 2 explained how modeling is likely to be selective, an expectation that was strongly supported by the development of the MSC. Another illustration of the incomplete copying is found in the WWF's choice not to immediately develop a seafood equivalent to the Global Forest and Trade Network. This was surprising given that the WWF was the key player backing the MSC and has been the central coordinator of the GFTN. Discussions about forming a seafood global trade network began to make headway in 2007 (Fiorillo 2007), but to date nothing equivalent to the GFTN has developed.

Finally, there was a general pattern in the development of programs, with the three global-first programs all emerging after 1996. By this time, many of the early-forming programs either were attempting to globalize or were already global and hence they were models from which to design new programs. This might mean that there has been a general progression of ideas: early programs formed locally first and then sought to globalize, whereas later-developing programs were global immediately. However, the Rainforest Alliance program and the SMBC bird-friendly program are both examples of efforts that solidified in the mid-1990s but were not immediately global. In fisheries and coffee, the empirical chapters also revealed other nascent local initiatives, and the choice of Fair Trade USA to leave the FLO highlights that different development paths remain possible.

REPRODUCTION AND CHANGE WITHIN CERTIFICATION PROGRAMS

Hypothesis 7: With local-first certification initiatives, the development of market demand creates resistance to change that can slow efforts to create a global program.

Hypothesis 8: Certification programs that are unable or choose not to respond to external pressures create opportunities for the emergence of new programs.

Hypothesis 9: When existing certification programs have a narrow policy scope or regulatory domain, new programs are likely to be complements; when early programs have a broad policy scope or regulatory domain, new programs are more likely to be competitors.

Hypothesis 10: When existing certification programs offer opportunities for influence from within, the likelihood of new programs developing is diminished.

Does initiation matter for the way programs adapt and change? Did the differences in the formation of certification discussed in the last section shape the development of individual programs? With reference to the hypotheses, this section reviews what the empirical chapters revealed, which provided support for the hypothesized effects. Remember that all four hypotheses (7 to 10) are relevant to how local-first programs evolve; only the last three (8 to 10) apply to global-first programs.

Local-First Programs

In this group of programs, the FSC took the shortest time to globally consolidate. It took six years from the first SmartWood certification in 1990 to when the FSC had endorsed its P&C, trademarked its on-product label, and had an operational accreditation service. As just noted, the ITTO provided a venue in which multiple interests were able to collect around the certification idea; as such, it tipped the scales in favor of those interests preferring a global program. The WWF was immediately involved and linked the program to work generating support among forest product buyers. This would become essential later on, and it set on track the development of producer-backed programs, discussed below. At first, however, it meant that efforts to create the FSC were on a scale greater than what any of the auditors were doing individually, particularly SmartWood and SCS. B&Q's role in this regard was critical.

The character of this support, when contrasted with developments in the coffee sector, highlights how the type of demand is significant for explaining why resistance to globalization did not develop. As chapter 4 documented, the demand for the FSC, up to when it became a global program in 1996, was mediated by the retail end of the supply chain and most especially the European sector, which itself was heavily targeted by NGOs. When the FSC launched, it was believed that consumer willingness to pay existed for environmentally friendly products (FSC 1999b). Yet without concerted marketing activities, it was a stretch to believe that consumer interest would translate into market premiums. Moreover, it would not just be a matter of generating supply, since product-tracking requirements meant intermediate steps between harvesting and the retail shelf would require vetting as well. Finally, there was no reason to assume that forest product producers would benefit from consumer demand. Retailers might capture most of these benefits instead. There were pockets of interest in certification, yet the logistical challenges posed significant problems for those trying to increase market penetration. This meant, overall, that there were few reasons for early-adopting companies to resist further entry by competitors. Collins Pine even advocated for greater adoption, arguing that without it, market demand was unlikely to develop (Hansen and Punches 1998). This was the case for the larger-volume producers in particular, and given the FSC rule requiring that labeled products contain 100 percent certified material.

Limited resistance from certifiers or the FSC's national affiliates also facilitated the quick consolidation. The certifiers' limited resistance is partly explained by the influence they had over the FSC's rules and procedures. SCS was represented on the Interim Board and also on the first FSC Board elected at the founding meeting in 1993 (FSC 2003). SmartWood representatives, for their part, helped draft early versions of the P&C. In addition, the FSC had yet to develop a trademarked logo, meaning early certified operations were using the logo of their chosen auditor. After the 1996 launch of its logo, the FSC still allowed the certifiers to display their own logos in addition to using the FSC's. Finally, the accreditation requirements were leniently applied. Though national initiatives would eventually develop local interpretations of the P&C, in the absence of such standards, the certifiers could use a generic checklist that they would localize. These were supposed to follow the structure of the P&C, yet this rule was loosely followed. The certifiers were allowed to continue using their own assessment standards and procedures so long as they provided a cross-reference document explaining its equivalence with the P&C (Counsell and Loraas 2002; Scientific Certification Systems 1995). All of this indicated a level of deference to the existing certifiers that lessened any immediate switching costs a shift to a global program might have imposed.

Efforts to consolidate a global producer-backed program took a total of seven years, measured from when the first certification standards were released by a national program in 1996 to when, in 2003, the PEFC adopted guidelines for endorsing national schemes around the world. Similar to the FSC, producer-backed programs had strong connections to intergovernmental processes, particularly the C&I processes of governments that took place after the UNCED. However, the process just discussed made certification unavoidable for the forestry industry. In addition, the opportunity for voice within the FSC was insufficient to outweigh the value of outside options—creating competitor programs. The specter of continued boycott pressure amplified the need for other action.

The producers' efforts to generate a global program were less about opportunities for individual companies and more about overcoming constraints imposed by the structure of the market. Developing a collective front was slowed by the limited preexisting organizational capacity of producers. Because the outcome was a collective good, producer programs are a closer fit to Prakash and Potoski's (2006, 2007a) green club conceptualization. They sought to provide an improved reputation for the entire industry, eventually trying to exclude those producers that were underperforming and therefore tarnishing the collective reputation (Sasser 2003). Yet even within the producer programs there were hints of tensions similar to those experienced by the FSC. Because of variation in PEFC standards across countries, as the program moved to labeling products, these differences began to matter. For instance, German PEFC producers reportedly were unhappy about competing with PEFC products from other countries that they argued faced lower standards.[2] If the argument in chapter 2 is correct, these tensions will only become more intense as more PEFC certifiers use the label. The discussion returns to this point in the section on sector-level patterns.

Turning to coffee, the speed of consolidation was markedly slower. With fair trade, it took from 1988, when the Dutch Max Havelaar formed, until 2003 for the FLO to issue a global label. Even after this, Fair Trade USA, the U.S. member of the FLO, continued to use its own label, and it officially ended its membership in the FLO as of January 2012. Unlike the forestry programs, national labeling initiatives such as Fair Trade USA were the main source of resistance to a unitary global program. Max Havelaar, as just noted, formed to secure market access for coffee grown by small Mexican producers. In only a few years, the initiative's coffee had a roughly 2 percent share of the Dutch market. Partly as a consequence, a wave of other national labeling initiatives followed. Thus, without an intergovernmental forum in which to build a global interest in labeling, fair trade quickly emerged as a network of loosely affiliated national initiatives. This pattern had enduring consequences for fair trade and, as the next section argues, patterns at the sector level.

Between 1988 and 1994, while labeling spread and market interest grew, efforts to coordinate were punctuated with disagreements over how to formalize relations. Because the FLO was formed to coordinate the national initiatives, less attention was given to the inclusion of other stakeholders. Rather than having direct membership, producers' groups were represented indirectly via the producer assembly and their relations with individual national initiatives. Producers became eligible for FLO membership only in 2006, having lobbied for access since the late 1990s. Needless to say, other groups faced similar challenges to influence the FLO's decisions from within.

While the FLO adapted its governance structures, worked to coordinate standards development, and began work to professionalize certification, the national initiatives continued to maintain control over functions that were otherwise being centralized. Given that national labeling initiatives were largely self-financing and operationally independent, the FLO faced a higher burden of proof to pull them together as a coordinated whole. For instance, Fair Trade USA continued to monitor the licensing of its label within the U.S. market and had its own producer support unit, two functions the FLO aimed to centralize. Additionally, as just noted, it took many years to release a single FLO label. Adopting the new label meant spending money to redesign packaging and promotional materials and also required time and resources for informing consumers of the change so as not to lose their trust.

With organics, the shift from local to global took thirty-two years for coffee and eleven years for aquaculture. Organic certification follows a similar model to that of the FSC: auditors conduct the field assessments; the IFOAM sets standards and, more recently, it has developed accreditation services. Thus, similar to the FSC, auditors and early adopters were a source of possible resistance to a global program. Yet unlike forestry, organic auditors had many more years in which to invest in their own rules and procedures. The IFOAM took until 1995 to release a coffee-specific standard and until 1997 to release a draft standard for aquaculture, which was formally endorsed only in 2005. Years before this, auditors were conducting organic assessments in both coffee and aquaculture. The first-ever coffee certification took place in 1967; they became more widespread in the 1980s; and by the mid-1990s there were thousands of certified coffee farmers. With aquaculture, interest in defining organic practices began in the late 1980s. The first audits took place in the mid-1990s.

Coffee and aquaculture were just two of many crops to which organic rules applied. Consequently, they were influenced by general efforts to globalize organic certification. These moves happened in the late 1980s. Until then, certification had been left to the individual certifiers. Recall that around forty certifiers were operational before the 1990s. These organizations built reputations around their standards and labels and were driving a dynamic period of growth. The quick growth led to an erosion of trust among the certifiers. There were also economic concerns for growers, who at the time were frequently members of the organizations conducting the certification assessments (for example, the CCOF).

With the increased expansion of organic production, differing private and public standards made the costs of fragmentation increasingly palpable and led to efforts in several countries to develop legislated definitions of organic practices. This development was important for two reasons. First, it impeded efforts to develop international accreditation procedures that were actually just commencing under the auspices of the IFOAM. Second, the choice illustrates how organic producers were seeking ways to regulate competitor entry. The legislated definition of organics in the United States was at least partially a barrier to prevent further entry to the organic market (Guthman 2004). The introduction of government-regulated organic standards and accreditation procedures did not dissuade those in the organic movement from taking steps as well. Through a series of initiatives, the IFOAM eventually developed a stand-alone accreditation program, which was then spun off as an independent organization—the IOAS—and soon had its own on-product label. Yet many certifiers did not seek accreditation, and use of the IFOAM label has been minimal. Because entry into markets such as the EU, the United States, and Japan is now regulated, many more certifiers have sought government accreditation. Thus, there were still issues of harmonization that confronted the organic certification, a set of issues that has been the focus of considerable discussion within the movement and with governments and intergovernmental organizations.

From this assessment of the developments across the sectors it is clear that the FSC consolidated quickly in part because limited demand for early-certified products dissuaded early participants from resisting globalizing the program. Fair trade's early success in gaining market acceptance, by contrast, gave those with vested interests in national labeling initiatives reasons to debate the merits of coordination. The individual national labeling initiatives had their own vision for how fair trade ought to work, and they felt coordinating might lessen their ability to control these decisions. With organics, the choice to seek government regulation for the definition of organics was significant in closing off a path toward a coordinated system of organic accreditation operated by the IFOAM and then the IOAS. It is important to remember, however, that coffee and aquaculture were just two of many crops under organic oversight. Organic husbandry had a long history in Europe and North America. When market interest in organics began to build in the 1980s, it would be these producers that sought ways to protect their market advantage. As chapters 6 and 8 revealed, in many countries they turned to government, asking for legislated definitions of organic practices.

The discussion also noted different dynamics at the sector level. Within coffee, demand created positive spillovers that other groups could tap. That fair trade was unable to address issues such as labor rights on coffee plantations further enhanced the likelihood of entry, an issue returned to in the next section. This limitation was also part of the reason that Fair Trade USA has chosen to go it alone. In this sense, unlike in forestry, where it was clear that the PEFC formed to compete with the FSC, many of the other programs to form for coffee have been framed as—at least partial—complements.

Global-First Programs

In this group of programs, the recently launched ASC took the shortest time to consolidate—from launch to the first certification took roughly two years. Next shortest is the MSC. It initiated in 1996 and was an independent organization with a global standard, accreditation process, and program label by 2000. Unlike in forestry, where the WWF was part of a larger community working to create a certification program, with fisheries, the WWF was the sole partner of Unilever. (Later it was the sole partner in working with the IDH to establish the ASC.) As the previous section argued, this narrowed the pool of ideas from which the MSC was constructed. The WWF was principally interested in the ecological facets of ocean systems, whereas Unilever was under pressure from Greenpeace and also felt dwindling ocean fish stocks were a threat to its business interests. Auditors such as SGS or SCS and NGOs such as Greenpeace were not directly involved in the initial talks that led to the MSC. The timing also affected the lessons the WWF and Unilever took from the FSC model. All told, the founders opted for a streamlined organization that they hoped could operate strategically to get the program running. A choice to remain focused also guided the program's standards development. It led the MSC to avoid aquaculture and remain focused on the ecological facets of ocean-capture fisheries production.

To an extent, the strategy was successful. The MSC was operational in just four years. However, the MSC began facing the top-down challenges of courting potential supporters and preventing entry by competitor programs. Because of its swift development, the program has been heavily scrutinized. Questions surrounded the certification of certain fisheries in relation to the goal of sustainability and how the program dealt with the social side of fisheries management, particularly in the developing world. Given the many millions of small-scale fishers and their lack of management capacity, there were concerns about whether certification could help. Social issues are a continuing concern, and the MSC has worked to address these needs through programs to make certification possible for smaller-scale, data-deficient fisheries. Nevertheless, the controversy and restricted options for voice within the MSC helped foster the emergence of alternatives.

The formations of the GAA and the RFS, separately and then as collaborators, mirror the producer-backed programs in the forestry sector. The RFS was launched by the NFI in 1997 and, not unlike the SFI, partly developed as a reaction to new regulatory threats presented by the reauthorized Magnuson-Stevens Fisheries Act. For aquaculture, dynamics followed species lines and were a response to NGO campaigns. Under heavy scrutiny, the shrimp-farming industry moved first to develop an aquaculture certification and labeling program. And although the RFS and the GAA joined forces, the attention remained squarely on aquaculture. In 2002, the GAA created a separate nonprofit—the Aquaculture Certification Council—to conduct certification for its standard.

Much like the MSC's relation to the FSC, Utz Kapeh modeled itself on the earlier work of fair trade. The program began as a partnership between a coffee buyer and coffee producers, each of which were motivated to signal their responsible practices compared with competitors. These founders were later joined by an NGO that felt Utz Kapeh could succeed where fair trade had been unable to by mainstreaming responsible coffee practices.

In all the global-first programs, the challenges faced have been different from those of the local-to-global group. They have had to localize their efforts to gain the confidence of those stakeholders and producers whose support is necessary for success. Thus, starting local appears to frontload the controversy, whereas starting global defers the challenges to sometime down the road during the program's implementation.

SECTOR-LEVEL CHANGE AND STABILITY

Chapter 2 introduced exit and voice as strategies actors might employ in the hopes of influencing a certification program. The argument held that exit would be preferred when opportunities for voice from within are—from the actor's perspective—less likely to be effective than outside options. This means that when a substitute exists or can be developed for less cost than the expected cost of seeking to influence the first-mover program, exit will be more likely. Creating an alternative program, therefore, should become more appealing with increased market demand and more limited possibilities for voice. Also, the ability and willingness of a program to update its functions to meet changing demands should affect whether actors feel a new solution is needed. This was the logic underlying hypotheses 8 through 10. The discussion below uses these insights to shed light on the patterns of program development within the three sectors.

Forestry

Starting with the FSC, at least four groups of supporters posed an exit threat: the certifiers, national initiatives, NGOs, and buyers and sellers of forest products. Consider what was at stake for the certifiers. Of the four initial certifiers, SGS arguably had the most to gain from the FSC's global consolidation; it was the only certifier that had a global presence, with offices in thirteen countries at the time (SGS 2002). As an illustration, in 1996 SmartWood was responsible for certifying the greatest proportion of FSC forests. By September 1997, however, SGS was the dominant auditor, having assessed nearly 70 percent of all the FSC-certified areas. These were spread around ten countries. SCS and SmartWood, by contrast, had certified operations in five and three countries respectively (Auld 2009). With the exception of SmartWood's initial certification in Indonesia, both auditors had assessed mostly U.S. forests.[3] This quick reversal, with SGS taking the lead, suggests that SGS benefited more from the globalization of the FSC. Why, then, did we not see resistance from SmartWood and SCS when it came to globalizing? As argued above, this can partly be explained by the access both groups had to the FSC's early decision-making processes: their early opportunities for voice were sufficient to diminish the apparent value of outside options.

However, chapter 4 documented that the discretion the FSC gave to certifiers was, to some extent, traded off against its relationship with national initiatives and certain NGOs. National initiatives felt that they should have control over what the FSC would mean within their jurisdiction, including the accreditation of certifiers, and local NGOs were typically key players vocalizing these positions. The incidents with WFP in British Columbia and J. D. Irving in the Canadian Maritimes both illustrate a struggle between the discretion given to the certifiers and what national initiatives felt should be their role within the FSC system. Those concerned with forests in one specific jurisdiction were not necessarily inclined to forgo advances on their own goals in order to advance the FSC as a whole. In reflecting on this period, Synnott (2005, 32) noted: "With hindsight, we should have backed up the endorsement of [contact persons] and [working groups] with a simple written agreement, right from the first endorsements in 1995, followed in due course by the more comprehensive legal agreements developed later. Much grief would have been avoided." Chapter 4 documented this tension. The fact that certain national groups have developed their own membership base amplified the tendency to consider the program in local rather than global terms.[4]

Finally, producers did take the exit option. Some connected this choice explicitly to the limited options for voice within the FSC; with others it was implicit. At first, producers' efforts were national, but eventually these were scaled up to offer a global FSC alternative. In doing so, they generated self-reinforcing processes, spurring more attempts to foster support for the FSC. The FSC was, for a few years, the only global program, which helped it secure support from buyers, many of which were members of the WWF buyer groups. Unlike a pure coordination effect, where a network externality can make one choice rational over alternatives, certification's benefits were like open-access goods. Efforts to build support for the FSC created positive spillovers that increased the value of outside options for producers. They were able to form alternative programs believing that buyers could be convinced to accept them as FSC substitutes and, moreover, that this project would be much easier than trying to work from within the FSC.

For those supporting the FSC, investments were made to counter this by trying to prevent spillovers from happening. In this respect, the launch of the FSC and subsequent support from the WWF 1995 Group generated a self-reinforcing process in which investments by producers worked to legitimize the certification idea (see Cashore, Auld, and Newsom 2004), and created positive feedbacks that reinforced the overall pattern of competition. The presence of producer-backed programs meant, moreover, that NGOs offering only tentative support for the FSC faced stronger incentives to bolster their support, given the possibility of market penetration by the competitor programs. Thus, although the forestry case is one of adaptation and change at the program level, this masks a more locked-in pattern at the sector level. It also presents an important illustration of how competition among private regulators can have positive effects (see also Overdevest 2010), a counterpoint to Avant, Finnemore, and Sell's (2010) proposition that competition is likely to undermine effectiveness.

Part of why this pattern has persisted to date is that the organization of buyers' groups raised the stakes of certification; these groups collectivized the decision, making it a competition between different programs more akin to a dispute over contesting technical standards. In this respect, it is not surprising that the disputes have been heated, since the outcomes would invariably involve big relative gains (or losses). Yet, because of the public good dimensions of the problem, the balance of power seems inherently unstable. The key mechanism leading to lock-in within politics—namely, the rule of law (Pierson 2004)—cannot be generated endogenously by those involved in certification. This is probably why both the PEFC and the FSC have sought recognition from the International Accreditation Forum (IAF), a group representing accreditation bodies around the world. Since article 2.4 of the Agreement on Technical Barriers to Trade requires member countries to use existing or nearly complete standards in applicable situations, gaining acceptance by the IAF provides a possible step toward hard-law acceptance. As it stands, the PEFC is now an associate member; the FSC, through the ISEAL Alliance, was denied entry (Humphreys 2006).

Moreover, building from Crouch and Farrell's (2004) discussion of change, there is still latent potential for other initiatives to develop. Naturland still has a production standard for organic forestry practices (Naturland 2007) and has reported certifying "almost all" the larger German municipal woodlands.[5] Likewise, forests have been certified against organic principles in Spain, though the focus is on wild-plant collection, not timber harvesting.[6] In addition, there are organizations such as the Tropical Forest Trust that work to help bring producers up to a standard where they might be able to achieve FSC certification. Although it does not include third-party verification, it does perform second-party assessments for the member companies that want to confirm the sources of the timber.[7] Finally, the formalization of outside critics such as FSC-Watch shows how some groups have already chosen to work from outside to push reforms. These tensions have indeed grown in recent years as forest certification has begun work on carbon offsets, an issue of significant concern to groups such as FERN and the Rainforest Foundation. FERN terminated its membership in the FSC over this issue, announcing its decision in June 2011 (FERN 2011).

All this highlights that although the story in the forestry sector was dominated by the two-program competition, there was also room for complementary programs and vocal criticism to develop. These may, in the future, serve as the starting point for new initiatives, which should be increasingly likely as other problems relevant to forests gain attention, including concerns over land-use change and climate change. Taking lessons from the fair-trade experience, how the FSC and other programs in the field adapt to address these emerging problems will be important for determining whether the two-program competition persists.

Coffee

Coffee certification emerged in three largely separate streams represented by organics, fair trade, and the RA-SAN initiative, and thus the immediate challenge was coordination. This proved difficult for three interrelated reasons. First, the experiences of organics and fair trade both illustrate that the policy scope (what issues to regulate) and domain (what actors to regulate) of early programs shapes the sector-level patterns. The first fair-trade labeling initiatives were created to help small producers and focused almost exclusively on market access. Organics began with attention to farm-level environmental impacts. However, the subsequent growing popularity of sustainable development ideas that merged social and environmental issues, and the later uptake of corporate social responsibility by many sectors, altered the focus within the coffee sector. This created the impression that neither fair trade nor organics was a sufficient solution.

Second, much like forestry, the success of organics and fair trade created positive spillovers, enhancing consumer interest in certification and labeling. This gave late-moving programs, including Utz Kapeh and the Rainforest Alliance, opportunities to quickly gain ground. Unlike forestry, these later-developing programs were not pure competitors. Rather, there has been a great deal more collaboration among programs, with efforts to harmonize understandings on standards and certification, such as through the Social Accountability in Sustainable Agriculture project undertaken from 2002 to 2004 by the FLO, Social Accountability International, the RA-SAN, and the IFOAM (Courville 2008). The 4C Association also illustrates an effort to generate a common baseline for the whole sector; this role has been further strengthened since Utz Kapeh, the Rainforest Alliance, and, most recently, the FLO have become 4C members. According to the 4C Association, "Complying with the 4C baseline sustainability standard empowers farmers to undertake additional compliance efforts required by other certified standards" (4C Association 2012). Although mutual recognition was attempted in forestry as well, within the coffee sector various programs have received it more favorably. For instance, while only the FSC is a member of the ISEAL Alliance, in coffee, the FLO, the IFOAM, and the Rainforest Alliance were all members for many years. Utz has now become a full member, whereas the IFOAM has dropped out. In this respect, the pattern of support for one program or another does not neatly mirror the two vying coalitions apparent in forestry (see Bernstein and Cashore 2007).

What organics and fair trade chose to focus on was not mere coincidence, of course. The discussion underscored how important the fall of the ICA was for propelling change in the coffee sector. First, it meant the need for other solutions was palpable. The price decline that occurred immediately after the collapse motivated the creation of Cafédirect, for instance, and generally spurred interest in the Max Havelaar model. The second drop in the coffee prices that occurred around 2000—dubbed the most recent "coffee crisis"—corresponded with growing interest in Utz Kapeh and the initiation of the 4C. Thus price instability in the post-ICA era has become a focal point for creating private action to assist coffee farmers. Arguably, this is an inherent source of instability within coffee markets that creates a reoccurring shock, spurring cyclical efforts to offset the downside effects of price volatility.

To recap, the internal challenges organics and fair trade faced in attempting to consolidate served as a window of opportunity for later-developing programs. Combined with the restricted domain of fair trade and the initial social-environment split between organics and fair trade, space was open for other programs. The entrances of Utz Kapeh, the individual initiatives of Starbucks and other specialty coffee roasters, and the 4C Association all illustrate how the combination of growing demand for responsible coffee along with fair trade's institutional design led to further fragmentation. Add to this the slowness of fair trade to include producers as formal members and the development of the FTO mark for fair-trade organizations, and the degree and continuation of fragmentation seems almost certain.

Fisheries

That organics struggled to consolidate quickly and the MSC was working to convince conservation groups that its program was legitimate created conditions facilitating the entry of new initiatives. And though a two-program competition similar to the forestry case was poised to emerge when the RFS-GAA collaboration formed, both these initiatives were reactions less to the MSC than to other NGO campaigns. Recall that the Ocean Trust was fighting the boycott campaigns and seafood buyer guides developed by Blue Ocean Institute and others. The push for fragmentation was enhanced still more due to the MSC's decision to not develop standards for aquaculture; this meant that even if NGOs had wanted to support the program as a solution for fisheries challenges, it would not have offered a comprehensive answer. Indeed, Wal-Mart made a commitment to selling shrimp certified by the GAA and it committed to purchasing MSC-certified ocean-capture seafood.

The current situation suggests that more fragmentation is due before there will be any consolidation among programs in the sector. Organic certifiers have begun creating ocean-capture programs; Friend of the Sea quickly got up and running with a global program for aquaculture and ocean-capture fisheries; the Packard Foundation and the WWF worked to develop an MSC equivalent for aquaculture—the ASC—which was launched in 2010; and the ISO has even entered the arena with work on a standard for ocean-capture fisheries and aquaculture production. Underlying all of this is the clear effect of the early choices of the MSC and the IFOAM on the direction of certification developments to date and likely into the future. Indeed, KRAV's and Naturland's work to develop ocean-capture organic certification standards illustrates continued forces for fragmentation. Most often, within organics, certifiers are the innovators pushing into new products and defining initial standards. The IFOAM and governments then follow and have to work to coordinate the diverse standards that are already operational.

A related point has to do with the MSC's choice not to have members. A tentative comparison with the development of the FSC suggests that this choice had long-term implications for the MSC. Certainly, governance was again and again a source of debate (Auld 2012; Auld and Gulbrandsen 2010). The argument here holds that by not giving organizations a direct stake in the MSC, it was easier for these other groups to stay outside the process, creating their own initiatives or raising criticisms about the program without having to then help implement those changes. Placing Naturland's activities in fisheries in contrast to its choice to join the German FSC working group and help to establish the German FSC standards illustrates how the absence of strong opportunities for influence within the MSC made the emergence of alternative programs that much more likely. Clearly the outside consultants hired to glean lessons from the FSC were concerned about the FSC's membership approach to stakeholder engagement. Yet even if the MSC had chosen to adopt a membership model, it is uncertain how this would have worked. Having been coordinated by Unilever and the WWF early on, it was hard to separate the MSC from these supporters. There was interest in the MSC from the beginning, as was apparent in the debates that occurred in *Samudra;* had the MSC provided a membership option, perhaps groups like the ICSF would have taken the opportunity.

Finally, the fact that the WWF and Unilever were the progenitors of the MSC highlights the fragmentation of the fisheries sector. NGOs in the sector were by no means acting as a coordinated group when things got under way. Rather, single-issue or species campaigns were the norm. Moreover, the fact that government regulation in certain countries, for instance, the United States, was serving as a useful tool to change behavior made the need for sectorwide certification less apparent.

IMPLICATIONS FOR THE STUDY OF PRIVATE GOVERNANCE

Social and environmental certification programs are one of a class of initiatives in which private actors play a role in the formation, implementation, and enforcement of rules. In examining the development of programs in the forestry, coffee, and fisheries sectors, this book has traced the influence that different program origins had on the processes of internal program consolidation and sector-level patterns of emergence. This final section reviews key insights the analysis revealed for existing work on private governance and, in certain cases, points to where further research would be useful.

Variation in Form

That the programs varied in several ways is an important stand-alone point. It underscores how finer-tuned attention to the institutional design of private governance requires further research. Three main conclusions follow from the analysis.

First, and in particular, scope conditions on the various claims made in the literature would help research to better understand the different forms of private governance and their different development dynamics. For instance, Prakash and Potoski (2007a) usefully note the forestry-specific focus of Cashore, Auld, and Newsom's (2004) work, questioning its generality. The comparison of forestry with coffee and fisheries underscores that there are indeed differences across the sectors with implications for how certification programs emerged and evolved. Features of the individual programs, including rules for membership, policy scope and domain, and governance structures varied and had clear implications for program development. In addition, the two-program competition apparent in forestry did not emerge in coffee or fisheries. A broader scan of other sectors reveals similar variation as well, such as the variety of apparel programs (Fransen 2011; Bartley 2007b). Such diversity becomes even more apparent, and arguably important, when certification is situated as one form of a broader and growing array of private rule makers that operate domestically and internationally, and when the clear lines of sectors are blurred for global challenges such as climate change or land-use change (Abbott 2012; Andonova, Betsill, and Bulkeley 2009; Hoffmann 2011; Auld 2014a). The discussion returns to this point below.

Second, chapter 1 discussed how shared-reputation benefits might not be, in all cases, why companies participate in certification programs, implying that scope conditions are also required for Prakash and Potoski's (2007a, 2006) conceptualization of certification initiatives as green clubs. In the empirical analysis of the forestry case, there were indications that a club good conceptualization was useful when thinking about producers acting collectively to offer an alternative to the FSC. Still, the forestry case showed that relative gains threaten to become more important as PEFC participants raise concerns about differences in national standards. The 4C Association appears to be aware of these dynamics and has included explicit rules that limit members from using the program to competitively disadvantage other members. It has also chosen not to adopt a label, which further helps to reduce the potential competitive struggles for private gain. Greater attention needs to be paid to these institutional choices to help understand how participants will act when programs offer collective benefits, private benefits, or some mixture of both. More generally, Prakash and Potoski's work was too static in treating the standard-setting body as a relatively fixed and accepted forum. The analysis in the preceding chapters gave clear evidence of how the rules and procedures of certification programs were in continual discussion and renegotiation, supporting the conclusions of other research that emphasizes how losers in one round of negotiations rarely give up hope that a future renegotiation cannot tip the balances back in their favor (Thelen 2003; Blyth 2002). And given that certification occupies the middle ground between markets and politics, the likelihood of contestation in private fields of governance seems that much higher.

Finally, research on these initiatives would be further enhanced by careful attention to the varying financing models. The framework in chapter 2 noted the importance of funders, and yet their role was beyond the scope of the analysis presented above. Bartley (2007a) shows how the U.S. funding community played a pivotal role in building market support for the FSC through careful and coordinated support for the FSC. Government as an additional funder merits its own careful attention. In addition, the research revealed that not all programs were equally reliant on outside funding. Foundation and government grants are critical for the FSC. Some of the FLO's national labeling initiatives, by contrast, receive upward of 50 percent of their revenue from logo licensing fees; the MSC is also now in this position—56 percent of its revenue came from logo licensing in fiscal year 2011–12 (MSC 2012). Interviews with program officials underscored the significance of funding issues. Hence, assessing the implications of these differences has both practical and theoretical significance. Practically, programs must find ways to generate sufficient funds to survive in the long run; theoretically, the power to generate revenue, like the state's ability to tax its citizens, would symbolize a significant degree of private authority.

Dynamics of Change

Much like Vogel's (1989) work detailing the ebb and flow of business influence in U.S. politics (see also Blyth 2002), the analysis underscores the dynamic contest over the terms of private governance. The analysis spoke to two issues: the role of demand and private regulatory competition.

Demand had two effects. First, with fair trade and organic certification, the demand for certified products, once it existed, lessened the willingness of various actors to seek a single global program for these respective policy areas. Many organic certifiers chose not to be accredited by the IOAS, and very few companies selling organic products licensed to use the late-released IFOAM label. Over the years, these organizations had nurtured their own reputations, meaning the IFOAM's label added little value. It was more important at the time to receive accreditation from the main importing markets. Similar dynamics occurred with fair trade, yet in this case, national labeling initiatives were the source of resistance. Second, in the case of the MSC, the demand for certified products, including a great deal of recent label use in certain markets, has fueled the creation of alternative programs. In this way, market demand for one certification program had the quality of an open-access good—it created positive spillovers that benefit later-developing programs.

Private regulatory competition was most apparent in the forestry sector. The analysis—adding to existing work on this dynamic (Cashore, Auld, and Newsom 2004; Humphreys 2006; Overdevest 2005, 2010)—provides initial evidence that competition increased the speed with which programs consolidated globally. In addition, it shows how program design mediates these processes. Membership provisions were important for lessening the threat of exit; without them, the incentives for forming alternative programs grew. This underlines the dynamic nature of program emergence. The threat of exit pushed programs to change, but there were instances in which internal inertia meant it was easier for new programs to address unattended issues than for existing programs to adapt. Thus, with greater demand, late movers have two options: join an existing program or form their own, as either a competitor or a complement to the existing program. When a first-mover program constructs high entrance barriers or carves a narrow policy niche, the likelihood of competitive entry rises. In the former situation, it is most likely to become a direct competitor. In the latter case, a late-developing program could become a complement.

These dynamics also highlight the ideational change certification helped to reinforce. Early programs were small organizations. Yet once these programs developed sufficient momentum, illustrating the value of the certification model, opportunities for emulation grew rapidly. This implies that the certification model has itself, to a large extent, locked out alternatives. Numerous complementary institutions and programs have emerged around certification to support its continued growth— initiatives such as the Tropical Forest Trust's work in the forest sector and Solidaridad's producer support network for Utz Kapeh. Even monitoring groups, such as FSC-Watch and the Tropical Commodity Coalition, represent spin-off organizations that derive their aims, at least in part, from the existence of certification.

However, by no means have actors entirely adapted their expectations and coordinated efforts around these new programs. Actors continue to exercise outside options, some of which were early alternatives against which the adoption of certification was weighed. For instance, Bartley (2003) discussed how Friends of the Earth shifted from boycotts and buyer guides to endorsing labeling and certification. Other examples include Silas Kopf's ecology tax and use of buyer guides for various products. Critically, these alternatives have not gone away. In this respect, the choice to develop certification initiatives did not involve climbing a branch and watching others wither and die, never again to be available. Rather, alternatives remain available and offer examples of Crouch and Farrell's (2004) mechanism for change, which notes how actors have redundant resources and capabilities that lie in wait, poised to chart a new direction when the conditions are right.

Certification and Governance

Although the private aspect of certification is frequently emphasized, these programs are closely coupled with domestic and international laws and agreements. Organics serves as the clearest example of what close collaboration with states and international organizations can mean for the development of certification programs. To date, it has created a patchwork of standards and accreditation programs, not all of which have an interest in coordinating around a single uniform approach. Lessons from this process have made other programs cautious about the role of states in officially sanctioning certification standards or accreditation processes, mainly because of the irreversibility of these decisions.

Nevertheless, it remains less clear how private governance ought to be organized. Is a unitary global system better than a fragmented network when it comes to addressing the environmental and social challenges of our time? How does the diversity of private governance processes interact with the diversity of intergovernmental processes that are directly or indirectly affecting a particular social or environmental problem? On the first question, a comprehensive answer is beyond the scope of this analysis. Across the sectors examined, research has documented positive effects of certification, measured by the improved social or environmental performance and situation of participating operators (for example, Auld, Gulbrandsen, and McDermott 2008; Le Mare 2008; Giovannucci and Potts 2008), although in many cases the balance of opinions remains mixed on the value of certification.[8] The uptake of certification has been quite notable, as chapters 4, 6, and 8 documented, yet the voluntary nature of these initiatives does still raise concerns that it is those operators that are closest to the standard that are participating, not those that are in the most need of improvements, if issues such as fisheries depletion, forest loss and degradation, and sustainable and fair coffee production are to be advanced comprehensively. Moreover, there are many problems certification programs are unable or poorly equipped to address, such as landscape-level processes or extrasectoral pressures (for example, pressures to convert forests to agricultural production) (Auld 2014b).

Thus, while certification programs have made laudable progress, they face an ongoing struggle to bring onboard more participants and adapt to the ever-changing perceptions of the environmental and social challenges. Returning to the counterintuitive relationship noted in chapter 1, demand for certified products is necessary, but it is not sufficient for individual programs to contribute to global governance. The challenge facing programs is threefold. First, for a program to reach its individual potential, it needs to take advantage of high reversal costs, complementarities, and network externalities to give actors reasons to support it over other alternatives. Second, it needs to find ways to prevent exit and free riding. Finally, programs must be adaptable to new understandings of social and environmental problems.

The second question on how the diversity of private governance initiatives interacts with the diversity of intergovernmental processes has become a central topic of interest for scholars of global governance focused on issues including energy (Colgan, Keohane, and Van de Graaf 2012), climate change (Abbott 2012; Keohane and Victor 2011; Michonski and Levi 2010; Hoffmann 2011; Andonova, Betsill, and Bulkeley 2009; Biermann et al. 2009), biodiversity (Oberthür and Gehring 2006; Oberthür and Stokke 2011), forests (Rayner, Buck, and Katila 2010; Overdevest and Zeitlin 2014), and even election monitoring (Kelley 2009; Hyde 2011). In the face of persistent roadblocks to ideal-type intergovernmental agreements in numerous issue areas, all of these scholars—in different ways and advancing different arguments—have begun to explore whether and how effective global governance can emerge from disparate and fragmented initiatives, and what criteria such an emerging system should be measured against.

A contribution this book makes to these discussions is to highlight that the relationship between private governance and intergovernmental processes varies across issue areas and through time. This has theoretical and practical implications for how we approach assessing the value of these interactions. Consider just two different patterns of interaction. First, a great deal of the growth in the voluntary carbon markets formed in anticipation of a soon-to-emerge international climate agreement (Newell and Paterson 2010); since the failure of the Copenhagen meeting in 2009 and the slow progress of subsequent rounds of negotiations under the UN Framework Convention on Climate Change (UNFCCC), trading of voluntary offsets—facilitated by a network of private standard setters, verification programs, offset registries, and trading venues (Green 2010, 2013; Hoffmann 2011)—has been more subdued (Peters-Stanley and Hamilton 2012). Second, the interactions of private forest governance began more as a gap-filling effort (as explained in chapters 3 and 4), but they have evolved to become about potential synergies. Forest certification is now examined to understand its potential as a complement to the growing legality verification rules developing within the EU, the United States, and more recently Australia and Japan (Overdevest and Zeitlin 2014; Cashore and Stone 2012) and to climate change–related efforts to advance mechanisms for reducing forest carbon emissions within the UNFCCC (Levin, Cashore, and Koppell 2009). These different conditions across sectors and over time complicate simple conclusions about the pattern of interactions that will or will not work well to advance effectiveness.

More research work advancing Abbott and Snidal's (2009b) ideas of orchestration or Oberthür and Stokke's (2011; Oberthür 2009) work on interplay management has the potential to unravel these complications. If the analysis in this book is correct, the likelihood that fragmentation persists is high. Given this, for certification to matter even more in the coming decades, it will be incumbent on research to advance our understandings of how and whether a suite of private initiatives might work in step with intergovernmental processes to tackle the ever-growing global challenges of our time.

1. Certain government policy instruments are similar to environmental and social certification. Many policy instruments are not coercive regulations but are rather designed to give actors flexibility in whether and how they accomplish certain societal goals; these include voluntary agreements, public-private partnerships, and information instruments (Howlett and Ramesh 1995). Partnerships come in many forms (Pauline V. Rosenau 1999). They can involve coordination to address rule or standard setting (Knill and Lehmkuhl 2002), implementation (Avant 2004), or service provision, where the relationship (from the state's perspective) can be classified as co-optation, delegation, coregulation, or self-regulation in the shadow of hierarchy (Börzel and Risse 2005). The last category is the closest analogue to certification programs. There are numerous examples of this form of self-regulation inspired by the potential of government intervention, such as Responsible Care in the chemical industry (Andrew A. King and Lenox 2000; Gunningham, Grabosky, and Sinclair 1998). These self-regulatory programs are also sometimes important precursors to the global private governance systems examined in this book (chapter 4). At the international level, the absence of hierarchy indicates some potential overlap between the challenges of interstate cooperation and the challenges certification programs face to enlist company participants. The best analogue to certification is a combined procedural-regulatory regime. Regulatory regimes, as defined by Young (1999), involve rules dictating specific actions. The rules may apply to the signatory state, corporations, NGOs, or other objects of the state's jurisdiction. With procedural regimes, the intent is to "provide mechanisms that allow actors to arrive at collective or social choices regarding problems that arise in the issue area" (Young 1999, 28). These combined procedural-regulatory regimes match many features of social and environmental certification programs. They seek to create cooperation to address social or environmental externalities

and they typically have monitoring, sanctioning, and dispute-resolution mechanisms (Levy, Young, and Zürn 1994).

2. This is distinct from delegated authority, in which the state either implicitly or
explicitly cedes authority to private actors (Cutler, Haufler, and Porter 1999a;
Cashore 2002; Clapp 1998; Falkner 2003; Cerny 1995; James N. Rosenau 1995;
Börzel and Risse 2005; Avant, Finnemore, and Sell 2010). Still, private governance is embedded in a system of state rules, including contract and property law,
which are not directly challenged by the programs (Meidinger 2006; Boström
2003; Gulbrandsen 2006; Howlett and Ramesh 2003; Bernstein and Cashore
2007).

3. Organizations are defined to have an "internal structure, an institutional framework governing the interactions of those persons who constitute the organization"
(Jack Knight 1992, 3).

4. I thank Tim Büthe for this way of formulating my central research questions.

5. *Global* is used as opposed to *international* because these programs aim to form
rules and procedures encompassing all of the operators relevant to a particular
combination of policy scope and actor domain.

6. I thank Tim Bartley for offering this way of expressing my central argument.

7. Openness connotes how much access an actor has to a decision-making process;
those with more access are seen to have greater potential influence over policy
outcomes.

8. Others have examined the inclusiveness, but not explicitly from the perspective
of how opportunities for participation affect the patterns of programs that emerge
in a given sector, as is done here. The degree of multistakeholderism has been
of interest more for scholars concerned with the democratic legitimacy of private
governance (Tollefson, Gale, and Haley 2008; Dingwerth 2007; Raynolds, Murray,
and Heller 2007), or how it affects the stringency of standards a program adopts
(Fransen 2011, 57–60).

9. Though their work draws from the ISO to develop the concept of a green club,
recent work is applying this concept to other such phenomena in the hopes of providing an overarching framework for understanding the institutional dimensions
of private voluntary programs (Potoski and Prakash 2009).

10. In their words: "Having more members helps advertise a club more broadly
among stakeholders as one member's progressive environmental activities generate positive reputational and goodwill externalities for other members" (Prakash
and Potoski 2006, 51).

11. Companies may in this case attempt to self-label as environmentally friendly
(Garcia-Johnson 2001), but the problem of credible signaling impedes this approach (Reinhardt 2000).

12. Note, in certain situations, there may be other reasons consumers pay more for a
responsibly produced product, including prestige, health, or warm glow (Andreoni 1990). In these cases, the action would not necessarily be other-regarding.

13. Oran R. Young (1999, 87) explains that because of the incentive to cheat, these
problems "are not only difficult to solve in the first instance but also require continual attention to be sure that individual parties do not succumb to the incentives
to violate rules they have accepted at the outset."

14. This follows Strange's (1983, 354) critique of regime analysis: "The dynamic
character of 'who-gets-what' of the international economy, moreover, is more

likely to be captured by looking not at the regime that emerges on the surface but underneath, at the bargains on which it is based."

15. Although selecting on the dependent variable presents risks (Gary King, Keohane, and Verba 1994), because social and environmental certification programs exist in limited sectors, choosing cases to create variation across an independent variable risked not capturing the key relationships of interest. The length of time for which programs have existed in each sector is also particularly useful for the third research question. It helps protect against drawing conclusions based on extreme values of the dependent variable that may be a product of stochastic rather than systematic factors. Observing the pattern over time through the use of process tracing helps ameliorate this problem (Geddes 2003, 125; George and Bennett 2005, 223).

16. Similarly, UK-based groups including Friends of the Earth and the WWF, along with the Body Shop and Safeway, organized a Green Consumer week in the fall of 1988 to coincide with the launch of the *Green Consumer Guide* (Elkington and Hailes 1988), a UK equivalent to *Shopping for a Better World* (Urry 1988).

17. Jon Elkington, one of the authors of the *Green Consumer Guide,* explained: "Consumer power is one lever among many, but as yet an under-exploited one. We make consumer choices much more often than we vote or lobby or demonstrate, so the potential for increased pressure on industry and government could be considerable" (Thomas 1988).

18. The only exception might be commodities for human consumption, where health considerations matter; though even with food, taste and shelf life likely remain critically important buying criteria (Shepherd, Magnusson, and Sjoden 2005).

19. See http://archive.org/web/web.php.

CHAPTER 2. DYNAMICS OF INITIATION, CONSOLIDATION, AND PROPAGATION

1. Hirsch and Gillespie (2001).

2. This work is a reminder that the modern state system represents a historical anomaly. Merchant law (*lex mercatoria*)—now private international trade law—existed as a means for merchants to self-regulate (Cutler 1999; Jack Knight 1992). Merchants also formed guilds that offered welfare protection for members and their families (Tilly 1992, 130).

3. Ruggie (2004) and others argue that the emerging "global public domain" is serving "not to replace states, but to embed systems of governance in broader global frameworks of social capacity and agency that did not previously exist" (519). See also Lipschutz and Fogel 2002; Bartley 2007b; Raynolds 2000, 2004; and Fridell 2007.

4. Two exceptions are Gulbrandsen (2010) and Fransen (2011), who examine how program design affects standard setting and the character of standards. See also Auld and Bull 2003

5. Article 2.4 of the agreement states: "Where technical regulations are required and relevant international standards exist or their completion is imminent, Members shall use them, or the relevant parts of them, as a basis for their technical regulations except when such international standards or relevant parts would be an ineffective or inappropriate means for the fulfilment of the legitimate objectives pursued, for instance because of fundamental climatic or geographical factors

or fundamental technological problems." http://www.wto.org/english/res_e/booksp_e/analytic_index_e/tbt_01_e.htm; see also WTO 2005; and Büthe 2010, 304.

6. Gulbrandsen (2010) also cites this point; however, he does not develop a framework in advance to systematically assess these processes. His book primarily studies the conditions that enable certification programs to emerge in two sectors, not the mechanisms and processes of emergence.

7. See also Verba 1971.

8. See also Farrell and Saloner 1985.

9. See also Egidi and Narduzzo 1997.

10. See also Tarrow 1998.

11. Similarly large financial institutions such as the World Bank, but increasingly also private banks and institutional investors (Conroy 2006, 121–47), have been targets to leverage material threats in the favor of particular behavioral changes (Keck and Sikkink 1998, 23).

12. Many analyses of the coffee sector use the "global commodity chain" perspective to examine the distribution of rents along the supply chain and the possibility that certification can meaningfully address social justice, development, and equity issues (see, e.g., Fridell 2007; Bacon et al. 2008; Jaffee 2007; Daviron and Ponte 2005).

13. Klooster (2005) highlights how the high-volume demands of large buyers in the forestry supply chain are inimical to the interests of small-scale forest producers. Another way of interpreting Klooster's argument is that there is a minimum scale of efficiency to participate as a seller to larger retailers.

14. Numerous factors influence the bargaining power of actors (see Porter 1998a). In research on certification, Espach (2005, 2006) claimed that supply chain pressures more likely work in industries with high asset specificity. Roberts (2003) found that chains with numerous intermediate steps between producers and consumers were inimical to this kind of pressure. (See also Oliver 1991; Schurman and Munro 2009.)

15. Numerous scholars have examined these dynamics with self-regulation of the chemical industry (Andrew A. King and Lenox 2000; Gunningham, Grabosky, and Sinclair 1998), ski areas (Rivera and deLeon 2004), tourism operations (Rivera 2002, 2004), and forestry (Sasser 2003; Reinhardt 2000).

16. See Pralle (2006) for analysis of the implications of these differences in a comparison of efforts to protect forests in British Columbia and California.

17. Uncertainty underlies DiMaggio and Powell's (1983) mimetic isomorphism: facing uncertainty, late-forming programs will tend to emulate similar organizations they view as legitimate and successful.

18. See also Tarrow (2005, 37) for discussion of modular repertoires, which follow a similar logic.

19. Oran R. Young (1991, 19) provides a useful definition of this kind of actor, one "who produces intellectual capital or generative systems of thought that shape the perspectives of those who participate in institutional bargaining and, in doing so, plays an important role in determining the success or failure of efforts to reach agreement on the terms of constitutional contracts in international society." Similar forms of leaders are discussed by others, under different names, for instance, bricoleurs or strategic leaders (Campbell 2005, 2004) and policy entrepreneurs (Kingdon 1984).

20. See also Tsebelis 1995, 1999.

21. Büthe (2012, 32) defines this group as "socio-political actors who either overtly call for indicators [or private rules] or value them to the point where they are willing to give credit or pay some cost for their provision."

22. This builds from Stigler's general hypothesis: "Every industry or occupation that has enough political power to utilize the state will seek to control entry" (5).

23. The comparison between performance and technology standards nicely illustrates this point. Under a performance standard for air emissions of SO_x from U.S. coal-fired power plants, certain plants would be able to reduce emissions by buying low-sulfur coal at a cost lower than what a scrubber would cost to achieve the same emissions reductions. With a technology standard requiring all companies to install scrubbers to accomplish the same emissions reductions, this cost advantage for certain firms would disappear. Thinking of this in the context of certification, if a program included a rule requiring scrubbers to meet some environmental performance outcome, those firms that installed scrubbers are likely to resist changing the rule to a performance standard if this eroded their cost advantage vis-à-vis competitors.

24. Where a company is located in a supply chain and its global scope should mediate these effects. Brand-sensitive companies will differ from primary producers (Garcia-Johnson 2001; Sasser 2003). Global companies are also better placed to benefit from coordination.

25. I thank Tim Büthe for noting the importance of deadlock as a possible mechanism for why change does not occur. In this case, some veto player whose cooperation is necessary to change a program defects because no cooperative outcome is preferable to the status quo (for discussion of the deadlock game, see Grieco 1988).

CHAPTER 3. MARKETS AND POLITICS IN THE FOREST SECTOR

1. In 2006, just over 1.827 billion m³ of wood was harvested for fuel for cooking, heating, and similar uses. Another approximately 1.684 billion m³ was extracted as industrial round wood (FAO 2007c).

2. In Africa nearly 98 percent of forests are public; Asia has similar ownership patterns. By contrast, in Central America, only 42.5 percent of the total forest area is owned publicly. Panama is an extreme case, with over 90 percent private ownership (FAO 2006, 202–7, table 5).

3. In Indonesia, for instance, 60 percent of the public lands are under private concessions, and around 45 percent of these lands are held by only ten corporations (White and Martin 2002). In British Columbia, Canada, only seventeen licensees controlled nearly 68 percent of the total annual allowable cut allocations in 1998 (Marchak, Aycock, and Herbert 1999).

4. In 2006, nine Latin American-based companies were top-ranking global pulp and paper companies; combined they produced nearly 27 percent (or 8.984 million metric tons) of the market-pulp production accounted for by the top one hundred companies. Only North America produced more, contributing 40.7 percent of the top one hundred total (Toland 2007).

5. In the United States in 1997, the four largest pulp companies accounted for 58.6 percent of the segment's total value of shipments. The four largest paper companies accounted for 33.6 percent of their segment's shipments; the top fifty accounted for 93.8 percent (U.S. Census Bureau 2001).

6. In Finland, for instance, forty-five enterprises (or just over 1 percent of all Finnish sawmills) accounted for 79 percent of total sawmill production (5.45 million m³) in 1992 (Fahys 1995).

7. In France, where around a third of production is from deciduous forests, the average facility was smaller, and there was less concentration among large producers (the top 66 largest mills accounted for only 21 percent of total production) (Fahys 1995). In the United States, another mixed producer, 4,024 companies owned sawmills in 1997, with the largest four accounting for only 16.8 percent of the value of shipments; the top 50 companies accounted for 48.1 percent of the total value (U.S. Census Bureau 2001).

8. http://www.census.gov/epcd/ec97/us/US000_44.HTM#N444.

9. The report noted: "While temperate forests seem to have reached a state of equilibrium, tropical forests are contracting rapidly as a result of expanding shifting agriculture, spontaneous settlement, planned colonization, clearance for plantations and ranching, cutting for fuel, and logging" (IUCN 1980, 54).

10. The WRI, UNDP, and World Bank report did not address the tropical forests of Australia, for instance (Hummel 1986).

11. See Humphreys (1996, 61) for further discussion of the openness of the ITTO to NGO participation. As he notes: "It is one of the most open arrangements offered by an IGO [intergovernmental organization] for NGO access."

12. According to Keck and Sikkink (1998, 154), Friends of the Earth–UK felt the ITTO might be useful owing to their experienced success at the IWC. Interview, former Friends of the Earth official, July 2012.

13. Poore (2003, 43) quotes the following from Dr. Freezailah's address: "What is crystal clear is that conservation of the tropical forests is one of the specific objectives of ITTO. Indeed, it can be said that conservation is a precondition for the survival of the tropical timber trade."

14. A total of 800,000 hectares of 828 million hectares of productive tropical forests remaining in 1985 were considered demonstrably under sustained yield management (Poore 2003, 54).

15. Interview, WWF International official, Geneva 2002.

16. The declaration was prepared by thirteen social and environmental organizations from around the world (see http://www.wrm.org.uy/).

17. Three reports were released in 1990 documenting shortcomings of the TFAP process: an internal review conducted by the FAO; one written for the WRI (Winterbottom 1990); and a joint report published by the WRM and the *Ecologist*. The scope and depth of criticism was strongest with the third report. It advocated an entire restructuring to achieve a truly "multi-disciplinary" and "cross-sectoral" approach to contending with tropical forest loss (Colchester and Lohmann 1990, 87–90).

18. Poore (2003, 65) explains: "For some time, there had been criticism of the effects of the forest policies and practices of some nations, notably Brazil and Malaysia, on their forest-dwelling and forest-dependent peoples, and this was brought to a head by outspoken criticism from the Swiss citizen, Bruno Manser, over the plight of the Penang people in Sarawak. It was at this stage that the question of indigenous peoples became a living issue in the deliberations of ITTO."

19. Interview, WWF official, Geneva, 2002.

20. The UK Timber Trade Federation—the industry association representing UK tim-

ber importers—responded by downplaying the significance of imports as a cause of the problem, explaining that imports make up 10 percent of removals and that the United Kingdom accounted for only a very small proportion of this total (Gowers 1985b). Interestingly enough, Friends of the Earth was aware of this contradiction but, fearing a backlash on the grounds that any other pressure would be cast as neocolonialism, the organization reasoned that a focus on the timber trade was the most palatable alternative (Jeanrenaud and Dudley 1997; Dudley, Jeanrenaud, and Sullivan 1995).

CHAPTER 4. THE RISE AND EVOLUTION OF FOREST CERTIFICATION

1. Interview, WWF official, December 2007. As an example, the Rainforest Alliance attended the fifth and sixth council sessions of the ITTO in November 1988 and May 1989, respectively (Gale 1998, 131, table 8.2). The WWF attended all of the sessions in the 1980s; many other groups, including Friends of the Earth International and its national affiliates, were also regular attendees.
2. Precursors to WARP coalesced in 1989 (Delaney 1990), but its founding meeting occurred in November 1990 (Synnott 2005).
3. Interview, Hubert Kwisthout, May 30, 2007.
4. Ibid.
5. Alan Knight, later B&Q's head of sustainability, explained how even the company's suppliers knew little about the origins of wood. To answer questions the company had been asked about its wood sourcing, B&Q surveyed its suppliers, and as Knight noted: "We had this bizarre statistic that over half our suppliers couldn't tell us where their timber was coming from, from the country level. But 90% of them reassured us they were from well-managed forests in the same sort of survey. More than that, over 25% of our suppliers were putting some form of claim or reassurance on their products about forestry" (cited in Cashore, Auld, and Newsom 2004, 275n16).
6. Interview, Hubert Kwisthout, May 30, 2007.
7. An earlier B&Q press release, issued on November 18, 1991, responded to the campaign by noting the company was supporting the FSC, which included a £14,000 donation to help it get under way (PR Newswire Europe 1991).
8. Interview, Hubert Kwisthout, May 30, 2007.
9. Other UK groups were also involved. CRISP-O (Citizen's Recovery of Indigenous People's Stolen Property Organization) undertook "ethical shop-lifting" tactics, removing mahogany products from UK stores, including Harrods, and delivering them to the attorney general's office, asking that they be returned to their rightful owners—the indigenous peoples of the Amazon (Zhouri 2000; see also Friends of the Earth 1995b).
10. Not all groups clearly supported or opposed boycotts. For instance, the RAN, a strong proponent of direct action and identified by Wille (1991) as favoring tropical forest boycotts, was a member of the CWG (Bartley 2007b), the key group that helped form the FSC.
11. These occurred in Brazil; British Columbia, Canada; Oregon and Washington in the United States; the United Kingdom; Malaysia; Ecuador; Ghana; Papua New Guinea; Peru; Sweden; and Switzerland (Synnott 2005; Dudley, Jeanrenaud, and Sullivan 1995).
12. Interview, Hubert Kwisthout, May 2007.

13. In the Washington and Oregon consultations, for instance, industry officials underscored the importance of plantations as an "effective way to satisfy demand for wood products" and as a way to "relieve the pressure on natural forests" (World Forest Institute 1993). Recall as well that the first-ever forest certification was of a teak plantation in Indonesia, indicating that these initial choices pushed decisions toward including rather than excluding plantations from the FSC system.

14. Interview, WWF official, Geneva, 2002; see also Dudley, Jeanrenaud, and Sullivan 1995, 146.

15. Interview, WWF official, Vancouver, 2007.

16. Interview, WWF official, Geneva, 2002.

17. For instance, Rettet den Regenwald, a German NGO, submitted a letter to the Founding Assembly outlining the flawed premise of the FSC. The author of the letter, Dr. Rosalind Reeve, wrote: "At best the FSC initiative is naive, at worst it provides a framework for the timber industry to achieve a much desired 'green veneer' and defuse pressure to attack the real issues of illegal trade, indigenous people's rights and over-consumption" (Reeve 1993). Yet the organization still became a member.

18. Later, the Rogue Institute and the Institute for Sustainable Forestry joined with the EcoForestry Institute Society and Silva Forest Foundation to form the Pacific Certification Council, a coalition aiming to develop certification standards for North America's west coast (Ghazali and Simula 1996).

19. Some early-certified companies did report premiums in the 3–5 percent range (Stevens, Ahmad, and Ruddel 1998; Humphries, Vlosky, and Carter 2001).

20. See Hansen and Punches (1998) for further discussion of the Collins Pine case.

21. Interview, WWF official, 2007.

22. Over time the groups' percentage share of membership has fallen to a degree. By June 2001, the WWF had twenty members of the FSC representing nineteen countries and the organization's international office in Geneva. Greenpeace had nine members and Friends of the Earth had six. However, the total membership had reached 488 (Auld 2009).

23. After meeting conditions from a preassessment, Flor y Fauna was formally certified by SmartWood in April 1995 (Donovan 1996). The audit was controversial because of purportedly shaky growth-and-yield predictions and pricing expectations (Centeno 1996). Although the affair raised several concerns (see Romeijn 1999), the key point here is it underscored that there were different understandings of what an FSC audit ought to entail. SmartWood argued that it was never within the scope of an FSC audit to check the validity of a company's financial analysis (Donovan 1996).

24. Commentators from industry and NGOs quickly flagged upcoming challenges: guaranteeing that the non-FSC wood was from "safe" sources and ensuring that companies committed to move toward 100 percent FSC over time (Tickell 1997c).

25. Searching for "Greenpeace," "clear-cut logging," and variants retrieved fifty-five articles in the Canadian *Globe and Mail* newspaper between 1990 and 2000. Before 1990, there were no articles containing the search terms and only one article in 2006 and 2007. Articles concentrated around the launch of the Greenpeace campaign in 1994 and began to wane in 1997, after MacMillan Bloedel announced intentions to stop clear-cutting. (Searches performed using www.lexis-nexis.com.)

26. This was not an isolated case. Another British company, Meyer International, also

joined the 1995 Plus Group in 1998, committing to seek FSC wood, and yet one of the company's divisions was still a campaign target for Friends of the Earth. The group noted the company's efforts but explained that the campaign would continue until Meyer withdrew from the mahogany trade (Timber & Wood Products 1998a). "Meyer is continuing to trade in Brazilian mahogany, so we are continuing our actions. . . . We will not stop just because they have joined the WWF Group" (Forestry & British Timber 1998).

27. Interview, Greenpeace official, August 2008.
28. Interview, FSC official, November 2002.
29. Interview, WWF official, December 2007.
30. By July 2000 MacMillan Bloedel, Lignum, Ltd., and the Forest Alliance were FSC members; Bill Dumont of WFP had also joined as an individual (FSC 2000b).
31. An official with the 1995 Plus Group emphasized this point to the UK timber industry, stating: "The WWF 1995 Plus Group sources from 76 counties. Does Mark Crichton Maitland [the head of the UK Timber Growers Association] want to be part of an international scheme with international recognition or does he think that the retailers should talk to growers in every country to develop individual schemes with every one?" (Timber Trades Journal 1997c).

CHAPTER 5. MARKETS AND POLITICS IN THE COFFEE SECTOR

1. See Bacon (2005) for discussion of coffee production by smallholders in Nicaragua; see Mendez (2008) for a similar discussion of El Salvadoran smallholders and Bray, Sanchez, and Murphy (2002) for smallholders in Mexico.
2. Overall, in 2003, total world demand hit 115 million (60-kilo) bags, of which 87 million bags were demand in importing countries and 28 million bags in producing countries (Lewin, Giovannucci, and Varangis 2004).
3. Instant coffee is an exception, given its longer shelf life (Pendergrast 2001).
4. Committed to keeping coffee prices down for its consumers, the United States had even instituted price controls in the postwar period (Pendergrast 2001; Bates 1997).
5. The Cuban revolution had taken place just two years earlier, giving Communism a foothold in the Americas (Fridell 2007, 140). Pendergrast (2001, 274) explains: "In 1960 Castro aligned himself with the Soviets and began nationalizing American companies, throwing the United States into a panic over Communist influence in Latin America and further propelling the United States toward support for the coffee agreement."
6. This calculation is based on production data from the FAO (2007a) and membership data from the International Coffee Organization (http://www.ico.org).
7. See http://www.ico.org/history.asp.
8. http://www.unctad.org/en/docs/ditccom2004ich17_en.pdf.
9. A year later, after the U.S. House of Representatives International Relations Committee passed a resolution calling for a Uganda coffee embargo, the five leading U.S. roasters announced they had stopped Ugandan imports (World News Digest 1978).
10. In 1983, for instance, the total aid bill reached approximately $273 million (Financial Times 1983).
11. It began with a TV advertisement aired by WHDH-TV, a CBS affiliate, that targeted Folgers, urging viewers: "Boycott Folgers Coffee. What it brews is misery,

destruction and death" (Jesse M. Harris 1990). P&G then pulled its advertise-
ments, worth around $1 million, from WHDH-TV, and the channel, after an
internal review, chose to terminate the ad (Palmer 1990).

12. In May 1985, President Reagan imposed an embargo against Nicaraguan imports,
claiming the Ortega government posed a threat to U.S. interests in the region.
Only Nicaraguan imports that had been "substantially altered" in a third country
were permissible; roasted coffee initially qualified (*New York Times* 1987).

13. However, by 1988, the United States sought to quell the remaining flow of Nicaraguan coffee, tightening the embargo to include all coffee, roasted or not (Kilborn
1988).

14. Michaels (1993) noted that the U.S. share of African exports fell from 4.1 percent
in 1983 to around 2 percent in 1998.

15. There were splits within the U.S. government. When the White House threatened to block African aid if more funds were not allocated to rebels in Nicaragua,
reporters for *Newsweek* quoted House Speaker Thomas P. O'Neill stating, "This
administration has shown that it is ready to starve Africans so that it can kill Latin
Americans" (Anderson et al. 1984).

16. Tallontire (2001) referred to this as "solidarity trading." Coffee was sold with the
pitch that purchases were an indication of "solidarity with the producer or producing country" (3).

17. Subsequent research has documented rent-seeking behavior in both Indonesia
(Bohman, Jarvis, and Barichello 1996) and Brazil (Jarvis 2005). In both cases,
considerable waste was incurred due to efforts taken to capture ICA quotas.

CHAPTER 6. THE RISE AND EVOLUTION OF COFFEE CERTIFICATION

1. It began importing Nicaraguan coffee in defiance of the Reagan administration's
embargo (Rice and McLean 1999).

2. Interview, Traidcraft official, May 2007.

3. http://www.european-fair-trade-association.org/Efta/index.php.

4. Interview, founder of Max Havelaar, February 2007.

5. Ibid.

6. Reports on the size of the market share varied. Kochen (2003) noted that within
a year, Max Havelaar had a 3 percent share (Vallely and McElvoy 1989; Walker
1989). More conservative estimates indicated that it took until 1995 for the label
to have a 2.3 percent share of the Dutch market (Rice and Ward 1996); others
reported the program capturing 2.2 percent by 1992 (Bruin 1993).

7. Interview, early organic farmer, February 16, 2007.

8. Ibid.

9. Interview, early organic participant, February 2007.

10. Interview, official involved in IFOAM accreditation program development, February 2007.

11. Naturland, for instance, by 1997 operated in Mexico, Guatemala, Peru, Costa Rica,
Bolivia, and Cameroon, where it had certified a total of twenty smallholder cooperatives with around fifteen thousand producers (ICO 1997).

12. Interview, Max Havelaar official, March 2007.

13. Ibid.

14. An in-house Certification Committee was initially in charge of certifying producers and registering traders, processors, exporters, importers, roasters, and

retailers. The FLO Board appointed members of the committee but had no other control over its decisions (Slob and Oldenziel 2003).

15. Information from presentations made by FLO staff at Biofach 2007, Nuremberg, Germany.

16. Interview, FLO staff, February 2007.

17. Ibid.

18. This perspective was expressed by a representative of Starbucks during a presentation at Yale School of Management, November 2007.

19. Interview, FLO official, March 2007.

20. http://www.rainforest-alliance.org/programs/agriculture/shop/index.html.

21. Between 2004 and 2006, the Rainforest Alliance had already sold around one thousand tons through Drie Mollen Holdings, a Dutch retailer (Panhuysen and Weiligmann 2006), which commentators in the Dutch market saw as a test run for the label.

22. The coffee was sold as "Cafe Salvador" and the selling sheet explained: "The peace in El Salvador cannot last without economic justice for all. When you buy Cafe Salvador, you are not only getting delicious coffee, you are helping to build the new El Salvador. We urge you to 'be a part of the peace'" (*Packaging Digest* 1994).

23. In 1998, the organization secured a grant from the Ford Foundation (Rice and McLean 1999).

24. This was the sentiment of one specialty industry commentator, Donald Schoen-holt, writing in the *Tea and Coffee Trade Journal* in 2001. He explained: "Through all of this hammering of specialty coffee there was no outcry by Fair Trade coffee advocates and organizations about the 92% of green coffee coming into the U.S. that is not specialty coffee. . . . Something is just wrong with this picture. Instead of befriending specialty coffee, the Fair Traders came at the weakest link with a truncheon, while leaving the guys that matter, the guys that can really help the cause of the farmer unscathed. . . . If the Fair Traders actually mean what they say, how come all the pressure was applied in the place it would affect the fewest number of green coffee bags purchased?" (2001, 105).

25. Interview, Utz Kapeh, February 2007.

26. http://www.hivos.nl/english/layout/set/print/english/activities_in_the_north/campaigns/coffee_coalition.

27. According to Ahold, it purchased around twenty thousand tons of green coffee, which accounted for around half the thirty-eight thousand potential tonnage under Utz Kapeh certification. (See http://www.ahold.com/page/4214.aspx.)

28. http://www.sustainable-coffee.net/download/2007/4C_Members-List_Feb07.pdf.

29. http://www.ifat.org/index.php?option=com_content&task=view&id=3&Itemid=11.

CHAPTER 7. MARKETS AND POLITICS IN THE FISHERIES SECTOR

1. See also Schrope 2008.

2. The fluctuations in pelagic capture come from the South American anchoveta fisheries, which are highly sensitive to ocean conditions influenced by El Niño effects in the Southeast Pacific (FAO 2007b, 8). According to Pauly et al. (2002), at least some of this fluctuation is also caused by overfishing.

3. For instance, Europe exported an average of 25 percent of its freshwater diadromous species production in the 1990s and Oceania exported 22 percent of its total crustacean production.

4. For instance, diadromous fish exports and imports both grew from around 10 percent in 1960 to over 30 percent in 2000.
5. http://www.fao.org/fishery/rfb/search.
6. Caddy and Seij (2005) suggest crashes in these waters where scientific understandings are most extensive are "[the] most disturbing evidence of the non-sustainability of marine fisheries." In a series of papers, Pauly and colleagues argue that historically, sustainability in fisheries rarely occurred due to policy (Pauly et al. 2002; Pauly, Watson, and Alder 2005). Rather, it happened because a large enough cohort of the breeding population resided outside the economically accessible areas, given available technology. Once technology opened these areas, stock abundance steadily and sometimes dramatically declined.
7. http://www.fao.org/fishery/topic/16149.
8. The IUU IPOA was one of four developed by the FAO. The others focused on sharks, seabirds, and over-capacity. See http://www.fao.org/fishery/code/ipoa/en.
9. See Cochrane and Doulman (2005) for discussion of the implementation challenges.
10. Dolphins caught in tuna nets and turtles in shrimp nets are two well-known examples (DeSombre 2000).
11. Paul Watson, one of the group's founders, had formerly helped launch Greenpeace (Shabecoff 1981).
12. Based on key word searches on www.lexis-nexis.com.
13. Although the population-level effects have not yet been thoroughly examined (Hilborn 2006) and the issue remains under debate (Krkosek et al. 2006; Brooks and Stucchi 2006), a study by Krkosek, Lewis, and Volpe (2005) found increased sea-lice infection in juvenile chum and pink salmon migrating past aquaculture pens in a series of inlets in British Columbia coastal waters. Much controversy has ensued, including during the recent Cohen Commission hearings investigating the status of the Fraser River sockeye salmon (Auld and McKee 2012).
14. As an example of this regulatory lag, the FAO Committee on Fisheries established a subcommittee focused on aquaculture only in 2001. See http://www.fao.org/fishery/about/cofi/aquaculture/en.

CHAPTER 8. THE RISE AND EVOLUTION OF FISHERIES CERTIFICATION
1. Interview, Soil Association official, June 4, 2007.
2. A formal statement of intent explained: "The MSC will be modeled on the successful Forest Stewardship Council (FSC), launched by WWF, other conservation groups and timber traders in 1993 to promote a market-led solution towards more sustainable forestry practices around the world," and that both the WWF and Unilever would "contribute matching funds into an extensive scoping exercise to explore how the FSC model [could] be adapted to meet the specific sustainability needs of global marine fisheries" (Michael Sutton 1996).
3. http://www.msc.org/html/content_470.htm.
4. National working groups were also formed for outreach and awareness building, but not standards development.
5. Murphy and Bendell (1997, 173) also discuss the initial apprehension of fish workers toward the MSC initiative, especially since it was being driven by a major buyer and a traditional opponent, the WWF.
6. The Audubon guide to seafood published in the May–June issue of its magazine

was a large success. Reports indicated that in a year the National Audubon Society had received eighty-five thousand reprint requests for the guide (Jung 1999). These were timely efforts given that stock-assessment reports required by the Magnuson Fishery and Conservation Act of 1996, released in late 1997, indicated that a third of U.S. commercial stocks, i.e., 96 of 279, were overfished (Tighe 1997).

7. Interview, official from the Marine Conservation Society, May 2007.

8. In 1999, the Nordic Council continued with this work independently, setting up a Technical Working Group on Ecolabeling Criteria. It released a report in 2000 that again emphasized the importance of government or intergovernmental bodies as the standards setters for eco labels (Stokke 2004).

9. http://web.archive.org/web/20010417011535/http://www.earthisland.org/map/.

10. They aimed to fashion a U.S.-based consumer campaign that would respect the concerns of local groups in the countries where shrimp farmers were spreading (Stonich and Bailey 2000).

11. Jason Clay, with the WWF, explained to a reporter how the MSC would first focus on large industrial fisheries, such as cod and haddock, avoiding the complications of tuna and shrimp fishing (Christensen 1997).

12. This was a quote attributed to Rob Rosenberry, the owner of an industry publication, *Shrimp News International*. (See also Kevin Hall 1997.)

13. In fact, industry players were also aware that a similar coordinated campaign was being mounted against the salmon farming industry.

14. According to the NFI, the eco label would be available to "industry members who endorse the Principles for Responsible Fisheries of RFS or GAA's Principles for Responsible Aquaculture, and incorporate these Principles into their business" (NFI 1999).

15. Their press releases explained: "Both programs are open to all segments of the industry (e.g., producer, importer, distributor, retailer or restaurant operator) and require the preparation of reports or plans that document implementation of the RFS/GAA principles" (NFI 1999).

16. The NFI noted its support for the U.S. forest industry's SFI, which implies that it realized the RFS might serve as a future competitor to the MSC (NFI 2000).

17. http://www.naturland.de/englisch/frame_defs/framedef.html.

18. "Kate Troll, fisheries specialist for the state Department of Commerce, said the law laid out four main criteria for certification: a designated harvest area, a management history, management that protects the environment and encourages sustained yields, and a demonstration that the producer added no prohibited substances" (Joling 1999).

19. See Earle (2000) for a discussion of the Thames herring fishery.

20. Interview, WWF International official, May 29, 2007.

21. The World Bank, the IUCN, and the Great Barrier Reef Marine Park Authority of Australia, for instance, released a report on global marine protection that identified 155 areas where new protection or better management of existing protection was highly recommended (Kenworthy 1995).

22. In Australia, jurisdiction over coastal waters is split between the federal, or commonwealth, government and the state and territorial governments. The latter have jurisdiction from the low-tide mark to three nautical miles offshore; the former controls from three nautical miles to the two-hundred-nautical-mile boundary of Australia's EEZ (Neil Stump 2005).

23. http://www.dec.wa.gov.au/mpra.
24. http://www.aquaculturecertification.org/accacti.html and http://www.aquaculture certification.org/accgov.html.
25. It reportedly intended to initially focus on frozen cod, canned herring, and fresh shrimp and crabs (Haland and Esmark 2002). See also Boström 2006.
26. http://www.worldwildlife.org/cci/aquaculture_projects.cfm. In 2009, the foundation's Web site listed a $1,000,000 grant to the WWF for "continued development of aquaculture standards" (cited in Auld 2009, 431). See also interview, official from the Marine Conservation Society, June 2007.
27. http://www.worldwildlife.org/cci/aquaculture_projects1.cfm.

CHAPTER 9. CERTIFICATION EMERGENCE AND
GROWTH ACROSS SECTORS

1. This assessment does not indicate how democratic or stakeholder-driven each organization was; it only notes how certain programs were easier to access than others. The overall categorization also neglects subtleties including how certain groups can have easier access than others, as the discussion in the empirical chapters detailed.
2. Interview, PEFC official, Stuttgart, December 2006.
3. Arguably as a way to increase its economies of scale, SmartWood later formed a network within the United States that housed the many existing regional initiatives such as the Institute of Sustainable Forestry and the Rogue Institute for Economy and Ecology.
4. Interview, FSC official, December 2006.
5. http://www.naturland.de/ourdistinguishingfeatures.html.
6. http://www.organic-europe.net/country_reports/spain/default.asp.
7. http://www.tropicalforesttrust.org.
8. This is particularly apparent in recent evaluations of the MSC program. Several studies have been published using different approaches to evaluating the performance of individual certified fisheries to draw conclusions about whether the MSC has been helping to advance fisheries' sustainability (compare Christian et al. 2013; Gutiérrez et al. 2012). These debates can be read as an extension of the controversies over the MSC detailed in chapter 8.

REFERENCES

Abbott, Kenneth W. 2012. "The transnational regime complex for climate change." *Environment and Planning C: Government and Policy* 30 (4): 571–90.

Abbott, Kenneth W., and Duncan Snidal. 2009a. "The governance triangle: Regulatory standards institutions and the shadow of the state." In *The politics of global regulation,* edited by Walter Mattli and Ngaire Wood, 44–88. Princeton, NJ: Princeton University Press.

———. 2009b. "Strengthening international regulation through transnational new governance: Overcoming the orchestration deficit." *Vanderbilt Journal of Transnational Law* 42:501–78.

Aberdeen Press and Journal. 1998. "Summer Isles salmon selling point is natural conditions." October 21, business: companies section, 14. http://web.lexis-nexis.com (accessed April 13, 2007).

Adweek. 1992. "For P&G, war drags on." A/S/M Communications, Inc., January 27, Takes, Same Old Grind section. http://web.lexis-nexis.com (accessed January 27, 2007).

AFPA. 2000a. *Application of the sustainable forestry (SFI) standard in Canada.* August. www.sfms.com/pdfs/sfiapplication.pdf (accessed October 22, 2001).

———. 2000b. *Fraser 3rd party certifies all its forestlands: Lands in Canada first outside U.S. to be independently audited under SFIsm.* Washington, DC: American Forest and Paper Association's SFI Program.

———. 2000c. *SFIsm AFF's American tree farm system® and AF&PA's Sustainable Forestry Initiative (SFI)sm program collaborate to expand the practice of sustainable forestry.* Washington, DC: American Forest and Paper Association's SFI Program.

Agardy, Tundi. 1999. "Creating havens for marine life." *Issues in Science and Technology* 16 (1): 37. www.lexisnexis.com/ (accessed August 13, 2007).

Agence France-Presse. 1991. "WWF slams tropical timber body as ineffective." May 23. http://web.lexis-nexis.com/ (accessed July 24, 2007).

———. 1993. "Global timber pact should be common forum for all timber trade, WWF." May 10. http://web.lexis-nexis.com/ (accessed July 24, 2007).

Aikman, Phil. 1997. "Industrial 'Hoover' fishing: A policy vacuum." Greenpeace International, January. http://archive.greenpeace.org/comms/cbio/hoovrpt.html (accessed August 8, 2008).

Akerlof, George. A. 1970. "Market for lemons: Quality, uncertainty and market mechanism." *Quarterly Journal of Economics* 84 (3): 488–500.

Alaska Oceans Program. 2007. "About us." October 26. www.alaskaoceans.net/aboutus/msc.htm (accessed August 17, 2008).

Aldrich, Howard E., and C. Marlene Fiol. 1994. "Fools rush in: The institutional context of industry creation." *Academy of Management Review* 19 (4): 645–70.

Allen, Carole. 1995. "Label this battle 'turtle-free.'" *Houston Press,* July 20.

Alpine, Daniel Mac. 1998. "Collins rolls out certified plywood." *Journal of the Certified Forest Products Council* (Winter). www.collinswood.com/MediaEvents/Resources/UnderstoryCertPly.html (accessed July 25, 2008).

Anderson, Harry, Tony Clifton, Jane Whitemore, and Ray Wilkinson. 1984. "Ethiopia: Too little—and too late." *Newsweek,* November 12. www.lexisnexis.com/ (accessed August 1, 2008).

Andonova, Liliana B., Michele M. Betsill, and Harriet Bulkeley. 2009. "Transnational climate governance." *Global Environmental Politics* 9 (2): 52–73.

Andreoni, James. 1990. "Impure altruism and donations to public-goods: A theory of warm-glow giving." *Economic Journal* 100 (401): 464–77.

Andresen, Steinar, and Shardul Agrawala. 2002. "Leaders, pushers and laggards in the making of the climate regime." *Global Environmental Change* 12 (1): 41–51.

Andresen, Steinar, and Tora Skodvin. 2008. "Non-state influence in the International Whaling Commission, 1970 to 2006." In *NGO diplomacy: The influence of non-governmental organizations in international environmental negotiations,* edited by Michele M. Betsill and Elisabeth Corell, 119–47. Cambridge, MA: MIT Press.

APP Newsfeed. 2000. "Vic: International foresters meet." October 28. www.lexisnexis.com/ (accessed April 17, 2008).

Arthur, W. Brian. 1989. "Competing technologies, increasing returns, and lock-in by historical events." *Economic Journal* 99 (394): 116–31.

Arthur, W. Brian, Yu M. Ermoliev, and Yuri M. Kaniovski. 1987. "Path-dependent processes and the emergence of macro-structure." *European Journal of Operational Research* 30 (3): 294–303.

ASC. 2012. "Vinh Hoan awarded first ASC certificate for responsible Pangasius farming" Aquaculture Stewardship Council, September 17. www.asc-aqua.org/index.cfm?act=update.detail&uid=132&lng=1 (accessed October 20, 2012).

Ashman, Darcy. 2001. "Civil society collaboration with business: Bringing empowerment back in." *World Development* 29 (7): 1097–113.

Aslam, Abid. 1997. "Environment: World Bank woos timber companies." IPS–Inter Press Service, November 21. www.lexisnexis.com/ (accessed July 14, 2008).

AssiDomän. 1998. "All AssiDomän forests FSC certified." June 30. www.asdo.se/english/presscenter/pressarchive.html (accessed November 30, 2001).

Associated Press. 1998a. "Environmentalists sue federal agencies to stop dolphin kills." April 13. http://web.lexis-nexis.com (accessed April 16, 2007).

———. 1998b. "Forest firms look at eco-friendly wood products." October 26. www.lexisnexis.com/ (accessed July 19, 2008).

Atyi, Richard Eba'a. 2006. "Forest certification in Gabon." In *Confronting sustainability: Forest certification in developing and transition countries,* edited by Benjamin Cashore, Fred Gale, Errol Meidinger, and Deanna Newsom, 443–72. New Haven, CT: Yale F&ES Publication Series, Report Number 8.

Audubon Society. 1998. "What's a fish lover to eat? The Audubon guide to seafood." *Audubon Magazine,* May–June. http://web.archive.org/web/20000815235804/magazine.audubon.org/seafood/guide/ (accessed April 17, 2007).

Auld, Graeme. 2006. "Choosing how to be green: An examination of Domtar Inc.'s approach to forest certification." *Journal of Strategic Management Education* 3:37–92.

———. 2009. "Reversal of fortune: How early choices can alter the logic of market-based authority." PhD diss., Yale University.

———. 2010. "Assessing certification as governance: Effects and broader consequences for coffee." *Journal of Environment and Development* 19 (2): 215–41.

———. 2012. "Marine Stewardship Council." In *Business regulation and non-state actors: Whose standard? Whose development?* edited by Peter Utting, Darryl Reed, and Ananya Reed, 148–59. London: Routledge.

———. 2014a. "Confronting tradeoffs and interactive effects in the choice of policy focus: Specialized versus comprehensive private governance." *Regulation and Governance* 8 (1): 126–48.

———. 2014b. "Private market-based regulations: What they are, and what they mean for land-use governance." In *Rethinking global land use in an urban era,* edited by Karen Seto and Anette Reenberg. Cambridge: MIT Press.

Auld, Graeme, Cristina Balboa, Tim Bartley, Benjamin Cashore, and Kelly Levin. 2007. "The spread of the certification model: Understanding the evolution of non-state market driven governance." Paper read at 48th Convention of the International Studies Association, February 27–March 3, Chicago.

Auld, Graeme, Steven Bernstein, and Benjamin Cashore. 2008. "The new corporate social responsibility." *Annual Review of Environment and Resources* 33 (1): 413–35.

Auld, Graeme, and Gary Q. Bull. 2003. "The institutional design of forest certification standards initiatives and its influence on the role of science: The case of forest genetic resources." *Journal of Environmental Management* 69 (1): 47–62.

Auld, Graeme, and Benjamin Cashore. 2013. "Mixed signals: NGO campaigns and NSMD governance in an export-oriented country." *Canadian Public Policy—Analyse de politiques* 39 (s2): 143–56.

Auld, Graeme, and Lars H. Gulbrandsen. 2010. "Transparency in nonstate certification: Consequences for accountability and legitimacy." *Global Environmental Politics* 10 (3): 97–119.

Auld, Graeme, Lars H. Gulbrandsen, and Constance McDermott. 2008. "Certification schemes and the impact on forests and forestry." *Annual Review of Environment and Resources* 33 (1): 187–211.

Auld, Graeme, and Jennifer McKee. 2012. "Enclosing aquaculture: The co-evolution of technology with public and private regulations." Paper read at SASE Mini Conference—"Regulating Labor and Environment: Beyond the Public-Private Divide," June 29–30, Boston.

Avant, Deborah. 2004. "Conserving nature in the state of nature: The politics of INGO policy implementation." *Review of International Studies* 30 (3): 317, 361–82.

Avant, Deborah, Martha Finnemore, and Susan K. Sell. 2010. *Who governs the globe?*

Edited by Christian Reus-Smit and Nicholas J. Wheeler. Vol. 114, Cambridge Studies in International Relations. Cambridge: Cambridge University Press.

Bacon, Christopher M. 2005. "Confronting the coffee crisis: Can fair trade, organic, and specialty coffees reduce small-scale farmer vulnerability in northern Nicaragua?" *World Development* 33 (3): 497–511.

Bacon, Christopher M., V. Ernesto Méndez, Stephen R. Gliessman, David Goodman, and Jonathan A. Fox. 2008. *Confronting the coffee crisis: Fair trade, sustainable livelihoods and ecosystems in Mexico and Central America.* Cambridge, MA: MIT Press.

Bain, Simon. 1993. "Supermarkets aid third world." *Scotsman*, October 17. www.lexis-nexis.com (accessed August 31, 2005).

Baird, I. G., and N. Quastel. 2011. "Dolphin-safe tuna from California to Thailand: Localisms in environmental certification of global commodity networks." *Annals of the Association of American Geographers* 101 (2): 337–55.

Baraibar, Barbara, and Helga Willer. 2006. "Crop information and statistics." In *The world of organic agriculture: Statistics and emerging trends, 2006,* edited by Helga Willer and Minou Yussefi, 52–68. Bonn, Germany: International Federation of Organic Agriculture Movements (IFOAM); Frick, Switzerland: Research Institute of Organic Agriculture (FiBL).

Bartley, Tim. 2003. "Certifying forests and factories: States, social movements, and the rise of private regulation in the apparel and forest products fields." *Politics and Society* 31 (3): 433–64.

———. 2007a. "How foundations shape social movements: The construction of an organizational field and the rise of forest certification." *Social Problems* 54 (3): 229–55.

———. 2007b. "Institutional emergence in an era of globalization: The rise of transnational private regulation of labor and environmental conditions." *American Journal of Sociology* 113 (2): 297–351.

Bass, Stephen. 1997. *Introducing forest certification: A report prepared by the Forest Certification Advisory Group (FCAG) for DGVIII of the European Commission.* Torikatu, Finland: European Forest Institute.

Bates, Robert H. 1997. *Open-economy politics: The political economy of the world coffee trade.* Princeton, NJ: Princeton University Press.

Beckman, Eric J. 2004. "Supercritical and near-critical CO_2 in green chemical synthesis and processing." *Journal of Supercritical Fluids* 28 (2–3): 121–91.

Beekman, Bert. 1998. "Fair trade and trade development." *ILEIA Newsletter* (December): 8–9.

Belliveau, Michael. 1996. "Marine Stewardship Council: The mantle of 'going green.'" *Samudra* 15: 21.

Bendell, Jem. 2000. *Terms of endearment: Business, NGOs and sustainable development.* Sheffield, UK: Greenleaf.

Bene, Christophe. 2005. "The good, the bad and the ugly: Discourse, policy controversies and the role of science in the politics of shrimp farming development." *Development Policy Review* 23 (5): 585–614.

Berger, I. E., P. H. Cunningham, and M. E. Drumwright. 2004. "Social alliances: Company/nonprofit collaboration." *California Management Review* 47 (1): 58–90.

Bergleiter, Stefan. 2008. "Organic aquaculture." In *The world of organic agriculture: Statistics and emerging trends, 2008,* edited by Helga Willer, Minou Yussefi-Menzler, and Neil Sorensen, 83–88. Bonn, Germany: International Federation of Organic

Agriculture Movements (IFOAM); Frick, Switzerland: Research Institute of Organic Agriculture (FiBL).

Bernstein, Steven. 2000. "Ideas, social structure, and the compromise of liberal environmentalism." *European Journal of International Relations* 6 (4): 464–512.

———. 2002. *The compromise of liberal environmentalism.* New York: Columbia University Press.

Bernstein, Steven, and Benjamin Cashore. 2007. "Can non-state global governance be legitimate? An analytical framework." *Regulation and Governance* 1 (4): 347–71.

Bernton, Hal. 2008. "Seattle trawlers may face new limits on pollock fishery." *Seattle Times*, October 11.

Betsill, Michele M., and Elisabeth Corell. 2008. *NGO diplomacy: The influence of nongovernmental organizations in international environmental negotiations.* Cambridge, MA: MIT Press.

Bhattacharya, Hrishikes. 2002. *Commercial exploitation of fisheries: Production, marketing, and finance strategies.* New Delhi: Oxford University Press.

Biermann, F., P. Pattberg, H. van Asselt, and F. Zelli. 2009. "The fragmentation of global governance architectures: A framework for analysis." *Global Environmental Politics* 9 (4): 14–40.

Bilder, Richard B. 1963. "The international coffee agreement: A case-history in negotiation." *Law and Contemporary Problems* 28 (2): 328–91.

Binnie, Kirsten. 1998. "Orkney-grown salmon takes organic lead: Sainsbury order won for produce." *Aberdeen Press and Journal*, September 16. http://web.lexis-nexis.com/ (accessed April 13, 2007).

Bird, Kate, and David R. Hughes. 1997. "Ethical consumerism: The case of 'fairly traded' coffee." *Business Ethics* 6 (3): 159–68.

Blackwell, David. 1991. "Value of timber organisation questioned." *Financial Times* (London), November 22, commodities and agriculture section, 30. http://web.lexis-nexis.com/ (accessed July 24, 2007).

Blyth, Mark M. 1997. "'Any more bright ideas?' The ideational turn of comparative political economy." *Comparative Politics* 29 (2): 229–50.

———. 2002. *Great transformations: Economic ideas and institutional change in the twentieth century.* Cambridge: Cambridge University Press.

———. 2003. "From comparative capitalism to economic constructivism: The Cornell Series in Political Economy." *New Political Economy* 8 (2): 263–74.

Bohman, Mary, Lovell Jarvis, and Richard Barichello. 1996. "Rent seeking and international commodity agreements: The case of coffee." *Economic Development and Cultural Change* 44 (2): 379–404.

Börzel, Tanja A., and Thomas Risse. 2005. "Public-private partnerships: Effective and legitimate tools of transnational governance?" In *Complex sovereignty: On the reconstitution of political authority in the 21st century,* edited by E. Grand and L. Pauly, 195–216. Toronto: University of Toronto Press.

Boston Globe. 1989. "Salvadoran coffee boycott is launched." December 8. http://web.lexis-nexis.com (accessed January 27, 2007).

Boström, Magnus. 2003. "How state-dependent is a non-state-driven rule-making project? The case of forest certification in Sweden." *Journal of Environmental Policy and Planning* 5 (2): 165–80.

———. 2006. "Regulatory credibility and authority through inclusiveness: Standardization organizations in cases of eco-labelling." *Organization* 13 (3): 345–67.

Botzem, Sebastian, and Sigrid Quack. 2006. "Contested rules and shifting boundaries: International standard-setting in accounting." In *Transnational governance: Institutional dynamics of regulations,* edited by Marie-Laure Djelic and Kerstin Sahlin-Andersson, 267–86. Cambridge: Cambridge University Press.

Boulton, Leyla. 1997. "Retailer backs stock saving plan." *Financial Times* (London), April 12, 6. http://web.lexis-nexis.com/ (accessed February 5, 2007).

Bovard, Jame. 1989. "Aid from the USA often hurts the hungry." *USA Today,* November 24. www.lexisnexis.com/ (accessed August 1, 2008).

Boyd, Claude E., and Aaron A. McNevin. 2012. "An early assessment of the effectiveness of aquaculture certification and standards." In *Toward sustainability: The roles and limitations of certification,* edited by Steering Committee of the State-of-Knowledge Assessment of Standards and Certification, A35–69. Washington, DC: RESOLVE.

Braithwaite, John, and Peter Drahos. 2000. *Global business regulation.* Cambridge: Cambridge University Press.

Bray, David B., Jose Luis P. Sanchez, and Ellen C. Murphy. 2002. "Social dimensions of organic coffee production in Mexico: Lessons for eco-labeling initiatives." *Society and Natural Resources* 15 (5): 429–46.

Brittain, Victoria. 1991. "UN session will test the West's commitment to recovering Africa's lost decade." *Guardian* (London), June 28. www.lexisnexis.com/ (accessed August 7, 2008).

Brooks, Kenneth. M., and Dario J. Stucchi. 2006. "The effects of water temperature, salinity and currents on the survival and distribution of the infective copepodid stage of the salmon louse (Lepeophtheirus salmonis) originating on Atlantic salmon farms in the Broughton Archipelago of British Columbia, Canada (Brooks, 2005): A response to the rebuttal of Krkosek et al. (2005a)." *Reviews in Fisheries Science* 14 (1–2): 13–23.

Brown, Amanda. 1990. "Thatcher will waste rainforest millions, claims green groups." Press Association, March 27. http://web.lexis-nexis.com/ (accessed July 22, 2007).

———. 2000. "Green groups urge caution on hardwood garden furniture." Press Association, April 21. www.lexisnexis.com/ (accessed July 20, 2008).

Brown, Elizabeth A. 1989. "Organic farming puts down roots." *Christian Science Monitor,* November 7. www.lexisnexis.com/ (accessed January 30, 2008).

Brown, Jackie. 1996. "Greenpeace targets dangers of fish 'Hoovering.'" Press Association, April 29. www.lexisnexis.com/ (accessed August 8, 2008).

Brown, Paul. 2004. "Crisis of credibility for 'green' fisheries: Drastic reforms urged to save watchdog from collapse." *Observer,* February 21. http://web.lexis-nexis.com (accessed February 5, 2007).

Bruin, Guido de. 1992. "Trade: Alternative channels needed for developing world goods." IPS–Inter Press Service, October 15. www.lexisnexis.com/ (accessed August 5, 2008).

———. 1993. "Netherlands: Buying chocolate with third world producers in mind." IPS–Inter Press Service, October 13. www.lexisnexis.com/ (accessed August 5, 2008).

Bryant, Dirk, Daniel Nielsen, and Laura Tangley. 1997. *The last frontier forests: Ecosytems and economies on the edge; What is the status of the world's remaining large, natural forest ecosystems?* Washington, DC: World Resources Institute, Forest Frontiers Initiative.

Buchanan, James M., and Viktor Vanberg. 1989. "A theory of leadership and deference in constitutional construction." *Public Choice* 61 (1): 15–27.

Bull, Gary, Warren Mabee, and Robert Scharpenberg. 1998. *Global fibre supply model.* Rome: Food and Agriculture Organization of the United Nations.

Burgmans, Antony. 2003. "Cooperation is catching." *Our Planet,* February. www.our planet.com/imgversn/134/burgman.html (accessed May 2, 2007).

Burros, Marian. 1998. "Eating well; serving no swordfish." *New York Times,* January 21. www.lexisnexis.com/ (accessed August 13, 2008).

Business Wire. 1995. "Agreement reached on international forest management consultations." July 1. www.lexisnexis.com/ (accessed April 2, 2008).

———. 1999a. "Coffee that's made in the shade: Starbucks and Conservation International debut shade grown Mexico." August 2. www.lexisnexis.com/ (accessed August 8, 2008).

———. 1999b. "Starbucks and Conservation International partner to support shade coffee in Mexico." February 24. www.lexisnexis.com/ (accessed August 8, 2008).

Büthe, Tim. 2010. "The power of norms; the norms of power: Who governs international electrical and electronic technology?" In *Who governs the globe?* edited by Deborah D. Avant, Martha Finnemore, and Susan K. Sell, 292–332. Cambridge: Cambridge University Press.

———. 2012. "Beyond supply and demand: A political-economy conceptual model." In *Governance by indicators: Global power through quantification and rankings,* edited by Kevin E. Davis, Angelina Fisher, Benedict Kingsbury, and Sally Engle Merry, 29–51. Oxford: Oxford University Press.

Büthe, Tim, and Nathaniel Harris. 2011. "Codex Alimentarius Commission." In *Handbook of transnational governance: Institutions and innovations,* edited by Thomas Hale and David Held, 219–28. Cambridge: Polity.

Büthe, Tim, and Walter Mattli. 2011. *New global rulers: The privatization of regulation in the world economy.* Princeton, NJ: Princeton University Press.

Butler, Brett J., and Earl C. Leatherberry. 2004. "America's family forest owners." *Journal of Forestry* 102 (7): 4–9.

Cabarle, Bruce. 1992. "Close encounters? NGOs and the TFAP." *Unasylva* 171 (4). www.fao.org/docrep/u7760e/u7760e06.htm.

Caddy, John F. 1999. "Fisheries management in the twenty-first century: Will new paradigms apply?" *Reviews in Fish Biology and Fisheries* 9 (1): 1–43.

Caddy, John F., and Robert C. Griffiths. 1995. *Living marine resources and their sustainable development: Some environmental and institutional perspectives.* Rome: FAO.

Caddy, John F., and J. C. Seij. 2005. "This is more difficult than we thought! The responsibility of scientists, managers and stakeholders to mitigate the unsustainability of marine fisheries." *Philosophical Transactions of the Royal Society B— Biological Sciences* 360 (1453): 59–75.

Cafédirect. 2006a. "Company history: 1989–1992." October 12. http://web.archive .org/web/20061012161805/www.cafedirect.co.uk/about/company.php (accessed January 30, 2007).

———. 2006b. "Company history: 1993–1995" October 12. http://web.archive .org/web/20061012162021/www.cafedirect.co.uk/about/comp_1993.php (accessed January 30, 2007).

Callejon, Diana Propper de, Tony Lent, Michael Skelly, and Charles A. Webster. 1998.

   Sustainable forestry within an industry context. Chicago: John D. and Catherine T.
      MacArthur Foundation.
Campbell, John L. 2004. *Institutional change and globalization*. Princeton, NJ: Prince-
      ton University Press.
————. 2005. "Where do we stand? Common mechanisms in organizations and
      social movements research." In *Social movements and organization theory*, edited
      by Gerald F. Davis, Doug McAdam, W. Richard Scott, and Mayer N. Zald, 41–68.
      Cambridge: Cambridge University Press.
Canada Newswire. 1998. "Greenpeace released a report." October 1. www.lexisnexis.
      com/ (accessed July 28, 2008).
Caron, D. D. 1989. "International sanctions, ocean management, and the law of the
      sea: A study of denial of access to fisheries." *Ecology Law Quarterly* 16 (1): 311–54.
Carpio, Ivan. 1993. "The Netherlands: Dutch promote alternative coffee trade." IPS–
      Inter Press Service / Global Information Network, July 2. www.lexisnexis.com
      (accessed August 31, 2005).
Cashore, Benjamin. 2002. "Legitimacy and the privatization of environmental gover-
      nance: How non-state market-driven (NSMD) governance systems gain rule-
      making authority." *Governance* 15 (4): 503–29.
Cashore, Benjamin, Graeme Auld, Steven Bernstein, and Constance L. McDermott.
      2007. "Can non-state governance 'ratchet up' global environmental standards?
      Lessons from the forest sector." *Review of European Community and International
      Environmental Law* 16 (2): 158–72.
Cashore, Benjamin, Graeme Auld, and Deanna Newsom. 2004. *Governing through
      markets: Forest certification and the emergence of non-state authority*. New Haven,
      CT: Yale University Press.
Cashore, Benjamin, Elizabeth Egan, Graeme Auld, and Deanna Newsom. 2007.
      "Revisiting theories of non-state market driven (NSMD) governance: Lessons
      from the Finnish forest certification experience." *Global Environmental Politics* 7
      (1): 1–44.
Cashore, Benjamin, and James Lawson. 2003. "Private policy networks and sustain-
      able forestry policy: Comparing forest certification experiences in the US North-
      east and the Canadian Maritimes." *Canadian American Public Policy*, March.
Cashore, Benjamin, and Michael W. Stone. 2012. "Can legality verification rescue
      global forest governance? Analyzing the potential of public and private policy
      intersection to ameliorate forest challenges in Southeast Asia." *Forest Policy and
      Economics* 18:13–22.
Cashore, Benjamin, G. Cornelius van Kooten, Ilan Vertinsky, Graeme Auld, and Julia
      Affolderbach. 2005. "Private or self-regulation? A comparative study of forest
      certification choices in Canada, the United States and Germany." *Forest Policy
      and Economics* 7 (1): 53–69.
Cashore, Benjamin, and Ilan Vertinsky. 2000. "Policy networks and firm behaviours:
      Governance systems and firm responses to external demands for sustainable for-
      est management." *Policy Sciences* 33 (1): 1–30.
Centeno, Julio Cesar. 1996. "Forest certification as a tool for greenwashing." *Treemail*,
      November 4. www.treemail.nl/teakscan.dal/files/greenwas.htm (accessed Octo-
      ber 1, 2007).
Cerny, Philip G. 1995. "Globalization and the changing logic of collective action."
      International Organization 49 (4): 595–625.

Chatterjee, Pratap, and Matthias Finger. 1994. *The earth brokers: Power, politics and world development.* London: Routledge.

Christensen, Jon. 1997. "As fish farming goes, it faces mounting environmental challenges." *New York Times,* March 1. http://select.nytimes.com/search/restricted/art icle?res=F30E17FA3B550C728CDDAA0894DF494D81 (accessed May 24, 2007).

Christian, Claire, David Ainley, Megan Bailey, Paul Dayton, John Hocevar, Michael LeVine, Jordan Nikoloyuk, Claire Nouvian, Enriqueta Velarde, and Rodolfo Werner. 2013. "A review of formal objections to Marine Stewardship Council fisheries certifications." *Biological Conservation* 161: 10–17.

Chuenpagdee, Ratana, Lance E. Morgan, Sara M. Maxwell, Elliott A. Norse, and Daniel Pauly. 2003. "Shifting gears: Assessing collateral impacts of fishing methods in US waters." *Frontiers in Ecology and the Environment* 1 (10): 517–24.

Clapp, Jennifer. 1998. "The privatization of global environmental governance: ISO 14000 and the developing world." *Global Governance* 4 (3): 295–316.

Clark, William, Ronald Mitchell, David Cash, and Frank Alcock. 2002. *Information as influence: How institutions mediate the impact of scientific assessments on global environmental affairs.* Cambridge, MA: John F. Kennedy School of Government, Harvard University.

Coase, Ronald H. 1960. "The problem of social cost." *Journal of Law and Economics* 3:1–44.

Cochrane, Kevern L., and David J. Doulman. 2005. "The rising tide of fisheries instruments and the struggle to keep afloat." *Philosophical Transactions of the Royal Society B—Biological Sciences* 360 (1453): 77–94.

Coffee Kids. 2008. "Mission." www.coffeekids.org/aboutus/ (accessed August 8, 2008).

Cohlmeyer, David. 1985. "Organic foods industry works on certification." *Globe and Mail* (Toronto), February 27. www.lexisnexis.com/ (accessed January 30, 2008).

Colchester, Marcus, and Larry Lohmann. 1990. *The tropical forestry action plan: What progress?* Penang, Malaysia: World Rainforest Movement; Sturminster Newton, Dorset, UK: Ecologist.

Colgan, Jeff D., Robert O. Keohane, and Thijs Van de Graaf. 2012. "Punctuated equilibrium in the energy regime complex." *Review of International Organizations* 7 (2): 117–43.

Commins, Ken. 2003. "IFOAM accreditation and the International Organic Accreditation Service." In *The organic guarantee system: The need and strategy for harmonization and equivalence,* edited by Christina Westermayer and Bernward Geier, 74–77. Tholey-Theley, Germany: IFOAM, FAO, and UNCTAD.

———. 2004. "Overview of current status of standards and conformity assessment systems." In *Harmonization and equivalence in organic agriculture,* edited by Ulrich Hoffman, Sophia Twarog, Antonio Compagnoni, Gunnar Rundgren, Nadia El-Hage Scialabba, and Selma Doyran, 1–23. Geneva: UNCTAD; Rome: FAO; Bonn: IFOAM.

Conner, Kathleen R. 1991. "A historical comparison of resource-based theory and five schools of thought within industrial organization economics: Do we have a new theory of the firm?" *Journal of Management* 17 (1): 121–54.

Connors, Tom. 1990. "A test of trade, not aid." *Journal of Commerce,* April 26. www .lexisnexis.com/ (accessed August 1, 2008).

Conroy, Michael E. 2006. *Branded: How the "certification revolution" is transforming global corporations.* Gabriola Island, British Columbia: New Society.

Constance, Dinzglas H., and Alessandro Bonanno. 1999. "Contested terrain of global fisheries: 'Dolphin-safe' tuna, the Panama Declaration, and the Marine Steward-ship Council." *Rural Sociology* 64 (4): 597–623.

Cooke, Edward S. 2004. Oral history interview with Silas Kopf, October 1. In *Nanette L. Laitman Documentation project for craft and decorative arts in America*. Easthampton, MA: Smithsonian Archives of American Art. www.aaa.si.edu/collections/oralhistories/transcripts/kopf04.htm (accessed October 1, 2008)

Counsell, Simon, and Kim Terje Loraas. 2002. *Trading in credibility: The myth and reality of the Forest Stewardship Council*. London: Rainforest Foundation.

Courville, Sasha. 2003. "Social accountability audits: Challenging or defending democratic governance?" *Law and Policy* 25 (3): 269–97.

———. 2008. "Organic and social certifications: Recent developments from the global regulators." In *Confronting the coffee crisis: Fair trade, sustainable livelihoods and ecosystems in Mexico and Central America*, edited by Christopher M. Bacon, V. Ernesto Mendez, Stephen R. Gliessman, David Goodman, and Jonathan A. Fox, 289–310. Cambridge, MA: MIT Press.

Cowan, R. 1990. "Nuclear-power reactors: A study in technological lock-in." *Journal of Economic History* 50 (3): 541–67.

Crouch, Colin, and Henry Farrell. 2004. "Breaking the path of institutional development? Alternatives to the new determinism." *Rationality and Society* 16 (1): 5–43.

Cumpiano, William. 2007. "Preservation through utilization? The paradoxes of rainforest protection." www.cumpiano.com/Home/Articles/Articles/rainforest.html (accessed November 1, 2007).

Cutler, A. Claire. 1999. "Private authority in international trade relations: The case of maritime transport." In *Private authority and international affairs*, edited by A. Claire Cutler, Virginia Haufler, and Tony Porter, 283–329. Albany: State University of New York Press.

Cutler, A. Claire, Virginia Haufler, and Tony Porter. 1999a. "The contours and significance of private authority in international affairs." In *Private authority and international affairs*, edited by A. Claire Cutler, Virginia Haufler, and Tony Porter, 333–76. Albany: State University of New York Press.

Cutler, A. Claire, Virginia Haufler, and Tony Porter, eds. 1999b. *Private authority in international politics*. Albany: State University of New York Press.

Cyert, Richard Michael, and James G. March. 1963. *A behavioral theory of the firm*. Englewood Cliffs, NJ: Prentice-Hall.

Dalton, R. J., S. Recchia, and R. Rohrschneider. 2003. "The environmental movement and the modes of political action." *Comparative Political Studies* 36 (7): 743–71.

Dankers, Cora, and Pascal Liu. 2003. *Environmental and social standards, certification and labelling for cash crops*. Rome: Food and Agriculture Organization of the United Nations.

Dauvergne, Peter. 1997. *Shadows in the forest: Japan and the politics of timber in Southeast Asia*. Cambridge, MA: MIT Press.

———. 2001. *Loggers and degradation in the Asia Pacific: Corporations and environmental management*. Cambridge Asia-Pacific Studies. Cambridge: Cambridge University Press.

David, P. A. 1985. "Clio and the economics of QWERTY." *American Economic Review* 75 (2): 332–37.

Daviron, Benoit, and Stefano Ponte. 2005. *The coffee paradox: Global markets, commod-*

ity trade and the elusive promise of development. London and New York: Zed Books in association with CTA Wageningen.

DCLM. 1997. "Marine reserve for Jurien Bay." Department of Conservation and Land Management, January 3. www.dec.wa.gov.au/news/minister-for-the-environment/marine-reserve-for-jurien-bay.html (accessed August 13, 2008).

———. 2003. "Jurien Bay Marine Park management plan: 2005–2015." Management Plan 49. Department of Conservation and Land Management. www.dec.wa.gov.au/park-finder/property/marine-parks-and-reserves/jurien-bay-marine-park.html (accessed August 12, 2008).

deFontaubert, A. Charlotte. 1995. "The politics of negotiation at the United Nations Conference on Straddling Fish Stocks and Highly Migratory Fish Stocks." *Ocean and Coastal Management* 29 (1–3): 79–91.

Delaney, Kevin. 1990. "Rare wood: Group encourages use of non-endangered species." *St. Louis (MO) Post-Dispatch,* November 27. www.lexisnexis.com/ (accessed November 1, 2007).

Delgado, Christopher L., Nikolas Wada, Mark W. Rosegrant, Seit Meijer, and Mahfuzuddin Admed. 2003. *Outlook for fish to 2020: Meeting global demand.* Washington, DC: International Food Policy Research Institute; Penang, Malaysia: WorldFish Center.

DeSombre, Elizabeth R. 2000. *Domestic sources of international environmental policy: Industry, environmentalists, and U.S. power; American and comparative environmental policy.* Cambridge, MA: MIT Press.

Development and Environment: The Founex Report. 1971. Founex, Switzerland: Carnegie Endowment for International Peace.

Dickenson, Nicole. 1993. "Catering for the ethical shopper: A look at a growing consumer trend." *Financial Times* (London), April 15. http://web.lexis-nexis.com/ (accessed July 9, 2007).

Dicum, Gregory, and Nina Luttinger. 1999. *The coffee book: Anatomy of an industry from crop to the last drop.* New York: New Press.

DiMaggio, Paul J., and Walter W. Powell. 1983. "The iron cage revisited: Institutional isomorphism and collective rationality in organizational fields." *American Sociological Review* 48 (2): 147–60.

Dimitrov, Radoslav S. 2006. *Science and international environmental policy: Regimes and nonregimes in global governance.* Oxford: Rowman and Littlefield.

Dingwerth, Klaus. 2007. *The new transnationalism: Transnational governance and democratic legitimacy; Transformations of the state.* Basingstoke, UK: Palgrave Macmillan.

Diringer, Elliot. 1990. "Bitter battle over the state's redwood." *San Francisco Chronicle,* October 29. www.lexisnexis.com/ (accessed May 30, 2005).

Dixon, Audrey. 1997. "Dodging the bullets from both sides." *Timber Trades Journal,* June 21. www.lexisnexis.com/ (accessed July 14, 2008).

DIY Week. 1997. "B&Q ups stance on environmental and social responsibility issues." October 31. www.lexisnexis.com/ (accessed July 20, 2008).

Djelic, Marie-Laure, and Kerstin Sahlin-Andersson. 2006. *Transnational governance: Institutional dynamics of regulation.* Cambridge: Cambridge University Press.

Donovan, Richard. 1996. "Smart Wood statement on Flor y Fauna." Posted comment. Forest List Archive, March 12. www.metla.fi/archive/forest/1996/03/msg00060.html (accessed March 30, 2008).

———. 2001. "Practical conservation through certified forestry: Observations on equity after ten years of Smartwood certification." Paper read at "Building Confidence among Forest Certification Schemes and Their Supporters," February 19–20, Rome.

Doulman, David J. 1995. *Structure and process of the 1993–1995 United Nations Conference on Straddling Fish Stocks and Highly Migratory Fish Stocks.* Rome: FAO.

Down to Earth: Science and Environment Online. 2006. "Coffee code: Wide agreement to improve industry practice." December 6. www.downtoearth.org.in/full6.asp?foldername=20041215&filename=news&sec_id=4&sid=39 (accessed August 28, 2008).

Dudley, Nigel, Jean-Paul Jeanrenaud, and Francis Sullivan. 1995. *Bad harvest? The timber trade and the destruction of the world's forests.* London: Earthscan.

Duffy, Robert W. 1992. "Turnabout exhibit spawns effort to educate woodworkers about conservation." *St. Louis (MO) Post-Dispatch,* May 4. www.lexisnexis.com/ (accessed November 1, 2007).

Dullforce, William. 1986. "Deadlock over tropical timber accord broken." *Financial Times* (London), July 30. http://web.lexis-nexis.com/ (accessed July 16, 2007).

Dunlap, Riley E. 1992. "Trends in public opinion toward environmental issues: 1965–1990." In *American environmentalism: The US environmental movement, 1970–1990,* edited by Riley E. Dunlap and Angela Mertig, 89–116. Philadelphia: Taylor and Francis.

Earle, Michael. 2000. "Marine Stewardship Council: Thames up or thumbs down?" *Samudra* 27:20–23.

Edeson, William. 2005. "FAO compliance agreement." UN Food and Agricultural Organization, 27 May. www.fao.org/fishery/topic/14766/en (accessed July 1, 2013).

Edwards, John. 1985. "Surprise deal on tropical timber." *Financial Times* (London), April 4. http://web.lexis-nexis.com/ (accessed July 16, 2007).

Edwards, Rob. 2000. "Supermarkets criticised over 'organic' fish." *Sunday Herald,* January 9. http://web.lexis-nexis.com/ (accessed April 13, 2007).

Egidi, Massimo, and Alessandro Narduzzo. 1997. "The emergence of path-dependent behaviors in cooperative contexts." *International Journal of Industrial Organization* 15 (6): 677–709.

Elkington, John, and Julia Hailes. 1988. *The green consumer guide: From shampoo to champagne, High-Street shopping for a better environment.* London: Victor Gollancz.

Elliott, Chris. 2000. *Forest certification: A policy network perspective.* Bogor, Indonesia: Centre for International Forestry Research (CIFOR).

Elliott, Chris, and Richard Donovan. 1996. Introduction to *Certification of forest products: Issues and perspectives,* edited by Virgilio M. Viana, Jamison Ervin, Richard Donovan, Chris Elliott, and Henry Gholz, 1–10. Washington, DC: Island.

Environmental Defense Fund. 1993. "Environmental group and leading organizations create task force: Seek to build environmental criteria into paper purchasing." August 18. http://web.archive.org/web/19991003015707/www.edf.org/pubs/NewsReleases/1993/Aug/c_paper.html (accessed April 16, 2007).

———. 1995. *Economics of manufacturing virgin and recycled-content paper.* White Paper 9. New York: Paper Task Force—Duke University, Environmental Defense Fund, Johnson & Johnson, McDonald's, the Prudential Insurance Company of American, and Time, December 19. www.environmentaldefense.org/documents/1619_WP9.pdf (accessed July 31, 2006).

EPA. 1998. *Environmental labeling: Issues, policies and practices worldwide.* Washington,

DC: Pollution Prevention Division, Office of Pollution, Prevention and Toxics, U.S. Environmental Protection Agency.

Equal Exchange. 2008. "Our story." www.equalexchange.com/story (accessed August 8, 2008).

Ertman, Thomas. 1997. *Birth of the leviathan: Building states and regimes in medieval and early modern Europe.* Cambridge: Cambridge University Press.

Ervin, Jamison. 1996. "The consultative process." In *Certification of forest products: Issues and perspectives,* edited by Virgilio M. Viana, Jamison Ervin, Richard Z. Donovan, Chris Elliott, and Henry Gholz, 13–32. Washington, DC: Island.

Espach, Ralph. 2005. "Private regulation amid public disarray: An analysis of two private environmental regulatory programs in Argentina." *Business and Politics* 7 (2): 1–36.

———. 2006. "When is sustainable forestry sustainable? The Forest Stewardship Council in Argentina and Brazil." *Global Environmental Politics* 6 (2): 55–84.

Esty, Daniel C. 2004. "Environmental protection in the information age." *New York University Law Review* 79 (1): 115–211.

EurepGAP. 2004. "EurepGAP Aquaculture Code launched." October 19. www.eurep gap.org/fish/Languages/English/news/134.html (accessed April 4, 2007).

———. 2005. "Aquaculture Code version 2.1 update published." June 13. www.eurep gap.org/fish/Languages/English/news/207.html (accessed April 4, 2007).

———. 2006. "About EUREPGAP." www.eurepgap.org/Languages/English/about .html (accessed March 19, 2006).

Evans, Bryan. 1996. "Technical and scientific elements of forest management certification programs." In *Economic, social and political issues in certification of forest management,* 1–24. Malaysia: University of British Columbia, Canada, and Universiti of Pertanian, Malaysia.

Evans, David W. 2001. *Status and trends reporting in fisheries: A review of progress and approaches to reporting the state of world fisheries.* Rome: Food and Agricultural Organization of the United Nations.

Evans, Peter. 1997. "The eclipse of the state? Reflections on stateness in an era of globalization." *World Politics* 50 (1): 62–87.

Fahys, J. 1995. *Survey of the structure of the sawmilling industry in the ECE/FAO region.* New York: United Nations.

Fair Trade Federation. 2007. "About us—history." www.fairtradefederation.org/ht/d/ sp/i/177/pid/177 (accessed August 7, 2008).

Fairtrade Foundation. 2003. "Annual review and financial statement." May 20. www .fairtrade.org.uk/includes/documents/cm_docs/2008/a/accounts2002.pdf (accessed March 30, 2008).

———. 2008. "Fairtrade and coffee plantations." www.fairtrade.org.uk/includes/ documents/cm_docs/2008/F/Fairtrade_and_Coffee_Plantations.pdf (accessed August 8, 2008).

Fair Trade USA. 2011a. "Fair trade for all: Innovation strategy." http://fairtradeforall .com/q-and-a/vision/will-you-reduce-fees-for-u-s-business-partners/ (accessed October 12, 2012).

———. 2011b. "Fairtrade USA announces innovative new strategy to double impact to farming communities by 2015." September 19. www.fairtradeusa.org/press -room/press_release/fair-trade-usa-announces-innovation-strategy-double -impact-farming-communit (accessed October 20, 2012).

———. 2012. "Triple pundit: Why Fair Trade USA parted ways with FLO." January 11. www.fairtradeusa.org/press-room/in_the_news/triple-pundit-why-fair-trade-usa -parted-ways-flo (accessed October 20, 2012).

Falkner, Robert. 2003. "Private environmental governance and international relations: Exploring the links." *Global Environmental Politics* 3 (2): 72–87.

FAO. 1980. *Tropical forest resources assessment project: Forest resources of tropical Asia.* Rome: Food and Agricultural Organization of the United Nations and the United Nations Environment Programme.

———. 1981. *Tropical forest resources assessment project: Forest resources of tropical Africa.* Vol. I. Rome: Food and Agricultural Organization of the United Nations and United Nations Environment Programme.

———. 1985. *Tropical forestry action plan.* Rome: Committee on Forest Development in the Tropics.

———. 1995. *State of the world's forests.* Rome: Food and Agriculture Organization of the United Nations.

———. 2000. *The state of the world fisheries and aquaculture.* Rome: Food and Agriculture Organization of the United Nations. www.fao.org/docrep/003/X8002E/ x8002e00.HTM (accessed August 13, 2008).

———. 2005. "Topics fact sheets: Processing fish and fish products." (Text compiled by Tina Farmer.) FAO Fisheries and Aquaculture Department, September 15. www.fao.org/fishery/topic/736 (accessed October 10, 2008).

———. 2006. *Global forest resources assessment 2005: Progress towards sustainable forest management.* Rome: Food and Agriculture Organization of the United Nations.

———. 2007a. *FAOSTAT.* Food and Agricultural Organization of the United Nations. http://faostat.fao.org/site/626/default.aspx (accessed May 20, 2007).

———. 2007b. *The state of the world fisheries and aquaculture, 2006.* Rome: Fisheries and Aquaculture Department, Food and Agriculture Organization of the United Nations.

———. 2007c. *State of the world's forests.* Rome: Food and Agriculture Organization of the United Nations, Electronic Publishing Policy and Support Branch, Communications Division.

———. 2012. *The state of world fisheries and aquaculture, 2012.* Rome: Food and Agriculture Organization of the United Nations.

Farrell, Joseph, and Garth Saloner. 1985. "Standardization, compatibility, and innovation." *Rand Journal of Economics* 16 (1): 70–83.

Faye, Denis. 1999. "Marine protection learning to give and take." *Ecos,* January 1. www.lexisnexis.com/ (accessed August 13, 2008).

Feder, Barnaby J. 1992. "Company news: For-profit foreign aid; seed money with a conscience." *New York Times,* June 25. www.lexisnexis.com/ (accessed August 8, 2008).

Feraru, Anne T. 1974. "Transnational political interests and the global environment." *International Organization* 28 (1): 31–68.

FERN. 2011. "FERN statement to the Forest Stewardship Council: Why FERN is withdrawing its FSC membership." June 2. www.fern.org/sites/fern.org/files/FERN leaving FSC_0.pdf (accessed July 5, 2012).

Financial Post (Toronto). 1993. "'Green' certification in forest." October 1, 6. http:// web.lexis-nexis.com/ (accessed August 8, 2006).

Financial Times (London). 1983. "El Salvador poses dilemma for U.S." January 21.
http://web.lexis-nexis.com/ (accessed January 28, 2007).

———. 1986. "Call to end timber pact deadlock." January 30. http://web.lexis-nexis
.com/ (accessed July 16, 2007).

Finlayson, Christopher Alan. 1994. *Fishing for truth: A sociological analysis of north-
ern cod stock assessments from 1977 to 1990.* Social and Economic Studies 52.
St. John's, Newfoundland: Institute of Social and Economic Research, Memorial
University of Newfoundland.

Fiorillo, John. 2007. "The Aquaculture Stewardship Council? Mangrove Action Project." September 12. www.mangroveactionproject.org/news/current_headlines/
the-aquaculture-stewardship-council/?searchterm=intrafish (accessed July 26,
2008).

Flanders, Karen. 1998. "WWF fisheries conference seeks solutions to current crisis."
M2 Presswire, September 16. http://web.lexis-nexis.com/ (accessed February 5,
2007).

Fliess, Barbara, and Tadatsuga Matsudaira. 1999. *Codes of corporate conduct: An inventory.* (TD/TC/WP(98)74/FINAL). Working Party of the Trade Committee: Organization for Economic Corporation and Development, May 3. http://appli1.oecd
.org/olis/1998doc.nsf/c16431e1b3f24c0ac12569fa005d1d99/c125692700622425
c12569a40038da6c/$FILE/04E95110.pdf (accessed July 26, 2005).

Fligstein, Neil, and Doug McAdam. 2012. *A theory of fields.* New York: Oxford University Press.

FLO. 1999. "Fair Trade: A viable alternative for small farmers." October 15. http://
web.archive.org/web/20010619230548/www.fairtrade.net/coffee.html (accessed
October 6, 2007).

———. 2003. *Shopping for a better world: Annual report 03/04.* Bonn, Germany:
Fairtrade Labelling Organizations International.

———. 2007. *Annual report 2006/07: Shaping global partnerships.* www.fairtrade.net/
fileadmin/user_upload/content/Final_FLO_AR_2007_03.pdf (accessed August
7, 2008).

———. 2011a. "An open letter from CEO on changes to the fairtrade system." September 16. www.fairtrade.net/single_view1+M572040838dd.html (accessed October
20, 2012).

———. 2011b. "Project assignment: Shrimp standards and pricing project." February 21. www.fairtrade.net/fileadmin/user_upload/content/2009/standards/
documents/Shrimps_Project_Assignment_14_03_2011_FINAL_VERSION.pdf
(accessed October 20, 2012).

Florini, Ann M. 2000. *The third force: The rise of transnational civil society.* Tokyo: Japan
Center for International Exchange; Washington, DC: Carnegie Endowment for
International Peace.

Forestry & British Timber. 1998. "Meyer's commits to timber certification." December.
www.lexisnexis.com/ (accessed July 20, 2008).

4C Association. 2006. "Rules of participation." January. www.4c-coffeeassociation.org/
uploads/media/4CDoc_002_Rules_of_Participation_v2.1_en.pdf (accessed October 20, 2012).

———. 2012. *Annual report 2011: Moving further.* Bonn, Germany: 4C Association.

Fowler, Penny, and Simon Heap. 2000. "Bridging troubled waters: The Marine Stewardship Council." In *Terms of endearment: Business, NGOs, and sustainable develop-ment*, edited by Jem Bendell, 135–48. Sheffield, UK: Greenleaf.

Franklin, Ben A. 1985. "Appeals court backs curbs on Japan whaling of U.S." *New York Times*, August 7. www.lexisnexis.com/ (accessed January 30, 2008).

Fransen, Luc W. 2011. *Corporate social responsibility and global labor standards: Firms and activists in the making of private regulation*. London: Routledge.

Fransen, Luc W., and Ans Kolk. 2007. "Global rule-setting for business: A critical analysis of multi-stakeholder standards." *Organization* 14 (5): 667–84.

Fridell, Gavin. 2004. "The fair trade network in historical perspective." *Canadian Journal of Development Studies* 25 (3): 411–28.

———. 2007. *Fair trade coffee: The prospects and pitfalls of market-driven social justice.* Studies in Comparative Political Economy and Public Policy. Toronto: University of Toronto Press.

Friend of the Sea. 2001a. "Friend of the Sea: Promoting sustainable fisheries for oceans and resources conservation." October 2. http://web.archive.org/web/2001 1002072104/http://www.friendofthesea.org/ (accessed September 6, 2008).

———. 2001b. "Preliminary analysis: Azorean tuna fishery." June 4. http://web .archive.org/web/20040615180057/www.friendofthesea.org/Azorean+Tuna +Fishery+Preliminary+Analysis.pdf (accessed September 7, 2008).

———. 2007. "Canadian BC salmon fishery is Friend of the Sea: Certified products on the shelves in Europe." October 9. http://web.archive.org/web/2007093016 4048/http://www.friendofthesea.org/ (accessed October 20, 2012).

Friends of the Earth. 1991a. "Hardwood chainstore massacre." Forests.org, November 11. http://forests.org/archive/europe/massacre.htm (accessed November 1, 2007).

———. 1991b. "UN agency stalls aid plan to save rainforests: Is this the end of the Tropical Forestry Action Plan?" November 20. http://nativenet.uthscsa.edu/ archive/nl/91d/0086.html (accessed November 19, 2007).

———. 1994. "Illegal mahogany trade." November 11. http://web.archive.org/web/ 19970225022636/www.foe.co.uk/pubsinfo/infoteam/pressrel/1994/19941115 172319.html (accessed July 17, 2008).

———. 1995a. "Boycott mahogany." February 13. http://web.archive.org/web/199702 25024410/www.foe.co.uk/pubsinfo/infoteam/pressrel/1995/19950213155820 .html (accessed July 17, 2008).

———. 1995b. "Illegal mahogany recovery." June 24. http://web.archive.org/web/1997 0225023728/www.foe.co.uk/pubsinfo/infoteam/pressrel/1995/19950623093246 .html (accessed July 17, 2008).

———. 1997a. "The good wood guide." February 25. http://web.archive.org/web/19 970225021736/www.foe.co.uk/camps/biohab/goodwood.html (accessed July 17, 2008).

———. 1997b. "Timber information sheet." February 25. http://web.archive.org/ web/19970225021930/www.foe.co.uk/camps/biohab/timbinfo.html (accessed July 17, 2008).

———. 1998. "Seeing the wood for the trees: What the UK timber industry doesn't tell you about the world's forests." January 16. http://web.archive.org/web/1998 0116161333/www.foe.co.uk/camps/biohab/ttf/briefing.htm (accessed July 17, 2008).

———. 2002. "Stop the chop: New guide to buying wood without wrecking forests." M2 PressWIRE, January 9. www.lexisnexis.com/ (accessed July 22, 2008).

Froese, Rainer, Maria Lourdes D. Palomares, and Daniel Pauly. 2000. "Estimation of life history: Key facts of fishes." February 2. www.fishbase.org/download/keyfacts .zip (accessed December 12, 2007).

FSC. 1994. "Principles and criteria for natural forest management." (Board approved version, June.) www.metla.fi/archive/forest/1994/07/msg00035.html (accessed July 22, 2008).

———. 1995. "FSC statutes" [document 1.3]. http://web.archive.org/web/19991009 014300/fscoax.org/html/noframes/1-3.htm (accessed July 28, 2008).

———. 1996. *FSC principles and criteria*. Oaxaca, Mexico: Forest Stewardship Council.

———. 1998a. "FSC endorses Swedish national forest standard." January 26. http:// web.archive.org/web/20001204001900/www.fscoax.org/not/noteng/noframe/ not2.html (accessed October 1, 2007).

———. 1998b. "FSC protocol for endorsing national initiatives" [document 4.1], February. http://web.archive.org/web/19990302024325/www.fscoax.org/html/ noframes/4-1.html (accessed August 20, 2007).

———. 1999a. "Forest Stewardship Council A.C. by-laws" [document 1.1], February. http://web.archive.org/web/20001202221500/www.fscoax.org/html/noframes/ 1-1.html (accessed August 20, 2007).

———. 1999b. "Frequently asked questions." February 18. http://web.archive.org/ web/19990218101843/www.fscoax.org/html/noframes/fsc_faq.html (accessed October 8, 2007).

———. 1999c. "FSC national initiatives: Contact details" [document 5.1.2], February. http://web.archive.org/web/19990302094042/www.fscoax.org/html/noframes/ 5-1-2.html (accessed August 21, 2007).

———. 1999d. *Revised FSC policy on percentage based claims: Draft for discussion.* Oaxaca, Mexico: Forest Stewardship Council.

———. 1999e. "Roles, rights, and responsibilities of FSC players" [document 2.10], May 31. http://web.archive.org/web/20010215153537/fscoax.org/html/noframes/ 2-10.htm (accessed September 29, 2007).

———. 2000a. *FSC annual report: 1999.* Oaxaca, Mexico: Forest Stewardship Council.

———. 2000b. "List of FSC members" [document 5.2.2] July 27. http://web.archive .org/web/20010603085633/fscoax.org/principal.htm (accessed July 27, 2008).

———. 2001. "List of FSC members" [document 5.2.2.]. June 12. http://web.archive .org/web/20010620143035/www.fscoax.org/html/noframes/5-2-2.html (accessed July 27, 2008).

———. 2003. *Forest Stewardship Council: US News and Views* 3 (6). www.fscus.org/ news/index.php?newsletter=8&action=Download (accessed May 8, 2008).

FSC-watch.org. 2008. "About." August 1. www.fsc-watch.org/about.php (accessed August 1, 2008).

GAA. 1998a. *Global Aquaculture Advocate* 1 (2). http://web.archive.org/web/199910 01173029/gaalliance.org/august98.html (accessed April 1, 2007).

———. 1998b. "Who we are." August 17. http://web.archive.org/web/19981205132 926/www.gaalliance.org/who.html (accessed April 1, 2007).

———. 1999. "GAA unveils codes of practice and eco-label." July 15. http://web .archive.org/web/19991105035426/www.gaalliance.org/codespress2.html (accessed April 2, 2007).

Gale, Fred P. 1998. *The tropical timber trade regime.* International Political Economy Series. New York: St. Martin's.

Galen, Michele. 1985. "Human rights: American senior citizens 'vacation' in Nicaragua coffee fields." IPS–Inter Press Service, February 20. http://web.lexis-nexis .com/ (accessed January 28, 2007).

Garcia, Serge M. 1992. "Ocean fisheries management: The FAO programme." In *Ocean management in global change*, edited by P. Fabbri, 381–418. London: Elsevier.

Garcia-Johnson, Ronnie. 2001. "Multinational corporations and certification institutions: Moving first to shape a green global production context." Paper read at the International Studies Association Convention, February 20–24, Chicago. www .nicholas.duke.edu/solutions/documents/rgj_isa_mncs.pdf (accessed August 9, 2005).

Garud, Raghu, and Peter Karnoe. 2001. "Path creation as a process of mindful deviation." In *Path dependence and creation*, edited by Raghu Garud and Peter Karnoe, 1–38. Mahwah, NJ: Lawrence Erlbaum.

Geddes, Barbara. 2003. *Paradigms and sand castles: Theory building and research design in comparative politics*. Ann Arbor: University of Michigan Press.

Geier, Bernward. 1999. "A look at the development of IFOAM in its first 25 years." International Federation of Organic Agriculture Movements. www.ifoam.org/ about_ifoam/inside_ifoam/pdfs/First_25_Years.pdf (accessed October 30, 2005).

George, Alexander L., and Andrew Bennett. 2005. *Case studies and theory development in the social sciences*. Cambridge, MA: MIT Press.

Gereffi, Gary, Ronie Garcia-Johnson, and Erika Sasser. 2001. "The NGO-industrial complex." *Foreign Policy*, July–August, 56–65.

Gereffi, Gary, Miguel Korzeniewicz, and Roberto P. Korzeniewicz. 1994. "Introduction: Global commodity chains." In *Commodity chains and global capitalism*, edited by Gary Gereffi and Miguel Korzeniewicz, 1–14. Westport, CT: Greenwood.

Ghazali, Baharuddin Haji, and Markku Simula. 1996. *Timber certification in transition: Study on the development in the formulation and implementation of certification schemes for all internationally traded timber and timber products*. Manila, Philippines: International Tropical Timber Organization.

Gibbens, Robert. 1991. "Ottawa backs off on pulp polluters." *Toronto Financial Post*, February 4, 1. www.lexisnexis.com/ (accessed September 12, 2007).

Gilbert, Christopher L. 1996. "International commodity agreements: An obituary notice." *World Development* 24 (1): 1–19.

Gilpin, Robert, and Jean M. Gilpin. 2001. *Global political economy: Understanding the international economic order*. Princeton, NJ: Princeton University Press.

Giovannucci, Daniele, and Freek Jan Koekoek. 2003. "The state of sustainable coffee: A study of twelve major markets." ICO, UNCTAD, and IISD. www.iisd.org/publi cations/pub.aspx?pno=579 (accessed March 13, 2006).

Giovannucci, Daniele, and Jason Potts. 2008. *Seeking sustainability: COSA preliminary analysis of sustainability initiatives in the coffee sector*. Winnipeg, Canada: Committee on Sustainability Assessment.

Globe and Mail (Toronto). 1988. "Dioxin testing ordered at Canadian pulp mills." January 26. www.lexisnexis.com/ (accessed September 11, 2007).

Goldman, Debra. 1991. "Shoppers still don't see green: Saatchi study sees paradox in attitude toward environment." *Adweek*, February 4. http://web.lexis-nexis.com/ (accessed July 9, 2007).

Good Wood Watch. 2001. "Good Wood Watch: Keeping forest certification meaningful in British Columbia." www.goodwoodwatch.org (accessed October 25, 2001).

Gordon, H. Scott. 1954. "The economic-theory of a common-property resource: The fishery." *Journal of Political Economy* 62 (2): 124–42.

Gottlieb, Robert. 1993. *Forcing the spring: The transformation of the American environmental movement.* Washington, DC: Island.

Gourlay, Candy. 1992. "North-south: Rich north can save poor south by 'fair' shopping." IPS–Inter Press Service, September 16. www.lexisnexis.com/ (accessed August 8, 2008).

Gowers, Andrew. 1985a. "Environmentalists attack tropical wood importers." *Financial Times* (London), May 3. http://web.lexis-nexis.com/ (accessed July 16, 2007).

———. 1985b. "Timber importers braced to meet challenge from environmentalists." *Financial Times* (London), June 4. http://web.lexis-nexis.com/ (accessed July 16, 2007).

Granovetter, Mark. 1985. "Economic-action and social-structure: The problem of embeddedness." *American Journal of Sociology* 91 (3): 481–510.

Green, Jessica F. 2010. "Private standards in the climate regime: The greenhouse gas protocol." *Business and Politics* 13 (2).

———. 2013. "Order out of chaos: Public and private rules for managing carbon." *Global Environmental Politics* 13 (2): 1–25.

Greenberg, Russell. 2000. *Criteria working group thought paper.* Washington, DC: Smithsonian Migratory Bird Center.

Greenberg, Russell, Peter Bichier, Andrea Cruz Angon, and Robert Reitsma. 1997. "Bird populations in shade and sun coffee plantations in central Guatemala. Poblaciones de aves en plantaciones cafetaleras en sombra y sol en la region central de Guatemala." *Conservation Biology* 11 (2): 448–59.

Greenpeace. 1994a. "Companies buy wood from the Kuusamo forest common." November 4. http://forests.org/archive/europe/gpfinfor.htm (accessed May 11, 2006).

———. 1994b. "Wanted: Clearcut-free forest products." Advertisement. *Globe and Mail* (Toronto), July 23.

———. 1995a. "Greenpeace national offices." http://web.archive.org/web/1999022 0201548/www.greenpeace.org/information.shtml (accessed August 27, 2008).

———. 1995b. "International NGOs join forces to save old-growth forests." Greenpeace, February 23. http://forests.org/archive/europe/trnfinla.htm (accessed May 11, 2006).

———. 2005. *A recipe for disaster: Supermarkets' insatiable appetite for seafood.* London: Greenpeace.

———. 2006. *A recipe for change: Supermarkets respond to the challenge of sourcing sustainable seafood.* London: Greenpeace.

———. 2008. *Carting away the oceans: How grocery stores are emptying the seas.* Washington, DC: Greenpeace.

———. 2009a. "Assessment of the Friend of the Sea fisheries and Aquaculture Certification Programme." June. www.greenpeace.org/usa/Global/usa/report/2009/7/assessment-of-friend-of-sea.pdf (accessed August 2, 2012).

———. 2009b. "Assessment of the Marine Stewardship Council (MSC) Fisheries Certification Programme." June. www.greenpeace.org/usa/Global/usa/report/2009/7/assessment-of-the-msc.pdf (accessed August 2, 2012).

———. N.d. *Just did it! The Vernon model of ecologically responsible forestry: Canada's first eco-certified forest. Clearcut-free?* Vancouver: Greenpeace.

Greenpeace Canada. 1997. "Greenpeace blockades Western Forest Products to save the Great Bear Rainforest: Forest actions coincide with Austrian protests and Ottawa legal action." May 21. www.greenpeace.org (accessed March 2, 2001).

Greenwire. 1991. "Birds: Warbler threatened by spraying." December 12. www.lexis nexis.com/ (accessed August 5, 2008).

———. 1996. "PCSD II: Gore presents awards to 15 programs." March 8. www.lexis nexis.com/ (accessed November 1, 2007).

Greig-Gran, Maryanne. 2004. *Following up on "Towards a sustainable paper cycle."* Geneva: World Business Council for Sustainable Development and International Institute for Environment and Development.

Gresser, Charis, and Sophia Tickell. 2002. "Mugged: Poverty in your coffee cup." Oxfam International. www.maketradefair.com/assets/english/mugged.pdf (accessed March 13, 2006).

Grieco, Joseph M. 1988. "Realist theory and the problem of international cooperation: Analysis with an amended prisoner's dilemma model." *Journal of Politics* 50 (3): 600–24.

Griffin, Larry J. 1993. "Narrative, event-structure analysis, and causal interpretation in historical sociology." *American Journal of Sociology* 98 (5): 1094–1133.

Griffiths, James. 2000. *Proposing an international mutual recognition framework.* International Forest Industry Roundtable.

———. 2001. *Proposing an international mutual recognition framework: Report of the working group on mutual recognition between credible sustainable forest management certification systems and standards.* International Forest Industry Roundtable.

Guber, Deborah Lynn. 2003. *The grassroots of a green revolution: Polling America on the environment.* Cambridge, MA: MIT Press.

Gulbrandsen, Lars H. 2004. "Overlapping public and private governance: Can forest certification fill the gaps in the global forest regime?" *Global Environmental Politics* 4 (2): 75–99.

———. 2005. "Explaining different approaches to voluntary standards: A study of forest certification choices in Norway and Sweden." *Journal of Environmental Policy and Planning* 7 (1): 43–59.

———. 2006. "Creating markets for eco-labelling: Are consumers insignificant?" *International Journal of Consumer Studies* 30 (5): 477–89.

———. 2010. *Transnational environmental governance: The emergence and effects of the certification of forests and fisheries.* Cheltenham and Northampton, UK: Edward Elgar.

Gunningham, Neil, Peter N. Grabosky, and Darren Sinclair. 1998. *Smart regulation: Designing environmental policy.* Oxford: Clarendon; New York: Oxford University Press.

Gunningham, Neil, Robert A. Kagan, and Dorothy Thornton. 2003. *Shades of green: Business, regulation, and environment.* Stanford: Stanford University Press.

Guppy, Nicholas. 1984. "Tropical deforestation: A global view." *Foreign Affairs* 62 (4): 928–65.

Guthman, Julie. 2004. *Agrarian dreams: The paradox of organic farming in California.* Berkeley: University of California Press.

Gutiérrez, Nicolás L., Sarah R. Valencia, Trevor A. Branch, David J. Agnew, Julia K. Baum, Patricia L. Bianchi, Jorge Cornejo-Donoso, Christopher Costello, Omar Defeo, Timothy E. Essington, Ray Hilborn, Daniel D. Hoggarth, Ashley E. Larsen,

Chris Ninnes, Keith Sainsbury, Rebecca L. Selden, Seeta Sistla, Anthony D. M. Smith, Amanda Stern-Pirlot, Sarah J. Teck, James T. Thorson, and Nicholas E. Williams. 2012. "Eco-label conveys reliable information on fish stock health to seafood consumers." *PLoS ONE* 7 (8): e43765.

Hacker, Jacob S. 2002. *The divided welfare state: The battle over public and private social benefits in the United States.* New York: Cambridge University Press.

Haland, Barb Lambrecht, and Maren Esmark. 2002. *Clean conscience consumption of seafood: A summary of eco-labels and environmental management systems for fisheries and aquaculture products.* Oslo: WWF-Norway.

Hall, Kevin. 1997. "Shrimp farms harvest aquaculture clash." *Journal of Commerce,* October 24. www.lexisnexis.com/ (accessed August 13, 2008).

Hall, Peter. 1986. *Governing the economy: The politics of state intervention in Britain and France.* New York: Oxford University Press.

Hall, Rodney Bruce, and Thomas J. Biersteker. 2002. *The emergence of private authority in global governance.* Cambridge: Cambridge University Press.

Hamilton, Gordon. 1995. "Eco-certified forest patch earns Greenpeace kudos: World-wide marketing plan tabbed for project." *Vancouver Sun,* December 1. www.lexisnexis.com/ (accessed July 24, 2008).

———. 1998a. "B.C. forest deals cancelled amid old-growth concerns: At least three European companies have informed B.C. forestry firms they will no longer buy their products unless old-growth logging ends or certain eco-standards are adopted." *Vancouver Sun,* April 3. www.lexisnexis.com/ (accessed November 17, 2007).

———. 1998b. "Greenpeace resumes action over WFP's Ingram practices: Company calls charges of watershed mismanagement frivolous, with its bid for eco-certification on line." *Vancouver Sun,* September 18. www.lexisnexis.com/ (accessed July 28, 2008).

———. 1998c. "Ingram logging opposed by Indians, eco-groups: Hereditary chiefs want one-year moratorium on harvest plans for watershed." *Vancouver Sun,* July 10, business section, F1. www.lexisnexis.com/ (accessed July 27, 2008).

Hammond, Susan. 2003. "SFF Eco-Certification Program." Silva Forest Foundation, January 31. www.silvafor.org/programs/ecocert/index.htm (accessed July 27, 2008).

Hamprecht, Jans. 2005. "Sustainable purchasing strategy in the food industry." PhD diss., University of St Gallen, Bamberg, Germany.

Hansen, Eric, and Heikki Juslin. 1999. *The status of forest certification in the ECE region.* New York: United Nations, Timber Section, Trade Division, UN-Economic Commission for Europe.

Hansen, Eric, and John Punches. 1998. "Collins Pine: Lessons from a pioneer." In *The business of sustainable forestry,* edited by the Sustainable Forestry Working Group, 6-1–6-16. Eugene: Oregon State University.

———. 1999. "Developing markets for certified forest products: A case study of Collins Pine Company." *Forest Products Journal* 49 (1): 30.

Hardin, Russell. 1982. *Collective action.* Baltimore: Published for Resources for the Future by the Johns Hopkins University Press.

Harris, Gillian. 1999. "The organic alternative." *Times* (London), July 30, home news section. http://web.lexis-nexis.com (accessed April 13, 2007).

Harris, Jesse M. 1990. "TV ad urges coffee boycott." Globe Newspaper Company, May 10, economy section, 90. http://web.lexis-nexis.com (accessed January 27, 2007).

Harrison, Kathryn. 1999. "Racing to the top or the bottom? Industry resistance to eco-labelling of paper products in three jurisdictions." *Environmental Politics* 8 (4): 110–36.

———. 2002. "Ideas and environmental standard-setting: A comparative study of regulation of the pulp and paper industry." *Governance* 15 (1): 65–96.

Haufler, Virginia. 2001. *A public role for the private sector: Industry self-regulation in a global economy.* Washington, DC: Carnegie Endowment for International Peace.

Haygreen, John G., and Jim L. Bowyer. 1996. *Forest products and wood science: An introduction.* 3rd ed. Ames: Iowa State University Press.

Helvarg, David. 2001. "On the blue frontier: Protecting the oceans." *E magazine* 12 (4): 26. www.lexisnexis.com/.

Hemmi, Kenzo. 1964. "International commodity agreements: Reality and the future." *Developing Economies* 2 (4): 358–72.

Herald (Glasgow). 1996. "Bid to combat overfishing." April 30, 4. www.lexisnexis.com/ (accessed August 1, 2007).

Hernes, Hans-Kristian, and Knut H. Mikalsen. 2002. "From protest to participation? Environmental groups and the management of marine fisheries." *Mobilization: An International Quarterly* 7 (1): 15–28.

Herrmann, Gerald A. 2003. "A short overview of IFOAM's organic guarantee system." In *The organic guarantee system: The need and strategy for harmonization and equivalence,* edited by Christina Westermayer and Bernward Geier, 71–73. Tholey-Theley, Germany: IFOAM, FAO, and UNCTAD.

Hettena, Seth. 1998. "Environmental groups protest Home Depot's sale of old-growth lumber." Associated Press State & Local Wire, October 14. www.lexisnexis.com/ (accessed November 1, 2007).

Hickman, Martin. 2006. "Cod taken off the shelves at ASDA to preserve stocks." *Independent* (London), March 28. www.lexisnexis.com/ (accessed August 1, 2012).

Highleyman, Scott, Amy Mathews Amos, and Hank Cauley. 2004. *An independent assessment of the Marine Stewardship Council.* Sandy River Plantation, ME: Wildhavens Consulting.

Hilborn, Ray. 2006. "Salmon-farming impacts on wild salmon." *Proceedings of the National Academy of Sciences of the United States of America* 103 (42): 15277.

Hilge, Volker. 2005. "Organic aquaculture in the world: Principles, public perception, markets, potential of products." Paper presented at the conference "Organic Aquaculture in the European Union: Current Status and Prospect for the Future," Brussels, October 12–13.

Hill, Brendan. 1997. "Label to protect shoal food." *Scotsman,* April 22. http://web.lexis-nexis.com/ (accessed February 5, 2007).

Hirsch, Paul M., and James J. Gillespie. 2001. "Unpacking path dependence: Differential valuations accorded history across disciplines." In *Path dependence and creation,* edited by Raghu Garud and Peter Karnoe, 69–90. Mahwah, NJ: Lawrence Erlbaum.

Hirschman, Albert O. 1970. *Exit, voice, and loyalty; Responses to decline in firms, organizations, and states.* Cambridge, MA: Harvard University Press.

Hirshleifer, Jack. 1983. "From weakest-link to best-shot: The voluntary provision of public goods." *Public Choice* 41 (3): 371–86.

H.O., Mohd Shahwahid. 2005. "Forest certification in Malaysia." In *Confronting sustainability: Forest certification in developing and transitioning countries,* edited by

Benjamin Cashore, Fred Gale, Errol Meidinger, and Deanna Newsom, 69–98. New Haven, CT: Yale F&ES Publication Series.

Hoberg, George. 1997. "Governing the environment; Comparing policy in Canada and the United States." In *Degrees of freedom: Canada and the United States in a changing global context,* edited by Keith Banting, George Hoberg, and Richard Simeon, 347–87. Montreal: McGill-Queens.

Hochstetler, Kathryn, and Margaret Keck. 2007. *Greening Brazil: Environmental activism in state and society.* Durham, NC: Duke University Press.

Hockerts, Kai. 2005. "The fair trade story." Oikos Sustainability Case Collection. www .oikos-foundation.unisg.ch/homepage/fairtrade.pdf (accessed September 12, 2006).

Hoffman, Andrew. J. 1999. "Institutional evolution and change: Environmentalism and the US chemical industry." *Academy of Management Journal* 42 (4): 351–71.

Hoffmann, Matthew J. 2011. *Climate governance at the crossroads: Experimenting with a global response after Kyoto.* New York: Oxford University Press.

Hogben, Dave. 1998. "Western seeks certification to satisfy European buyers." *Vancouver Sun,* June 5, F2.

Home Depot. 1996. "White House honors the Home Depot and Collin's Pine Company." March 7. http://web.archive.org/web/19970129011028/www.homedepot .com/FI/pcsd.htm (accessed November 1, 2007).

———. 1997. "Ten year selected financial and operating highlights." http://web.ar chive.org/web/19971212054615/http://www.homedepot.com/ (accessed October 1, 2007).

———. 2007. *Form 10-K* (annual report), March 29. http://ir.homedepot.com/reports .cfm (accessed December 8, 2007).

Hoobanoff, Shaye. 2004. "Coffee industry to adopt conduct code." *Deutsche Welle,* October 9. www.dw-world.de/dw/article/0,2144,1324034,00.html (accessed August 25, 2008).

Houston Economic Summit. 1990. "Houston Economic Declaration." G7 Houston Economic Summit, July 10. www.g7.utoronto.ca/g7/summit/1990houston/com munique/index.html (accessed June 19, 2002).

Howard, Steven, and Justin Stead. 2001. *The forest industry in the 21st century.* Godalming, UK: WWF International.

Howlett, Michael, and M. Ramesh. 1995. *Studying public policy: Policy cycles and policy subsystems.* New York: Oxford University Press.

———. 2003. *Studying public policy cycles and policy subsystems.* Vol. 2. Toronto: Oxford University Press.

Hume, Stephen, Alexandra Morton, Betty C. Keller, Rosella M. Leslie, Otto Langer, and Don Staniford. 2004. *A stain upon the Sea: West coast salmon farming.* Madeira Park, British Columbia: Harbour.

Hummel, Fred. 1986. "Report in reports: Tropical forests; A call for action." *Environment* 28 (4): 25–27.

Humphreys, David. 1996. *Forest politics: The evolution of international cooperation.* London: Earthscan.

———. 2004. "Redefining the issues: NGO influence on international forest negotiations." *Global Environmental Politics* 4 (2): 51–74.

———. 2006. *Logjam: Deforestation and the crisis of global governance.* London: Earthscan.

Humphries, Shoana, Richard P. Vlosky, and Douglas Carter. 2001. "Certified wood products merchants in the United States: A comparison between 1995 and 1998." *Forest Products Journal* 51 (6): 32–39.

Hunt, John. 1991. "Retailers agree WWF hardwood initiative." *Financial Times* (London, December 11. http://web.lexis-nexis.com/ (accessed July 24, 2007).

Hunter, Beth, and Sarah King. 2008. *Out of stock: Supermarkets and the future of seafood.* Toronto: Greenpeace, Canada.

Hyde, Susan D. 2011. *The pseudo-Democrat's dilemma: Why election monitoring became an international norm.* Ithaca, NY: Cornell University Press.

ICFA. 1996. "World's fishery groups urge policies to go beyond sustaining current seafood production." December 10. http://web.archive.org/web/20020118093327/http://icfa.net/ (accessed August 21, 2008).

———. 1997. "Annual meeting." September 29. http://web.archive.org/web/20020118093327/http://icfa.net/ (accessed August 21, 2008).

ICO. 1997. *Agricultural and economic analysis of organically grown or "organic" coffee.* London: International Coffee Organization.

———. 2012. "All exporting countries: Total production." www.ico.org/historical/2000–09/PDF/TOTPRODUCTION.pdfs (accessed October 23, 2012).

IFAT. 2008. "Monitoring: Building trust in fair trade." July 3. www.ifat.org/index.php?option=com_content&task=view&id=21&Itemid=68 (accessed August 7, 2008).

IFCNR. 2001. "United they stand . . . against sustainable fisheries." April 4. www.fisheries.ifcnr.com/article.cfm?NewsID=113 (accessed April 5, 2007).

IFOAM. 2001. *IFOAM annual report 2000.* www.ifoam.org/about_ifoam/inside_ifoam/annual_reports.html (accessed August 5, 2008).

———. 2005. "Report of the IFOAM world board to the IFOAM General Assembly." September 25. www.ifoam.org/pdfs/IFOAM_Report.pdf (accessed August 1, 2007).

IIED. 1996. *Towards a sustainable paper cycle.* London: International Institute for Environment and Development.

Ince, Peter J. 1999. "Global cycle changes the rules for US pulp and paper." *PIMA's North American Paper Maker* 81 (12): 37–42.

International Paper. 2006. "International Paper agrees to sell 5.1 million acres of U.S. forestland for approximately $6.1 billion." April 4. http://investor.internationalpaper.com/phoenix.zhtml?c=73062&p=irol-newsArticle&ID=838517&highlight (accessed December 8, 2007).

IOAS. 2006. "History." March 21. www.ioas.org/WEBSITE/0410_History.htm (accessed April 1, 2006).

Islas, Jorge. 1997. "Getting round the lock-in in electricity generating systems: The example of the gas turbine." *Research Policy* 26 (1): 49–66.

ITS Global. 2005. *Evaluation and assessment of the Cerflor-Brazilian forest certification scheme against the requirements of the PEFC Council.* Melbourne: International Trade Strategies Global.

ITTO. 1992. *ITTO guidelines for the sustainable management of natural tropical forests.* Yokohama, Japan: Forest Research Institute of Malaysia.

IUCN. 1980. *World conservation strategy: Living resource conservation for sustainable development.* Gland, Switzerland: IUCN, UNEP, and WWF.

Jack, Andrew. 1990. "Fair trade set to join free-range as a USP—consumer awareness." *Financial Times* (London), October 11. http://web.lexis-nexis.com/ (accessed January 29, 2007).

Jaffe, Roberta, and Christopher M. Bacon. 2008. "From differentiated coffee markets toward alternative trade and knowledge networks." In *Confronting the coffee crisis: Fair trade, sustainable livelihoods and ecosystems in Mexico and Central America,* edited by Christopher M. Bacon, V. Ernesto Mendez, Stephen R. Gliessman, David Goodman, and Jonathan A. Fox, 311–36. Cambridge, MA: MIT Press.

Jaffee, Daniel. 2007. *Brewing justice: Fair trade coffee, sustainability, and survival.* Berkeley: University of California Press.

James, Deborah. 2000. "Justice and java: Coffee in a fair trade market." *NACLA Report on the Americas* 34 (2): 11–14.

Jamieson, Robert L. 1994. "Why coffee is taking a toll on songbirds." *Seattle Post-Intelligencer,* May 5. www.lexisnexis.com/ (accessed August 5, 2008).

Jarvis, Lovell S. 2005. "The rise and decline of rent-seeking activity in the Brazilian coffee sector: Lessons from the imposition and removal of coffee export quotas." *World Development* 33 (11): 1881–1903.

Jeanrenaud, Jean-Paul, and Nigel Dudley. 1997. "The role of NGOs in the forest debate." Paper presented at the XI World Forestry Congress, Antalya, Turkey, October 13–22.

Jespersen, Claus, Kim Christiansen, and Brent Hummelmose. 2000. *Cleaner production assessment in fish processing.* Nairobi: United Nations Environment Programme and Danish Environmental Protection Agency.

Joling, Dan. 1999. "Pilot projects aim toward organic label for Alaska seafood." Associated Press State & Local Wire, June 23. http://web.lexis-nexis.com/ (accessed October 4, 2006).

Jones, Bryan D. 1999. "Bounded rationality." *Annual Review of Political Science* 2(1): 297–321.

Jung, Carolyn. 1999. "Fish-depletion concerns constrain San Francisco–area restaurants." *San Jose Mercury News,* September 7. www.lexisnexis.com/ (accessed August 13, 2008).

Kalfagianni, Agni, and Philipp Pattberg. 2013. "Fishing in muddy waters: Exploring the conditions for effective governance of fisheries and aquaculture." *Marine Policy* 38: 124–32.

Katz, Ian. 1992. "Knock, knock, knocking wood: Friends of the Earth has called for a consumer boycott of wood products from DIY stores." *Guardian* (London), January 10, features section, 27. www.lexisnexis.com/ (accessed November 1, 2007).

Kay, Jane. 1997. "Home Depot bans ancient redwoods." *Portland Oregonian,* May 9. www.lexisnexis.com/ (accessed November 1, 2007).

Keck, Margaret E., and Kathryn Sikkink. 1998. *Activists beyond borders: Advocacy networks in international politics.* Ithaca, NY: Cornell University Press.

Kelley, Judith. 2009. "The more the merrier? The effects of having multiple international election monitoring organizations." *Perspectives on Politics* 7 (1): 59–64.

Kemp, Rene, Arie Rip, and Johan Schot. 2001. "Constructing transition paths through the management of niches." In *Path dependence and creation,* edited by Raghu Garud and Peter Karnoe, 269–300. Mahwah, NJ: Lawrence Erlbaum.

Kennedy, Bob. 1999. "Orkney salmon goes organic." *Aberdeen Press and Journal,* April 21, fishing: salmon section, 21. http://web.lexis-nexis.com/ (accessed April 13, 2007).

Kenworthy, Tom. 1995. "Marine protection sites proposed; World Bank, conservation groups offer ambitious preservation plan." *Washington Post,* June 24. www.lexis nexis.com/ (accessed August 13, 2008).

Keohane, Robert O., and Joseph S. Nye Jr. 1998. "Power and interdependence in the information age." *Foreign Affairs* 77 (5): 81–94.

Keohane, Robert O., and David G. Victor. 2011. "The regime complex for climate change." *Perspectives on Politics* 9 (1): 7–23.

Khindaria, Brij. 1982a. "Conference hopes to halt forest decline." *Financial Times* (London), June 8. http://web.lexis-nexis.com/ (accessed July 16, 2007).

———. 1982b. "Timber accord may lead the way." *Financial Times* (London), June 29. http://web.lexis-nexis.com/ (accessed July 16, 2007).

Kiewiet, D. Roderick, and Mathew D. McCubbins. 1991. *The logic of delegation: Congressional parties and the appropriations process.* Chicago: University of Chicago Press.

Kilborn, Peter T. 1988. "U.S. moves to ban Nicaraguan coffee." *New York Times,* April 5. http://web.lexis-nexis.com/ (accessed January 27, 2007).

King, Andrew A., and Michael J. Lenox. 2000. "Industry self-regulation without sanctions: The chemical industry's Responsible Care Program." *Academy of Management Journal* 43 (4): 698–716.

King, Gary, Robert O. Keohane, and Sidney Verba. 1994. *Designing social inquiry: Scientific inference in qualitative research.* Princeton, NJ: Princeton University Press.

Kingdon, John. 1984. *Agendas, alternatives, and public policies.* Glenview, IL: Scott Foresman.

Kinnaird, Margaret F., Eric W. Sanderson, Timothy G. O'Brien, Hariyo T. Wibisono, and Gillian Woolmer. 2003. "Deforestation trends in a tropical landscape and implications for endangered large mammals." *Conservation Biology* 17 (1): 245–57.

Kitschelt, Herbert P. 1986. "Political opportunity structures and political protest: Antinuclear movements in four democracies." *British Journal of Political Science* 16 (1): 57–85.

Klein, Naomi. 1999. *No logo: Taking aim at the brand bullies.* New York: Picador.

Klooster, Daniel. 2005. "Environmental certification of forests: The evolution of environmental governance in a commodity network." *Journal of Rural Studies* 21 (4): 403–17.

Knight, Alan. 2000. *Seeing the customer and the trees: A proposed revised buying policy for B&Q for beyond 2000 for consultation.* Chandlers Ford, Eastleigh, Hampshire, UK: B&Q.

Knight, Danielle. 1997. "Gabon-environment: Forest Council acts to decertify logging firm." IPS–Inter Press Service, November 18. www.lexisnexis.com/ (accessed July 15, 2008).

———. 1998. "Environment: Corporate gaints abandon 'old-growth' forest products." IPS–Inter Press Service, December 9. www.lexisnexis.com/ (accessed July 19, 2008).

Knight, Jack. 1992. *Institutions and social conflict: Political economy of institutions and decisions.* Cambridge: Cambridge University Press.

———. 1995. "Models, interpretations, and theories: Constructing explanations of institutional emergence and change." In *Explaining social institutions,* edited by Jack Knight and Itai Sened, 95–119. Ann Arbor: University of Michigan Press.

Knight, Peter. 1991. "Business and the environment: Timber trade gets green credentials." *Financial Times* (London), October 30, section 1, 20. www.lexisnexis.com/ (accessed November 1, 2007).

———. 1993a. "Business and the environment: Poised for the big leap forward—The campaign for 'green labels' on wood products." *Financial Times* (London), July 7. http://web.lexis-nexis.com/ (accessed July 24, 2007).

———. 1993b. "Timber watchdog ready to bark." *Financial Times* (London), October 6, 1993, 12.

———. 1996. "Forests for life: Eco-label; The mark of good management." *Observer*, September 29, 96.

Knill, Christoph, and Dirk Lehmkuhl. 2002. "Private actors and the State: Internationalization and changing patterns of governance." *Governance* 15 (1): 41–63.

Kochen, Marlike. 2003. "History of fair trade." International Federation of Alternative Trade, December. www.worldshops.org/fairtrade/netw/2004_FinalHistory_of _FairTrade.doc (accessed March 13, 2006).

Kolk, Ans. 1996. *Forests in international environmental politics: International organisations, NGOs and the Brazilian Amazon.* Alexander Numankade, Netherlands: International Books.

Kolk, Ans, Rob van Tulder, and Carlijn Welters. 1999. "International codes of conduct and corporate social responsibility: Can transnational corporations regulate themselves?" *Transnational Corporations* 8 (1): 143–80.

Konefal, Jason, Michael Mascarenhas, and Maki Hatanaka. 2005. "Governance in the global agro-food system: Backlighting the role of transnational supermarket chains." *Agriculture and Human Values* 22 (3): 291–302.

Kopf, Silas. 1993. "Responsible woodworking: A personal odyssey." In *Conservation by design,* edited by Scott Landis, 35–36. Providence, RI: Museum of Art, Rhode Island School of Design; Easthampton, MA: Woodworkers Alliance for Rainforest Protection.

Korutz, Bryon J. 2003. *Industry surveys: Paper and forest products.* New York: Standard and Poor's.

Kotchen, Matthew J., and Klaas van 't Veld. 2009. "An economics perspective on treating voluntary programs as clubs." In *Voluntary programs: A club theory perspective,* edited by M. Potoski and A. Prakash, 67–86. Cambridge, MA: MIT Press.

Kozak, Robert, and Kerstin Canby. 2007. "Why China prefers logs: Explaining the prevalence of unproccessed wood in China's timber imports." In *Information bulletin: China and East Asia* 9:1–5. Washington, DC: Forest Trends and Rights and Resources Group.

Krasner, S. D. 1991. "Global communications and national power: Life on the Pareto frontier." *World Politics* 43 (3): 336–66.

———. 2001. "Sovereignty." *Foreign Policy* 122:20–29.

KRAV. 2002. "Project description: Eco-labelling of wild capture fish and shellfish." KRAV—Ekonomisk Forening, December 9. http://arkiv.krav.se/arkiv/internatio-nellt/projdes1.pdf (accessed June 9, 2007).

Krier, Jean-Marie. 2005. "Fair trade in Europe, 2005: Facts and figures on fair trade in 25 European countries." Fair Trade Advocacy Office, December. www.worldshops .org/news/new/FairTradeinEurope2005.pdf (accessed March 13, 2006).

Krkosek, Martin, Mark A. Lewis, and John P. Volpe. 2005. "Transmission dynamics of parasitic sea lice from farm to wild salmon." *Proceedings of the Royal Society B— Biological Sciences* 272 (1564): 689–96.

Krkosek, M., Mark A. Lewis, John P. Volpe, and Alexandra Morton. 2006. "Fish farms and sea lice infestations of wild juvenile salmon in the Broughton Archipelago: A rebuttal to Brooks (2005)." *Reviews in Fisheries Science* 14 (1–2): 1–11.

Krugman, Paul. 1991. "History versus expectations." *Quarterly Journal of Economics* 106 (2): 651–67.

Kura, Yumiko, Carmen Revenga, Eriko Hoshino, and Greg Mock. 2004. *Fishing for answers: Making sense of the global fish crisis.* Washington, DC: World Resources Institute.

Kurien, John. 2000. "Behind the label: Are eco-labels the answer to sustainable fishing?" *New Internationalist* 325: 25–27.

Kysar, Douglas A. 2004. "Preferences for processes: The process/product distinction and the regulation of consumer choice." *Harvard Law Review* 118 (2): 525–642.

Landis, Scott. 1993. *Conservation by design.* Providence, RI: Museum of Art, Rhode Island School of Design; Easthampton, MA: Woodworkers Alliance for Rainforest Protection.

Langman, Mary. 1992. "Memories and notes on the beginning and early history of IFOAM." International Federation of Organic Agriculture Movements. http://infohub.ifoam.org/sites/default/files/page/files/early_history_ifoam.pdf (accessed October 30, 2005).

Lawson, James, and Benjamin Cashore. 2001. *Autopoiesis and forest certification.* Auburn, AL: Auburn University Forest Policy Center.

Lehman, Stan. 2000. "Environmentalists turn to consumers for help in curbing Amazon forest devastation." Associated Press Worldstream, April 11. www.lexisnexis.com/ (accessed July 21, 2008).

Le Mare, Ann. 2008. "The impact of fair trade on social and economic development: A review of the literature." *Geography Compass* 2 (6): 1922–42.

Levi, Margaret. 1997. "A model, a method and a map: Rational choice in comparative historical analysis." In *Comparative politics: Rationality, culture and structure,* edited by Mark I. Lichbach and Allan S. Zuckerman, 19–41. Cambridge: Cambridge University Press.

Levin, Kelly, Benjamin Cashore, and Jonathan Koppell. 2009. "Can non-state certification systems bolster state-centered efforts to promote sustainable development through the Clean Development Mechanism (CDM)?" *Wake Forest Law Review* 44:777–98.

Levy, Marc A., Oran R. Young, and Michael Zürn. 1994. *The study of international regimes.* Laxenburg, Austria: International Institute for Applied Systems Analysis.

Lewin, Bryan, Daniele Giovannucci, and Panos Varangis. 2004. *Coffee markets: New paradigms in global supply and demand.* Agriculture and Rural Development Discussion Paper 3. International Bank for Reconstruction and Development, Agriculture and Rural Development Department, March. http://lnweb18.worldbank.org/ESSD/ardext.nsf/11ByDocName/CoffeeMarketsNewParadigmsinGlobalSupplyandDemand/$FILE/CoffeeMarkets-ArdDp3.pdf (accessed September 1, 2005).

Lienert, Sam. 1999. "Marine protection parks not needed, says Seafood Council." AAP Newsfeed, January 14. www.lexisnexis.com/ (accessed August 13, 2008).

Lindblom, Charles. 1977. *Politics and markets: The world's political economic systems.* New York: Basic Books.

Linton, April. 2004. "Partnering for sustainability: Business–NGO alliances in the coffee industry." *Development in Practice* 15 (3–4): 600–614.

Linton, April, Cindy Chiayuan Liou, and Kelly Ann Shaw. 2004. "A taste of trade justice: Marketing global social responsibility via fair trade coffee." *Globalizations* 1 (2): 223–46.

Lipschutz, Ronnie D. 1992. "Reconstructing world-politics: The emergence of global civil society." *Millennium: Journal of International Studies* 21 (3): 389–420.

Lipschutz, Ronnie D., and Cathleen Fogel. 2002. "'Regulations for the rest of us?' Global civil society and the privatization of transnational regulation." In *The emergence of private authority in global governance*, edited by Rodney Bruce Hall and Thomas J. Biersteker, 115–40. Cambridge: Cambridge University Press.

Lober, Douglas J., and Mark D. Eisen. 1995. "The greening of retailing: Certification and the home improvement industry." *Journal of Forestry* 95 (4): 38–41.

Lober, Douglas J., and Donald Philip Green. 1994. "NIMBY or NIABY: A logit model of opposition to solid-waste-disposal facility siting." *Journal of Environmental Management* 40 (1): 33–50.

Lunn, Stephen. 1999. "Fishermen snarling at no-go zones." *Weekend Australian*, December 11. www.lexisnexis.com/ (accessed August 13, 2008).

Lush, Patricia. 1991. "Europeans join B.C. logging fight." *Globe and Mail* (Toronto), June 10. www.lexisnexis.com/ (accessed September 11, 2007).

———. 1995. "Forest companies to sell ecologically certified products: Move to label goods from sustainable areas intended to please customers, end boycotts." *Globe and Mail* (Toronto), December 28. www.lexisnexis.com/ (accessed July 19, 2008).

———. 1998. "Loggers covet the green logo." *Globe and Mail* (Toronto), June 11. www.lexisnexis.com/ (accessed October 1, 2008).

Luttinger, Nina, and Gregory Dicum. 2006. *The coffee book: Anatomy of an industry from crop to the last drop.* Rev. ed. New York: New Press.

Luxner, Larry. 1996. "Zoo hosts sustainable coffee congress." *Tea and Coffee Trade Journal* 168 (11): 84–87. www.luxner.com/cgi-bin/view_article.cgi?articleID=81 (accessed March 14, 2006).

Mabbett, Terry. 2007. "Stored coffees come of age." *Tea and Coffee Trade Journal* 179 (5). www.teaandcoffee.net/0507/coffee.htm (accessed January 27, 2014).

MacLean, Pamela A. 1989. "Judge orders observers aboard tuna boats." United Press International, January 17. http://web.lexis-nexis.com/ (accessed April 16, 2007).

MacMillan Bloedel, Ltd. 1998. "MB plans to stop clearcutting." *MB Journal* 18 (7).

Madeley, John. 1989. "UN agency accepts criticism of 'old-fashioned' forestry policy." *Financial Times* (London), September 5, section 1, commodities and agriculture, 40. http://web.lexis-nexis.com/ (accessed July 22, 2007).

Mahoney, James. 2000. "Path dependence in historical sociology." *Theory and Society* 29 (4): 507–48.

Makabenta, Leah. 1993. "Environment: Eco-labelling, an idea whose time has come." IPS–Inter Press Service, June 4. www.lexisnexis.com/ (accessed September 1, 2007).

Malone, James L. 1983. "The United-States and the Law of the Sea after UNCLOS-III." *Law and Contemporary Problems* 46 (2): 29–36.

Mangrove Action Project. 2005. *The MAP News.* Mangrove Action Project, December 5. www.mangroveactionproject.org/news/the-map-news/mapnews165/?searchterm=walmart (accessed August 16, 2008).

Manuel, Anne. 1985. "Human rights: New report on Nicaraguan rebel abuses." IPS–Inter Press Service, March. http://web.lexis-nexis.com/ (accessed January 28, 2007).

Marchak, M. Patricia, Scott L. Aycock, and Deborah M. Herbert. 1999. *Falldown: Forest policy in British Columbia.* Vancouver: David Suzuki Foundation and Ecotrust Canada.

Marine Parks and Reserves Authority. 1999. *Annual Report: 1 July 1998–30 June 1999.* Department of Conservation and Land Management, November 18. www.dec .wa.gov.au/mpra (accessed August 16, 2008).

———. 2000. *Annual Report: 1 July 1999–30 June 2000.* Department of Conservation and Land Management, November 18. www.dec.wa.gov.au/mpra (accessed August 16, 2008).

Market Wire. 2007. "HQ sustainable receives ACC certification: First major tilapia company certified, highlights quality of HQS's toxin-free products." December 21. www.lexisnexis.com/ (accessed August 16, 2008).

Marlin, Alice Tepper, Jonathan Schorsch, Emily Swaab, and Rosalyn Will. 1991. *Shopping for a better world.* New York: Council on Economic Priorities and Ballantine Books.

Marshall, George. 1991. "FAO and tropical forestry." *Ecologist* 21 (2): 60–72.

Martin, Lisa L., and Beth A. Simmons. 1998. "Theories and empirical studies of international institutions." *International Organization* 52 (4): 729–57.

Martinelli, Enzo. 1998. *Fair trade in Europe: Facts and figures on the fair trade sector in 16 European countries.* Maastricht: European Fair Trade Association.

Matas, Robert. 1996. "The changing West: Part six of seven." *Globe and Mail* (Toronto), January 8. www.lexisnexis.com/ (accessed July 19, 2008).

Mathew, Sebastian. 2004. "Sustainable development and social well-being: Which approach for fish trade?" *Bridges* 4 (3): 11–14.

Mattli, Walter, and Tim Büthe. 2003. "Setting international standards: Technological rationality or primacy of power?" *World Politics* 56 (1): 1–42.

Max Havelaar, Switzerland. 2008. "Quality label." March 1. www.maxhavelaar.ch/en/ maxhavelaar/quality-label/ (accessed July 26, 2008).

May, Brendan, Duncan Leadbitter, Mike Sutton, and Michael Weber. 2003. "The Marine Stewardship Council (MSC): Background, rationale and challenges." In *Eco-labelling in fisheries: What is it all about?* edited by Bruce Phillips, Trevor Ward, and Chet Chaffee, 14–33. Oxford: Blackwell.

McAlexander, Jamee, and Eric Hansen. 1998. "J. Sainsbury plc and Home Depot: Retailers' impact on sustainability." In *The business of sustainable forestry: Case studies.* Sustainable Forestry Working Group. Chicago: John D. and Catherine T. MacArthur Foundation.

McDermott, Constance L. 2003. "Personal trust and trust in abstract systems: A study of Forest Stewardship Council–accredited certification in British Columbia." PhD diss., University of British Columbia.

McDermott, Constance L., Emily Noah, and Benjamin Cashore. 2008. "Differences that 'matter'? A framework for comparing environmental certification standards and government policies." *Journal of Environmental Policy and Planning* 10 (1): 47–70.

McNichol, Jason Hall. 2002. "Contesting governance in the global marketplace: A sociological assessment of business-NGO partnerships to build markets for certified wood." PhD diss., University of California, Berkeley.

Meidinger, Errol E. 2006. "The administrative law of global private-public regulation: The case of forestry." *European Journal of International Law* 17 (1): 47–87.

Mendez, V. Ernesto. 2008. "Farmers' livelihoods and biodiversity conservation in a coffee landscape of El Salvador." In *Confronting the coffee crisis: Fair trade, sustainable livelihoods and ecosystems in Mexico and Central America*, edited by Christopher M. Bacon, V. Ernesto Mendez, Stephen R. Gliessman, David Goodman, and Jonathan A. Fox, 207–34. Cambridge, MA: MIT Press.

MHR, Viandes Meats. 1999. "History of organic farming." February. www.mhr-viandes.com/en/docu/docu/d0000153.htm (accessed August 20, 2005).

Michaels, Marguerite. 1993. "Retreat from Africa." *Foreign Affairs* 72 (1): 93–108.

Micheletti, Michele. 1999. "Put your money where your mouth is! The virtues of shopping for democracy." Paper read at the Nordic Political Science Association conference, October 28–29, Uppsala, Sweden.

Michelsen, Johannes. 2001. "Recent development and political acceptance of organic farming in Europe." *Sociologia Ruralis* 41 (1): 3–20.

Michonski, Katherine E., and Michael A. Levi. 2010. *The regime complex for global climate change.* New York: Council on Foreign Relations.

Migdal, Joel S. 2001. *State in society: Studying how states and societies transform and constitute one another.* Cambridge: Cambridge University Press.

Mintzberg, Henry. 1978. "Patterns in strategy formation." *Management Science* 24 (9): 934–48.

Mitchell, Chip. 1998. "Bittersweet: As competition brews among coffee fair traders, a movement comes of age." *Monthly Newsletter of the Resource Centre of the Americas* 15 (8). www.web.net/~bthomson/fairtrade/fair67.html (accessed August 10, 2007).

Mitchell, Ronald B. 2011. "Transparency for governance: The mechanisms and effectiveness of disclosure-based and education-based transparency policies." *Ecological Economics* 70 (11): 1882–90.

Morgan, Dan. 1977. "U.S. coffee companies major source of Amin's revenue." *Washington Post,* November 5, A2. http://web.lexis-nexis.com/(accessed January 28, 2007).

MSC. 1999a. "About." January 25. http://web.archive.org/web/19990125101405/http://www.msc.org/ (accessed March 23, 2007).

———. 1999b. "MSC structures: The Marine Stewardship Council structure and governance." January. http://web.archive.org/web/19990125101405/http://www.msc.org/ (accessed May 15, 2007).

———. 2000a. "Environmental organisation praises Migros for its leadership and vision in providing sustainable seafood to customers." November 15. www.msc.org/html/ni_46.htm (accessed October 2, 2006).

———. 2000b. "Marine Stewardship Council awards sustainability label to Alaska salmon." September 9. www.msc.org/html/ni_54.htm (accessed October 2, 2006).

———. 2000c. "MSC structures: The Marine Stewardship Council structure and governance." October 2. http://web.archive.org/web/20001002235224/http://www.msc.org/structure.html (accessed May 15, 2007).

———. 2000d. "Support grows for the Marine Stewardship Council certification programme." September 23. www.msc.org/html/ni_50.htm (accessed October 2, 2006).

———. 2000e. "World's first sustainable seafood products launched." March 3. www.msc.org/html/ni_55.htm (accessed October 2, 2006).

———. 2001a. "Alaska salmon processors/distributors pleased with eco-label." November 13. www.msc.org/html/ni_31.htm (accessed October 2, 2006).

———. 2001b. "Board members." May 4. http://web.archive.org/web/2001050 4221048/www.msc.org/templates/template3.asp (accessed August 16, 2008).

———. 2001c. "Governance review commission." January 18. http://web.archive.org/ web/20010118151300/http://www.msc.org/ (accessed August 14, 2008).

———. 2001d. "MSC announces new governance structure." July 27. www.msc.org/ html/ni_36.htm (accessed October 2, 2006).

———. 2003. "Board members." February 2. http://web.archive.org/web/20030202 102425/http://www.msc.org/ (accessed August 14, 2008).

———. 2004. "MSC to convene objections panel to review objection on determination for the Gulf of Alaska pollock fishery." October 22. www.msc.org/newsroom/ press_releases/archive-2004/msc-to-convene-objections-panel-to-review (accessed August 17, 2008).

———. 2005a. "Gulf of Alaska pollock: Conclusion of objections process." April 11. www.msc.org/newsroom/press_releases/archive-2005/gulf-of-alaska-pollock -conclusion-of-objections (accessed August 1, 2008).

———. 2005b. *MSC stakeholder council.* London: Marine Stewardship Council.

———. 2006. "MSC not to develop aquaculture standard: MSC Board statement." November 20. www.msc.org/html/ni_290.htm (accessed June 9, 2007).

———. 2007a. *Annual report 2005/2006.* www.msc.org/assets/docs/MSC_annual _report_05_06.pdf (accessed June 9, 2007).

———. 2007b. "Certified fisheries and fisheries in assessment." April. www.msc.org/as sets/docs/fishery_certification/MSC_fisheries_06–07.pdf (accessed June 9, 2007).

———. 2012. *Trustees' report and accounts for the year end 31st March 2012.* London: Marine Stewardship Council.

Muhtaman, Dwi Rahmad, and Ferdinandus Agung Prasetyo. 2006. "Forest certification in Indonesia." In *Confronting sustainability: Forest certification in developing and transitioning countries,* edited by Benjamin Cashore, Fred Gale, Errol Meidinger, and Deanna Newsom, 33–68. New Haven, CT: Yale F&ES.

Mui, Ylan Q. 2008. "Grocers' rules follow wave of sustainably farmed fish." *Washington Post,* July 16, suburban edition. www.lexisnexis.com/ (accessed August 3, 2012).

Murphy, David F., and Jem Bendell. 1997. *In the company of partners: Business, environmental groups and sustainable development post-Rio.* Bristol, UK: Policy Press.

Myers, Norman. 1984. *The primary source: Tropical forests and our future.* New York: Norton.

Naturland. 2006. "Background information: Coffee code or 4C Code (Common Code for the Coffee Community)." December. www.naturland.de/fileadmin/MDB/ documents/International/English/4C_background_information.PDF (accessed August 25, 2008).

———. 2007. *Naturland standards on production.* Gräfelfing, Germany: Naturland.

Naylor, Rosamond L., Rebecca J. Goldburg, Jurgenne H. Primavera, Nils Kautsky, Malcolm C. M. Beveridge, Jason Clay, Carl Folke, Jane Lubchenco, Harold Mooney, and Max Troell. 2000. "Effect of aquaculture on world fish supplies." *Nature* 405 (6790): 1017–24.

Nelson, Richard R., and Sidney G. Winter. 2002. "Evolutionary theorizing in economics." *Journal of Economic Perspectives* 16 (2): 23–46.

Nesmith, Jeff. 1998. "Old growth forest protests an old story for Canadian loggers." Cox News Service, October 28. www.lexisnexis.com/ (accessed July 19, 2008).

Newell, Peter, and Matthew Paterson. 2010. *Climate capitalism: Global warming and the transformation of the global economy.* Cambridge: Cambridge University Press.

New Hampshire Business Review. 1991. "The Home Depot scrutinizes products' environmental claims." 13 (20): 26. www.lexisnexis.com/ (accessed November 1, 2007).

New York Times. 1974. "Japanese and Soviet whaling protested by boycott of goods." June 20, 8.

———. 1987. "Nicaraguan coffee available." March 25, C6. http://web.lexis-nexis.com/ (accessed January 27, 2007).

———. 1989. "A bigger sea around us." January 7, section 1, 26. www.lexisnexis.com/ (accessed February 15, 2008).

———. 1998. Display ad 61, G2.

NFI. 1997a. "NFI Board approves industry code for responsible fishing, new executive vice president." May 6. http://web.archive.org/web/19980712140533/nfi.org/News_Room/pr9713.htm (accessed March 30, 2007).

———. 1997b. "Seafood coalition announces 'Principles for responsible fisheries' to promote sustainable fisheries." March 20. http://web.archive.org/web/19980712140614/nfi.org/News_Room/pr9709.htm (accessed March 30, 2007).

———. 1998. "The Responsible Fisheries Society of the United States." December 3. http://web.archive.org/web/19981202141742/www.nfi.org/RFSUS.htm (accessed March 30, 2007).

———. 1999. "RFS and GAA merge fisheries and aquaculture eco-labeling programs: Partnership increases participation in industry's sustainable fisheries program." June 22. http://web.archive.org/web/20010429031406/nfi.org/pressreleases/1999/pr9940.htm (accessed March 30, 2007).

———. 2000. "NFI supports Sustainable Forestry Initiative (SFI) Program." April 18. http://web.archive.org/web/20010420052951/nfi.org/pressreleases/2000/pro011.htm (accessed March 30, 2007).

Ngangoue, Nana Rosine. 1997. "Gabon-environment: NGOs want eco-label stripped from German firm." IPS–Inter Press Service, January 26. www.lexisnexis.com/ (accessed July 14, 2008).

Nix, Mede. 1988. "Environmentalists protest killing of dolphins." United Press International, January 21. http://web.lexis-nexis.com/ (accessed April 16, 2007).

Noble, Kimberley. 1989. "Ontario pulp, paper firms must monitor their pollution." *Globe and Mail* (Toronto), March 3. www.lexisnexis.com/ (accessed September 12, 2007).

Norr, Serena. 2007. "Swiss water process: The 100% chemical free decaf coffee." *Tea and Coffee Trade Journal* 179 (3). www.teaandcoffee.net/0307/retail.htm (accessed December 12, 2007).

North, Douglass C. 1991. *Institutions, institutional change and economic performance.* New York: Cambridge University Press.

Nossiter, Bernard D. 1983. "New sea wars on the horizon." *New York Times,* January 30, section 4, 4. www.lexisnexis.com/ (accessed Febuary 13, 2008).

NRDC. 1996. "Shrimp cocktail: Recipe for disaster." August 16. http://web.archive.org/web/19961019030716/www.nrdc.org/status/ocshrsr.html (accessed April 16, 2007).

Oberthür, Sebastian. 2009. "Interplay management: Enhancing environmental policy integration among international institutions." *International Environmental Agreements: Politics, Law and Economics* 9 (4): 371–91.

Oberthür, Sebastian, and Thomas Gehring. 2006. "Institutional interaction in global environmental governance: The case of the Cartagena Protocol and the World Trade Organization." *Global Environmental Politics* 6 (2): 1–31.

Oberthür, Sebastian, and Olav Schram Stokke. 2011. *Managing institutional complexity: Regime interplay and global environmental change.* Cambridge, MA: MIT Press.

Ocean Trust. 2000. "Responsible Fisheries Society." October 3. http://web.archive.org/web/20001003160901/www.oceantrust.org/news/index.htm (accessed October 1, 2008).

———. 2001. "Seafood guides from the Audubon Society, Monterey Bay Aquarium, Natural Resources Defense Council, Environmental Defense & Chefs Collaborative." January 1. http://web.archive.org/web/20011216110318/www.oceantrust.org/brief_book/chefs_guide_01_2001.htm (accessed October 26, 2008).

OECD. 2005. "Private certification of a fishery as sustainable." In *Environmental requirements and market access,* edited by OECD, 253–67. Paris: Organisation for Economic Co-operation and Development.

Oliver, Christine. 1991. "Strategic responses to institutional processes." *Academy of Management Review* 16 (1): 145–79.

Olson, Mancur. 1971. *The logic of collective action: Public goods and the theory of groups.* Cambridge, MA: Harvard University Press.

Organic Consumers Association. 2007. "Seafood: Bringing fair trade and sustainability concerns together." February 13. www.organicconsumers.org/articles/article_4131.cfm (accessed June 9, 2007).

O'Riordan, Brian. 1997. "Marine Stewardship Council: Who's being seduced?" *Samudra* 18:10–11.

———. 1998. "Sticky labels." *Samudra,* December. http://oldsite.icsf.net//jsp/publication/samudra/pdf/english/issue_21/art07.pdf?null (accessed May 2, 2007).

O'Rourke, Dara. 2003. "Outsourcing regulation: Analyzing nongovernmental systems of labor standards and monitoring." *Policy Studies Journal* 31 (1): 1–29.

Osterlund, Peter. 1985. "A global strategy to save tropical forests." *Christian Science Monitor,* October 23, national section, 3. http://web.lexis-nexis.com/ (accessed July 16, 2007).

Ostrom, Elinor. 1986. "An agenda for the study of institutions." *Public Choice* 48:3–25.

———. 1990. *Governing the commons: The evolution of institutions for collective action.* Cambridge: Cambridge University Press.

Overdevest, Christine. 2004. "Codes of conduct and standard setting in the forest sector: Constructing markets for democracy?" *Relations industrielles—Industrial Relations* 59 (1): 172–97.

———. 2005. "Treadmill politics, information politics and public policy: Toward a political economy of information." *Organization and Environment* 18 (1): 72–90.

———. 2010. "Comparing forest certification schemes: The case of ratcheting standards in the forest sector." *Socio-economic Review* 8 (1): 47–76.

Overdevest, Christine, and Jonathan Zeitlin. 2014. "Assembling an experimentalist regime: Transnational governance interactions in the forest sector." *Regulation and Governance* 8 (1): 22–48.

Oxfam. 1994. *Action on trade.* Oxford: Oxfam.

Oxfam GB Archive. 1989–98a. Bodleian Library, Oxford. Marketing Directorate correspondence, Fairtrade Foundation, R0647.

———. 1989–98b. Bodleian Library, Oxford. Marketing Directorate correspondence, Fairtrade Foundation, R0674.

Ozinga, Saskia. 2001. *Behind the logo, an environmental and social assessment of forest certification schemes.* Moreton-in-Marsh, UK: FERN.

Packaging Digest. 1994. "Coffee bags with a socio-economic message." 31 (12): 70–72. www.lexisnexis.com/ (accessed August 10, 2007).

Page, Scott E. 2006. "Path dependence." *Quarterly Journal of Political Science* 1:87–115.

Palmer, Thomas. 1990. "P&G will resume ad on channel 7 in '91." Globe Newspaper Company, December 12, economy section, 73. http://web.lexis-nexis.com/ (accessed January 27, 2007).

Panhuysen, Sjoerd, and Baerbel Weiligmann. 2006. *Coffee barometer 2006: Certified coffee in the Netherlands.* Amsterdam: Dutch Coffee Coalition.

Paper Task Force. 1995. *Paper Task Force recommendations for purchasing and using environmentally preferable paper.* New York: Environmental Defense Fund.

Pattberg, Philipp H. 2005. "The Forest Stewardship Council: Risk and potential of private forest governance." *Journal of Environment and Development* 14 (3): 356–74.

———. 2007. *Private institutions and global governance: The new politics of environmental sustainability.* Cheltenham, UK: Edward Elgar.

Pauly, Daniel, Villy Christensen, Sylvie Guenette, Tony J. Pitcher, U. Rashid Sumaila, Carl J. Walters, R. Watson, and Dirk Zeller. 2002. "Towards sustainability in world fisheries." *Nature* 418 (6898): 689–95.

Pauly, Daniel, and Marie-Lourdes Palomares. 2005. "Fishing down marine food web: It is far more pervasive than we thought." *Bulletin of Marine Science* 76 (2): 197–211.

Pauly, Daniel, R. Watson, and Jackie Alder. 2005. "Global trends in world fisheries: Impacts on marine ecosystems and food security." *Philosophical Transactions of the Royal Society B—Biological Sciences* 360 (1453): 5–12.

Pearce, Fred. 1992. "Green timber merchant turns on ecologists." *New Scientist* 133 (1814): 18.

———. 2003. "Can ocean friendly labels save dwindling stocks?" *New Scientist* 178 (2395): 5.

Pearlstine, Norman. 1974. "Wailing over whaling." *Wall Street Journal,* June 26.

PEFC. 1998. "PEFC memorandum." October 27. http://web.archive.org/web/2000 1208212400/www.pefc.org/Ramme2.htm (accessed July 25, 2008).

———. 2002. "Basis for certification schemes and their implementation." November 22. http://web.archive.org/web/20030714165528/www.pefc.org/TechDocs/ Annex3_Implementation_2002-11-22.pdf (accessed July 25, 2008).

———. 2008. "About PEFC: A short history." July 2. www.pefc.org/internet/html/ about_pefc/4_1137_498.htm (accessed July 30, 2008).

Pelline, Jeff. 1993. "Certifiably 'green' lumber comes to market." *San Francisco Chronicle,* October 8, business section, B1. www.lexisnexis.com/ (accessed October 8, 2007).

Pendergrast, Mark. 2001. *Uncommon grounds: The history of coffee and how it transformed our world.* New York: Basic Books.

Percival, Robert V., Christopher H. Schroeder, Alan S. Miller, and James P. Leape. 2003. *Environmental regulation: Law, science, and policy.* 4th ed. New York: Aspen.

Perfecto, Ivette, Robert A. Rice, Russell Greenberg, and Martha E. VanderVoort. 1996. "Shade coffee: A disappearing refuge for biodiversity." *Bioscience* 46 (8): 598–608.

Petersen, Elizabeth H. 2006. *Institutional economics and fisheries management.* Cheltenham, UK: Edward Elgar.

Peters-Stanley, Molly, and Katherine Hamilton. 2012. *Developing dimensions: State of voluntary carbon markets, 2012.* Washington, DC: Ecosystem Marketplace; New York: Bloomberg New Energy Finance.

Petit, Charles. 1989. "Rain forest group urges wood boycott." *San Francisco Chronicle,* November 3, A17. www.lexisnexis.com/ (accessed November 1, 2007).

Petty, Ross D. 1992. "FTC advertising regulation: Survivor or casualty of the Reagan revolution?" *American Business Law Journal* 30 (1): 1–34.

Philadelphia Inquirer. 1992. "Coffee boycott ends." March 21, C11. http://web.lexis-nexis.com/ (accessed January 27, 2007).

Phillips, Matt. 2001. "Green campaigner: Business power must be checked." *Observer,* July 8, business section, 15. www.lexisnexis.com/ (accessed July 22, 2008).

Pierson, Paul. 2004. *Politics in time: History, institutions, and social analysis.* Princeton, NJ: Princeton University Press.

Pitt, David E. 1993. "U.S. seeks to 'fix' mining provision of sea treaty." *New York Times,* August 28. www.lexisnexis.com/ (accessed February 14, 2008).

Pittsburgh Post-Gazette. 1997. "Redwood Boycott." February 12. www.lexisnexis.com/ (accessed November 1, 2007).

Polanyi, Karl. 1944. *The great transformation.* New York: Farrar and Rinehart.

Ponte, Stefano. 2004. *Standards and sustainability in the coffee sector.* Winnipeg: International Institute for Sustainable Development.

Poore, Duncan. 2003. *Changing landscapes: The development of the International Tropical Timber Organization and its influence on tropical forest management.* London: Earthscan.

Porter, Michael E. 1998a. *Competitive advantage: Creating and sustaining superior performance.* New York: Free Press.

———. 1998b. *Competitive strategy: Techniques for analyzing industries and competitors.* New York: Free Press.

Potoski, Matthew, and Aseem Prakash. 2005. "Green clubs and voluntary governance: ISO 14001 and firms' regulatory compliance." *American Journal of Political Science* 49 (2): 235–48.

———. 2009. *Voluntary programs: A club theory perspective.* Cambridge, MA: MIT Press.

Prakash, Aseem, and Matthew Potoski. 2006. *The voluntary environmentalists: Green clubs, ISO 14001, and voluntary regulations.* Cambridge: Cambridge University Press.

———. 2007a. "Collective action through voluntary environmental programs: A club theory perspective." *Policy Studies Journal* 35 (4): 773–92.

———. 2007b. "International Standards Organization as a global governor: A club theory perspective." Paper read at American Political Science Association, August 30–September 2, Chicago.

———. 2010. "The International Organization for Standardization as a global governor: A club theory perspective." In *Who governs the globe?* edited by Deborah D. Avant, Martha Finnemore, and Susan K. Sell, 72–101. Cambridge: Cambridge University Press.

Pralle, Sarah Beth. 2006. *Branching out, digging in: Environmental advocacy and agenda setting.* Washington, DC: Georgetown University Press.

Price, Wendy. 1997. "A sustained effort." *Timber Trades Journal,* March 15. www.lexis nexis.com/ (accessed July 20, 2008).

Printing World. 1997. "Falling off a logo." January 27. www.lexisnexis.com/ (accessed April 5, 2008).

PR Newswire. 1990. "Organic foods industry moves to standardize: Agreements to protect farmers, suppliers and consumers nationwide." January 3. www.lexis nexis.com/ (accessed February 16, 2008).

———. 1992. "Home Depot announces environmental greenprint(sm)." June 3, financial news section. www.lexisnexis.com/ (accessed November 1, 2007).

———. 2005. "New certification for Wal-Mart shrimp another example of environmental leadership: Adopting best aquaculture practices for farm-raised shrimp ensures quality product for consumers around the world—harvested with sustainability in mind." November 17. www.lexisnexis.com/ (accessed August 17, 2008).

PR Newswire Europe. 1991. "B&Q position on Friends of the Earth timber campaign." November 8. www.lexisnexis.com/ (accessed July 20, 2008).

———. 2007. "First major DIY retailer supports WWF 1995 timber deadline." September 26, general and city news section. www.lexisnexis.com/ (accessed November 19, 2007).

Pulp and Paper Report. 2003. "Expansions in Brazil and Chile adding 3.7 million tonnes of eucalyptus and pine pulp." 5 (14).

PWC. 2006. "Global forest, paper and packaging: industry survey." www.pwc.com/gx/ eng/about/ind/fpp/pwc_gfpp-survey2006_final.pdf (accessed August 12, 2006).

Quarto, Alfredo, Kate Cissna, and Joanna Taylor. 1996. "Choosing the road to sustainability: The impacts of shrimp aquaculture and the models for change." Paper read at the International Live Aquatics Conference, October 13–15, Seattle.

Rainforest Action Network. 1997. "Burger King cancels rainforest beef contracts." http://web.archive.org/web/19970526015435/www.ran.org/ran/victories/ burgerking.html (accessed November 2, 2007).

Rainforest Alliance. 2005. *Sustainable agriculture standard: Sustainable Agriculture Network.* New York: Rainforest Alliance.

———. 2007. "Reflecting trend toward global companies embracing sustainability, McDonald's UK puts Rainforest Alliance certified coffee on the menu." January 8. www.rainforest-alliance.org/news.cfm?id=mcdonalds (accessed February 15, 2007).

Raloff, Janet. 1979. "Bloody harvest." *Science News* 115 (13): 202–4.

Rama, D.B.K., and K. Jaga. 1992. "Pesticide exposure and cholinesterase levels among farm workers in the Republic of South Africa." *Science of the Total Environment* 122 (5): 315–19.

Ramaswami, Rama. 1992. "Green coffee for a cleaner planet (organically grown coffees have their niche in the market)." *Tea and Coffee Trade Journal* 164 (4): 21–26.

Ramirez, Anthony. 1990. "From coffee to tobacco, boycotts are a growth industry." New York Times Company, June 3. http://web.lexis-nexis.com/ (accessed January 27, 2007).

Ramsar Convention on Wetlands. 1997. "Industrial Shrimp Action Network (ISA Net): Global group formed to counter destructive industrial shrimp farming." October 24. www.ramsar.org/about/about_shrimp_action.htm (accessed April 4, 2007).

Rayner, Jeremy, Alexander Buck, and Pia Katila. 2010. *Embracing complexity: Meeting the challenges of international forest governance; A global assessment report prepared by the Global Forest Expert Panel on the International Forest Regime.* Geneva: IUFRO.

Raynolds, Laura T. 2000. "Re-embedding global agriculture: The international organic and fair trade movements." *Agriculture and Human Values* 17 (3): 297–309.

———. 2004. "The globalization of organic agro-food networks." *World Development* 32 (5): 725–43.

Raynolds, Laura T., Douglas Murray, and Andrew Heller. 2007. "Regulating sustainability in the coffee sector: A comparative analysis of third-party environmental and social certification initiatives." *Agriculture and Human Values* 24 (2): 147–63.

Reed, Matthew. 2001. "Fight the future! How the contemporary campaigns of the UK organic movement have arisen from their composting of the past." *Sociologia Ruralis* 41 (1): 131–45.

Reese, April. 2001. "Forests: Industry, enviros tussle over 'mutual recognition'; framework." Greenwire, July 21. www.lexisnexis.com/ (accessed April 16, 2008).

Reeve, Rosalind. 1993. "The Forest Stewardship Council aims, principles and criteria: A critical examination predicting failure." Rettet den Regenwald e. V, September 30. http://forests.org/archive/general/fsc.htm (accessed December 5, 2006).

Reich, Robert B. 2007. *Supercapitalism: The transformation of business, democracy, and everyday life.* New York: Knopf.

Reinhardt, Forest L. 2000. *Down to earth: Applying business principles to environmental management.* Boston: Harvard Business School Press.

Rice, Robert A., and Jennifer McLean. 1999. *Sustainable coffee at the crossroads: A White Paper prepared for the Consumer's Choice Council,* October 15. www.greenbeanery.ca/bean/documents/sustainableCoffee.pdf (accessed March 14, 2006).

Rice, Robert A., and Justin R. Ward. 1996. *Coffee, conservation, and commerce in the Western Hemisphere: How individuals and institutions can promote ecologically sound farming and forest management in northern Latin America.* Washington, DC: Smithsonian Migratory Bird Center.

Richard Burbidge. 1999. "Richard Burbidge Ltd. denies investing in rainforest destruction as named in Greenpeace report." PR Newswire Europe, October 1. www.lexisnexis.com/ (accessed July 20, 2008).

Richards, Laura J., and Jean-Jacques Maguire. 1998. "Recent international agreements and the precautionary approach: New directions for fisheries management science." *Canadian Journal of Fisheries and Aquatic Sciences* 55 (6): 1545–52.

Rivera, Jorge. 2002. "Assessing a voluntary environmental initiative in the developing world: The Costa Rican Certification for Sustainable Tourism." *Policy Sciences* 35 (4): 333–60.

———. 2004. "Institutional pressures and voluntary environmental behavior in developing countries: Evidence from the Costa Rican hotel industry." *Society and Natural Resources* 17 (9): 779–97.

Rivera, Jorge, and Peter deLeon. 2004. "Is greener whiter? Voluntary environmental performance of western ski areas." *Policy Studies Journal* 32 (3): 417–37.

Rivera, Jorge, Peter deLeon, and Charles Koerber. 2006. "Is greener whiter yet? The sustainable slopes program after five years." *Policy Studies Journal* 34 (2): 195–221.

Robbins, Chandler S., John R. Sauer, Russell S. Greenberg, and Sam Droege. 1989. "Population declines in North American birds that migrate to the neotropics."

Proceedings of the National Academy of Sciences of the United States of America
86:7658–62.

Roberts, Sarah. 2003. "Supply chain specific? Understanding the patchy success of ethical sourcing initiatives." *Journal of Business Ethics* 44 (2): 159–70.

Rogue Institute for Ecology and Economy. 1997. "Green certification." *Community Ecology* (fall). http://web.archive.org/web/19990420133853/id.mind.net/~roguinst/riee5.html (accessed October 1, 2008).

———. 1999. *Smartwood certified forestry: Oregon guidelines, 1999.* Ashland, OR: Rogue Institute for Ecology and Economy.

———. 2000. "History of achievements." June 9. http://web.archive.org/web/20000609180547/id.mind.net/~roguinst/history.htm (accessed October 1, 2008).

Roheim, Cathy A., and Jon G. Sutinen. 2006. *Trade and marketplace measures to promote sustainable fishing practices.* Geneva: International Centre for Trade and Sustainable Development (ICTSD) and High Seas Task Force (HSTF).

Romeijn, Paul. 1999. *Green gold: On variation of truth in plantation forestry.* Heelsum, Netherlands: Treemail.

Rose, Carol M. 1991. "Rethinking environmental controls: Management strategies for common resources." *Duke Law Journal* 1 (February): 1–38.

Rosenau, James N. 1995. "Governance in the twenty-first century." *Global Governance* 1 (1): 13–43.

Rosenau, Pauline V. 1999. "Introduction: The strengths and weaknesses of public-private policy partnerships." *American Behavioral Scientist* 43 (1): 10–34.

Rosenberg, David. 2003. "Introducing the EUREPGAP coffee reference code." September. www.eurepgap.org/documents/webdocs/Introducing_EUREPGAP_Coffee.pdf (accessed March 4, 2006).

Rotherham, Tony. 2005. *The trade and environmental effects of ecolabels: Assessment and response.* Nairobi: United Nations Environment Programme.

Rue, Steve La. 1997. "Efforts surfacing to save fish." *San Diego Union-Tribune,* January 8. www.lexisnexis.com/ (accessed August 8, 2008).

Ruggie, John G. 2002. "Taking embedded liberalism global: The corporate connection." Paper read at Canadian Congress of the Social Sciences and Humanities, May 29, University of Toronto.

———. 2004. "Reconstituting the global public domain: Issues, actors, and practices." *European Journal of International Relations* 10 (4): 499–531.

Rundgren, Gunnar. 2007. "Certification bodies: Almost 400 organic certifiers in more than 70 countries." In *The world of organic agriculture: Statistics and emerging trends, 2007,* edited by Hellga Willer and Minou Yussefi, 69. Bonn, Germany: International Federation of Organic Agriculture Movements (IFOAM); Frick, Switzerland: Research Institute of Organic Agriculture (FiBL).

Salter, Liora. 1999. "The standards regime for communication and information technologies." In *Private authority and international affairs,* edited by A. Claire Cutler, Virginia Haufler, and Tony Porter, 97–128. Albany: State University of New York.

Sandler, Todd, and John Tschirhart. 1997. "Club theory: Thirty years later." *Public Choice* 93 (3–4): 335.

Sasser, Erika N. 2003. "Gaining leverage: NGO influence on certification institutions in the forest products sector." In *Forest policy for private forestry,* edited by Larry Teeter, Benjamin Cashore, and Daowei Zhang, 229–44. Oxon, UK: CAB International.

Sasser, Erika, Aseem Prakash, Benjamin Cashore, and Graeme Auld. 2006. "Direct targeting as an NGO political strategy: Examining private authority regimes in the forestry sector." *Business and Politics* 8 (3): 1–34.

SCAA. 2005. "Draft comparison codes for communication purposes—Comparing coffee codes: Organic, fair trade, Rainforest Alliance certified, Utz Kapeh and the common code." August 17. www.scaa.org/pdfs/SCAAComparingCoffeeCodes_Aug2005.pdf (accessed March 15, 2005).

———. 2007. "Specialty coffee retail in the USA, 2006." www.scaa.org/pdfs/news/specialtycoffeeretail.pdf (accessed August 24, 2008).

Schapiro, Mark. 1994. "The cult of coffee." *Atlanta Journal and Constitution*, December 4. www.lexisnexis.com/ (accessed August 5, 2008).

Scharpe, Alberik. 2003. "The EU regulation." In *The organic guarantee system: The need and strategy for harmonization and equivalence*, edited by Christina Westermayer and Bernward Geier, 24–29. Bonn, Germany: International Federation of Organic Agriculture Movements.

Schmidt, Carl-Christian. 1999. "The Marine Stewardship Council: A market-based management approach." In *ACP-EU fisheries research report number 5*, edited by Daniel Pauly, Villy Christensen, and Lucilia Coelho. Brussels: European Commission, Directorate General for Development and Directorate General for Research. http://cordis.europa.eu/inco/fp5/acprep33_en.html (accessed January 27, 2014).

Schoenholt, Donald N. 2001. "The fair trade ideal: The ultimate answer for sustainability? (The coffee crisis part 2)." *Tea and Coffee Trade Journal* 173 (11): 103–6.

Schoon, Nicholas. 1990. "Aid could destroy rain forest." *Independent* (London), March 22. http://web.lexis-nexis.com/ (accessed July 22, 2007).

———. 1991. "Ecolabels used on tropical timber imports 'suspect.'" *Independent* (London), June 11. www.lexisnexis.com/ (accessed November 19, 2007).

———. 1992. "Ecological wood product labels planned." *Independent* (London), March 16, 2.

Schreurs, Miranda A. 2002. *Environmental politics in Japan, Germany, and the United States.* Cambridge: Cambridge University Press.

Schrope, Mark. 2008. "Overfishing worse than thought." *Nature News,* July 9. www.nature.com/news/2008/080709/full/news.2008.942.html.

Schurman, Rachel, and William Munro. 2009. "Targeting capital: A cultural economy approach to understanding the efficacy of two anti–genetic engineering movements." *American Journal of Sociology* 115 (1): 155–202.

Schwarz, Walter. 1992. "Small world, fair deal." *Guardian* (London), September 18. http://web.lexis-nexis.com/ (accessed January 29, 2007).

———. 2004. "Protection, not perfection: The Marine Stewardship Council aims to do for fish what the Soil Association does for organic food." *Guardian* (London), March 10. http://web.lexis-nexis.com/ (accessed February 5, 2007).

Scialabba, Nadia El-Hage, and Caroline Hattam. 2002. *Organic agriculture, environment and food security.* Rome: Food and Agriculture Organization of the United Nations.

Scientific Certification Systems. 1995. *The Forest Conservation Program: Program description and operations manual.* Oakland, CA: Scientific Certification Systems.

———. 1999a. *The Forest Conservation Program: Forest lands certified as "well managed."* Oakland, CA: Scientific Certification Systems.

———. 1999b. *Scientific Certification Systems: Overview of evaluation and certification programs.* Oakland, CA: Scientific Certification Systems.

———. 2000. "Public summary for the MSC certification of the Western Rock Lobster Fishery, Western Australia." Scientific Certification Systems Marine Fisheries Certification Program, April. www.msc.org (accessed August 13, 2008).

Scott, Anthony. 1955. "The fishery: The objectives of sole ownership." *Journal of Political Economy* 63 (2): 116–24.

Scott, Colin. 2002. "Private regulation of the public sector: A neglected facet of contemporary governance." *Journal of Law and Society* 29 (1): 56–76.

Scrase, Hannah. 1994. "SCS certification label reaches critical mass in the hardlines industry: Retailers and manufacturers praise SCS's scientific approach to verifying claims, resolving environmental problems and raising consumer awareness." PR Newswire, August 15. www.lexisnexis.com/ (accessed July 26, 2008).

———. 1995. "The Forest Stewardship Council: Its contribution to independent forest certification." *Commonwealth Forestry Review* 74 (3): 192–95.

Sea Shepherd Conservation Society. 2008. "About Sea Shepherd Conservation Society." www.seashepherd.org/about-sscs.html (accessed January 30, 2008).

Sea Turtle Restoration Project. 1999. "History and accomplishments." November 13. http://web.archive.org/web/19991113204154/http://www.seaturtles.org/ (accessed April 17, 2007).

SeaWeb. 2008. "History." www.seaweb.org/aboutus/history.php (accessed August 8, 2008).

Senter, Al. 1998. "Ethical business: Fair trading group aims to bring bigger firms on board." *Observer,* January 11, business section, 7. http://web.lexis-nexis.com/ (accessed January 29, 2007).

SGS. 2002. *Annual report 2001.* Geneva: SGS Société Générale de Surveillance.

Shabecoff, Philip. 1981. "Rusty trawler to lead battle against whale hunts." *New York Times,* May 31, 1. www.lexisnexis.com/ (accessed January 30, 2008).

———. 1982. "Commission votes to ban hunting of whales." *New York Times,* July 24. www.lexisnexis.com/ (accessed February 5, 2008).

———. 1985a. "Judge upsets U.S.-Japanese whaling accord." *New York Times,* March 6. www.lexisnexis.com/ (accessed February 7, 2008).

———. 1985b. "U.N. gets rescue plan for tropical forests." *New York Times,* October 29. http://web.lexis-nexis.com/ (accessed July 16, 2007).

———. 1988. "Senate panel urged to toughen curbs on killing of dolphins." *New York Times,* April 14. www.lexisnexis.com/ (accessed January 30, 2008).

Shapiro, Ian. 2002. "Problems, methods, and theories in the study of politics; or, What's wrong with political science and what to do about it." *Political Theory* 30 (4): 596–619.

Shaw, Teri. 1991. "Rain forest reprieve: Designers are switching to ecologically correct woods." *Washington Post,* November 14, home section, T16. www.lexisnexis.com/ (accessed November 1, 2007).

Shepherd, R., M. Magnusson, and P. O. Sjoden. 2005. "Determinants of consumer behavior related to organic foods." *Ambio* 34 (4–5): 352–59.

Shepsle, Kenneth A., and Mark S. Bonchek. 1997. *Analyzing politics: Rationality, behavior, and institutions.* New York: Norton.

Short, Katherine. 2003. "The WWF perspective." In *Eco-labelling in fisheries: What is it all about?* edited by Bruce Phillips, Trevor Ward, and Chet Chaffee, 109–13. Oxford: Blackwell.

Sibaja, Marco Antonio. 1993. "El Salvador: U.S. groups buy coffee to support peace process." IPS–Inter Press Service, April 15. www.lexisnexis.com/ (accessed August 8, 2008).

Simons, Theresa. 1990. "Epic struggle over redwoods." *California Journal*, March 1. www.lexis-nexis.com/ (accessed May 30, 2005).

Simpson, David. 1992. "Co-op coffee aims to help third world farmers." Associated Press, April 27. www.lexis-nexis.com/ (accessed August 31, 2005).

Skodvin, Tora, and Steinar Andresen. 2003. "Nonstate influence in the International Whaling Commission, 1970–1990." *Global Environmental Politics* 3 (4): 61–86.

Skonhoft, A. 2012. "Port state measures." UN Food and Agricultural Organization, 7 July. www.fao.org/fishery/psm/en (accessed July 1, 2013).

Slob, Bart, and Joris Oldenziel. 2003. *Coffee and codes: Overview of codes of conduct and ethical trade initiatives in the coffee sector.* Amsterdam: SOMO.

SMBC. 2001. "Update 2000: Winging into the new millennium." http://nationalzoo .si.edu/ConservationAndScience/MigratoryBirds/About_us/smbc_report2001 .pdf (accessed August 5, 2008).

———. 2002. *Norms for production, processing, and marketing of "bird friendly" coffee.* Washington, DC: Smithsonian Migratory Bird Center, National Zoo.

———. 2008. "Bird friendly® coffee program history and quick facts." Smithsonian National Zoological Park. http://nationalzoo.si.edu/printpage/default.cfm (accessed August 5, 2008).

Smith, W. Brad, Patrick D. Miles, John S. Vissage, and Scott A. Pugh. 2003. *Forest resources of the United States, 2002.* St. Paul, MN: U.S. Department of Agriculture, Forest Service, North Central Research Station.

Snidal, Duncan. 1985a. "Coordination versus prisoners-dilemma: Implications for international-cooperation and regimes." *American Political Science Review* 79 (4): 923–42.

———. 1985b. "The game-theory of international-politics." *World Politics* 38 (1): 25–57.

———. 1996. "Political economy and international institutions." *International Review of Law and Economics* 16 (1): 121–37.

Soil Association. 2004. "Fish farming and organic standards: Information sheet." www.soilassociation.org/web/sa/saweb.nsflibrarytitles/19426.html (accessed January 12, 2007).

Solidaridad. 2006. *Annual report 2005.* Utrecht: Solidaridad Foundation.

Sommer, Adrian. 1976. "Attempt at an assessment of the world's tropical moist forests." *Unasylva* 28 (112–13): 5–25.

Sommer, Mark. 1993. "Beyond the forest summit." *Christian Science Monitor*, April 22. www.lexisnexis.com/ (accessed September 1, 2007).

Spar, Deborah L., and Lane T. La Mure. 2003. "The power of activism: Assessing the impact of NGOs on global business." *California Management Review* 45 (3): 78–101.

Stanbury, William T. 2000. *Environmental groups and the international conflict over the forest of British Columbia 1990 to 2000.* Vancouver: SFU-UBC Centre for the Study of Government and Business.

Starbucks. 2007. *Form 10-K annual report* [SEC filing]. November 29. http://investor .starbucks.com/phoenix.zhtml?c=99518&p=irol-sec (accessed December 12, 2007).

Stark, Judy. 1992. "Saving the rain forest." *St. Petersburg Times*, July 21. www.lexisnexis.com/ (accessed October 10, 2007).

Steele, Jonathan. 1985. "Trying to stop the famines of tomorrow: Background report on the long-term problems of Ethiopia." *Guardian* (London), July 16. www.lexisnexis.com/ (accessed August 10, 2007).

Stevens, James, Mubariq Ahmad, and Steve Ruddel. 1998. "Forest products certification: A survey of manufacturers." *Forest Products Journal* 48 (6): 43–49.

Stevis, Dimitris. 2006. "The trajectory of the study of international environmental politics." In *Palgrave advances in international environmental politics,* edited by Michele Betsill, Kathryn Hochstetler, and Dimitris Stevis, 13–53. New York: Palgrave MacMillian.

Stigler, George J. 1971. "Theory of economic regulation." *Bell Journal of Economics and Management Science* 2 (1): 3–21.

Stokke, Olav Schram. 2004. "Labelling, legalisation and sustainable management of forestry and fisheries." Paper read at The Fifth Pan-European International Relations Conference, September 9–11, The Hague, Netherlands.

Stonich, Susan C., and Conner Bailey. 2000. "Resisting the blue revolution: Contending coalitions surrounding industrial shrimp farming." *Human Organization* 59 (1): 23.

Strange, Susan. 1983. "Cave! hic dragones: A critique of regime analysis." In *International regimes,* edited by Stephen D. Krasner, 337–45. Ithaca, NY: Cornell University Press.

Stump, Ken, and Dave Batker. 1996. "Sinking fast: How factory trawlers are destroying U.S. fisheries." Greenpeace, August http://web.archive.org/web/20060902082012/www.greenpeace.org/raw/content/usa/press/reports/sinking-fast-how-factory-tra.pdf (accessed August 1, 2008).

Stump, Neil. 2005. "Marine protected areas in Australia: Towards a coordinated rock lobster industry position." *New Zealand Journal of Marine and Freshwater Research* 39 (3): 765–74.

Sullivan, Francis. 1990. "Time to open the FAO fortress." *Financial Times* (London), October 18. http://web.lexis-nexis.com/ (accessed July 25, 2007).

Sustainable Agriculture Network. 2002. "Generic standards for coffee farm evaluation." Rainforest Alliance and the Sustainable Agriculture Network, January 14. www.rainforest-alliance.org/programs/agriculture/pdfs/coffee.pdf (accessed February 4, 2007).

———. 2012a. "History." http://sanstandards.org/pdfs/standards_policy_dev_hand book.pdf (accessed October 20, 2012).

———. 2012b. "Sustainable Agriculture Network and Rainforest Alliance expand certification system." June 1. http://sanstandards.org/sitio/ (accessed October 20, 2012).

Sutton, David. 2003. "An unsatisfactory encounter with the MSC: A conservation perspective." In *Eco-labelling in fisheries: What is it all about?* edited by Bruce Phillips, Trevor Ward, and Chet Chaffee, 114–19. Oxford: Blackwell.

Sutton, Michael. 1996. "Marine Stewardship Council: New hope for marine fisheries." *Samudra* 15:15–18.

———. 1998. "Marine Stewardship Council: An appeal for co-operation." *Samudra* 19:26–30.

Sutton, Michael, and Caroline Whitfield. 1996. "A powerful arrow in the quiver." *Samudra* 16:33–34.

Synnott, Timothy. 2005. *Some notes on the early years of FSC.* Saltillo, Mexico.

Tacon, Albert, and Deborah Brister. 2002. "Organic aquaculture: Current status and future prospects." In *Organic agriculture, environment and food security,* edited by Nadia El-Hage Scialabba and Caroline Hattam. Rome: Food and Agriculture Organization of the United Nations. www.fao.org/docrep/005/Y4137E/y4137e00 .HTM (accessed August 16, 2008).

Talbot, John M. 2004. *Grounds for agreement: The political economy of the coffee commodity chain.* Lanham, MD: Rowman and Littlefield.

Tallontire, Anne. 2001. "Fair trade and development." Working paper. Natural Resources Institute, Natural Resources and Ethical Trade Programme. Greenwich: University of Greenwich.

Tallontire, Anne, and Peter Greenhalgh. 2005. "Establishing CSR drivers in agribusiness." Final Report for Foreign Investment Advisory Service International Financial Corporation and World Bank. Natural Resources Institute, August. www.ifc .org/ifcext/economics.nsf/AttachmentsByTitle/CSR-FINAL+Report+on+CSR +Drivers+in+Agribusiness/$FILE/FIAS+CSR+drivers+final.pdf (accessed August 20, 2008).

Tarmann, Kevin Francis. 2002. "The fair trade coffee movement: Norm change or niche marketing?" PhD diss., University of Virginia.

Tarrow, Sidney G. 1998. *Power in movement: Social movements and contentious politics.* New York: Cambridge University Press.

———. 2005. *The new transnational activism.* Cambridge Studies in Contentious Politics. New York: Cambridge University Press.

Taylor, J. Gary, and Patricia J. Scharlin. 2004. *Smart alliance: How a global corporation and environmental activists transformed a tarnished brand.* New Haven, CT: Yale University Press.

Thanksgiving Coffee. 2008. "Time line." www.thanksgivingcoffee.com/timeline (accessed August 8, 2008).

Tharian, George K. 1987. "International commodity agreements: The case of natural rubber." *Social Scientist* 15 (4–5): 77–86.

Thelen, Kathleen. 1999. "Historical institutionalism in comparative politics." *Annual Review of Political Science* 2:369–404.

———. 2003. "How institutions evolve: Insights from comparative historical analysis." In *Comparative historical analysis in the social sciences,* edited by James Mahoney and Dietrich Rueschemeyer, 208–40. Cambridge: Cambridge University Press..

Thomas, Harford. 1988. "Society tomorrow (ecologue): Growing demand from the new conscious consumers." Guardian (London), January 6. www.lexisnexis.com/ (accessed August 10, 2007).

Thomson, Bob. 1995. "A history of fair trade labels." August. http://ca.geocities.com/ bthomson100/label_history.html (accessed August 10, 2007).

Tice, Carol. 1998. "Is there certified wood in your future?" *National Home Center News ProDealer Supplement,* June 8. www.lexisnexis.com/ (accessed July 22, 2008).

Tickell, Oliver. 1994. "Kindest wood cuts of all." *Times* (London), June 11. www.lexis nexis.com/ (accessed May 22, 2006).

———. 1997a. "FSC cracks down on certifier despite 'approval.'" *Timber Trades Journal,* October 25. www.lexisnexis.com/ (accessed July 15, 2008).

———. 1997b. "Greens disagree." *Timber Trades Journal,* May 3. www.lexisnexis.com/ (accessed July 14, 2008).

———. 1997c. "Part-certified products may carry FSC logo." *Timber Trades Journal*, January 18. www.lexisnexis.com/ (accessed July 20, 2008).

Tighe, Michael. 1997. "Nearly one-third of valuable fish stocks are overfished, government says." Associated Press, October 6. www.lexisnexis.com/ (accessed August 8, 2008).

Tilly, Charles. 1984. "Social movements and national politics." In *Statemaking and social movements: Essays in history and theory*, edited by Charles Bright and Susan Friend Harding, 297–317. Ann Arbor: University of Michigan Press.

———. 1992. *Coercion, capital, and European states, AD 990–1992*. Cambridge, MA: Blackwell.

Timber & Wood Products. 1998a. "FoE protests at Meyer's mahogany policy." Timber & Wood Products, October 24. www.lexisnexis.com/ (accessed July 20, 2008).

———. 1998b. "SGS rebukes Greenpeace for misuse of FSC name." Timber & Wood Products, October 31. www.lexisnexis.com/ (accessed July 15, 2008).

———. 1998c. "Targets under fire." Timber & Wood Products, August 29. www.lexisnexis.com/ (accessed July 15, 2008).

———. 1999a. "From the margins to the mainstream." Timber & Wood Products, November 6. www.lexisnexis.com/ (accessed April 8, 2008).

———. 1999b. "Small forest owners to launch new Euro-scheme." Timber & Wood Products, February 13. www.lexisnexis.com/ (accessed April 2, 2008).

Timber Trades Journal. 1997a. "FSC approves fifth certifier." February 1. www.lexisnexis.com/ (accessed July 15, 2008).

———. 1997b. "FSC investigates Isoroy's Gabon certification." February 8. www.lexisnexis.com/ (accessed July 15, 2008).

———. 1997c. "Retailers get bad advice from WWF, says Timber Growers chairman." March 15. www.lexisnexis.com/ (accessed July 15, 2008).

Times (London). 1989. "Stores fail to check rain forest damage." July 16. http://web.lexis-nexis.com/ (accessed July 16. 2007).

Toland, Justin. 2007. "Slimmed down IP still dwarfs the rest." *PPI* 49 (9): 25.

Tollefson, Chris, Fred P. Gale, and David Haley. 2008. *Setting the standard: Certification, governance, and the Forest Stewardship Council*. Vancouver: UBC.

TransFair USA. 2000a. "History." April 28. http://web.archive.org/web/20000817012835/www.transfairusa.org/about/history.html (accessed March 17, 2007).

———. 2000b. "Market opportunity assessment executive summary." April 28. http://web.archive.org/web/20010418232256/www.transfairusa.org/about/reports/moa.html (accessed October 6, 2007).

Tratensek, Dan, and Chris Jensen. 2006. "Annual report: Retail DIY market profile." *Hardware Retailing* 191 (16): 24–34.

Trenor, Casson. 2010. *Carting away the oceans*. Washington, DC: Greenpeace.

———. 2012. *Carting away the oceans VI*. Washington, DC: Greenpeace.

Tropical Commodity Coalition. 2012. "Coffee barometer 2012." www.newforesight.com/sites/default/files/newforesight/TCC_CoffeeBarometer2012.pdf (accessed October 20, 2012).

Troy, Terry. 1992. "Policing environmental claims (made by consumer product manufacturers)." *HFD: The Weekly Home Furnishings Newspaper* 66 (20): 98–99.

Tsebelis, George. 1995. "Decision-making in political-systems: Veto players in presidentialism, parliamentarism, multicameralism and multipartyism." *British Journal of Political Science* 25: 289–325.

———. 1999. "Veto players and law production in parliamentary democracies: An empirical analysis." *American Political Science Review* 93 (3): 591–608.

———. 2000. "Veto players and institutional analysis." *Governance* 13 (4): 441–74.

UCIRI. 2005. UCIRI: "Unión de comunidades indígenas de la región del istmo (Union of indigenous communities of the isthmus region)." Paper read at the Second International Conference on Gross National Happiness, "Rethinking Development: Local Pathways to Global Wellbeing," June 20–24, Antigonish, Nova Scotia.

Ullman, Richard H. 1978. "Human rights and eonomic power: The United States versus Idi Amin." *Foreign Affairs* 56 (3): 529–43.

UN. 1948. *Havana charter for an international trade organization.* Havana: United Nations.

———. 1998. *The United Nations convention on the law of the sea.* Geneva: United Nations.

UNCED. 1993. *Agenda 21.* Geneva: UN Conference on Environment and Development.

UNGA. 1968. *Problems of the human environment.* New York: United Nations.

———. 1971. *Development and environment.* New York: United Nations.

———. 1992. *Report of the United Nations Conference on Environment and Development, Annex III: Non-legally binding authoritative statement of principles for a global consensus on the management, conservation, and sustainable development of all types of forests.* Geneva: United Nations.

Ungeheuer, Friedel. 1972. "Woodstockholm." *Time,* June 19.

Unilever. 2002. "Sustainability initiatives: Fish." November 28. http://web.archive .org/web/20021017195744/www.unilever.com/environmentsociety/sustainability initiatives/fish/ (accessed March 24, 2007).

Upton, Christopher, and Stephen Bass. 1996. *The forest certification handbook.* 2 vols. Delray Beach, FL: St. Lucie.

Urry, Maggie. 1988. "Campaign to put the green into shopping." *Financial Times* (London), September 12, www.lexisnexis.com/ (accessed August 10, 2007).

U.S. Census Bureau. 2000a. *Establishment and firm size (including legal form of organization): 1997 economic census, accommodation and foodservices subject series.* Washington, DC: U.S. Department of Commerce, Economics and Statistics Administration.

———. 2000b. *Establishment and firm size (including legal form of organization): 1997 economic census, manufacturing subject series.* Washington, DC: U.S. Department of Commerce, Economics and Statistics Administration.

———. 2000c. *Establishment and firm size (including legal form of organization): 1997 economic census, retail trade subject series.* Washington, DC: U.S. Department of Commerce, Economics and Statistics Administration.

———. 2001. *Concentration ratios in manufacturing.* Washington, DC: U.S. Department of Commerce, Economic and Statistics Administration.

U.S. Department of Labor. 1997. *By the sweat and toil of children.* Washington, DC: U.S. Department of Labor, Bureau of International Labor Affairs.

USLEAP. 1995. "Starbucks code out: Now comes the hard part." December 1995. www.usleap.org/print/425 (accessed August 6, 2008).

———. 1997. "Starbucks reneges on code, campaign for coffee workers to resume." April. www.usleap.org/print/424 (accessed August 6, 2008).

———. 2000. "Slow pace of Starbucks criticized: Guatemalan coffee worker survey released." March. http://usleap.org/print/422 (accessed August 6, 2008).

U.S. Newswire. 1990. "World Wildlife Fund withdraws support for UN tropical forestry action plan." October 1. http://web.lexis-nexis.com/ (accessed July 25, 2007).

Utz Certified. 2007. "Interim chairman for UTZ Board." April 25. www.utzcertified .org/index.php?pageID=145&showItem=198&searchFor=roozen&filterCat=A,B, C,D (accessed August 6, 2008).

Utz Kapeh. 2004. "Who is who at Utz Kapeh." May. http://web.archive.org/web/ 20040116052333/http://www.utzkapeh.com/ (accessed August 6, 2008).

Vallejo, Nancy, and Pierre Hauselmann. 2004. *Governance and multistakeholder processes.* New York: Sustainable Commodity Initiative, a joint venture of the United Nations Conference on Trade and Development and IISD.

Vallely, Paul, and Anne McElvoy. 1989. "Capturing the flavour of justice: Labelling, the good life." Times Newspapers, July 19. www.lexisnexis.com/ (accessed May 9, 2006).

Vandenbergh, M. P. 2005. "The private life of public law." *Columbia Law Review* 105 (7): 2029–96.

———. 2007. "The new Wal-Mart effect: The role of private contracting in global governance." *UCLA Law Review* 54 (4): 913–70.

Vaupel, Suzanne. 1999. "National organic standards: Lessons from the US experience." In *Quality and communication for the organic market,* edited by Willie Lockeretz and Bernward Geier, 81–88. Tholey-Theley, Germany: International Federation of Organic Agriculture Movements.

Verba, Sidney. 1971. "Sequence and development." In *Crises and sequences in political development,* edited by Leonard Binder, 283–316. Princeton, NJ: Princeton University Press.

Vertinsky, Ilan B., and Dongsheng Zhou. 1999. *Products and process certification: Systems, regulations and international marketing strategies.* Vancouver: Center for International Business Studies, University of British Columbia and Department of International Business, Chinese University of Hong Kong.

Viana, Virgilio, Jamison Ervin, Richard Donovan, Chris Elliott, and Henry Gholz. 1996. *Certification of forest products: Issues and perspectives.* Washington, DC: Island.

Vigneron, Franck, and Lester W. Johnson. 1999. "A review and a conceptual framework of prestige-seeking customers." *Academy of Marketing Science Review* 3 (1): 1–15.

Vilhinen, Laura, Eric Hansen, Heikki Juslin, and Keith Forsyth. 2001. *Forest certification update for the ECE region, summer 2001.* New York: UN, ECE.

Visseren-Hamakers, I. J., and P. Glasbergen. 2007. "Partnerships in forest governance." *Global Environmental Change* 17 (3–4): 408–19.

Vogel, David. 1989. *Fluctuating fortunes: The political power of business in America.* New York: Basic Books.

———. 1995. *Trading up: Consumer and environmental regulation in a global economy.* Cambridge, MA: Harvard University Press.

———. 2008. "Private global business regulation." *Annual Review of Political Science* 11 (1): 261–82.

Walker, Ruth. 1989. "The price tag on social justice." *Christian Science Monitor,* October 5. http://web.lexis-nexis.com/ (accessed March 5. 2007).

Wapner, Paul Kevin. 1995. "Politics beyond the state: Environmental activism and world civic politics." *World Politics* 47 (3): 311–40.

———. 1996. *Environmental activism and world civic politics.* Albany: State University of New York Press.

Washington, Sally, and Lahsen Ababouch. 2011. *Private standards and certificaton in fisheries and aquaculture: Current practices and emerging issues.* Rome: Food and Agriculture Organization of the United Nations.

Watson, R., and Daniel Pauly. 2001. "Systematic distortions in world fisheries catch trends." *Nature* 414 (6863): 534–36.

Webb, Kernaghan. 2002. *Voluntary codes: Private governance, the public interest and innovation.* Ottawa: Carleton University Research Unit for Innovation, Science and the Environment.

Wenban-Smith, Matthew. 2001. *Soil Association woodmark.* Bristol, UK: Soil Association.

Wesseling, C., D. Antich, C. Hogstedt, A. C. Rodriguez, and A. Ahlbom. 1999. "Geographical differences of cancer incidence in Costa Rica in relation to environmental and occupational pesticide exposure." *International Journal of Epidemiology* 28 (3): 365–74.

Wessells, Cathy Roheim, Kevern Cochrane, Carolyn Deere, Paul Wallis, and Rolf Willmann. 2001. *Product certification and ecolabelling for fisheries sustainability.* Rome: Food and Agriculture Organization of the United Nations.

Westermayer, Christina, and Bernward Geier. 2003. *The organic guarantee system: The need and strategy for harmonization and equivalence.* Bonn, Germany: IFOAM, FAO, and UNCTAD.

Western Forest Products. 1998. "WFP to pursue green certification." Canada Newswire, June 3. www.lexisnexis.com/ (accessed July 27, 2008).

Wetzstein, Cheryl. 1990a. "Consumer attitudes growing more green, but wallets aren't." *Washington Times,* August 1, C10. http://web.lexis-nexis.com/ (accessed July 9, 2007).

———. 1990b. "Green seal will mean good deal for globe." *Washington Times,* June 15, C1. www.lexisnexis.com/ (accessed November 1, 2007).

Weyler, Rex. 2004. *Greenpeace: How a group of journalists, ecologists and visionaries changed the world.* Emmaus, PA: Rodale.

White, Andy, and Alejandra Martin. 2002. *Who owns the world's forests? Forest tenure and public forests in transition.* Washington, DC: Forest Trends and Center for International Environmental Law.

White, Andy, Xiufang Sun, Kerstin Canby, Jintao Xu, Christopher Barr, Eugenia Katsigris, Gary Bull, Christian Cossalter, and Sten Nilsson. 2006. *China and the global market for forest products: Transforming trade to benefit forests and livelihoods.* Washington, DC: Forest Trends.

Wilkinson, John. 2006. "Fish: A global value chain driven onto the rocks." *Sociologia Ruralis* 46 (2): 139–53.

Wille, Chris. 1991. "Buy or boycott tropical hardwoods?" *American Forests,* July–August. http://findarticles.com/p/articles/mi_m1016/is_n7-8_v97/ai_11012459/print (accessed August 1, 2007).

———. 2004a. *A brief history of the evolution of the Sustainable Agriculture Network and Rainforest Alliance certified.* London: UK Department for International Development.

———. 2004b. "Certification: A catalyst for partnership." *Human Ecology Review* 11 (3): 288–91.

Williamson, Oliver E. 1985. *The economic institutions of capitalism: Firms, markets, relational contracting.* New York: Free Press; London: Collier Macmillan.

Wilson, Jeremy. 1998. *Talk and log: Wilderness politics in British Columbia, 1965–96.* Vancouver: UBC.

Winterbottom, Robert. 1990. *Taking stock: The Tropical Forestry Action Plan after five years.* Washington, DC: World Resources Institute.

Wood Technology. 1999. "Westvaco, home stores join certification movement." 126 (10): 22.

World Forest Institute. 1993. *Feasibility study regarding forest product certification in Oregon, Washington and British Columbia.* Portland, OR: World Forest Institute.

World News Digest. 1978. "U.S. importers boycott coffee." Facts on File World News Digest, June 2, other nations: Uganda section. http://web.lexis-nexis.com/ (accessed January 28, 2007).

WTO. 2005. "Technical information on technical barriers to trade." August 29. www.wto.org/english/tratop_e/tbt_e/tbt_info_e.htm (accessed May 7, 2010).

WWF. 1996. "The FSC makes its mark." February 16. http://web.archive.org/web/19970216214053/www.panda.org/news/wwfnews/WWF_News_Spring/FSC.htm (accessed July 17, 2008).

———. 1997. "World Bank and WWF join forces to conserve earth's forests." July 26. http://web.archive.org/web/19980212111531/panda.org/news/press/news_130.htm (accessed July 17, 2008).

———. 1998. "Certified forest area hits 10 million hectares." June 30. http://web.archive.org/web/20010212020330/www.panda.org/forests4life/news/300698_certfor.cfm (accessed July 17, 2008).

———. 1999a. "Certification hits more than 15 million hectares worldwide." January 21. http://web.archive.org/web/20010212020125/www.panda.org/forests4life/news/210199_15cert.cfm (accessed July 17, 2008).

———. 1999b. *WWF's global forests and trade initiative.* Washington, DC: World Wildlife Fund.

———. 2000. "New hope for the Amazon." April 11. http://web.archive.org/web/20001215201200/www.panda.org/news/press/news.cfm?id=1916 (accessed July 17, 2008).

———. 2001a. "Certification: Mutual recognition of schemes." August. http://assets.panda.org/downloads/po3iiimutualrecognition.pdf (accessed July 30, 2008).

———. 2001b. "Environmental NGOs call for credible forest certification and reject IFIR mutual recognition proposal." February 19. http://web.archive.org/web/20020803235942/panda.org/forests4life/news/pr_rome.cfm (accessed July 30, 2008).

———. 2001c. "Global forest and trade network." February 21. http://web.archive.org/web/20010221005206/www.panda.org/forests4life/certify_ftncntact.cfm (accessed July 20, 2008).

———. 2007. "Salmon aquaculture dialogue." April 2. www.worldwildlife.org/cci/dialogues/salmon.cfm (accessed April 2, 2007).

———. 2012. "Aquaculture: Salmon." www.worldwildlife.org/what/globalmarkets/aquaculture/dialogues-salmon.html.

WWF, Fern, Friends of the Earth, and Greenpeace. 1998. *NGO statement on forest certification and chain of custody for European Working Group on Timber Chain of Custody.* www.fern.org/pubs/archive/etc.html (accessed July 17, 2008).

Young, Oran R. 1991. "Political-leadership and regime formation: On the development of institutions in international society." *International Organization* 45 (3): 281–308.

———. 1999. *Governance in world affairs*. Ithaca, NY: Cornell University Press.

Zammuto, Rick, Bill Barclay, Tamara Stark, and Phil Aikman. 1998. *Western Forest Products logging practices and the Forest Stewardship Council's principles and criteria: An indicative assessment*. Vancouver: Greenpeace.

Zarocostas, John. 1995. "ISO: Enviros say Canadian forestry plan is too weak." Greenwire, May 30. www.lexisnexis.com/ (accessed Aprl 1, 2008).

Zhouri, Andréa. 2000. "Transnational campaigns for the Amazon: NGO strategies, trade and official responses." *Ambiente & sociedade* 3 (6–7): 31–63.

Zonneveld, Luuk. 2003. "2001–2002: The year in review." Fairtrade Labelling Organizations (FLO) International, February. http://web.archive.org/web/200302 20131324/www.fairtrade.net/sites/news/onetonine/two.htm (accessed July 28, 2008).

Zugarramurdi, Aurora, Maria A. Parin, and Hector M. Lupin. 1995. *Economic engineering applied to the fishery industry*. Rome: Food and Agriculture Organization of the United Nations.